Nice Fellow

First published in 2001 by
Mercier Press
PO Box 5, 5 French Church Street, Cork
Tel: (021) 4275040; Fax: (021) 4274969
e.mail: books@mercier.ie
16 Hume Street Dublin 2
Tel: (01) 6615299; Fax: (01) 6618583
e.mail: books@marino.ie

Trade enquiries to CMD Distribution
55a Spruce Avenue
Stillorgan Industrial Park
Blackrock County Dublin
Tel: (01) 294 2556; Fax: (01) 294 2564

© T. Ryle Dwyer 2001

ISBN   Hardback: 1 85635 368 0
       Paperback: 1 85635 379 6

10 9 8 7 6 5 4 3 2 1
A CIP record for this title is available from
the British Library

Cover photograph courtesy of
Colman Doyle

Cover design by Penhouse
Printed in Ireland by ColourBooks,
Baldoyle Industrial Estate, Dublin 13

NICE FELLOW

A BIOGRAPHY OF JACK LYNCH

T. RYLE DWYER

MERCIER PRESS

To Gerard, Siobhán, Audrey,
Ruth and Sarah Colleran

CONTENTS

PART TWO

PREFACE

In October 1983, Jack Lynch launched *De Valera and His Times*, a collection of papers that had been read at a conference held to mark the centenary of Éamon de Valera's birth the previous year. Lynch quoted extensively from a review that I had written which had been published in that morning's *Irish Times*, but he took issue with my conclusion that the compilation of essays was unbalanced because, for the most part, they showed only the good side of the Long Fellow. Lynch argued that there was no other side. I got a first-hand insight into the humanity of the man that day. He had not realised that I was present at the launch. On being told that I was there, he asked to meet me. He immediately apologised and expressed the hope that I was not offended by his comment.

Frankly, I was flattered that he had quoted so extensively from the review and did not take the least offence at his remarks, but it was touching that he should be so concerned that he might have offended someone. This helps to explain why he was so popular, because he was always considerate, a thorough gentleman.

During the conversation, he spoke about his relationship with de Valera, mentioning that the Long Fellow had a very good sense of humour and a tremendous capacity to surprise. He said that de Valera was not a man to tell jokes, except when they were at his own expense.

In private, he had the endearing quality of being able to laugh at his own failings. On one occasion, Lynch said he had visited de Valera at Áras an Uachtarán with King Baudouin of Belgium. The king had been told that Lynch was a famous hurler and de Valera talked about hurling. The Long Fellow picked up a hurley stick, but held the wrong way round, with the boss facing downward instead of upward. He had a *sliotar* in his hand; he threw it in the air and, to Lynch's amazement, proceeded to strike the ball with the upside-down hurley. De Valera was almost totally blind at the time and Lynch remarked that he did not think the President could have hit the Áras with the hurley, much less the *sliotar*.

In the course of a wide-ranging discussion, Lynch mentioned that he kept no diaries and had a very bad memory. A woman had written to him that week, thanking him for what he had done for her daughter, but he said that he did not remember anything about the woman, her daughter or what he had done for her. In the middle of the conversation, apropos of nothing in particular, he seemed to become very reflective, as if something was bothering him. 'You know,' he said, 'in politics you sometimes have to do something you don't want to do, and you will have to live with that for the rest of your life.'

In the early 1960s the Taoiseach, Seán Lemass, gave Lynch the task of preparing Ireland for entry into the European Economic Community. It would be a long road, taking over a decade, but at the end the Irish people voted so overwhelmingly in favour of joining Europe that all further debate on the issue became superfluous for the rest of Lynch's life. If he had done nothing else but provide leadership on this issue, Lynch would deserve to be remembered, but there was much more to his career besides.

He enjoyed enormous electoral popularity. He inherited a minority government but within a year achieved the unique feat of turning it into a majority regime by winning a succession of by-elections. He then caused a surprise by securing an overall majority in the general election of 1969. Although Fianna Fáil increased its percentage vote in the next general election of 1973, the party narrowly lost power. It returned to office in 1977, however, with the largest majority ever enjoyed by the party.

Yet throughout his leadership, Fianna Fáil was racked by internal divisions. Although he managed to purge the party of his most vociferous critics, there was always a disgruntled rump, and that section would come back to plague him again and again. Some blamed him for the turn of events in Northern Ireland, while others argued that his greatest achievement was keeping the Republic of Ireland out of the Northern Ireland conflict.

Clouds of confusion were created by both friends and foes who tried to manipulate him and his legacy. The aim of this book is to penetrate that confusion, not to glorify or denigrate, but to present a balanced assessment of Jack Lynch's career.

I would like to thank the staffs of the various libraries and archives mentioned in the bibliography; T. P. O'Mahony for the generous loan of the taped interviews that he used for his earlier Lynch biography; Tom Maguire of RTÉ for his valuable help in providing access to the volume of archival material in RTÉ Cork; Michael Costello at Kerry County Library; Joe W. Specht, Director of McMurry University Library, Abilene, Texas; the *Irish Examiner* for permission to use its extensive collection of photographs; Pat Malony, Suzanne Crosbie, Brian O'Connell and Paul McCarthy in the *Irish Examiner* library, Lilian Calverley in the *Irish Examiner* photographic department and Brian Looney and Tim Vaughan of the *Irish Examiner* for their assistance; Colman Doyle and Martyn Turner for providing photographs and cartoons respectively. Finally I would like to thank and pay tribute to the professionalism of Jane Casey in editing the manuscript.

TRD

Tralee

August 2001

PART ONE

1

FAMOUS SPORTSMAN

1917–1948

John Mary Lynch was born on 15 August 1917 at St Anne's Shandon, Cork, on the second floor of his family home, which was within yards of the famous Shandon Bells. From his youth he was called Jack.

His father, Daniel Lynch, was one of three sons reared on a small farm at Baugorm, south of the town of Bantry, County Cork. One brother emigrated to the United States and another stayed on the farm while Dan moved to Cork city around the turn of the century. He began as an apprentice tailor and initially shared digs with J. J. Walsh, who would later become Minister for Posts and Telegraphs in the first Free State government. In 1908, Dan married Nora O'Donoghue, who came originally from Glaunthaune, a short distance from Cork city. By the time they met, her family had moved to the city.

Nora was one of nine children and was already a seamstress when Dan met her. After they married, she would help him by doing hand-stitching at home. They had seven children. The first five were boys, one of whom died before Jack, the youngest of the boys, was born. Theo was the eldest, followed by Charlie and

Finbar. After Jack there were two girls, Rena and Eva. It was a happy home.

Jack remembered his father as 'a strict but fair' man. 'A tall, dignified-looking man, quiet and modest in all his doings,' was how Jack would later describe him. 'He liked a drink occasionally and was interested in sports.' He was a very quiet man who did not speak much, except after a few drinks. In his younger days he had played Gaelic football in Bantry and later with a Cork City team, but he was interested in all sports, despite the ban imposed on foreign games by the Gaelic Athletic Association. Dan Lynch attended rugby, soccer, Gaelic football and hurling matches and would take his boys with him. His main recreations, when Jack was young, were walking and road-bowling, which was a particularly popular sport in Cork.

Nora was an outgoing woman, deeply interested in music. She attended the Opera House almost every Thursday night, and passed on a love of music to Jack, who was very attached to her. He had the reputation of being the wild one of the family. 'He was always getting up to some devilment and, because he was the youngest of four boys, always getting away with murder at home,' his brother Theo recalled. Jack was the bane of the sexton's life at the church across the lane. His early memories were of playing pranks in the graveyard by the church, and it was not uncommon to see him being chased among the headstones by the sexton, who used to call him 'bullet-eyes'.

Jack played handball against the wall of the nearby butter market, and often played hurling, using the market's doorposts as a goal. He was also a keen swimmer, swimming in the Lee or the public baths, as the local swimming pool was called.

He began school at St Vincent's Convent, Peacock Lane in 1923 and remained there for two years before going to the Christian Brothers school, the North Monastery, where he spent the next eleven years. He would later say that teachers like Pat

Callanan, John Moore and Dan Moore had had a profound influence on him, as did Christian Brothers like Brothers Malone, Lawlor and Moynihan. The last, who was called 'Tango' by the students, later became Provincial of the Southern Province of the Christian Brothers. Like each of his older brothers, Jack spent some years as an altar boy.

In his final year of primary school, he secured a corporation scholarship. At the time there were just ten scholarships and he finished in a tie for tenth place, so an eleventh was specially awarded that year.

In October 1930, when Jack was thirteen, his mother took ill and went into the North Infirmary. It was thought to be a comparatively minor ailment, but she suffered a heart attack in the infirmary and died suddenly. Jack had been particularly close to her and he was 'absolutely shattered' by her death, according to himself. It was totally unexpected, and to make matters worse, she had been due to come home the following day.

'A nurse rushed up to the house from the North Infirmary to tell us that she had died,' he recalled. 'I walked around the streets in a daze for hours before coming back home and for years later I was deeply affected by the loss.'

With so many young children to look after, Dan decided to move the family in with Nora's married sister, Statia O'Reilly, and her husband and family. The O'Reillys had six children, the eldest of whom was just a few weeks younger than the youngest of the Lynch girls, so they became like one continuous family.

The two families first lived in 5 Vernon View on the South Douglas Road, but this meant that the Lynch boys were living some three or four miles from their school at the North Monastery, so the two families moved to 22 Redemption Road on the north side of the city, nearer the school. The two eldest Lynch boys had grown up and moved away from home by then, but they still thought of the family house as home and returned there for holidays. When they were all together, there were fifteen people in the house.

It was a happy home – so much so that some of them would look back and say that there was never even an argument in the house, but that is never the way with large families. Theo remembered that Jack and his sister Rena were always quarrelling, but this was also a sign of affection, as they were to be the closest members of the family throughout life.

'When we moved into our aunt's house, there were twelve of us in all, so you can imagine there was never a dull moment,' Rena recalled. 'Jack was the liveliest of the lot: a great mimic and easily the brainiest of the family.'

Among Jack's childhood friends were Michael Twomey, the son of a local butcher; Tadhg Carey, the future president of University College Cork; Leo Skentelberry, a future Irish ambassador to Argentina and Australia; and Tadhg Carroll, future secretary of the Department of Labour. Lynch's teachers remembered him as a very good student, but he was an even better hurler and actually made the school's senior hurling team when he was just fourteen years old. He was injured in one of the earlier games when he was hit in the back of the head with a hurley in a game with St Finbarr's College, Farrenferris. Those were the days before they wore any protective headgear. Lynch believed that the accident was caused by his own hesitation. From then on, he believed that 'you either get in or stay out.'

Jimmy Barry, who would train the Cork team for many years, remembered noticing Lynch as a schoolboy. 'I was refereeing a match between the "Mon" and Farrenferris,' he recalled. 'The clever movements of the young fellow playing centre-back for the "Mon" caught my eye. He had the best idea of playing centre-back that I had seen for a long time.' After the game, as the players were heading for the dressing rooms, Barry asked Jack his name. Lynch told him and then followed him to ask why he had wanted to know. 'I told him that if he continued to hurl as he did that day, he would soon wear the Cork jersey.'

Lynch was a member of the school team that won the Munster Colleges Championship – the Dr Harty Cup – in 1935, and he captained the side to retain the trophy the following year. He also had the distinction of playing on the team that won the double by taking the Munster Colleges football title as well. As a seventeen-year-old, he was so fit that he never looked too bulky when fully dressed, but when togged out, he had a powerful, athletic build and weighed twelve and a half stone. By then he had already won a senior County Championship medal with Glen Rovers, played for the Cork minors and had been selected to play on the Cork senior team in the National League while still in his fifth year at secondary school.

'I think it was recognised fairly early that I had an ability as a hurler and frankly I took advantage of this for missing an occasional class, as I used to have allowances made for me by the teachers, who were convinced I was otherwise preoccupied – which may not always have been the case,' he recalled.

His brothers Theo, Charlie and Finbar had all joined the Glen Rovers hurling club at a young age, so it was natural that Jack would follow suit. There he came under the influence of Paddy O'Connell, one of the great father figures of the club. Paddy recognised young Jack's potential and took a particular interest in his progress.

'He used to take me to some of the big Munster Championship matches and point out facets of the play to me, and the techniques of the various players,' Jack recalled. 'For instance, I remember him getting me to watch Mickey Cross, the Limerick half-back in the early thirties. He was one of Paddy's own favourites. I noted how he moved towards a ball, how he sized up to it, how occasionally he would let it pass him in order to create greater pace for himself, etc. I learned quite a lot about tactics and, I suppose, to think about the game during those outings.'

'I have a distinct recollection of Jack going off to a Munster final in Thurles with Paddy O'Connell and wearing a lovely new coat that was bought for him a day or two earlier,' his brother Theo recalled. 'He came back from the match all right, but there was no sign of the coat, which was left behind in the excitement of the day. He was like that, despite all my father said to him.' This might well have been one of the earliest signs of his later forgetfulness.

He played his first championship match with Cork the following year. After securing his Leaving Certificate in 1936, he took up a temporary position with the Dublin District Milk Board. Seán Brennan, one of the leading lights of the Civil Service GAA Club, was in charge of the board at the time, and Lynch's involvement with the club undoubtedly enhanced his prospects of getting a permanent position in the civil service.

After four months in Dublin he moved back to Cork at Christmas and took up a position in the Circuit Court Office on 29 December 1936. 'The County Registrar asked me to sit with him in court and after a while he let me take over as acting registrar, sitting in the court on my own until 1943.'

During those years he played hurling with Glen Rovers and was one of the few to win County Championship medals in each of the club's famous eight victories in a row from 1934 to 1941, but this was a particularly bleak period for senior hurling in the county. He also played with St Nicholas, the Glen's sister football club that he helped to win the County Championship in 1938, and again in 1941. But Cork was in the GAA doldrums for much of the period. After winning the all-Ireland hurling title in 1931, Cork was beaten in the Munster final the following year and did not reach another Munster final until 1939, when Lynch captained the team to victory over all-Ireland champions Limerick in what many witnesses said was the greatest hurling game ever played. With just a minute to go Limerick were leading by a point until Cork got a goal and won the match.

Jimmy Barry, the team trainer and coach, thought that Lynch made an ideal captain. 'He was in a very strong position to dictate to others,' Barry explained, 'because he always played well himself, and besides, others had a tremendous respect for him. Training him was simple. He was always very sincere and straightforward and this made him easy to mould.'

The all-Ireland final against Kilkenny was played on 3 September 1939. That morning the British Prime Minister Neville Chamberlain made his famous broadcast announcing that Britain was at war with Germany. It had been a wet morning but the day developed beautifully. The game began in bright sunshine, but it would be remembered as the 'thundering and lightning final', because it ended in a storm.

The young Cork team got off to a nervous start as Kilkenny scored two early goals, and Cork were still six points down at the halfway stage. The broadcast of the match was actually interrupted by a newsflash that France had declared war on Germany.

In the second half Cork began their fightback with Lynch playing a major role at centre field. Late in the game Cork got a twenty-one-yard free kick and Lynch tried to blast for a goal, but it was saved. With just two minutes left to play, Cork finally drew level. The last couple of minutes were played out in a frightening thunderstorm and a deluge of rain. With the approach of the full-time whistle, Kilkenny were awarded a 'seventy'. Cork managed to clear the *sliotar* but only to Jimmy Kelly of Kilkenny, some sixty-five yards from the goal. He drove it over the bar for the winning point.

'As a young man it took me a long, long time to forget the defeat by one point, the very last puck of the game,' Lynch recalled almost fifty years later. 'I can remember every inch and every movement of that final puck and I felt I could have stopped it.' Europe may have been in convulsions, but Lynch was more upset by Cork's defeat. 'I was much more concerned that evening about our losing the match,' he said. He had an added weight on his mind: not only did he think that he might have been able to block the final point somehow, but there was also the realisation of what might have been if he had tapped the twenty-one-yard free kick over the bar.

He did go on to captain the team to victory in the National League, in which the famous Christy Ring made his debut on the Cork senior hurling team. In Lynch's estimation, Ring was to become 'the greatest hurler of all times'.

Cork qualified for the Munster final again in 1940. It was another epic encounter. 'Scribblers are bankrupt for phrases,' one reporter noted. 'Our vocabulary is exhausted.' A new language was needed to describe the superlative match, which ended in a draw. The replay the following week was every bit as good. At the start of the second half, Limerick went into a seven-point lead by notching up ten points in the first ten minutes. Lynch then began a revival by scoring a goal, but it was too late to make up the whole deficit and Limerick won by two points, going on to capture the all-Ireland title that year.

The National League was suspended for the remainder of the Second World War, or the 'Emergency' as it was known in Ireland. The championship itself was disrupted by travel restrictions in 1941, as a result of a foot-and-mouth epidemic. Cork were supposed to play Tipperary, but there were severe travel restrictions placed on Tipperary and the game could not take place, so it was decided that Cork would play all-Ireland champions Limerick for the right to represent Munster in the all-Ireland final. The winner would play Tipperary in the Munster final, to be held after the all-Ireland final. Cork duly hammered Limerick (8–10 to 3–2) and then trounced Dublin (5–11 to 0–6) on the last Sunday in September. Lynch was playing well in the final until he was injured and had to go off.

Cork won that all-Ireland Hurling Championship after playing just two games and neither of the opponents got within even six goals of them, but they were to be upset in the Munster final on the last Sunday in October, when Tipperary won (5–4 to 2–5). Lynch thus had the distinction of being a member of the first team to win an all-Ireland title even though a different team won the provincial championship. That same year he also played on the St Nicholas team that won the Cork county football championship.

During this period Lynch became particularly friendly with Christy Ring, who obviously looked up to him. In 1941, Ring had a dispute with his club, Cloyne, and refused to play with the team again. At the time he was earning his living as a driver and was facing prosecution for a driving offence. He was deeply worried that he might lose his licence and sought the help of Lynch, who assured him that he would only be fined about ten shillings. When this turned out to be the case, Ring was profoundly grateful to Lynch, who invited him to join Glen Rovers. The rest is history. Ring went on to win a record eight all-Ireland medals.

While working in the courthouse, Lynch watched the lawyers in action and became interested in the legal profession himself. Watching the barristers working, he thought they were a mediocre lot and that he could do the job easily – the only difference being that they had a degree. In 1941, therefore, he began taking evening classes in law at University College Cork under C. K. Murphy, a practising solicitor, and the barrister Denis P. O'Donovan. Another of his lecturers was Alfred O'Rahilly, an intriguing character who served for many years as president of the college before retiring, a widower, to enter the priesthood. The only other student doing law with Lynch at the time was David Marcus, who later distinguished himself as a novelist and the literary editor of the *Irish Press*.

'He would come home for his tea and study from seven to twelve midnight,' according to his brother Theo, 'and then he would get up again early in the morning to study again before going to work, and at the same time he was playing hurling and football. Frankly, I don't know how he did it.'

In 1942, Lynch again captained Cork in the hurling championship, in which the most difficult match was in the first round, against old rivals Limerick. After winning that, Cork had little difficulty in the rest of the championship, easily beating Tipperary in the Munster final, Galway in the all-Ireland semi-final, and Dublin by seven points in the final. He therefore had the distinction of being presented with the Liam McCarthy Cup.

The following summer was a particularly busy one for Lynch. He was playing as a wing-back on the Cork football team which had almost caused a sensation against Kerry in the Munster semi-final in Killarney. Cork had not beaten Kerry for thirty years, and as a result Kerry tended to take Cork rather lightly. They were very lucky to get away with a draw on the day. Thus, Kerry were ready for the replay at the Athletics Grounds in Cork, but much to their surprise, Cork were even better. There was a record gate for the game, which Cork won by the narrowest of margins, but even the *Kerryman* newspaper concluded that they should have won by more. Cork went on to beat Tipperary in the Munster final but lost out to Cavan in the all-Ireland semi-final.

The Cork hurlers went all the way again 1943. Their five-point win over Waterford in the Munster final was their closest game of the whole championship. Immediately after that game, Lynch went on holidays with some friends to Glengarriff. There was a group of girls staying at the hotel and the two groups teamed up to go hiking, swimming and dancing. One of them was Máirín O'Connor, with whom Lynch fell in love.

He was only able to do the first two years of the legal course at UCC, so he had to move back to Dublin to attend King's Inns if he wished to continue his studies. He therefore secured a transfer within the civil service to Dublin, where Máirín, the daughter of a judge, was living. Their relationship blossomed.

'My transfer to Dublin, within the civil-service structure, was again facilitated because of my sporting connections,' he explained. 'Paddy Ó Ceallaigh, a principal officer in the Department of Finance and also chairman of the Civil Service Football Club, arranged my transfer to Dublin and I joined the club.'

'I was attached to the District Court Clerks' Branch, which is near what is now the entrance to the new wing of Leinster House, close to where ministerial cars are parked when the Dáil is sitting,' Lynch continued. 'I was able to get off work there during term-time at 4.30 to attend lectures in the King's Inns.' Shortly afterwards he was transferred to the Department of Justice, where he became private secretary to the secretary of the department, Stephen A. Roche, who allowed Lynch time off to continue his studies. It was while working for him that Lynch first visited the Dáil in Leinster House. Roche sent him to seek out Fionán Lynch, the Fine Gael deputy from Kerry South, so that he could be formally notified of his appointment as a judge to the Circuit Court.

In 1944 Jack Lynch was chosen to play on the Munster teams for the Railway Cup in both football and hurling. For the first time ever, Cork players filled a majority of the places on the football team, but they were beaten decisively by Ulster in their first game. Cork went out to Tipperary in the first round of the football championship but the hurlers qualified to meet Limerick in what was called 'The Great Bicycle Final' in Thurles. The transportation system was severely disrupted by the wartime fuel shortages, so a horde of cyclists descended on Thurles and were rewarded with a thrilling game that ended in a draw. The replay a fortnight later lived up to expectations and was another thriller that was only decided in the final minute with a goal by Christy Ring. After a narrow win over Galway in the all-Ireland semi-final, Cork went on to take the title by beating Dublin easily in the final. It was the first time that any county had won four all-

Ireland hurling titles in a row, and Lynch was one of nine players who had started in all four finals.

While in Dublin he played for the Civil Service Club, and he helped it to win its first Dublin County football championship in 1944. 'Playing with the civil service, I began, really for the first time, to take football seriously and play in the company of players to whom football was their only sporting interest. I think it helped me greatly.' He was an accomplished all-round sportsman, as he demonstrated that year after Tipperary knocked out Cork in the first round of the 1945 hurling championship. Cork got a measure of revenge by beating Tipperary by the narrowest margin in the football championship, in which Jack moved to the wing forwards. In the Munster final at Killarney, Cork surprised Kerry.

'Apparently nothing was learned from the defeat in 1943,' complained a disgusted reporter in the *Kerryman*. Cork were much fitter and ran out easy winners. Cork were trailing by a point in the first half when Lynch scored a couple of points to put them into a lead from which they never looked back. They were leading by seven points in the final quarter when Lynch finished off a dazzling move with a goal, but it was disallowed, as he was adjudged to have been 'inside the square'. Minutes later, he had another opportunity to score a goal, but he drove the ball wide. Yet Cork still won by five points.

After beating Galway in the all-Ireland semi-final, Cork beat Cavan in the all-Ireland final to avenge their defeat two years earlier. Lynch was unlucky in the first half to have his shot for goal come back off the upright, but he played a vital part in the final minute of the game by passing the ball which led to Cork's second goal, as the team won by 2–5 to 0–7. It was Cork's first time winning the Sam Maguire Cup, and it would be the county's only all-Ireland senior football title between 1911 and 1973.

In late 1945 Lynch was called to the bar and was faced with the difficult decision of whether or not to stay in the security of the civil service, in which he was clearly progressing. 'To be quite honest, as a career it got me down,' he admitted. 'I tossed a coin, heads or tails I'd resign from the civil service.' He decided to quit and moved back to Cork, where he set up in private practice as a barrister. He continued to play football and hurling. The Cork footballers were beaten by Kerry in the first round of the 1946 championship, but the hurlers had an eight-point victory over Clare at the same stage.

Lynch was not long back in Cork when he was approached by friends in Fianna Fáil – Maurice Forde, Pat McNamara, Bill Barry and Garret McAuliffe of the Brothers Delaney *cumann* of the party – to stand for the Dáil in a Cork City by-election in June 1946, called to fill the seat vacated as a result of the retirement of William Dwyer, the founder of the Sunbeam Woolsey textile firm. Jack had never taken any active part in politics, other than carrying a banner as a fourteen-year-old in a parade for Éamon de Valera when he came to Cork as Fianna Fáil leader during the 1932 general-election campaign. 'There was a great feeling for Dev at the time,' he later recalled. 'I was conscious of him being a marvellous, romantic figure.'

He did not remember either of his parents being politically inclined, but his father's people were strongly anti-Treaty, and the Lynch boys went to stay with them on holidays near Bantry every year. Jack figured that 'some of their instinctual feelings' were transmitted to him, but he never knew how his father voted.

'Politics were never discussed,' Jack explained. No doubt part of his father's political reserve would have been prompted by the fact that part of his business was providing uniforms for Army officers, who would all have been strongly pro-Treaty, at least prior to 1932.

Lynch declined the invitation to stand for the Fianna Fáil nomination in 1946, because it would have meant opposing Patrick 'Pa' McGrath, who had been working actively within Fianna Fáil for years. Jack indicated, however, that he would be interested in standing for the party at the next general election. He then campaigned for McGrath, for whom he made his first political speech from a platform that he shared with Frank Aiken at Blackpool Bridge. McGrath won the seat comfortably on the second count, on transfers from the independent Tom Barry, the hero of the War of Independence. Barry's fame did not translate into votes at the ballot box in this, his first and only venture into electoral politics. He finished at the bottom of the poll, well behind even Michael O'Riordan, a proclaimed socialist who was the lone standard-bearer for the Communist Party of Ireland for many years.

Cork defeated Waterford, Limerick and Galway – with at least three goals to spare in each game – to qualify for the all-Ireland hurling final against Kilkenny. On 10 August 1946 Jack and Máirín were married. From the outset, she was prepared to support him in anything that he wished to do, as she wanted to see him happy. It made for a very successful relationship.

Cork defeated Kilkenny easily in the all-Ireland final and Lynch won his sixth senior medal in a row – a feat that was never before achieved, nor has been equalled since. He always looked back on the year that followed that victory as the happiest of his life. Newly married and building up a practice at the bar, he obviously relished the challenges. At the outset he was warned that it was going to be particularly difficult.

'You know, young man,' the senior barrister Jim Maher warned him, 'you come in here to a sow that has a big litter and she has only a limited number of tits, and unfortunately there's none left for us.' But of course Lynch had one enormous advantage over any other barrister starting out. As he had acted as registrar of the Circuit Court for so many years, solicitors had regularly been in contact with him about when their cases would be called, so they already knew him: hence they were more likely to bring him business. The fact that he was not seen as political in those days also probably helped him. The solicitor who brought him most business had strong ties with Fine Gael: Michael Collins-Powell, a nephew of the famous Michael Collins.

Lynch described himself as a 'journeyman barrister' in that he did not specialise in any particular form of law; he just took whatever cases were offered to him. He got the reputation of being 'quietly efficient'. His first case involved 'cattle-rustling'. His client, a butcher, had slaughtered a stray, but Lynch managed to get him off, as two different juries failed to reach a verdict. Thus it was seen as a victory for Lynch. Another of his more memorable cases involved a compensation claim on behalf of a youngster from his own Blackpool area. In the course of the case, heard before Judge Joseph O'Connor, Lynch made a number of technical arguments, to the amazement of some of his childhood neighbours. 'He's able to talk up to them, boy!' one spectator was heard to say in a tone that betrayed as much surprise as admiration.

Jack Lynch never lost the common touch, no matter how successful he became. His old acquaintances always thought of him as one of the lads. Even as a barrister, he continued to play football and hurling. In 1947, the Cork hurlers again made it all the way to the all-Ireland final. Lynch was still playing in the demanding position at centre field, but Cork went down by the narrowest margin to Kilkenny, who won with two late points. Lynch blamed himself for this defeat because he missed two chances to equalise in the dying moments, driving both shots wide.

In 1947, the new political party Clann na Poblachta, which had been formed the previous year from much the same background as Fianna Fáil, began making inroads into Fianna Fáil's republican support. The new party won two by-elections in October and was preparing to put up enough candidates at the following general election to form a majority government. Lynch was approached by Paddy Murphy, a butcher friend, to stand for Clann na Poblachta, but he refused, on the grounds that his interest lay with Fianna

Fáil. At the time, Fianna Fáil seemed under threat, but Éamon de Valera met the challenge head-on by calling a surprise general election in February 1948, even though the existing Dáil still had another fifteen months to run.

Lynch's friends from the Brothers Delaney *cumann* again asked for his permission to nominate him at the party's selection convention. He discussed the move with Máirín. She would have preferred him to stay out of politics, but she knew that he wanted to get involved in it and she supported him fully. 'I would have had more of him to myself, I suppose,' she explained, 'but if he had not entered politics, he would not have been happy, and my happiness depends on his. If he was miserable outside politics, I would be too.'

He therefore agreed to allow his name to go forward. It was only after he was nominated to stand with McGrath, Walter Furlong and Seán McCarthy that he formally joined the party.

The cost of living and the economic shortages were the main election issues. Lynch's own power base was in the Glen Rovers Club, whose members canvassed for him. But it was a highly personalised campaign. They were supporting Jack Lynch, not Fianna Fáil, whose top brass were particularly unhappy when club members began circulating polling cards that merely called for support for Lynch. 'I asked Glen Rovers not to do it,' Lynch explained, 'but they argued that it was purely a private matter for them and didn't involve the Fianna Fáil party. I went so far as to impound the personal canvass cards, but they got another supply.' There was tension with the other Fianna Fáil candidates until Tom Crofts persuaded the Glen Rovers canvassers to ask for support for the others as well.

Lynch met Éamon de Valera for the first time when he came to Cork for an election rally. They met in a private house in Blackpool before the rally.

De Valera was keen to be briefed on local issues before he

addressed the people. He then left the city in order to make a processional entry. 'I had a reverential awe for him,' Lynch said, 'but at that meeting, I found him very human.'

It was not a particularly good election for Fianna Fáil, which had been in power for sixteen years. People wanted change, so they voted for various opposition parties. Lynch headed the Fianna Fáil panel, with McGrath just behind him. They retained the two seats for Fianna Fáil, which lost its overall majority and was replaced in government by a National Coalition comprised of no fewer than six parties and a number of independents.

Although Lynch had moved into politics, he did not yet hang up his hurling boots. He continued to play for another couple of years. But he brought the lessons he had learned on the sporting field into politics with him. 'I made friendships practically all over the country and this, I suppose, helped in the political sphere afterwards,' he explained. 'I learned from hurling and football a discipline and a self-control, how to be part of a team and how to cope with both victory and defeat. All players acquire these qualities in time, if they are to survive, and they apply well to life outside sport.'

Throughout his whole playing career he remembered losing his temper only twice. Once was in a county championship match when an opponent made an extremely offensive comment; the other time was a dangerous foul tackle in an inter-county game. In politics he would make a name for himself with the same kind of quiet control that he displayed on the playing pitch, but he would make his greatest impact as a good team player in the political game.

2

BUDDING POLITICIAN

1948–1951

Having been in power for so long, Fianna Fáil took a while to acclimatise to being in opposition. Lynch was soon appointed secretary to the parliamentary party and put in charge of research. He was expected to draft de Valera's speeches and index the Dáil debates and newspaper articles, as well as preparing briefs for the members of the front bench.

'I got on very well with Dev and liked him a lot,' Lynch explained. 'One of his traits I noticed particularly was his meticulous attention to the words he used in public speeches. I used to help him on his speeches from 1948 to '49 and I learned a lot of the need for precision in speech from Dev.' But his role as research assistant and speechwriter was so time-consuming that his legal practice suffered.

'I stayed with the job for a year but after that I went to Dev and told him that I couldn't afford to continue to neglect my legal duties completely,' Jack recalled. 'He understood my position and he took in Pádraig Ó hAnnracháin as his own private secretary and this relieved me of most of the work I had been doing.' In 1950 Jack returned to his practice on the Cork Circuit.

Even as a Dáil deputy he continued to line out with Cork in the hurling championship, but he was losing some of his pace and moved into the full-forward line. Some 40,000 people saw Cork defeat Limerick in Thurles in 1948, but the team then lost by a point to Waterford in the Munster final. The Waterford team went on to win the all-Ireland title that year.

Jack played again in 1949 when Cork had a couple of epic games against Tipperary. The first game was in injury time when Tipperary managed to score a goal to tie. As full forward, under the existing rules Lynch would have been expected to charge the goalkeeper and the story circulated afterwards that after Jack challenged him, Tony Reddan, the Tipperary goalkeeper, warned him that if he tried that again, there would be a by-election in Cork.

With just five minutes left in the replay, Cork were four points down. Lynch went out in the field to collect a ball and raced through the Tipperary defence to score a goal. Cork added a point shortly afterwards to tie up the game at 3–10 each. Lynch scored 1–6 of that total. For the first time ever in the championship, extra time was played, before Tipperary eventually won.

Afterwards one of the great talking points of the game was of a goal that was never given to Cork. Many people claimed that the *sliotar* hit the stanchion holding the wire net in the goalmouth. The ball came out so quickly that others claimed that it never went in. The following year it was decided to do away with wire netting and use cord instead.

Lynch played his final championship game in the Munster Hurling Final at Killarney in 1950, when Tipperary won by 2–17 to 3–11. The game ended in a bit of a shambles when the crowd spilled onto the pitch for the final minutes. Jim Barry, the Cork trainer, complained that it was the worst stewarding he had ever seen. At one point he claimed that Cork should have had a 'seventy' but the umpires could not see, with all the people on the end line.

Although Lynch was one of the youngest members of the Dáil, he was able to secure a political profile by asking parliamentary questions, or by engaging in debate on the few opportunities that were allowed to him as a backbencher. The Dáil was still somewhat polarised by Civil-War politics. Although the Civil War had been over for more than a quarter of a century, the bitterness still remained, as most of the principal figures in both Fine Gael and Fianna Fáil had been active in the conflict.

Lynch was a member of a new breed of politicians with no political baggage. Although he was among the country's most famous sportsmen, he had always been modest about his own accomplishments. There was never anything of the braggart about him during his playing days and he was just as modest when he entered the Dáil. He avoided the Civil-War invective that frequently permeated debates. He was polite to everyone. As a result, he was liked on all sides of the Dáil.

One of his earliest Dáil speeches was during an adjournment debate on the Workman's Compensation Act in April 1949. The minimum payment had been raised to 50 shillings a week in 1948 but if the courts had previously ordered that an individual should get the previous maximum of 30 shillings a week, those people would still only get that amount. Lynch complained that this was unfair and he instanced three specific cases in which this had happened. William Norton, the Tánaiste and leader of the Labour Party, rebuked him mildly by suggesting that Lynch should consult a lawyer on the matter. 'If he gets some legal advice, he will find that these people can recover a greater rate of compensation than he or some of those for whom he speaks appear to realise,' Norton said. As Lynch had qualified as a barrister, Norton's suggestion was highly insulting, but the insult was not intended. Norton had only thought of him as a sportsman, not as a barrister. He admitted that he was 'completely unaware' of Lynch's professional qualifications. 'Insofar as the reply purported to be even in the remotest degree a reflection on his professional qualifications,' Norton told the Dáil in apology next day, 'I withdraw any such unintended reflection.' Whether Lynch was right or not would be for the courts to decide, but Norton was at pains to emphasise that no personal or professional slight was intended. 'I want to assure him that I had no such thought in my mind and I would ask him to accept that,' Norton repeated.

'I accept that explanation unreservedly,' Lynch replied. Such gracious exchanges tended to stand out because members on opposite sides of the Dáil were so often at each other's throats.

Lynch assured the Dáil that he was not calling for more money to encourage malingering. Thirty years later, when he stepped down as Taoiseach, there was an anomaly within the system in which people would take home more in unemployment insurance than they would have received if they had been earning, because the benefits were not taxed.

It was ironic that one of Lynch's other questions in the Dáil concerned the building of swimming pools. In March 1949 he asked the Minister for Local Government, Brendan Corish, if his department would honour the commitment of his Fianna Fáil predecessor to provide local authorities with up to 60 per cent of the cost of 'indoor and outdoor swimming facilities within their administrative areas.'

The Fianna Fáil minister had made the promise but Corish noted that no provision had been made in the estimates for the money. In other words, it was just political posturing. As far as the new government was concerned, swimming pools were strictly a matter for the local authorities themselves. An Olympic-sized swimming pool would not be built in the country during Lynch's lifetime.

Other questions raised by Lynch concerned emigration – which was over 30,000 annually in 1948 – and the number of private premises being rented by the state or semi-state organisations in

Dublin. At the time, there were twenty-seven different private premises being occupied by officials in the state sector.

On 1 December 1949 he questioned Paddy McGilligan, the Minister for Finance, about the failure to pass on an increase in civil-service pensions to those who had retired before the increase. Those people had also been hit by the rise in the cost of living that the increase covered. He noted that Fianna Fáil had made provisions for those already retired when it had last raised pensions in 1946.

Talk of pensions tended to be a touchy subject, since the Cumann na nGaedheal government had cut a shilling off the old-age pension in 1924. It was the kind of mean and insensitive cost-cutting measure that had to be endured by one of the weakest sections of society. Whatever it may have saved the exchequer, it cost the government far more in terms of political support, because Fianna Fáil politicians berated their opponents for the shilling reduction for decades afterwards. Paddy McGilligan, the Minister for Finance, had been a member of that government and, as such, he was a convenient target for Fianna Fáil ridicule. While Lynch did not engage in any posturing theatrics to exploit the issue, he did not have to, because everybody who had any interest in Irish politics was well aware of the saga of the shilling.

Lynch took part in the detailed discussions on amendments at the committee stage of the Criminal Justice Bill in 1949 in a constructive way. He objected to giving district judges the power to imprison somebody for as long as twelve months, because the district courts were only supposed to deal with summary justice. He also advocated that free legal aid should be provided for people who could not afford legal representation.

He complained about the amount of foreign travel being undertaken by Seán MacBride, the Minister for External Affairs, whom he had heard 'referred to as the External Minister for Affairs'. There was too much entertaining as far as Lynch was concerned. He complained about the lavish way in which the government was entertaining some foreign guests. 'On occasions recently I have seen where distinguished visitors have been entertained to luncheon at Iveagh House and to dinner that same evening in Áras an Uachtaráin,' he said. 'I think we are being somewhat extravagant in this respect, considering our resources as a nation.'

Lynch also objected to the government's establishment of the Irish News Agency, on the grounds that it would hurt the employment of journalists. He argued that the agency would be supplying copy and that there would not be room for stories by journalists because of the shortage of newsprint. He also accused the government of establishing too many committees, authorities and boards. 'It is a saga of "passing the buck" as has never been known under any administration, not only in this country but in any country,' Lynch said. 'The time has come when ministers must be made to bear their own responsibilities for their own particular departments.' Specifically, he objected to allowing members of the new Industrial Development Authority to determine investment in private industries.

'I suggest again that it is a dangerous precedent to allow men appointed by the minister to this authority to have control over the expenditure of moneys in the establishment of industries that are being contemplated by private individuals,' he argued. 'It is a continuation of a principle which has been accepted by this government, of setting up outside bodies to control administration, relieving ministers of responsibilities which they should themselves retain.'

Lynch also asked questions about teachers' pay and conditions, about unemployment insurance, about contributions under the National Health Insurance, and about food subsidies.

In April 1951 the political world was rocked by the mother-and-child controversy when Noël Browne was forced to resign as

Minister for Health because he baulked at accepting the dictat of the Catholic hierarchy. They had opposed the government's bill because in the opinion of some bishops, especially the Archbishop of Dublin, John Charles McQuaid, it smacked of creeping socialism. He insisted that the bill should include a means test, whereas Browne wanted the scheme to cover as many people as possible in order to tackle the country's disgracefully high infant-mortality rate. It would go down as one of the most significant political controversies of the second half of the twentieth century, but Lynch took no part in the debate. Under de Valera, Fianna Fáil stood back and allowed deputies of the government parties to savage each other in a particularly bitter debate. De Valera's only contribution was at the very end of the exchanges when, with a politically majestic touch, he dismissed the whole controversy with a single sentence. 'I think,' he said, 'we have heard enough.'

The issues involved were of monumental significance. If Fianna Fáil had intervened, it would probably have tended to promote unity within the government parties, but as it was, they split among themselves and the government soon collapsed. Lynch's one contribution to the whole controversy was after the defeat of the mother-and-child scheme, when he asked if health officers in Cork would be consulted before any new bill was drafted.

In reality, none of his contributions from the opposition benches amounted to much. They just showed where his own interests lay. The first National Government came tumbling down as a result of its own internal difficulties, rather than anything Fianna Fáil had done.

3

PARLIAMENTARY SECRETARY

1951–1954

After the general election that ensued as a result of the collapse of the government, Fianna Fáil was returned to power. Éamon de Valera was elected Taoiseach with the help of some independents, including Noël Browne and a deputy from Kerry South, Jack Flynn, who had served as a Fianna Fáil deputy in the Dáil from 1932 to 1943 but had been forced to stand down as a candidate by de Valera in 1943 for 'womanising'. As they used to put it delicately at the time, he got a young woman 'into trouble' and she happened to be the niece of a prominent cleric. In the circumstances, Flynn had to bow out of politics for a while.

But he was elected again in 1948 as an independent deputy, and after he was re-elected in 1951 he found himself in the happy position of being one of a few independent deputies who held the balance of power. He supported de Valera and, his past indiscretions soon forgiven, was welcomed back into the party fold.

When Lynch arrived for the inauguration of the new Dáil, he was greeted with the news that he was likely to be offered a position by de Valera. 'I got the first hint that I was to be promoted to government office when I went to my pigeon-hole in Leinster

·House to collect my mail on the day the Dáil resumed.' The new Fine Gael deputy from North Kerry, whose name was also Jack Lynch, handed him a letter that he had opened mistakenly, thinking it was for himself.

'He said something to the effect that the news would please me,' the Corkman recalled. 'It was a letter from Dev informing me of my appointment and asking me to come to see him.'

It was the first time that Lynch had ever been in the Taoiseach's office. 'He informed me that he was appointing me to a new position, Parliamentary Secretary to the Government, with roving responsibilities for the Gaeltacht and the congested districts.' Jack was assigned the 'task of the coordination and initiation of schemes designed to develop the Gaeltacht economically and otherwise.'

Helping the disparate Gaeltacht areas was a major problem, because they tended to be the most economically deprived parts of the country, with poor land and no industrial base. For over a century, use of the Irish language had been declining, because many of the native speakers tended to view the language as a badge of backwardness. They therefore insisted that their children should be raised speaking English. One child reared in such circumstances was Michael Collins. Both of his parents were native Irish speakers, but they only used the language at home when they did not want their children to know what they were talking about. Some of those authorities who wished to revive the language contributed to this mentality by their own attitude.

Comdháil Náisiúnta na Gaeilge had reservations, for instance, that if industries were set up in the heart of the Gaeltacht there was a danger that this 'might tend to spread the use of the English language and so anglicise those areas.' Jack Lynch, who disagreed with that viewpoint, wanted the areas to develop economically rather than have Gaeltacht areas preserved as 'a kind of museum showpiece.'

'To create or maintain a condition of poverty amongst the

residents of the Fíor-Ghaeltacht areas is the surest possible way to kill the language,' Lynch argued. 'I am sincerely convinced of this, that unless these people get a decent way of living within the confines of their own Fíor-Ghaeltacht areas, they will be justified in abandoning those areas, and if they forget the language as a result of that, it will not be their fault.'

The work being done for Gaeltacht areas was already dispersed among different ministries and departments of state, such as the departments of lands, forestry, agriculture and education. 'I was supposed to have equal access to all departments, with the result that I came to be regarded as a sort of "mendicant", a nuisance,' he explained.

Some people suggested that a 'Bord na Gaeltachta' should be established to coordinate reforms. At de Valera's suggestion, an inter-departmental committee of senior civil servants from each of the departments involved was set up to examine the question. Those who were calling for a new board failed to come up with 'even the bones of a comprehensive scheme' on how the available money could best be spent, however. They did not suggest any 'practical scheme', according to Lynch. In true bureaucratic style, the committee argued that there was 'no inherent demand from the people of the Gaeltacht for such a board', with the result that the inter-departmental committee could undertake the task itself.

Lynch would demonstrate throughout his political career that he was loath to interfere with his civil servants. On this occasion, for instance, he ruled out the establishment of a special ministry for Gaeltacht areas on the grounds that 'it would be difficult and impracticable to divest the different departments such as lands, forestry, agriculture and education' of their existing functions and vest the administration in the Gaeltacht areas 'in a Minister for the Gaeltacht.'

Having criticised the previous government for establishing too many committees, authorities and boards, it was ironic that the first thing that Lynch was to do in government was establish the new inter-departmental committee, to consider the establishment of a new board. Oifig na Gaeltachta (the Gaeltacht Office) was then set up without any actual planned functions. He secured the necessary legislative approval to establish the office and relied on the civil servants to figure out what to do next.

'The sum which the Dáil has been asked to vote has reference only to the salaries and expenses of the office which has been created,' Lynch told the Dáil. 'There is no provision for any development in undertakings at the moment.' It was symptomatic of his slow, cautious style brought about by his heavy dependence on his civil servants. James Dillon, the Minister for Agriculture in the outgoing government, wrote to Lynch with certain suggestions, but officials at the Department of Agriculture were opposed to Dillon's ideas and even threw cold water on some of the projects that Dillon had initiated himself.

'Being a deputy from a city area with some little knowledge of the Gaeltacht, but not such a sufficient knowledge as to be able to tackle the job with which I was charged in a proper manner,' Lynch explained, 'I decided to go quietly around the Gaeltacht areas and visit as many of the places as possible or meet as many of the people as I could and talk to them about their particular problems.'

He privately informed those members of the Dáil and Senate who represented Gaeltacht areas of his plans, but he soon found this was a mistake because the various politicians used the occasion to emphasise their own concern for the welfare of their constituents, and everywhere that Lynch visited he inevitably found himself at large, unwieldy public meetings.

Seán Collins, the Fine Gael deputy from Cork South-west and older brother of the famous Michael Collins, derided Lynch's Gaeltacht meetings as 'nothing but hot air'.

Lynch responded that he had played down his visits. He only informed respective deputies and senators privately. 'I tried to give these visits as little publicity as possible,' he said. 'I tried, in the best manner I could, to go to the scene of operations, meet the people concerned and discuss their problems with them and help in their solution.'

James Dillon was also critical of the Gaeltacht meetings, which he dismissed as a charade, but he blamed the Taoiseach. Dillon complained that the establishment of the Office of the Gaeltacht was 'a political stunt' or 'a dirty racket' designed by de Valera to shore up Fianna Fáil's declining fortunes in the west of Ireland. Dillon was a brilliant orator, though his theatrical style of speaking was more suited to the political past. He engaged in the kind of posturing point-scoring that often had nothing to do with political realities. It impressed his own followers, because of the drabness of routine politics. His oratory also impressed – or at least amused – the journalists who covered politics, but it never had much appeal for uncommitted voters.

Throughout most of Lynch's political career, Fine Gael never seemed to realise that there was little political benefit in preaching to their own convinced supporters while essentially ignoring the desires and aspirations of the rest of society. Dillon, who would take over as leader of Fine Gael before the end of the decade, was a master of outdated techniques. He spent most of his time ridiculing Fianna Fáil in general and de Valera in particular, just as Fine Gael had been doing since he helped to establish the party in 1933. Dillon certainly delivered his withering invective with more style than his colleagues, but he was no more effective, because he was only appealing to his own supporters, and in the process he frequently repulsed those who held the middle ground, especially those of the younger generation who had not been infected by the bitterness arising from the events of the Civil War.

Lynch, who used to meet de Valera regularly to discuss Gaeltacht affairs, acknowledged that he owed his position to the Long Fellow, for whom he developed a warm personal affection. 'There was no single problem confronting him or confronting the Gaeltacht that I did not discuss with him,' Lynch later explained. 'I was given permission on any occasion to go to the Cabinet with any problem that I might have on my hands, having first advised the Taoiseach, and having then prepared whatever submission I had for the government through the appropriate minister,' Lynch noted. 'Even if that minister did not see eye-to-eye with the proposition, he was at least bound, being the minister responsible for that aspect of administration, to place it before the Cabinet and give me an opportunity of arguing my case before the government and enabling me to get the government's decision on it.'

Having become personally fond of de Valera, Lynch resented Dillon's tendency to twist his criticism of any department into an attack on the Taoiseach. Therefore when criticism of the Gaeltacht office became an assault on de Valera, Lynch responded with a rare personal attack on Dillon, whom he accused of being motivated by an irrational hatred of de Valera. 'That hatred is born of a certain amount of jealousy of the status which the Taoiseach has achieved in this country and of the importance of the Fianna Fáil Party throughout the country,' he contended, as he defended his own visits to the Gaeltacht as strictly non-partisan.

'I took the utmost precautions to ensure I would get the goodwill of everyone in carrying out these visits and in trying to get what benefit I could out of them,' Lynch explained. 'I tried, in the best manner I could, to go to the scene of operations, meet the people concerned and discuss their problems with them, and help in their solution.' He later admitted to the Dáil that the visits got out of hand, as he had never intended them to turn into the kind of large public meetings that inevitably became mere platforms for the grandstanding of local and aspiring politicians. As a result, there was little opportunity for the kind of personal interaction that Lynch desired.

Once the initial meetings proved unwieldy, Lynch changed his approach and went to other areas quietly, just to meet 'small groups of influential people who had any reasonable suggestion to make.' He concluded that the Gaeltacht's problems could be tackled in about half a dozen different ways, including the provision of facilities and amenities such as parish halls and playing pitches, as well as improving the infrastructure. These areas were so backward at the time that their roads were still unpaved and the housing had no electricity, running water or sewerage.

To tackle the economic plight of the people, Lynch argued that they needed to make proper use of their land by resettlement and afforestation, as well as the use of fertilisers on what was generally inferior land. He also recognised a potential to exploit a tourist market, especially among those anxious to learn the Irish language. 'More people would visit the Gaeltacht if suitable accommodation were available for them,' Lynch contended. 'The people of the Gaeltacht would provide such accommodation if financial assistance were available.' Organisations that sponsored courses for young students wishing to learn Irish had been complaining that there was not sufficient accommodation available in the immediate vicinity. He therefore moved to ensure that grants would be available to provide for additional accommodation and to ensure that the accommodation had 'an adequate water supply and sewerage facilities.'

Efforts to attract industries in order to provide employment in the Gaeltacht areas never amounted to much during his period in office, though some fringe areas did benefit. The inter-departmental committee met around forty times in the next two and a half years, but when Fianna Fáil lost power in 1954, the new government promised to set up a Department of the Gaeltacht and the moribund committee became lethargic.

Lynch was largely a political facilitator who was as good as the civil servants who worked under him, because he depended on them for his drive and imagination. He essentially established the new Gaeltacht office, but from the outset he relied on others to come up with the ideas to promote it. He showed neither imagination of his own nor much drive when it came to implementing decisions, if those met with opposition.

He was greatly impressed, for instance, by the woollen and knitwear products marketed by Gaeltarra Éireann, as those were produced 'almost entirely in the Fíor-Ghaeltacht area by Irish-speaking people.' Those goods were 'equal to the best produced in any part of the world,' he said. While he acknowledged that there were 'difficulties with regard to design and finish', he contended that those were largely overcome by establishing a finishing centre in Mayo. Lynch was convinced of the potential of Gaeltarra Éireann to provide more employment in the Gaeltacht, but he was still slow to act, because this would amount to providing state assistance to certain companies, which would be to the disadvantage of their competitors in English-speaking areas.

'I had a strong feeling, amounting almost to conviction, that the establishment of a special board for the industry section of Gaeltacht Service would be a better thing and would make for an expansion of employment in Gaeltacht areas and would, in general, make Gaeltarra Éireann a more efficient company,' he told the Dáil afterwards. 'There were certain objections. Such a company would to a large extent, initially at least, have to be sponsored by the government. Being then in open competition with other producers, it would possibly be regarded with suspicion and might even raise a good deal of opposition from companies not subsidised by the government.

'I insisted that a scheme of training be established by sending young people from the Gaeltacht to the large textile centres in England so that when the time came, they would be capable of taking over the management and technical control of these Gaeltacht factories and be at the same time in a position to ensure, as natives of the Gaeltacht, that Irish would be used insofar as that was possible.'

The main idea was to promote employment in Gaeltacht areas so that the native speakers would be able to find work and settle in the locality, thereby helping to keep Irish speakers within the area. It was hardly an imaginative programme and it was not very successful.

Lynch would later admit that the civil servants were much too conservative. 'It was my own experience that, when ideas were put to me which appeared, prima facie, to have some sound prospects of success, cold water was thrown on most of them by the Department of Agriculture.

'It is easy for technicians in any line to beat down an untrained opinion, no matter how enthusiastic or well-informed that opinion may be,' he continued. 'That is the position that I frequently found myself to be in and I do not confine that criticism to the Department of Agriculture alone. I feel that the department's mentality and outlook is too conservative and it is time that they forgot the training of Sir Horace Plunkett and those that followed him.' Plunkett had been the inspiration behind the cooperative movement around the turn of the century.

Lynch argued that growing tomatoes in glasshouses would help to solve the problems of the Gaeltacht. The glasshouses could be heated with native peat, which was plentiful in those areas. 'Unless we do something visionary like that,' he warned, 'I do not see much prospect of retaining in the west even the number of people living there at the present time.'

Agriculture was the only way of retaining people in the west, as far as he could see. To that end he advocated the drainage of the blanket bog in the west of Ireland and experimentation with the growing of grass meal on the reclaimed bogland. These were called 'congested areas', which seemed like a misnomer in view of the high emigration from the area. In the forty years between 1911 and 1951 some 400,000 people had emigrated; 50,000 of those came from County Mayo alone. Yet, he noted, there was so little productive land that these areas were still too densely populated.

'Any scheme that would make more land available to these people or make undeveloped land productive should have been pursued and expanded,' Lynch observed. His own remedy was the Grass Meal Act of 1953, which met with ridicule in the more traditional agricultural circles. 'That project was as daft as a sixpenny watch and anybody who knows anything about it at all knows that it was daft,' James Dillon declared. 'Can you imagine any country with 12 million acres of arable land, the finest grass-growing land not only in Europe but in the whole world, who, when they want to grow grass as the raw material for the feeding stuffs of our own farmers, repair to the most remote bogs of Bangor Erris on which to grow it? There are 12 million acres of land in this country, every one of which will grow better grass than any land in Europe, and yet these people, when they wanted to grow grass meal, went to the bogs of Bangor Erris.'

When Dillon returned as Minister for Agriculture in the second Inter-Party Government in 1954, he promptly scrapped the grass-meal scheme. 'We closed it down because it was all cod, and anybody who knows anything about agriculture in this country knows it is cod,' he said.

While much of the world enjoyed an economic boom in the mid-1950s, the Republic of Ireland was economically depressed. Pursuing the conservative economic thinking that limited international trade in order to protect native industries, the country made little economic progress. De Valera was already in his seventies and virtually blind, yet he clung to the leadership of Fianna Fáil after losing power in 1954.

4

BACK IN OPPOSITION

1954–1957

Lynch returned to his practice at the bar when Fianna Fáil went back into opposition in 1954. Without his previous political-research responsibilities, he was able to obtain a higher profile in the Dáil itself. Rather than engaging in political point-scoring with government ministers, or political posturing for the sake of media attention, Lynch's style in opposition was to concentrate on asking questions that were of particular interest to people in the Cork area, especially in his own constituency. But he did not seek particular attention for himself alone. Almost all of his questions were submitted jointly in his own name and that of Pa McGrath, his party and constituency colleague.

Many of those questions related to the ongoing need for housing accommodation for some 4,000 families in Cork, where the new housing schemes that were being built required services like public lighting and proper roads. They also asked about for a new school for Mayfield and new garda stations at Gurranebraher, Spangle Hill and Ballyphehane, as well as other thickly populated areas of Cork where new housing schemes were well advanced. Despite the serious housing shortage in Cork, Lynch was confident the problem would be tackled, if for no other reason than 'that no government can afford the political unpopularity that a housing crisis would bring in its wake. Therefore, while not viewing the problem with any degree of complacency, I am not, at the same time, very much alarmed that the difficulties now being encountered will not be overcome to the satisfaction of everybody.'

With the growing population of Cork, he and McGrath also asked questions regarding the need for an airport to serve the area, the building of a new bridge and traffic control in the city as well. They also asked questions about the appointment of a local engineer, the staffing of Cork sanatorium and the need for a telephone kiosk on the South Douglas Road, and they raised questions about workmen's compensation as well as the desirability of increasing the pensions of members of the old IRA and Cumann na mBan. These questions and others like them were easy for members of the Opposition to ask, because they did not have to find the money to finance the various projects.

Lynch also appealed to the government to set up a radio orchestra in Cork. As a deputy for the city, he admitted that he would be expected to put forward such a case, but in this instance he said that he personally felt strongly about the issue. Over the years, he had not had much time for that kind of music, until he was obliged to attend performances given in Cork by some orchestras, and this sparked his interest. 'Strangely enough,' he said, 'I got interested in it and I found a much greater pleasure in sitting and listening to an orchestra than ever I did in listening to it over the air.' Hence he developed 'a great degree of interest in that type of music.' His latent love of such music may well have been inherited from his late mother.

In his capacity as Fianna Fáil spokesman for Gaeltacht affairs, Lynch accused the new government of not implementing any new ideas and not doing enough to attract industries to remote areas. In October 1956, he objected to the appointment of Paddy Lindsay as Minister for the Gaeltacht on the grounds that he did not know what the office was about or whether the government had any plans for it.

This criticism really ran against the grain of Lynch's usual Dáil contributions, because he normally avoided personal attacks, but in this case his objection was not so much that Lindsay was being appointed as that anybody was being appointed, because the groundwork for a full ministry had not yet been prepared 'from the administrative and the staff-structure point of view.' When he had been appointed to take charge of Gaeltacht affairs himself, he admitted that he had had no idea of what the office entailed, but he noted that there had been no intention of appointing him as a full minister.

On another, earlier occasion, Lynch seized on the opportunity to denounce an apparent abuse of the language-revival efforts. He asked the Minister for Defence about a press report that an Irish air corps plane, piloted by two air corps officers, had recently carried three high-ranking officers to Wales to examine three ensigns of the Irish Naval Service in their competence in the use of Irish while they were engaged on a technical training course in Wales.

Seán MacEoin, the Minister for Defence, replied that the two pilots were testing the aircraft and they made a virtue out of necessity by flying the examiners in the course of their test, with the result that the whole venture in fact cost less than four pounds.

Like most men of his age, Lynch had joined the Auxiliary Defence Forces during the Emergency period, so he took some interest in the needs of the army. He and McGrath asked Dáil questions about the unsatisfactory living quarters at Collins Barracks, for instance, and he denounced the segregation within the military, which was a holdover from the British period. 'I object strenuously to this segregation of classes within the army,' he told the Dáil. 'Our army is too small for that kind of thing.'

Discipline was understandable when confined to the professional activities of army life, but beyond that he felt that soldiers and their families should be free to circulate as they wished among their neighbours. In particular, he resented the idea that junior officers were forbidden to date the daughters of men in the ranks. 'I think that is a deplorable attitude to adopt, and more deplorable still,' he said, 'is the fact that the wives of NCOs and junior officers are segregated in church services.'

Usually there was a ready remedy for the things about which Lynch was raising questions. He did not normally take issue just to embarrass his opponent. He frequently objected to the practice of blaming past governments for present misfortunes, such as the opposition tactic that involved accusing Fianna Fáil of undermining farming during the 'economic war' of the 1930s. 'I first came to political intelligence during that period,' he said. Most people in the farming community supported Fianna Fáil. It was the larger farmers who gravitated to the 'Blueshirts', and he was critical of their illegal activities. 'It ill-becomes any deputy, no matter on what side of the House he stands, to boast of any part taken by any party or individual or group of individuals against our properly constituted and elected government of that day,' he told the Dáil.

It was necessary to be thick-skinned in public life, but he complained of the farcical efforts of some Fine Gael deputies who 'to make themselves appear to be the saviours of the country would get under the hide of an elephant.' They engaged in mud-slinging merely in the hope that some of it would stick. In particular he resented accusations by Paddy Donegan of Fine Gael about low standards in Fianna Fáil.

'I joined the Fianna Fáil Party and if I felt it aspired only to such low standards as have been attributed to it, I would leave it today,' Lynch said. Little over a decade later Lynch would be presiding over a government in which one of his own ministers accused his own colleagues of low standards. Intra-party rivalries were normal among deputies from the same constituency, but that was never Lynch's style. He went out of his way to cooperate with Pa McGrath until the latter's death on 20 June 1956.

Lynch complained at budget-time about the apparent hypocrisy of those on the other side of the Dáil who had criticised the taxation policy of the previous Fianna Fáil government but then did nothing when they got into power to rectify the things they criticised in opposition. He also involved himself in a controversy over the appointment of a postman in Drinagh, County Cork. A man who had been appointed was let go after six weeks and told that he had not been successful in his appointment because, Lynch believed, a supporter of Michael Pat Murphy, the Labour deputy for Cork West, was found for the job.

The first man had been appointed before Deputy Michael P. Murphy advised one of his supporters to go to the labour exchange and register instead of receiving the sickness benefits which he had been getting at the time the vacancy was declared, Lynch contended. The position for the postman was then re-advertised and the young man who had got the job honestly was put out of it after six weeks.

'It is nothing short of disgraceful that a young man, fully competent of doing the duties assigned to him, should be displaced for no other reason than that he was not a supporter of the Labour Party in West Cork,' Lynch declared. 'The man who was subsequently appointed had a family, it may be said, while the original appointee had not. That is not the point at issue here. The real point in this matter is that no man can feel secure in his position unless he is *persona grata* with the local deputy who supports the government for the time being. That is a disgraceful situation which should not be allowed to exist.'

The first man was actually working as a temporary postman without the minister's knowledge at the time of his appointment by the Department of Posts and Telegraphs. The minister, Michael J. Keyes, a member of the Labour Party, made no apologies for reversing the decision. He said that he did not know the second man was a chairman of the Labour Party. All he knew was the man's name and the fact that he had a wife and five young children, whereas the other was a young man of only nineteen years. 'In view of the fact that the man who had a wife and five children was unemployed,' Keyes said, 'I had no hesitation in giving the decision in his favour. Since then, the other young man has been engaged on temporary relief work and we have done anything we could for him, short of giving him priority over a married man with a family.'

Such interventions were really the exception in Lynch's case. He was one of the few members of the Dáil who usually avoided partisan politics and he was even prepared to give credit to his opponents. 'I have my own opinion about the leaders of the different parties in the House, particularly the men who led the government and the opposition parties twenty and twenty-five years ago, and irrespective of what policies they supported in the past, I have the utmost respect for them, because I believe that individually most of them would have made their mark in a much more remunerative fashion if they ignored the problems of this country and applied themselves to whatever vocation they felt they were best suited for.'

The second coalition government, which came to power in 1954, ran into economic difficulties over fluctuations in the British market, which had an adverse effect on Irish exports. This was exacerbated by undisciplined and ill-advised government spending, which seriously depleted the country's external assets. The banks publicly called on the government to cut back drastically on its spending in the autumn of 1956 and the panic measures adopted by the government caused massive confusion in the industrial sector. The building industry – frequently seen as an economic barometer – was virtually closed down, and unemployment soared to a record high of 84,093 in December 1956.

Many things seemed to conspire against the government. The winter of 1956–7 was particularly wet and led to massive flooding around the country. There was an oil shortage due to the Suez Crisis and the war between Israel and Egypt. Rationing books were circulated for petrol, bringing back memories of the deprivations endured in the Emergency period of the Second World War. On top of all this, the IRA began its border campaign, blowing up customs posts along the border and raiding police stations for arms in Northern Ireland. The War of Independence had begun with similar raids for arms and there was a genuine concern that Northern Ireland might erupt into a similar conflict, but in such a divided society there was bound to be communal strife into which the rest of the island could easily be sucked.

Clann na Poblachta, with its more republican views on the national question than Fine Gael, withdrew its support for the government and indicated that it would support a motion of no confidence tabled by Fianna Fáil when the Dáil reconvened for its first session of the new year on 12 February 1957. The coalition government was clearly doomed, so the Taoiseach, John A. Costello, did not wait for the debate but asked the President to dissolve the Dáil and call a general election for March 1957.

The outcome was largely predictable, as Fianna Fáil campaigned to put the country back to work. Under the coalition, the country's economic prospects had seemed extremely gloomy, so Fianna Fáil romped home to a comfortable electoral majority – nine seats to spare over all the other parties combined. Even that belied the actual majority, because four Sinn Fein deputies did not take their seats, so Fianna Fáil had more than a dozen seats to spare in forming a majority government.

5

Minister for Education

1957–1959

Jack Lynch had built up a practice as a barrister and he was reluctant to give it up to go into government in 1957. From the outset, de Valera made it clear that he wished to have him in the Cabinet, but Lynch had reservations.

At de Valera's request he arrived at Leinster House early on the first day of the new Dáil. The High Court was in session in Cork that day, and Lynch arrived with his 'bag full of briefs'. De Valera offered him the post of Minister for Education and the Gaeltacht. 'As I hadn't got a family,' Lynch later said, 'I felt I wasn't risking too much by going back into politics full time. My wife would very much have preferred me to stay at the bar, but I felt I had an obligation to accept the offer once it was made. I was, of course, flattered to be offered a ministry at all.'

Seán Moylan, who had been Minister for Education in the previous Fianna Fáil government, is reputed to have remarked that Lynch's appointment 'proves that Dev still has a sense of humour'. Lynch openly admitted that he did not consider himself 'an expert or anything like an expert on education.'

While de Valera was in charge, Cabinet meetings tended to be very long and there were usually two meetings a week. The Taoiseach liked to engage everyone around the table. He never took a vote, but sought consensus. As he had a seemingly inexhaustible store of patience himself, he would allow items to be discussed over days until he eventually got the consensus that he was seeking himself. To that extent, he was a kind of 'unique dictator', to use the title of one of his earlier biographies.

There were a number of very forceful characters in the government. Lynch noted that Seán McEntee was 'precise on every subject' and 'very forceful' as Minister for Health and Social Welfare; so was Paddy Smith, the Minister for Agriculture, but in an earthy way. Smith quickly brought topics down to basics. Frank Aiken was forceful, too, in External Affairs. As Minister for Finance, Jim Ryan introduced the First Programme for Economic Expansion, which was to have a profound effect on the country's economy. It took only one meeting to approve the publication of Ken Whitaker's *Economic Development*, largely because it conformed to the thinking of most members of the Cabinet, especially Seán Lemass. 'We very quickly appreciated its worth and of course Lemass supported it vigorously,' Lynch noted.

Although he was one of the youngest members of the government, Lynch found a ready ally in de Valera. 'I had very little difficulty in getting things through Cabinet,' he noted. 'Dev, who had been Minister for Education at one time for a few months, was sympathetic to any demands I made. He used to ring up every now and again to inquire how things were going.'

It was Lynch's first administrative job, but his own background in the civil service was a great help. 'I didn't find it difficult to cope,' he noted. 'I had been in the civil service myself and had a good idea how the civil service worked. I never read only the top document on a file – usually a summary of what was written elsewhere – I always flipped over to read the conflicting arguments for and against a proposal. I also usually approached relatively junior civil servants in connection with an issue when they were the people directly involved and when their memos impressed me.'

The education portfolio did not rank highly. In May 1922, when Michael Collins concluded the infamous election pact with de Valera, they agreed to share Cabinet posts on a 5-to-4 ratio if they won the election. This was obviously in violation of the Anglo-Irish Treaty, but supporters of Collins tried to placate the British by indicating that de Valera would be appointed to a ministry with little influence. 'What would it matter if de Valera were appointed Minister for Education?' Kevin O'Higgins asked the British. For his part, de Valera actually suspected that he would be appointed to Education, and he was determined to refuse the post.

As a former teacher, however, de Valera professed a particular interest in education and actually assigned himself to the Department of Education for the school year of 1939–40, when he was already functioning in the crucial positions of Taoiseach and Minister for External Affairs. The Second World War had already begun on the Continent and this was a time of considerable diplomatic activity, as Ireland was striving to stay out of the war; therefore even he probably never regarded Education as more than a third-rate ministry.

Between 1935 and 1944 there was an average of between eight and nine resolutions on educational matters at each Fianna Fáil *ard fheis*, but after the war, education dropped down the list of the party's priorities. 'One finds that education almost disappeared as an issue during the 'fifties,' Maurice Johnson argued in his master's thesis on education in Irish politics.

In 1948 when the first National Coalition was formed, the Fine Gael leader, Richard Mulcahy, was unacceptable to Clann na Poblachta as Taoiseach, because of the part that he had played as head of the Free State Army during the Civil War. John A. Costello therefore became the first and only Taoiseach in the history of the state to be elected without being the leader of his own party. In a manner that was reminiscent of the way that Michael Collins and his colleagues had planned to sideline de Valera back in 1922, Mulcahy was essentially pushed aside by being appointed Minister for Education in the 1948 government and again in 1954 when the second National Coalition was formed.

He allowed himself to be downgraded in the interest of ousting Fianna Fáil. He never thought the post provided him with much scope for action. Instead, he believed his department should have no real input into education, other than providing the money to finance the whole thing. As far as he was concerned, educational policy was effectively determined by the authorities of the Roman Catholic Church, with parents essentially having no say. They merely provided the children.

Lynch came into office with no real plans of his own. Indeed, he still had no definite plans after almost two months in office.

'Personally,' he told the Dáil, 'I think I would have a cheek to come in here after one month in the department and try to promulgate a policy that should be followed.' Instead he relied on continuing the policy of his predecessor, who had planned to cut the education budget. One of Lynch's first acts as Minister for Education was to announce a 10 per cent reduction in the capital grants paid to secondary schools and a 6 per cent cut in the money for vocational education. The decision to cut the budget had already been taken and hinted at in the estimates by Richard Mulcahy. The cuts really ran counter to the general trend of increasing educational spending in Europe, but since Lynch was implementing a Fine Gael plan, there was little real opposition in the Dáil, other than some criticism that he sought to play down the bad news by announcing it in a speech that was wholly in Irish.

Government ministers rarely gave the Opposition credit for much, but Lynch was glad to give his predecessor the full credit for that decision. 'I had no part in drawing up the estimate,' he said, as he praised Mulcahy for having had the political courage to take such a difficult decision. 'I regret he found it necessary,' Lynch added, 'but I regret more so that I found it impossible, in the light of the financial situation, to restore the cut.' The money was indeed restored in the estimates the following year and, like a true politician, Lynch took the full credit for restoring them.

Although he had very little involvement in third-level education, he did appoint a Committee on Accommodation Needs of the National University of Ireland, with the future Chief Justice and later President, Cearbhall Ó Dálaigh, as chairman in September 1957. Nine months later the committee reported that the college should be expanded. But acquiring property in the area of Dublin where the university was based would be extremely expensive, so they proposed building upward, which naturally sparked a controversy. 'It was then that the massive Belfield project got under way,' Lynch noted. It was decided to transfer University College Dublin from Earlsfort Terrace to Belfield, where the college already owned 252 acres of land.

Professor J. J. O'Meara suggested that UCD should amalgamate with Trinity College instead. The Catholic hierarchy, which had long been discouraging Catholics from attending Trinity College, had essentially banned them, with the result that Trinity was known as a Protestant university and UCD as its Catholic counterpart. John Cardinal D'Alton, the Catholic primate of all Ireland, essentially killed the amalgamation proposal by complaining that it would mean a union of incompatibles.

A number of educational issues perennially generated discussion and even controversy. One was the need to raise the school-leaving age, set at fourteen at the time. Another was the reduction of class sizes. The question of whether the controversial Primary Certificate examination should be abandoned also sparked fierce arguments. In addition, there was much heated debate over the use of corporal punishment, the shortage of teachers and the deplorable state of many school buildings, not to mention the best way of reviving the Irish language, which had been a major issue ever since the foundation of the state.

'There was a tendency in the 1950s to identify education with the restoration of the Irish language,' according to one educational authority. 'In any discussion on education, one could be sure that, sooner or later, the language question would be introduced, with people becoming vehement in supporting or opposing government policy.' De Valera had long maintained that the revival of the language was his main political priority.

Lynch seemed to waste no time in fitting into the traditional mould. In his first major address as Minister for Education he announced his intention to examine the possibility of introducing an oral Irish test as part of the Intermediate Certificate examination. Symbolically, it was a gesture which seemed to suggest that the revival of the language was the most pressing educational issue facing the country. Nothing actually came of that proposal but in 1958 he formally announced that an oral Irish test would be included in the Leaving Certificate examination from 1960 onwards. 'This was to highlight the importance of speaking the language,' Lynch explained. 'I tried to establish that as much attention as possible be given to the spoken language.'

Otherwise he was content to allow things to remain the same, because he realised that public indifference was a big obstacle to the revival of the language. 'In common with many other deputies I am not satisfied with the progress that has been made,' Lynch explained to the Dáil. 'Many more people know and understand Irish now than did twenty years ago, but I share the view very strongly that there is some reticence among those of us who know the language to speak it among ourselves.' Pressurising voters to do something they did not want to do was not likely to be popular, and Lynch was determined above all to be popular.

As the youngest member of the Cabinet in 1957, he seemed to adhere to the old ways of doing things and, even though the country was on the brink of dramatic change, he showed little ministerial imagination during his tenure at education. Of course, he could always plead that the lack of finances hampered him initially.

Most politicians shied away from questioning the Church's enormous sway in educational matters. As Minister for Agriculture in 1956, for instance, James Dillon had sought to set up an agricultural institute. But when it became known that this institute would be placed under the supervision of Trinity College, the Catholic hierarchy requested an urgent meeting with the then Taoiseach John A. Costello. He met Bishops Michael Browne of Galway and Cornelius Lucey of Cork. They made it brutally clear that, in their consideration, they had a proprietorial interest in the National University of Ireland and that it, not Trinity College, should have control of the teaching of agriculture at the new institute.

The teaching of agriculture had nothing to do with 'faith or morals' as far as Costello was concerned, so he told the bishops that their objections were too late, because the decision to place the institute under the auspices of Trinity College was already an accomplished fact. The bishops approached de Valera, but he refused to intervene on their behalf.

Bishop Lucey therefore denounced the government's plans as 'socialism of a gradual, hidden and underhand' kind. He noted that Trinity College, 'if not wholly Protestant, is free-thinking or indifferent as regards religion.' Thus he argued that it should not have a position of equality with the colleges of the National University of Ireland. Dillon was greatly offended by Lucey's remarks. 'The plain truth is that the intervention of individual bishops in public controversy is becoming a serious evil, and if it continues, irretrievable damage will be done,' Dillon wrote.

The secretary of the conference of bishops warned the government that the plan for the agricultural institute was 'another incursion of the state into the sphere of higher education.' The hierarchy essentially considered that the education of the vast majority of the Irish people was their preserve. Confronted with this attitude and fearing a repetition of the mother-and-child controversy in the sphere of agricultural education, Costello and Dillon were compelled by their colleagues to concede to the demands of the bishops.

Lynch therefore moved very gingerly when it came to any educational issue that was likely to provoke the hierarchy. Of course, Noël Browne had had few qualms about confronting church leaders ever since the mother-and-child controversy. He demanded action on a whole range of educational issues, such as the school-leaving age, the number of unqualified teachers, class sizes and the physical state of school buildings as well as the continued use of corporal punishment. He believed the state should take over education, but Lynch argued that education should be a partnership between church and state, and as minister he was not prepared to use his financial clout to force change.

As education was compulsory only to the age of fourteen, some 40 per cent of children left school at that age, and more than half had left by the age of sixteen. Lynch wanted to raise the school-leaving age, but he realised the problem was 'a matter of providing increased educational facilities rather than extending compulsorily the age limit.' The facilities were already strained.

One in five – or 2,097 – lay teachers did not have teacher training and almost one in three (32 per cent) of the religious teachers were unqualified. Each year the teacher-training colleges produced 418 new teachers, but an average of 334 trained teachers retired annually. Classes tended to be overcrowded in urban areas, with sixty to seventy pupils in a class, whereas educational authorities argued that the maximum number should be thirty. In such large classes the teacher was inevitably preoccupied with keeping control rather than actually teaching.

There was a shortage of over 3,000 trained teachers when Lynch took over as Minister for Education. In view of the high rate of attrition from teaching, it would take over three and a half decades to make up the shortfall, much less find the extra 4,000 teachers that would be necessary to reduce class sizes, or the more than 400 teachers that would be needed if the school-leaving age was raised to sixteen. Lynch accepted that both goals were desirable. 'It is a target we should endeavour to achieve in the shortest possible time,' he told the Dáil in May 1957.

At the existing rate at which new teachers were being introduced, it would take almost ninety years to produce enough teachers, but there was one glaringly obvious remedy. The high rate of attrition from teaching was largely due to a ban on married women teachers. Once a woman teacher got married, she had to retire. The ban had been introduced in October 1933 at the height of the Great Depression for a variety of reasons. It was introduced by the Department of Education, over the objections of the Irish National Teachers' Organisation, while the Catholic bishops refused to take a stand one way or the other. Yet many people blamed the bishops.

It was said that the Roman Catholic hierarchy, in its wisdom, considered that pregnant teachers would somehow be a bad example to pupils. Of course, to their way of thinking, the example would have been even worse if the married women did not become pregnant, because as far as the Church was concerned a woman's primary role in society was in the home as a mother. There had been a report in the *Irish Press* that the Department of Education was considering the removal of the ban on married women teachers, but Lynch denied any knowledge of this and emphasised that the report had certainly not been inspired by him, even though he clearly had reservations about the ban. 'I think that it is a great waste of teaching power that women teachers, on marriage, are obliged to retire at the present time,' he admitted.

People who, for one reason or another, were unable to get into teacher-training college frequently made up for the shortage of teachers. The qualification of Junior Assistant Mistress was awarded to women who had sought but not achieved entry to one of the training colleges.

Since education was considered to be, in political terms, the preserve of the churches, most politicians shied away from the whole area (except Noël Browne, who tackled the issue with the enthusiasm of a hungry dog after a bone). The solution to the problem of unqualified teachers was obvious, and Browne could not understand why the government did not remove the ban on married women immediately. But then, the righteous manner with which he tackled such issues frequently irritated his political colleagues. He even managed to antagonise Lynch – the most accommodating of ministers.

'They ought to make Deputy Dr Browne a dictator,' Lynch snapped at one point. 'Perhaps he might get on with the job then.' Of course, he quickly regretted his intemperance. 'If the deputy were less aggressive,' Lynch explained, 'he might get a more reasonable reply.'

'I am quite satisfied,' Browne replied in typical fashion. 'I did not expect anything better from the minister.'

Over 800 school buildings were considered so defective that Lynch admitted that they 'should be replaced'. His department sanctioned the building of 136 of the required new buildings, but at that rate of replacement, it would take at least fifteen years 'to provide new schools in all the cases where existing schools are regarded as in need of replacement.'

As Minister for Education, one might have thought that Lynch should have put the welfare of the pupils first, but it was obvious that he thought of other considerations as paramount, whether it was the social views of local Catholic Church leaders, the financial considerations of the government or the fears of parents. When Charles J. Haughey, a first-term member of the Dáil, asked about 'making education compulsory for blind children', for instance, Lynch was clearly reluctant, on the grounds that the parents of those children might object.

'Compulsion in such cases, involving the bringing of children and young people from their homes to schools, is something which would be regarded as anathema by ordinary parents,' he explained. 'Indeed, it is something which I do not think I would be prepared to stand over. On the other hand, I am very anxious that as many blind children as possible should avail of the tuition provided in these schools; there is plenty of room for them. The only thing I can do is encourage parents to avail of the facilities afforded.'

James Dillon advocated the introduction of a positive incentive to promote the use of the Irish language by giving free secondary education to children competent in Irish at primary school, and then giving university scholarships to those who got honours in Irish in the Leaving Certificate.

Many people objected that proficiency in the use of Irish was a compulsory requirement for entry into the National University or to secure a position in the civil service. There were also objections that Irish-speaking students had their marks boosted for doing other subjects through the medium of Irish.

When asked about the teaching of Irish, Lynch adopted a moderate stand. 'I'm not a fanatic,' he said. 'I'm realistic enough to see that it's never going to replace English, but I would like to see it rank as an equal. I feel that, if we can make it something more than just another school subject, something children will want to learn for its own sake, they will acquire a love for it as the language of their forebears, a language of great antiquity and culture.' In February 1958 the Parliamentary Secretary to the Taoiseach announced an inquiry into the teaching of Irish in schools. It was the first of a number of such inquiries, but it had the effect of shielding Lynch from further consideration of the language issue until the inquiry was completed.

Having openly admitted at the outset that he was not 'anything like an expert on education', he moved very gradually, growing more confident as he went along, especially as he was able to rely on 'the assistance of experts'. There was enormous political potential in the job for an imaginative and ambitious minister, because there was a great need for educational reform. The existing system was antiquated and seriously run-down, with the result that there was tremendous scope for conspicuous achievement, especially as Lynch's predecessors tended to the belief that the government should have no real say in educational policy. Seán O'Connor, an assistant secretary of the department, was convinced that little would happen until a minister took the reins as the prime mover in educational policy, but he realised that 'no minister new to the job would risk what he saw as confrontation with the Church authorities'. Yet O'Connor believed that the problem was not that the Catholic hierarchy was seeking authority over education so much as the fact that the politicians had simply abdicated their responsibility.

The educational system in Britain had been undergoing a quiet revolution since the end of the Second World War. Before the war, it was taken for granted that anything beyond a primary education was available only to those who could afford it, or to a small number of particularly deserving students who obtained scholarships. But soldiers of all classes were called on to make equal sacrifices in the war and there was a recognition therefore that all their children should have equal opportunities.

Britain was the first country in Europe to provide a secondary education for all children and to raise the school-leaving age to fifteen. Sweden, France and Luxembourg, as well as parts of Germany, soon followed. The children of the great post-war 'baby boom' were reaching secondary-school age in the late 1950s, with the result that education took on added significance around the globe, and Ireland was no exception. Since so many young people were emigrating from Ireland, the demand for reform to provide children with a proper education became all the more pressing.

As the prospect of greater ties with the countries in Europe became more likely, the call for the teaching of Continental languages instead of classical Latin and Greek began to grow, and with that came the realisation that much of the system was in need of reform. Within the next decade there would be very few aspects of the educational system that did not undergo change.

The de Valera era was slowly coming to a close. When Lynch addressed the annual conference of the Association of Secondary Teachers of Ireland (ASTI) in April 1958 he was still emphasising the importance of education as a means of instilling 'a sense of national, cultural and ethical values'. Much of the impetus for educational change in Ireland would later be attributed to the publication in 1958 of the famous white paper *Economic Development*, drawn up by T. K. Whitaker. It emphasised the need for educational change, especially in the field of vocational education, in order to facilitate planned economic reform.

'The vocational organisation is more flexible than the primary and secondary systems and those concerned with it are imbued with an enthusiasm which, in large areas of rural Ireland where the system is still a novelty, gives something of a missionary character to the work involved,' Whitaker wrote. It was therefore significant that in April 1959 Lynch was telling the Congress of Vocational Teachers about 'courses of instruction which are contributing in an increasing way to our economic development.' This marked a distinct change in educational thinking. Henceforth the economic role would become a major consideration, whereas hitherto cultural and spiritual considerations had dominated Irish educational thinking. The fruits of the new approach became more apparent in the coming decade.

Education was soon seen as a panacea for the economic ills of the country, and there was a growing recognition of the need to afford an equal opportunity to all children. Hence the recognition of the need both to expand secondary education and to reform the vocational educational system in order to eliminate its second-class status. The 260 vocational schools did not provide access to third-level education for any of their 23,000 pupils, as the Group Certificate examination at the age of fifteen or sixteen was purely terminal. Pupils at those schools could not even sit the Inter-mediate Certificate examination, and the transfer of students was only one way, from secondary to vocational, and never the other way around. Vocational education had been treated as distinctly inferior or second-class.

All of the country's 480 secondary schools were in private hands, usually under the control of diocesan priests or a religious order which employed the teachers and ran the schools, with the state providing most of the money by way of grants. It also fell to the state to provide the money for new school buildings and Lynch recognised that this would entail more state input into the overall system.

'If the State were directly, as suggested, to subsidise the building of secondary schools, it would, because of its public character and responsibility, be forced to intervene to a much greater degree that at present in matters connected with the establishment of schools, such as their location, the pupils attending them and so forth,' Lynch told the ASTI conference in April 1958. He warned that this could lead to problems in relation to the admission of non-recognised pupils. 'Indeed,' he said, 'the whole question of entry to secondary school might have to be considered.'

The following month he decided to scrap the marriage ban, and he even adopted an apologetic tone towards Noël Browne as he explained that he had not given the matter proper consideration the previous year when he first addressed the issue. He apparently forgot that he had actually expressed his own misgivings about the ban at that time.

'I answered him, without examining the question very carefully,' Lynch explained in May 1958. He announced that 400 women teachers would be re-employed in a temporary capacity, especially in remote areas where his department had been unable to find qualified teachers to replace women who had been forced to retire as a result of the marriage ban. As it stood, each of those graduating from teacher-training college had a choice of two to three jobs, which meant that the more remote areas had little attraction for young teachers. It was 'unjustified and intolerable' that those who were forced out by marriage were inevitably replaced by unqualified teachers such as the Junior Assistant Mistresses, as far as Lynch was concerned. 'The employment of so many untrained teachers is educationally indefensible,' he said. Henceforth, he announced, married women teachers could hold on to their posts from 1 July 1958.

He had obviously cleared the move with Archbishop John Charles McQuaid of Dublin in advance. 'I cannot say what opposition there was among members of the hierarchy, indeed if any, but I know that in Archbishop McQuaid I had a powerful ally in effecting this very necessary reform,' Lynch later explained. At its June meeting the hierarchy expressed no dissent to a memorandum from the Department of Education explaining the changes in relation to women teachers.

As usual there were some complaints from members of the Opposition, but in this case they actually denounced him for 'taking the easy way out'. Richard Mulcahy described the shortage of teachers as 'a very pressing problem', but he seemed to think that Lynch should have done things the hard way, or concentrated on other problems. As usual when a government minister implemented a popular reform, the Opposition accused him of doing too little too late. What would happen to women teachers who got married in May, before the new scheme came in effect in July, Mulcahy asked.

'I do not think anybody will get married in May now,' Lynch replied. He apparently had no intention of facilitating those who might be in a hurry to get married. But then, of course, people who rushed the nuptials tended to be the source of local scandal in those days, with the result that facilitating them was not considered politically expedient.

Another of the more controversial issues during Lynch's tenure as Minister for Education was the issue of corporal punishment, which was denounced as 'an utterly medieval and barbarous practice' by Noël Browne. 'I think it is always wrong for an adult to beat a child,' Browne emphasised.

'Some corporal punishment is necessary,' Lynch argued. 'The rule, as deputies know, is that children may be slapped on the open hand.' That may have been the law but it was grossly abused at the time. For instance, the law did not permit the leather strap, which was used by Christian Brothers for over thirty years. In September 1956 Richard Mulcahy moved to legalise the strap, but there was such outrage that he dropped the proposal that December. Nevertheless, the Christian Brothers continued to ignore the law and neither Lynch nor the Department of Education dared to interfere with them.

Lynch did not cite any scientific study to support his views on the effects of corporal punishment. Instead, he cited the Papal encyclical *Divini Illius Magistri,* in which Pope Pius XII stated that disorderly inclinations amongst children must be corrected. While the word of the Pope may have been authoritative enough for Lynch, it clearly did not carry that much weight with Browne.

'Generally,' Lynch said, 'I do not think Deputy Dr Browne will deny the parents' right to correct their children in a fair manner. The child, as we seek to establish in this country, is given into the custody of the school manager, and while the child is there, the manager is *in loco parentis* and, to a large extent, he carries all the powers and rights of the parent. Certainly, by implication, he carries the power of correction, whether or not it is delegated to the teacher. Irish teachers are not sadists and only in very rare instances do we get a case where a teacher might have gone beyond the limits.'

Many pupils from that era could probably testify to the inaccuracy of that statement. It was even more absurd of Lynch to say that 'there are remedies for that and they are readily availed of'.

'Surely it is unnecessary on any occasion?' Noël Browne asked.

In March 1959 Browne asked about 'the case of a child forcibly removed to an industrial school from his father's care, against the declared wishes of the father and the child, for not attending school or Mass.' Lynch replied that he had 'no functions in regard to the committal of children to industrial schools, which is a matter for the court of jurisdiction.' In the light of some of the horrific abuses – sexual and physical – that occurred in these schools during this period, the attitude taken did not reflect to Lynch's credit, any more than did the fact that such abuse continued during his tenure.

The pressure to reform education was building slowly as the press began to take greater interest in the issues. Under the headline 'Your Children Have to Suffer', the *Sunday Independent* carried a particularly caustic editorial on 29 December 1958, charging that the educational system was not preparing children for life, especially those who finished at the age of fourteen, who were being compelled to emigrate. 'The facts are beyond controversy,' the editorial contended. 'These children face the world as semi-illiterates.'

Lynch talked about the need for school replacements. He sympathised with those who were unhappy at the rate at which new schools were being built. 'I do not know where all the blame lies,' he told the Dáil, 'but I intend to find out, and I hope that the tempo will increase in the coming years.' In 1959 he initiated plans to bring down the pupil-teacher ratio, and it continued to fall in the following years.

Lynch was Minister for Education for only two years, during which the Department of Education underwent a fundamental change in direction. Successors like Paddy Hillery, George Colley and Donogh O'Malley were quicker to engage with their briefs, but then the new direction was already set. In comparison with most of his predecessors – who never really got involved in education policy at all – Lynch was an innovator. He was essentially the first minister to assert the department's right to reform educational policy, though most of the much-needed reforms were implemented by his successors.

As Minister for Education, he was undoubtedly a qualified success as a cautious innovator, especially in comparison with those who preceded him. During his time, a growing emphasis was placed on the practical economic applications of education, in addition to inculcating spiritual and cultural values. The conservative civil servants who had been dominating the Department of Education had previously ignored the economic aspect of education. But things were changing with the advent of Seán O'Connor, who was to become arguably the most progressive and dynamic secretary in the history of the Department of Education. He was to do for education what another of his contemporaries, T. K. Whitaker, was to do for economic thinking.

Lynch got on very well with the civil servants at his department and he was smart enough to give a degree of latitude to O'Connor, who later credited him with opening up the Department of Education and initiating the climate for the major changes that were implemented by his successors. In addition to forming a good rapport with the civil servants, Lynch got on well with his ministerial colleagues and was very much a team player. He generally kept to his own brief, but he did speak out in the Dáil in support of colleagues, including his defence of the Minister for

External Affairs, Frank Aiken, against Fine Gael charges of being soft on communism because he supported a proposal to discuss the admission of communist China to the United Nations Organisation in 1957.

'Perhaps Ireland's most direct interest in the mainland of China is the number of Irish missionaries who have gone there in the past to spread the Catholic faith,' Lynch explained. 'Many of them were imprisoned, many of them suffered and most of them were expelled. We believe that if Red China could be induced to practice tolerance there would be new hope for these missionaries, and not only for the missionaries but for the people who are dominated by the Peking government.'

At the time the issue was not whether communist China was entitled to represent China at the United Nations but whether the organisation should even discuss the admission of 'Red China'. 'Surely there is an elementary principle that if any organisation purports to represent the entire world, an organisation that excludes 500 million people is not, in fact, a united-nations organisation,' Lynch argued. 'If a cancerous growth is left un-attended, is it not certain that no medical or other power on earth will prevent that growth from consuming the victim? If the cancerous growth of communism is left to grow and develop in the mainland of China, is it not only reasonable to assume that the millions of people who still resist the Peking government will ultimately be consumed by that communist growth?'

Fine Gael spokesmen complained that Aiken was gratuitously insulting the United States and aligning Ireland with the Chinese communists against the Americans. 'To suggest that we have so outraged all American opinion that we have seriously prejudiced our position vis-à-vis the United States is, I think, ridiculous,' Lynch contended. He went on to note that some prominent Americans had actually supported another of Aiken's suggestions – that both the Allies and the Soviets should withdraw their troops from Europe. 'If we as a nation are to command respect, we must act with some degree of independence of mind in these international assemblies,' Lynch said. 'So long as our suggestions are made in good faith and without any intention of injuring those people who are our friends, it ought to be our duty – if we see in our suggestions and actions a means of promoting world peace, of curbing the spread of communism and of creating freedom of action for free people and for the missionaries we have who want to spread the gospel abroad – to take such action.'

Probably the greatest tribute that could be paid to Lynch's handling of his first Cabinet post was his promotion to Minister for Industry and Commerce when Seán Lemass took over as Taoiseach in June 1959 following the election of Éamon de Valera as President of Ireland. Lemass was primarily interested in economic matters and had spent the bulk of his ministerial career as Minister for Industry and Commerce, with the result that his appointment of Lynch as his successor was unquestionably an endorsement of his ministerial record.

6

MINISTER FOR INDUSTRY

AND COMMERCE

1959–1961

'I had enormous respect for Lemass, especially his direct approach and capacity to make quick decisions,' Lynch noted. 'He wanted to move me from Education to Industry and I was none too keen on the change. In the first place, I felt I had a better command of the issues related to Education than I had of the multifarious issues connected with the Department of Industry and Commerce, which incidentally included at the time responsibility for transport and power. Secondly, I felt I was just on the verge of achieving something in education and didn't want to leave just at that point.'

'I want you to sit at this desk,' Lemass said, when Lynch entered his office.

'I suppose I had little choice,' Lynch noted. 'I transferred over to Industry and Commerce, where I was to stay for six years.'

As Minister for Education, there had been little for him to do by way of legislation. He was never the most imaginative of ministers but he inherited probably the most dynamic department in the government. The country had already started the move towards industrialisation. From 1953 to 1957, manufacturing output had increased less in Ireland than in any of the twelve western European countries, but there was a dramatic turnaround under Lemass in 1958 and 1959, when Ireland had the fifth-highest rate of increase.

Investment in Irish factories had come from a wide variety of countries, including Great Britain, Germany, the USA, Canada, the Netherlands, France, Sweden, Belgium, Norway, Italy and Switzerland. From April 1957 to June 1959, some 214 new industrial concerns were established in the country and the rate of foundation of new industrial schemes was actually increasing. In the twelve months leading to September 1959, for instance, ninety-two new industries were started up and construction was begun on a further twenty-six factories. The volume of industrial production for the quarter in which Lynch took over ministerial responsibilities at Industry and Commerce was the highest ever recorded at that time of year.

Much of this industrial expansion depended on the export of transportable industrial goods. These stood at about £17.5 million in 1958, and there was a phenomenal increase of about £6 million, or 30 per cent, in the twelve months leading up to September 1959. Of course, just building factories and producing goods was not going to be sufficient to secure employment; it was necessary to ensure the factories had markets in order to guarantee their survival. Even though there had been a marked increase in industrial production, there was actually a slight drop in the value of Irish exports in 1959, as a result of a drop in exports of cattle, butter and bacon.

'It took me some time to settle in at Industry and Commerce but I felt in command of the job after a while and got considerable satisfaction from it, even though it virtually shattered my private life,' Lynch later recalled. 'Constant demands were being made on ministerial time, at public functions and engagements throughout and outside the country. There were a number of occasions during which I was called back from holiday because of strikes, and my wife and I lost a few holiday deposits during that period. Sometimes when we were able to get away, for example on holiday weekends, it was at short notice and we often failed to get a booking. It was during this period that we decided we would get a small holiday home sometime, somewhere.'

The Department of Industry and Commerce had already prepared an extensive amount of legislation as part of the government Programme for Economic Expansion. Lynch therefore inherited a whole raft of prepared bills dealing with a wide range of matters, from the promotion of industrialisation to facilitate training and trade, to matters regarding working conditions, like wages and holiday entitlements.

Industrial-credit legislation was created to allow industrialists to reclaim from the state up to two-thirds of the cost of expanding their plants. Initially there was a ceiling of £50,000 on the amount that could be claimed, but Lynch secured Dáil approval to remove the limit for factories in areas that had been designated as underdeveloped in order to encourage industrialists to set up in more remote districts. The Apprenticeship Act was designed to raise the standard of apprenticeship schemes in order to improve the quality of employees available to new industries. 'We must ensure that they will not be short of highly trained workers in the critical years that lie ahead,' Lynch explained, because it was only a matter of time before the country would have to join either the Common Market or the European Free Trade Area.

The Hire-Purchase (Amendment) Act was designed mainly to protect consumers. It authorised the Minister for Industry and Commerce to regulate the minimum deposits and maximum periods of payment in connection with hire-purchase agreements and credit-sale transactions, which had increased dramatically in recent years. The new legislation stipulated that the agreement had to be in writing. In the event of default, goods on which more than a third of the price had been paid could only be recovered with a court order, which had to be obtained in the court nearest to where the purchaser was residing. Moreover, the defaulter would have a right to pay off the outstanding amount and keep the goods. Prior to that, anyone who defaulted would not have the right to pay off the outstanding amount and the goods could be repossessed, even though almost the full amount had been paid.

The Insurance Act was amended at Lynch's behest in order to promote exports by providing insurance coverage for them, with the approval of the Minister for Finance. Under the Insurance Act of 1953, the aggregate liability of the Minister for Industry and Commerce was not to exceed £2 million, but this was raised to £5 million. On the domestic front, his department arranged for a 'Buy Irish' campaign.

The Industrial Relations (Amendment) Bill, 1958, dealt with wages and conditions of employment of agricultural workers within the sphere of the Labour Court, providing for registration by the court of employment agreements between workers' and employers' organisations. It also introduced legislation governing vacation time for workers. It specifically provided double time for working on bank holidays and it reduced the qualifying period for a worker to be eligible for an annual holiday.

In addition to matters relating to industrialisation, Lynch was also charged with implementing plans in relation to tourism, mineral exploration and fish farming. Thus he had to guide an enormous amount of legislation through the Dáil, which he did with little difficulty, as he was a politician who rarely provoked opposition.

Time and time again, Liam Cosgrave, his Fine Gael counterpart, would welcome the proposed legislation. There were some amendments to improve the bills, and Lynch would often accept those in the spirit in which they were offered. 'I certainly appreciate, since I came into office as Minister for Industry and Commerce, the help and cooperation that has been given to me from that side of the House,' Lynch told the Dáil in March 1961. 'I think I put it on record before and it gives me pleasure to do so again.'

Lynch inherited the project to build a new airport for Cork city when it was already at a fairly advanced stage; this was of great political advantage to himself. 'I know I am Minister for Industry and Commerce for the entire country, but the welfare of Cork is naturally very dear to me,' he told the Dáil. Hence he took a particular interest in the project. Preliminary drainage work had already been done on the site and they had already reached the stage of inviting tenders for construction of the airport, which was due to go into operation in 1961.

One of his earliest tasks was to introduce a bill to reorganise Córas Trachtála as a statutory board to carry on the functions of promoting, assisting and developing exports. He recognised that its dependence on an annual vote for funding by the government had retarded development, so he proposed that the company be afforded what he called 'security of venture', giving it semi-state status and the right to plan its long-term activities.

Córas Trachtála had been established in 1951 to stimulate exports by supplying Irish companies with export information on overseas markets, organising collective marketing and supplying importers in overseas countries with information on Irish goods. The company also provided information on distribution channels and advice on the selection of agents overseas, and it arranged participation in foreign trade fairs. It played a vital part in the economic development of the state, and opposition spokesmen like Liam Cosgrave of Fine Gael and William Norton of the Labour Party were highly complimentary of the work done by Coras Trachtála, but James Dillon, the Fine Gael leader, was not impressed. A brilliant old-style orator, weaned on posturing politics and a captive of the past, Dillon was now too old to change. He seemed to be convinced that any change suggested by Fianna Fáil was bound to be bad. 'Is there to be no end to this fraud and codology?' Dillon asked. In 1932, he said, he had met a civil servant wandering along a corridor with papers in his hand. 'Where are you going with that sheaf of papers?' Dillon asked.

'Well, to tell you the truth,' the civil servant replied, 'I am carrying out my minister's instructions to look for an alternative market for eggs that I know does not exist. I am paid to go and look for it.' Just because one civil servant was a waster hardly justified doing nothing about securing markets for evermore, but it seemed to be enough for Dillon.

'This bill is cod,' he insisted. 'It has been introduced for no purpose other than to create the impression that the Taoiseach, since he got into power, is like a human dynamo, and that is all.' As far as Dillon was concerned, 'There is only one thing more dangerous to our export programme than lethargy, and that is misguided zeal. Incalculable harm can be done by rushing out to promote markets for a particular product and then discovering, when the orders come in, that you are not in a position to supply them.'

While Dillon was Minister for Agriculture in the two coalition governments, his thinking was to produce as much as possible rather than obtaining or making sure there was a market in the first place. Increased production did not mean increased profit, because once a glut developed, the price dropped. In recent months agricultural exports had been dropping and it was well for the country that Lemass had the vision to move towards industrialisation.

Even when it came to agricultural production, Dillon exhibited a kind of change-nothing conservatism. Lynch was appalled by the backwardness of some areas and recognised the need to develop them in some way. 'When I had just been appointed a parliamentary secretary with special responsibility for the western areas, and visited some part of the west and went to the bog in the Glenamoy area,' he told the Dáil, 'I was amazed at the extent of the wasteland that I saw there.' The Fianna Fáil government therefore made provisions to put up the money for a grass-meal company in Bangor Erris, County Mayo, in 1953, but after Dillon became Minister for Agriculture in the second coalition government, the plug was pulled on the project. On returning to power in 1957, Fianna Fáil appointed a committee to investigate the whole thing and it reported in November 1958, unanimously recommending that grass meal could be produced competitively on reclaimed bogland. This certainly justified Lynch's earlier stance.

When he moved legislation on 14 July 1959 to give effect to the proposals, Dillon was again highly critical. 'This is a peculiarly daft Fianna Fáil aberration,' the Fine Gael leader declared. 'People who go daft in this way lose all capacity for perspective. This is a silly political stunt to revive the waning fortunes of a few poor old Fianna Fáil deadbeats in north Mayo. We all know that.

'You could grow grass on Nelson's hat on the top of Nelson's Pillar or on the carpet of Dáil Éireann if you were prepared to spend enough money in the operation. You can grow grass anywhere. You could grow grass on the Minister's head or on my head, if you were prepared to undergo the inconvenience.'

Tourism was another area in which the Fianna Fáil government saw potential for expansion. The previous government had cut back drastically on tourist marketing in the United States in 1955. By the time Lynch took over ministerial responsibility for tourism in 1959, Bord Fáilte was spending 29 per cent less on the American market than in 1955. Most of the cuts were in the area of advertising, which was down 56 per cent, and to make matters worse there had been a 50 per cent rise in publicity costs. As a result, Bord Fáilte was effectively doing less than a quarter of the advertising that it had been doing five years earlier. It concentrated much more on attracting British tourists instead. It practically doubled its spending on the British market, opening new offices in Manchester and Glasgow. But Irish tourism from Britain was seriously affected by the IRA's border campaign, which began in late 1956.

Lemass had recognised the potential for development of the tourist industry and his department had already prepared legislation before he became Taoiseach. Thus Lynch inherited that prepared legislation and he moved the second stage of the Tourist Traffic Bill on 9 July 1959 to provide more money to Bord Fáilte to enable it to provide financial assistance for the development of major tourist resorts and the provision of additional bedroom accommodation in hotels, because the shortage of accommodation was hampering the development of tourism. The tourist season was so short that it was difficult to persuade hotels and guesthouses to expand. In 1958 the Government authorised Bord Fáilte to encourage hotels and motels to build extra en suite rooms by providing grants of up to a fifth of the cost, and in 1960 a further incentive was introduced in the form of an annual depreciation allowance of 10 per cent in respect of capital expenditure incurred on the construction of new hotels and the extension of existing buildings.

With the decline of advertising in the United States, the drop-off in American tourism should have been predicted, but when the number of Americans who visited Ireland declined in 1959, it still caught the tourist industry by surprise. Bord Fáilte therefore opened a new office in Chicago and Lynch predicted that there would be an increase in American visitors in 1960.

In addition to introducing legislation, Lynch also urged the community as a whole to become more conscious of the needs of tourists by ensuring that high ditches were lowered so that the tourists would have a better view of the countryside. 'There is, perhaps, nothing so frustrating for tourists as to find that some particularly appealing view which they would like to enjoy is shut off by high walls and hedges,' he complained.

Expenditure by visitors to Ireland in 1960 reached £42.4 million, which amounted to an 11 per cent increase on the previous year and a 30 per cent increase from 1957. The country's share of the American traffic to Europe had increased from 6 to 10 per cent in the past decade, but he recognised that there was even more potential in the British market. Only about 1 per cent of the British who took a vacation abroad visited Ireland. 'If, instead of 1 per cent, we could attract 2 or perhaps 3 per cent, the effect on our tourist earnings would be electrifying,' Lynch noted.

The scope of his ministerial responsibilities involved him in other areas also, such as wage and price disputes. The price of bread was a particularly contentious issue after the Fianna Fáil government eliminated food subsidies. Lynch accused the Opposition of playing politics with the issue.

When a previous Fianna Fáil government had cut the subsidies in 1952, the Opposition did not restore them when they returned to power in 1954, despite the fuss they kicked up over the issue. Seán Casey, a Labour deputy from Cork, recalled that people campaigning for Lynch attached bread to sticks in 1957 in an attempt to exploit the issue of the cost of bread. 'The minister's party and supporters in Cork went around with loaves of bread on sticks and were referring to the price of bread,' Casey contended.

'If we decided to import all our wheat rather than grow it here at home, we could put bread on the tables of our consumers at a much lower price,' Lynch explained, 'but it is equally true that we would then lose to the national economy several million pounds a year which the farmers get for growing wheat.'

As a result of a particularly wet summer in 1958 there was a poor wheat yield and it was necessary to import large quantities of foreign wheat, which was much cheaper than the native produce. As a result the price of bread dropped. But there was a bumper wheat harvest in 1959, so imports were cut and the price of bread went up again by a farthing on a two-pound batch loaf.

In the midst of so much economic expansion it was probably inevitable that there should be a degree of industrial unrest over wages, with high-profile strikes in Coras Iompar Éireann (CIÉ) and the Electricity Supply Board (ESB). 'For the first time since the war the increases were not related to the consumer price index,' according to Lynch. The cost of living had gone up slightly in February 1959, but it dropped back again to the 1958 level in 1960.

As a backbencher, Lynch had told the Dáil that deputies should stay out of industrial disputes and not become involved at the invitation of one side, unless also invited by the other side, because 'it often happens that when a person in public life intervenes, the effect is to prolong the particular dispute.' Hence he suggested that the newly founded Labour Court should engage in conciliation as well as arbitration, and he was quite content to follow his own advice as a minister.

During 1961, however, he found himself dragged into a couple of major labour disputes. There had been relative tranquillity among bus-workers in CIÉ for more than a decade, until March 1961, when busmen went on strike for better weekend re-muneration 'for working unsocial hours'. Their grievance had been submitted to the Labour Court, which recommended that instead of their normal rate, they should be paid time-and-a-quarter for Saturdays after 1 p.m. The Irish Transport and General Workers' Union (ITGWU) rejected the recommendation and demanded time-and-a-half on Saturdays and double-time on Sundays. To press this claim, the union called for a series of weekend strikes, beginning on Saturday 4 March. The chairman of the board of CIÉ, Todd Andrews, was a hard-headed man with fixed ideas that he was not afraid to express to anyone. He was prepared to accept the Labour Court's recommendations, but the union rejected them, much to his disgust.

As Minister for Industry and Commerce, Lynch was in charge of labour matters. He was anxious to avoid involvement for as long as possible, as the principals on each side tended to be intransigent, but he found himself reluctantly dragged into the dispute. 'Lynch was not particularly interested in the affairs of CIÉ, finding it a political burden,' Andrews noted. 'I got the impression that he found me also something of a burden; my abrasive manner was offensive to his nice gentle personality.'

When Lynch invited the management and unions to talks, Andrews felt the invitation was a mistake, because it diminished the authority of the Labour Court and encouraged the unions to hold out for better terms. There could be little real empathy between him and a conciliatory minister like Lynch.

Striking only on the weekends was comparatively easy for the union because it caused a minimum of inconvenience to the public, and it was also comparatively cheap, as the men could work the remainder of the week. The whole thing offended the chairman's sense of patriotism and he decided to force the issue by locking the men out if they withdrew their services again the following weekend.

Lynch tried to avert the confrontation by offering independent arbitration that would be binding on both sides, but the union demanded that its workers should have a right to vote on any recommended settlement. John Conroy, the president of the ITGWU, explained that the men were distrustful of tribunals as long as they did not have a working-class majority. He seemed to think that 'all employers were enemies'.

Andrews, who was from a working-class background himself, had no time for class pretensions. Ireland was now a classless society in his view. 'For me, the public service was the most honourable form of employment,' he wrote, 'and I looked on CIÉ as the property of the whole nation. I felt that the trade unions should recognise that the board and management of CIÉ and other semi-state companies were of the same social origin as themselves and had nothing to gain by treating their employees unfairly.'

'Our experience has been that an offer made in negotiation immediately becomes a commitment for the board, even though it may be rejected at the time,' Andrews explained publicly. 'It is the springboard from which, in subsequent proceedings, the unions seek to gain advantage.' He added that 'it is well-nigh impossible to reach finality in direct negotiations with the unions.'

The lockout, which began on Monday, 13 March 1961, affected some 6,000 workers. It evoked memories of the infamous 1913 lockout involving the union leader James Larkin and William Martin Murphy of Dublin United Tramways. The Irish Congress of Trade Unions (ICTU) and the three unions involved in CIÉ got behind the workers. James Larkin Jr, the general secretary of the Workers' Union of Ireland, charged that Andrews was essentially challenging the workers' right to strike.

On the Thursday Lynch announced that he had proposed the formation of a special three-man court of inquiry, chaired by the Supreme Court judge and future President Cearbhall Ó Dálaigh, to investigate the dispute. He was joined by Leo Crawford, joint secretary of the ICTU, and Frank Lemass, the general manager of CIÉ who also happened to be the Taoiseach's brother. If the court could not come to a decision, it was agreed that Ó Dálaigh would issue his own recommendations and these would be put to a ballot of the workers. The lockout was lifted and the workers returned to work on Friday, but insisted on resuming their weekend action.

After four days of deliberation, the inquiry recommended that the increase suggested by the Labour Court should be more than doubled. It was proposed that the men be paid time-and-a-half from 1 p.m. on Saturdays and time-and-three-quarters on Sunday. The workers accepted the recommendations by a more than 2-to-1 majority.

Cearbhall Ó Dálaigh was appointed Chief Justice of the

Supreme Court later that year, while Lynch got the political credit for settling the dispute, despite the intransigence of Andrews. But the latter was convinced that the minister had undermined the normal bargaining procedures by his intervention. 'Ministers' interventions in strikes can never be anything but disastrous,' Andrews concluded in his memoirs.

In August 1961 Lynch intervened in a strike involving some 2,600 electricians by calling for a conference of representatives of both sides at the Department of Industry and Commerce. Although less than a third of the strikers were employed by the ESB, there was a real threat to the national power supply. As a result of Lynch's intervention, terms were quickly agreed between the representatives, with the addition of an extra penny an hour on the previous offer of a seven-pence-an-hour increase, but this was rejected by the workers. Lynch had to try again. Another penny an hour was added and the unions recommended this to the workers, but they rejected this offer too. Another penny an hour was added, and this was accepted to end the two-week-old strike.

Afterwards Lynch explained that it was 'generally desirable that the State should not lead in the matter of wages, that those should be fixed by agreement between employers and employees in the private sector and that the remuneration of state workers should follow the rates voluntarily fixed.'

Lemass called a general election for October 1961 when the existing Dáil was well into its final year. It was a favourable time for Fianna Fáil, as the economy was performing magnificently. The contrast with the previous government going into the election could hardly have been starker. Prior to 1957 the economy had been stagnating for years and disillusionment was rife in the community, whereas the economy was growing at an unprecedented rate in 1961.

Some of the credit for arresting the economic slide should be attributed to the policies introduced by Gerard Sweetman in the final year of the Second Coalition, but most of the credit went to T. K. Whitaker's Programme for Economic Expansion of 1958. It aimed at 2 per cent annual growth. That figure had been achieved in 1959 and was doubled in 1960, which was the last year for which figures were available at the time of the election. Lynch was in the happy political position that the figures for the various advances were actually announced while he was Minister for Industry and Commerce. Exports in 1960, for instance, attained the record level of £152.4 million, which represented a 16.6 per cent increase over the previous year. Unemployment dropped by 7.5 per cent on the previous year. Thus the economic indicators favoured the government in general and Lynch in particular during the general-election campaign. In political terms, the real question was whether Fianna Fáil would benefit more from its own magnificent performance in government than it had benefited from the public reaction to the apparently dismal performance of the other parties in government in the run-up to the last election. Of course, the dismal aspect of that performance was more apparent than real, since Gerard Sweetman had initiated the unpopular policies that were needed to turn the economy around.

Lemass was not complacent. 'I warned my party that any member who used such a phrase as "You never had it so good" would be promptly repudiated by me,' he explained on 11 October 1961. 'In every speech I made during the campaign, I emphasised my view that economic progress should be regarded as only beginning and that the rate of progress would have to be accelerated before we could achieve the aims we have set ourselves.'

From Lynch's political perspective, Cork seemed to do particularly well out of the industrialisation. Irish Steel had been in financial trouble but the government intervened to provide the company with money to build what amounted to 'a new steelworks' on the site of the existing one in his own constituency. The government had indicated its intention of providing over £3 million to Irish Steel as early as 1958, so Lynch could not be accused of unduly favouring his own constituency, especially as the proposal had been welcomed by the Fine Gael spokesman.

Lynch insisted that he did not interfere with bodies like the Industrial Institute when it came to influencing their policies. Certainly he met with and listened to those who complained about the institute's decisions on grants and the placement of factories, but he said that he never interfered personally with the selection of any new factory sites. 'I have repeated, time and again, to people who have asked me to use my influence with An Foras Tionscal that I do not intend to use any influence with that body,' he told the Dáil. 'There is no attempt on my part, or on the part of my department, to influence An Foras Tionscal in any way. That applies, in particular, to the location of industries.' Cork was the second-largest industrial centre in the country and it was inevitable that it would benefit from the industrialisation; Lynch just happened to be in the right place at the right time.

For the first time in his political career he headed the poll, with more than half a quota to spare, but Fianna Fáil was not able to reach the dizzying heights it had attained in 1957. The party's vote actually dropped by 4.5 per cent nationally. In Cork City the decline was 2.4 per cent, which was enough to cost the party one of its three seats. Fianna Fáil ended up three seats short of an overall majority, but since nine independent deputies were elected around the country, Fianna Fáil was the only party that could realistically hope to form a government.

Before the Dáil voted on his nomination for Taoiseach, Lemass announced that he had not even approached any of the in-dependents for their support. He said he was standing on the Fianna Fáil platform and if elected he would implement Fianna Fáil policies, and he was duly elected without difficulty.

7

MINISTER FOR INDUSTRY

AND COMMERCE

1961–1965

Throughout the whole of the seventeenth Dáil, Jack Lynch served as Minister for Industry and Commerce. He had inherited the most dynamic department in the government from Lemass, and the department continued to play an important role under Lynch as the economy flourished. He had the primary responsibility for implementing the Second Programme for Economic Expansion.

The new Dáil convened under very different circumstances to its predecessor. At the end of 1956, emigration was running at around 40,000 people a year and unemployment had reached over 95,000. The country was in the midst of a depression that was dramatically lifted during the lifetime of the sixteenth Dáil, from 1957 to 1961.

'It was little wonder then that there was despondency through-out the country and that doubts prevailed as to the capacity of the country to make any solid or regular progress at all,' Lynch observed, recalling the way things were when de Valera formed his last government. 'Public confidence was at such a low ebb that it was obviously necessary for somebody, and particularly for the government, to redefine the national objectives. This was done in a very realistic way through the medium of the First Programme for Economic Expansion.'

The success of the Whitaker Plan inspired public confidence. 'In the four years up to 1962 the gross national product had increased by 18.5 per cent and in every individual sector of our economic activity there was significant, and in many cases spectacular, progress,' Lynch contended. The main aim of the policy was to generate industrial employment. The unemployed register in the same period was reduced from about 78,000 on average to 58,000. The volume of production in manufacturing industries had increased by about 50 per cent between 1957 and the end of 1963. The Whitaker Plan had envisaged an annual 2 per cent increase in the gross national product, but this was actually more than doubled. The momentum continued into the life of the new Dáil. The gross national product for 1961 increased by 8.7 per cent. Although there was a dip in the rate of progress in 1962, when the increase dropped to 4.9 per cent, it was at 5 per cent in the first half of 1963 and it then jumped back up to 8 per cent in the second half of the year.

The average number of people engaged in industry rose from 141,000 in 1957 to 167,000 in 1963. In the six years from 1958 to 1963, some 226 new industrial enterprises were opened around the country, many with the help of outside investment.

Nobody suggested that Lynch deserved the credit for the economic boom. Whitaker was recognised as its architect. Lynch was the minister who facilitated things, and he was quite content to allow others to shine. While the Taoiseach assumed a super-visory role, Lynch's responsibilities were recognised as the most onerous within the government. Those responsibilities were modified at the establishment of the new government in 1961, when tourism was transferred to the Minister for Transport and

Power instead. 'Shortly, there will be nothing left of the Department of Industry and Commerce but the minister and the building in Kildare Street,' James Dillon commented sarcastically.

'Industry and Commerce at the time was also responsible for all labour matters,' Lynch noted, 'and I was being constantly called into the settlement of strikes.' Lemass also depended on him to play a major role in negotiations with the Common Market on Ireland's application for membership.

'I think the main responsibility for these negotiations must rest on myself as Taoiseach,' Lemass told the Dáil, 'but I contemplate that the actual conduct of negotiations, where it involves the attendance of a minister at meetings in Brussels or elsewhere, will most likely be entrusted to the Minister for Industry and Commerce.' Lynch was a particularly good choice because of his ability to get on with the Opposition, which had promised that it would act in the national interest. This was a far cry from the 1920s and 1930s, when Fianna Fáil first and then Fine Gael opposed each other for party-political considerations, often without regard for the national interest.

Now both parties were much more inclined to cooperate on matters such as Ireland's possible membership of the European Economic Community (EEC). Lemass formally presented the Irish case for membership on 18 January 1962 in Brussels, and there were further discussions in May, but the Irish government did not press its application strongly, because of problems with the British application. Lemass and Lynch visited each of the EEC capitals and talked with the various leaders, none of whom expressed opposition to Ireland's prospective membership. On 22 October 1962 the EEC unanimously agreed to open negotiations on the Irish application. The biggest stumbling block was the attitude of the British government at the time.

Three-quarters of all Irish exports and four-fifths of the country's agricultural exports went to Britain. Ireland could not therefore afford to lose the British market by joining the Common Market while Britain was outside it. The British were reluctant to cut their trading ties with Commonwealth countries and fellow members of the European Free Trade Area (EFTA), which had been set up as a rival to the Common Market. In the past, Britain had essentially tried to undermine the EEC before it got going properly. Now France was in no hurry to facilitate the British, but there was no such hostility towards Ireland. For one thing, Ireland had not joined the EFTA, because it had not included agriculture. The Irish government was always more interested in the EEC, as it offered tremendous prospects for Irish beef exports.

At a press conference on 14 January 1963, the French President Charles de Gaulle said that the British were not yet ready to join the Common Market because of their reservations, their calls for restrictions, and demands for preferential arrangements for their Commonwealth trading partners. Britain's application was therefore shelved for the time being and the Irish application was put on hold too.

'This deadlock is, we hope, purely temporary,' Lemass told the Dáil. 'Our desire is that a way will be found before long to enable all European countries which share the aims expressed in the Treaty of Rome to participate fully in a wide Community.'

Throughout his early ministerial career in the 1930s, Seán Lemass had been a strong proponent of trade tariffs for industrial protection, but he adopted a very different approach as Taoiseach as he presided over a government that began tearing down the barriers he had done so much to establish himself. The Opposition naturally highlighted the policy contradictions.

It fell to Lynch to defend the Taoiseach's policy. 'We did no more than follow the traditional industrial policy which every country in the world has followed,' he argued. 'In the pre-war years, tariffs were the order of the day, and not peculiar in any way to this country. Tariff walls were built up in every country in Europe against every other country in Europe in those days.' But those walls began to come down with the establishment of the Common Market in 1956. The Fianna Fáil government immediately recognised that the country's future lay within the EEC, rather than the EFTA. 'We did say at that time that, insofar as our interests lay in Europe, they lay with the countries then forming the European Economic Community, and that the most desirable arrangement for us would be a common market in which we would be members with Britain,' Lynch explained.

'In the light of the failure to gain membership of the Common Market, we were keen to change the nature of our relationship with the British, to take account of our move towards free trade and to alter the unfair trading relationship between us and Britain on agricultural produce,' Lynch added. 'Lemass and I visited the then British Prime Minister, Harold Macmillan, in London, but there was no political will in Britain at the time to engage in a venture such as this. It wasn't until the Labour Party came to power in 1964 that we were able to open negotiations on what was to become the Anglo-Irish Free Trade Agreement, which was signed in 1965.'

Lynch considered Ireland's eventual membership of the Common Market virtually inevitable, despite the French government's blocking of Britain's application. Much of his ministerial time was consumed in preparing for membership – steering through new legislation to modernise the country's economic structures, reforming company law, gradually dismantling the country's tariff barriers and modernising industries so that they could compete with their Continental counterparts.

'Enormous changes occurred in our industrial life,' Lynch noted. 'The high walls of protection gave way to freer trade, the Control of Manufacturers Act was repealed and foreign industry assiduously courted into Ireland.' Fifteen American factories were set up in Ireland from 1957 to 1961.

These provided much-needed employment, which was generally welcomed, though Noël Browne asked if 'the money spent by various government envoys touting for business over the years was money well spent in the circumstances?' Many industries – such as Irish Steel, Verolme Cork Dockyard, the different motor-assembly plants and flour mills – would not survive if Ireland joined the EEC, according to Browne.

'I have lost no opportunity in public speeches or elsewhere of emphasising to manufacturers the urgent need for assessing their prospects in free-trade conditions and for taking steps to improve their competitiveness,' Lynch replied. A committee on industrial organisation had been set up to conduct a comprehensive survey of the industrial sector in order to determine which industries were strong enough to benefit from EEC membership, which would be viable after a transition period, and which would need and deserve government help, as well as those that deserved no sympathy because they had merely sheltered behind protectionism without attempting to become competitive. Those companies would have to 'readapt themselves while there is still time,' he warned.

The report of the Committee on Industrial Organisation, which was published in 1962, prompted the government to provide additional grants for technical assistance to improve productivity and efficiency in various industries. On 7 July 1962 Lynch proposed that previous grants for up to a third of the cost should be increased to half of the total cost.

The country's industrialisation was actually proceeding faster than expected. Lynch had to ask for supplementary finance for the IDA on 28 February 1962, because the expanded programme undertaken by the Authority had led to a number of projects not foreseen in the annual estimate. By the end of January 1962, there were seventy projects in production in undeveloped areas being assisted by the IDA, and there were a further fifty-two projects in various stages of development, according to Lynch. Those 122 projects were expected to employ about 10,000 workers.

There was little opposition to this industrialisation in the Dáil. The main criticism was from the two members of the National Progressive Democratic Party, Noël Browne and Jack McQuillan, who had originally been elected to the Dáil as members of Clann na Poblachta. Following the mother-and-child debacle, Browne joined Fianna Fáil for a period, but then broke with it to found his own party. He and McQuillan objected to the haphazard way in which these industries were being located. They thought industrialists were being allowed to do what they liked.

'The promoter will start his industry to suit himself, not to suit the rural area or to fit into some overall picture that may be in the minds of the government,' McQuillan argued. 'He may want to live in the locality. If he likes Killarney, he will go to Killarney and start his industry there, destroying the picturesque countryside with his buildings.' This was a patently obvious reference to Liebherr crane factory in Killarney. The government even provided the foreign industrialists with state aid, without adequate safeguards to ensure that they would not just leave when it suited them. Nobody was objecting, as long as the factories were providing employment. 'If there is a bit of employment given in a locality,' McQuillan said, 'people will sell their immortal souls, and the countryside with them.'

'I do not see any foundation for the suggestion that these people, having availed of the grants paid to them here, can abscond overnight, leaving us holding the baby,' Lynch argued in reply. Even if the industrialists absconded, their structures would be left behind, with the result that these amounted to an investment in the industrial infrastructure. 'We do not want to tell these people how to run their business,' he insisted. 'We do not want to breathe down their necks every time they turn in their factories or sit at their office desk. I do not think that to do that would prove successful. It would deter to a considerable extent the number of people likely to come here.'

Lynch also dealt with the issue of location. 'The other criticism was that I should have more control over the amount of the grants and the location of the industry,' he noted. 'If the minister were the person who decided first whether a grant should be given, the amount of the grant and the location, would anybody in his sane senses believe that he would not be influenced in some way by political motives?'

St Patrick's Copper Mine in Avoca posed a particular problem, because the mine, which employed 500 people, was in financial trouble. 'I feel responsible, as Minister for Industry and Commerce, for their employment,' Lynch explained. To ensure the viability of the mine, he called on the Dáil on different occasions for further assistance to the company.

Part of the problem was that the price of copper had dropped to £170 a ton, from the £430 it had fetched when the mining lease had been assigned to the company in January 1956. The parent company, Consolidate Mogul of Canada, asked for help from the Irish government in 1958. A loan of £1,368,000 was provided and commercial production was commenced in October of that year. They then ran into further difficulties, and the state guaranteed a further loan of £550,000 in December 1959. The company sought another £600,000 in 1962, saying that they were not able to raise any of the necessary capital privately, but the government decided not to provide any more state funds. A receiver was appointed and the state was called upon to honour its guarantees, which meant that the whole project really cost the state about £2.25 million. By this time the state was the virtual owner of the mine, even though the Canadians had invested about £2 million themselves. 'We would not be justified in expending the taxpayers' money in rescuing private capital adventured on a commercial risk,' Lynch explained, but he wished to afford the promoters 'every opportunity of rendering their enterprise successful', principally for the sake of the employees. Hence another £240,000 was advanced to keep the mine running while the viability of the whole project was assessed independently.

If Lemass had tried to do that, there would have been complaints of favouritism and charges that he was gambling recklessly with taxpayers' money, but Lynch never provoked such criticism. He was untainted by Civil-War baggage. It was not his style to try to score political points off his opponents, and they usually did not try to score them off him. He personally attracted very little opposition. Hence Lemass relied on him a great deal. This was particularly important because Fianna Fáil had only a minority government. Liam Cosgrave, the Fine Gael spokesman on Industry and Commerce, welcomed Lynch's approach to the problem as 'the only obvious decision that could be taken.'

As part of a broad overall plan to prepare for EEC membership, Lynch sought to update the country's company legislation. On 14 November 1962 he moved the second stage of the Companies Bill, which he described as 'the biggest piece of legislation which has been put before the Oireachtas since the establishment of the state.' In all it had some 400 sections and thirteen schedules. A special Dáil committee to examine the legislation was set up, with the agreement of Fine Gael.

Other legislation to prepare for broader international co-operation and membership of the EEC included the Restrictions of Imports Bill, and Lynch moved bills to amend the 1927 act covering copyright, trademarks and patents. All of this legislation was welcomed by the Fine Gael opposition spokesman, Liam Cosgrave.

The Committee on Industrial Organisation had undertaken surveys of twenty-four different industries with a view to their preparation for EEC membership. As those reports were being published individually, Lynch was in a better position to introduce legislation necessary to help the various industries in different ways, such as allowing the IDA to take a more active role. In January 1963, for instance, he moved an amendment to the Industrial Grants Act and the Underdeveloped Areas Act to allow the IDA to extend and increase grants to different industries and to permit a single composite grant for buildings and equipment.

Rather than give a grant to Nitrigin Éireann, legislation was introduced 'to provide for repayable interest-bearing advances' from the exchequer to enable the company to establish a nitrogenous fertiliser factory in Arklow. The money advanced to the company was to be repayable with interest.

In July 1963 Lynch moved to help Verolme Cork Dockyard, which had been set up in 1959. There was a worldwide depression in the shipbuilding industry and it had been necessary for various governments to rescue well-established shipyards in other countries. The Industrial Credit Company provided a £4.76 million loan to Verolme, which employed 850 workers in Cork. Special funding was also provided for Irish Steel in Cork.

James Dillon, the Fine Gael leader, later questioned why an additional £350,000 subsidy had been given to Cornelius Verolme to meet the contract price for building the bulk cargo carrier for the Netherlands Freight and Tanker Company of the Hague. Verolme was also chairman of that company, so there was an apparent cosy circle in which one of his companies was paid a subsidy so that he could make the price to sell the ship to another of his companies. At this time another vessel was being built for the Liberian National Shipping Company, in which Verolme had a 25 per cent share. When Dillon raised the matter on 17 June 1964, however, he demanded answers from the Taoiseach rather than Lynch.

Even though questions were asked about wasting government money on Verolme Cork Dockyards and Irish Steel, there was no uproar, or even the usual mock-indignation on the other side of the Dáil about Lynch showing favouritism to companies in his own constituency. This was a measure of the way that Lynch's style was helping to break down traditional political barriers. Hence he was frequently used as a government troubleshooter, especially when it came to strikes and wage demands. Industrial relations came under his ministerial remit and he had a double interest in this area, as the spiralling wage costs would inevitably damage the country's competitiveness, but he moved cautiously.

Lemass took the lead in encouraging the unions and employers to devise a joint national strategy to ensure the organised development of industrial relations as the economy grew. In July 1962 the National Employer-Labour Conference between the Federated Union of Employers (FUE) and the ICTU representative and experts on behalf of both began meetings. In February 1963 the government published a white paper with the main aim of promoting the orderly increase in wages in conjunction with the growth of national production.

'Most people in the country accept the white paper for what it is, a request for the exercise of restraint in wage demands in the interests of the national economy as a whole,' Lynch argued. The government provided the machinery to help achieve settlements through the Labour Court. 'Where unusually high increases are obtained,' he argued, 'the tendency will be for every other wage group to seek pro rata increases. When this happens, it sets a dangerous pattern, not so much that anybody desires to depress wages but because everybody desires a reasonable pattern of wage increase consistent with national production.'

In order to draw attention to the situation, the white paper called for short-term restraint in wage demands and advocated that the Labour-Employer Conference establish a long-term cure 'of haphazard increases and wage adjustments' by holding periodic conferences between representatives of employers and workers to make objective assessments so that salary rates could be established in the private sector, ensuring an 'orderly relationship' between wage increases and production. Lynch moved carefully, emphasising that he was only looking for advice, rather than personally proposing any set procedure.

Following the ESB strike, he said that he had his department review the existing industrial-relations machinery in consultation with other departments, but he was waiting for proposals from a subcommittee of the Labour-Employer Conference to guide him on whatever proposals he would ultimately table. 'Even now,' he stressed, 'the white paper does not put forward any proposal for general adoption.'

The government was not attempting 'to impose any particular system on workers and employers,' he stressed. 'It would prefer to maintain what is the position heretofore; to maintain and support a sound system developed by these interests themselves. The government, instead of proposing a revision of negotiating machinery, has waited for a proposal from the Labour-Employer Conference.'

Observing that James Dillon, the Fine Gael leader, had referred rather disparagingly to economists, Lynch explained that he had a much greater regard for them. Ultimately this trust in economists was to have a profound effect on his political career. 'If economists warn the government of certain trends, and the government, having examined that warning, are convinced that certain trends are there, it is the duty of the government to acknowledge them,' he argued.

There was a bus strike in March 1963 over CIÉ's plans to introduce one-man buses. The three unions involved had accepted the principle of one-man buses the previous year, but they then sought to use this for bargaining purposes in order to secure better pensions, sickness benefits and travel concessions. As the issue had been discussed since 1959, it was felt that it would be extremely difficult for anyone to mediate, but Lynch had intervened on 22 March by proposing to establish a three-man commission to examine the demands of the workers. This was the way the previous lockout had been settled in 1961. The unions accepted this proposal and CIÉ agreed to postpone the introduction of the new system, but the workers rejected the proposal by a three-to-one margin in a secret ballot. They insisted that the arbitration would not be binding and that they should be free to ballot on the recommendations of the proposed commission. Lynch was ready to accede to the men's demand.

'The bus stoppage went on for a month, with the political pressure on the government mounting all the time, until finally the Taoiseach, Seán Lemass, decided that the lockout should be lifted,' Andrews noted in his memoirs.

'Jack Lynch telephoned me to say that "the Boss" (i.e. Lemass) wanted me to take the men back,' Andrews recalled. 'I told him I would refuse to do so unless I got a directive either from the Taoiseach or from himself as Minister for Industry and Commerce.'

'At Lynch's suggestion, I decided to discuss the position personally with the Taoiseach and reiterated my demand for a formal public directive,' Andrews continued. 'I said to Lemass that in every man's life there comes a time when he must make a stand. There would be no compromising on the question of the lockout unless it was made clear that the decision had been taken out of the hands of CIÉ.'

'All right,' Lemass replied. 'I'll tell the minister to issue the directive.'

When Andrews returned to his office there was already a message from Lynch summoning him to a meeting. 'We agreed on the form of the directive and he promised to send it to the press,' Andrews continued. 'Later he phoned to say that he had read over the directive to "the Boss", who agreed with the wording but did not think it was necessary to publish it. I replied that unless it was published, the lockout would not be lifted by me. He phoned back in due course to say that publication had been arranged.'

'I have informed the unions that if they can procure the endorsement of my proposals with this modification, I will direct the board of CIÉ to accept them,' Lynch wrote to the secretary of the company. 'The unions have intimated to me that they could have a ballot carried on the amended proposals and the result conveyed to me before Monday 8 April. I therefore strongly request that your board defer the operation of one-man scheduled bus services until that date.'

The wording was rather clumsy, because Lynch had really exceeded his ministerial authority. He did not have the authority to direct the board of CIÉ in such matters. When Noël Browne and Jack McQuillan called on the government to compel the chairman of CIÉ to withdraw the one-man bus proposal, for instance, Lynch pointed out that he did not have the authority to do so.

'I have no statutory power to issue directions to CIÉ in relation to trade disputes between the company and its employees,' he explained. Under the Minister and Secretaries Act, he did have the authority 'to make a strong request to the company', which he did. 'The company knew well that I had no power to direct them to do anything, but knew I was making an attempt to solve the strike, and they agreed to accept my direction in the matter,' he explained. In other words, the members of the board accepted his direction even though they knew he had no right to direct them. However, the whole thing merely postponed the strike for a week.

On 8 April 1963 some 4,150 men went on strike. In his frustration, Lynch accused Browne and McQuillan of sabotaging his efforts to end the dispute. 'I have in my hand a photostat copy of a pamphlet issued by those two deputies, copies of which were handed to members of the Irish Transport and General Workers Union as they were exercising their ballot,' Lynch said. 'It is a document which I would describe as the most pernicious piece of political perfidy I ever saw and it contains an enticement to action which is communist policy.' Using smear tactics – Red or otherwise – was out of character for Lynch, but on this occasion it was a measure of his exasperation with Browne, who would have tried the patience of a saint.

During the strike, which lasted from 8 April to 12 May 1963, the Army was called in to provide transport, but there were not enough Army lorries to meet the demand. After five weeks, the strike was resolved when the employees agreed to go back to work and operate the one-man buses in return for an increase in sickness benefits and a promise of a commission to consider workers' pension rights.

During the final weeks of 1963 and into the new year, Lemass tried to persuade the unions and employers' organisations to agree on a national wage agreement. This was finally concluded in January 1964 and was intended to run until the end of June 1966. The economy was projected to grow by 8 per cent, but the government persuaded the employers to agree to a 12 per cent wage increase in an attempt to ensure industrial peace. For six months it seemed to be working, but then in June the Dáil deputies awarded themselves a 50 per cent pay increase. They were getting only £1,000 a year at the time, so raising that to £1,500 could hardly be described as overpaying themselves, but this was more than most people were earning; the politicians were calling on everybody else to hold a line while they breached the guidelines themselves.

Before the summer was over, some 20,000 building workers went on strike in Dublin. The tradesmen and general workers in the building trade did not return to work after their annual holiday. They went on strike for a forty-hour week. The employers rejected the claim as a breach of the national wage agreement, which included a stipulation that employees agreed to 'existing weekly working hours.' The workers' new demand was a clear breach of the agreement, but the politicians were hardly in a position to take a stand, because of the 50 per cent increase the Dáil deputies had awarded themselves.

The strike, which began on 18 August 1964, was confined almost exclusively to County Dublin. It was the first major strike in the building industry since 1937, when, after a seven-month strike, all the men had to show for their troubles was an extra penny an hour.

The dispute was referred to the Labour Court and two different deals were worked out between the representatives of the employers and the unions, with the help of the Labour Court's conciliation officer, but both agreements were rejected when referred back to the seventeen unions involved. Initially the union representative agreed to a deal that cut half an hour off the forty-two-and-a-half-hour working week in Dublin, but after this was rejected by the unions, they agreed to a cut of an hour and to the establishment of a forty-hour week by the following winter. Even though the strike was confined mainly to Dublin, the unions balloted their members nationwide, and the latest deal was rejected by twelve of the unions.

Lynch tried to avoid involvement initially. In fact, he came in for some criticism because he remained totally aloof in relation to this issue. He was actually abroad on holidays and made no effort to return when the strike began. It was only after the ITGWU called for the strike to be extended nationwide that Lynch met with the ICTU to stop the whole thing spreading. He got the unions and employers together again, much to the annoyance of Paddy Smith, the Minister for Agriculture. At the Cabinet meeting on Tuesday 6 October, Smith complained bitterly and things became quite heated before he stormed out of the meeting. Next day he wrote a letter of resignation to Lemass, denouncing the unions as a dishonest, incompetent and tyrannical plague. Time and again the union representatives would agree to terms, only to have the workers reject them.

'Those so-called leaders of the trade union movement whom our Minister for Industry and Commerce have [sic] been chasing around for years now could not lead their grandmothers,' Smith wrote. 'When reason and decency is [sic] abandoned there are only two courses – fight or surrender. I believe a stand like this will be in the interest of all in the end and I feel thousands of others see with me in this – even real trade union leaders should.'

Lemass apparently hoped that Smith would reconsider his resignation as the crisis surrounding the strike was put at the top of the agenda for the next Cabinet meeting, on 9 October, but on the eve of that meeting Smith released his letter of resignation to the press and called a press conference. He was not only annoyed that the government was caving in to the unions which were breaking the National Wage Agreement, but convinced that the government had an urban industrial bias that rendered it virtually indifferent to the plight of agricultural workers. 'Although I disagreed with his views at the time,' Lynch later explained, 'he was representing a growing tension between the industrial and agricultural sectors as the industrial one boomed under the expansionary Fianna Fáil policies at the time and the agricultural sector lagged behind.'

Smith's resignation had the potential to cause a major political crisis. He had first been brought into government in 1939 as parliamentary secretary to the then Taoiseach Éamon de Valera, and he was first promoted to Minister for Agriculture in 1947. He had been a minister in every Fianna Fáil Cabinet since then. His resignation could have destabilised the minority government easily, had the Taoiseach not acted quickly.

Lemass, who learned around 11.15 a.m. that Smith had announced his resignation publicly, moved to ensure that a replacement was appointed so quickly that the new appointment would make as much news as the resignation. He summoned Charles Haughey and Brian Lenihan to his office. He told Haughey that he was appointing him Minister for Agriculture and Lenihan that he intended to appoint him to the Cabinet in Haughey's place as Minister for Justice. Lenihan's promotion from parliamentary secretary necessitated the approval of the Dáil, which was not due to meet for another three weeks. Ironically, the

Dáil chamber was in the process of being renovated but this work was being delayed by the strike. The Taoiseach therefore assigned the Justice portfolio to himself, and by 12.20 p.m. he had convened the Cabinet to formalise Lenihan's appointment as parliamentary secretary to the Minister for Justice as a temporary measure until his formal appointment to the Cabinet could be given the necessary approval of the Dáil.

'Lemass was a great politician,' Haughey later claimed. 'He had a great capacity to anticipate things, to be ahead of the developments, not having to react to them. The new appointments made as much news as Smith's resignation. He didn't allow any atmosphere to build up, it was all over and done with before most people knew what was happening.'

The next day the new appointments did, in fact, provoke more comment than anything Smith might have said at his press conference. 'Dublin was agog last night with speculation about Mr Haughey's chances of making a go of Agriculture,' one *Irish Times* reporter noted. In a separate editorial the newspaper wondered about Haughey's aptitude for agriculture, because he was seen as the epitome of the new urban politician. 'His urban and urbane background, his knowledge of law and accountancy, and even horses and horsemanship, do not seem at first glance to fit him for the post,' the leader writer contended. 'We can only wait and see whether he can sufficiently adapt his considerable talents to a new and challenging position.' If Smith had hoped to provoke a government crisis by his resignation, he was totally outmanoeuvred.

It had been rumoured, however, that Lemass was planning a major reshuffle of his Cabinet when the Dáil reconvened. It was widely believed that he intended to replace senior ministers like Jim Ryan, Seán McEntee and Gerald Bartley, all of whom were in their seventies. If the Taoiseach had, indeed, planned on such a reshuffle, Smith's resignation forced him to put the whole thing on hold.

Meanwhile, the building workers' strike continued. Lynch's initiative in calling the two sides together at the Department of Industry and Commerce led to another breakthrough the following Tuesday. The two sides agreed that the working week in Dublin would be cut by an hour and a quarter immediately and by a similar amount in a year's time, to bring it down to forty hours. It was also agreed that Lynch would appoint an independent commission to examine the issue nationwide.

The government suffered a serious economic setback later that month when the British government announced a 15 per cent surcharge on all industrial imports. Lemass protested vigorously both to the British ambassador in Dublin and in person in London, where he was accompanied by Lynch for talks with Prime Minister Harold Wilson and his colleagues. The Taoiseach argued that the surcharge would have 'an exceptionally severe effect' on Irish trade, because of the country's dependence on the British market. The surcharge was going to hit 21 per cent of Ireland's total exports, whereas it only applied to about 5 per cent of exports from Western European countries in either the Common Market or the EFTA.

Wilson expressed regret but he made it clear that his government had no alternative and Dublin would have to assume that the measure would last for six months. Lemass and his Cabinet colleagues considered the possibility of making an immediate application for membership of the EEC, but this was not feasible at the time, though it was a long-term alternative. 'We see in membership of the EEC the means of escaping from excessive dependence on the British market and from the danger that the bilateral agreement, under which our trade is now conducted, could be set aside or temporarily suspended, as has happened in Britain,' the Taoiseach explained. As soon as the British could overcome their temporary difficulties, he proposed, Dublin and London should conclude a free-trade agreement.

Lynch could not have known it but he was coming to the end of his tenure as Minister for Industry and Commerce. The country had enjoyed a period of unparalleled prosperity. Political criticism of him was largely confined to the carping comments of the few frustrated socialists in the Dáil.

'Deputy Dr Browne gave us his usual homily on socialism,' Lynch complained on one occasion. 'At least he appeared to have the merit of sincerity, but he had the demerit of making extravagant and almost hysterical charges against individuals.' When Browne 'referred to the past seven years as seven wasted years in the economic advance of the country', Lynch was able to point out with justification that the country's exports more than doubled in those so-called 'wasted years', that the number of industrial jobs had dramatically increased, and 'for the first time in generations, we succeeded in reversing the trend of emigration.'

In the midst of the economic prosperity there was little talk of the partition issue, but at the start of the new year *The Irish Times* asked both Lynch and Brian Faulkner, the Minister for Commerce in Northern Ireland, if they would be willing to meet each other. 'I would be willing to meet Lynch any time,' Faulkner replied. Lynch, too, welcomed the idea.

But before they could meet there was an even more momentous meeting when Seán Lemass travelled north for a meeting in Belfast with Prime Minister Terence O'Neill of Northern Ireland on 14 January 1965. Three weeks later, Faulkner met with Lynch in Dublin. 'Our talks covered the possibility of cooperation in the economic field, with particular reference to trade and industrial research,' Lynch explained afterwards. 'We have arranged that discussions will take place at official level, after which I expect I shall meet Mr Faulkner again.'

In March 1965 there was a by-election in mid-Cork. With just a minority government, Lemass was acutely conscious of the damage that losing the seat would do. The previous February, when he faced by-elections in Cork and Kildare, he warned that he would call a general election if Fianna Fáil lost either of the contests. The ploy obviously worked, because the party won both seats. This was similar to the tactic employed by the French president Charles de Gaulle, who repeatedly called referenda and threatened to resign if his proposals were defeated. In March 1965 Lemass tried the same ploy again in a Mid-Cork by-election, but the seat was won by Eileen Desmond of Labour, and Lemass called a general election.

This time Fianna Fáil missed the overall majority by the narrowest margin possible, winning 72 of the 144 seats.

8

MINISTER FOR FINANCE

1965–1966

Seán Lemass was re-elected Taoiseach without any difficulty on 21 April 1965. The big change in his new government was the appointment of Jack Lynch as Minister for Finance in place of a member of the party's old guard, Dr Jim Ryan, who had retired from politics. The appointment of Lynch was particularly significant, because the Taoiseach was also coming to the end of his political career and had decided that this would probably be his last term in the Dáil.

Of course, the public was not aware that this was the case. Lemass was not considered to be particularly old, seeing that he still had more than a decade to go before he would reach the age at which de Valera had stood down, but there was a general consensus that the Long Fellow had stayed on too long. Lemass was not about to make that mistake.

Although the country was still in the midst of an economic boom, there had been a hiccup in the economy, with a number of disturbing features. Government expenditure had gone up by a staggering 30.4 per cent, largely as a result of pay adjustments for the civil service, the Army, teachers, and those employed by the health authorities. There was considerable unrest in the workplace, with disruptive strikes in the ESB, the banks and the newspaper industry.

The economy itself had been growing steadily for the previous seven years at an annual average of 4.3 per cent, but there were signs of a slowdown in late 1965. This was partly due to external forces. Irish exports were seriously hit by the British surcharge on imports, and there was a decline in the flow of capital into Ireland, because of the apparent economic slowdown. This led to a dramatic decline in the trade balance. Economists contended that a significant amount of the increase in imports was new machinery and raw materials for use in industry, which was part of the price to be paid for increased productivity. But although productivity had increased, the markets began to fall.

The Irish economy was further hit by a growth in borrowing, increased public spending, and wage rises that were increasing faster than productivity, with the result that temporary import levies were imposed by the government on non-essential goods, mainly luxury items and goods which could be supplied in sufficient quantities from Irish sources.

These moves, which were contrary to the general trend, in which the country had been opening up rather than restricting trade, were necessary as a temporary measure in response to the British surcharge. Lemass had been the main architect of dismantling the tariffs, for which he had been largely responsible during the 1930s. These tariffs had supported inefficiency and high costs, thereby rendering much Irish production uncompetitive on the international market.

Lemass had approached the government of Harold Macmillan with a view to expanding Anglo-Irish trade, but Macmillan was in a precarious political position, and his successor, Sir Alex Douglas-Home, was even weaker, so it proved impossible to make progress with the British until the change of governments brought Harold Wilson of the Labour Party to power. In November 1964 Lemass was accompanied by Lynch and Haughey to talks with Wilson and his colleagues. This led to talks between officials of the two governments in early 1965, but progress was slow.

Meanwhile Lynch introduced his first budget on 11 May 1965. In his address he highlighted an increase in social-welfare benefits. Pensions such as the non-contributory old-age pension and the blind and widows' pensions were raised by an extra ten shillings a week, which was to be recovered by raising the taxes on petrol, beer, wine, spirits and tobacco. 'We are in the happy position that the yield from all these commodities has shown a marked buoyancy and it is clear that the increases I propose can be borne without serious adverse effects,' he noted.

'All in all, a wise budget, if not an imaginative one,' *The Irish Times* observed. 'What the budget boils down to is that, if the government did not feel an obligation to increase social-welfare payments, we could have had a standstill – that is, little or no change from last year. As things are, many categories of people entitled to better benefits are to get them. Thus election promises, largely spurred by pressure from the two opposition parties, have been honoured.'

One of Lynch's reforms was to curtail the amount of Dáil debate on financial business. Under the existing system there would be four financial debates in rapid succession. The first was on the so-called Vote on Account. This was a device to request money to tide over the government for the first four months of the financial year until the budget could be formulated and enacted. The second debates would follow shortly afterwards, when the government estimates were announced, and the third would be on the budget, while a fourth debate would ensue on the Finance Bill introduced to give force to the budget proposals. Lynch proposed that the vote on account be eliminated because it inevitably took place before the figures were available. As a result, speakers were usually only speculating. He proposed that henceforth the necessity for the vote could be eliminated if each government was authorised to spend up to four-fifths of the amount that had been allocated for each particular service in the preceding financial year.

Fine Gael welcomed his proposal. 'I am satisfied,' the opposition spokesman on finance, T. F. O'Higgins, explained, 'that what is proposed in this bill will not involve any lessening of the necessary control this House should exercise.'

But Lynch did come in for some criticism when it became apparent that there was a discrepancy in his budget figures in relation to capital expenditure. He announced projects totalling some £103.75 million but when the figures for capital expenditure in the Second Programme for Economic Expansion were published following the budget, these envisaged spending of £95.5 million, and that was the figure that was officially authorised in the enabling legislation. As a result, the budget figures were out by more than £8 million, or 8.6 per cent in this instance. This, of course, was a clerical foul-up on the part of the civil servants – another instance of Lynch's heavy dependence on his advisers.

When the discrepancy became apparent in July, the Taoiseach admitted the mistake, and Lynch announced that the expenditure would be cut back to the authorised £95.5 million. The Opposition was naturally critical. Gerard Sweetman ridiculed Lynch by comparing him with a new bride who was unable to read a cookbook properly and created a dish comprised of the start of one recipe and the end of another.

In July, Lemass kick-started the stalled negotiations with the British. Accompanied by Lynch, Haughey and Paddy Hillery, he went to London to reinvigorate the talks between the officials, which had run into trouble earlier in the year. Following these talks, the civil servants again took up the running. Members of the two governments then finalised negotiations, and the Anglo-Irish Free Trade Agreement was signed in London on 14 December 1965.

'As it turned out, we got what we sought in most respects and the fall-back positions in others,' Lemass told the Dáil. 'I must say that I do not believe that this could have happened but for the personal intervention of the British Prime Minister, Mr Harold Wilson, at the final and crucial stages of the negotiations when, as is perhaps not unusual in these matters, the main purpose of the negotiations was becoming obscured by arguments about details.'

Lynch sought no publicity for himself. He was just one of the team. On the other hand, Haughey made front-page news by explaining the benefits for Irish agriculture. When Lynch made the newspapers, it seemed that he was propelled by events, whereas Haughey constantly sought publicity, aided by his friend John Healy, who wrote the popular 'Backbencher' column in *The Irish Times*. Hardly a week went by that Haughey, Brian Lenihan or Donogh O'Malley were not mentioned in the column, in which they were branded 'the three musketeers'. They were the new breed of high-living, urban politician. Lynch, on the other hand, kept a low social profile. He was very rarely mentioned in Healy's column, and then only in passing. Yet Healy recognised that Lynch was more popular than any of the other three without even trying.

Fine Gael put up only token opposition to the new agreement. Liam Cosgrave, who had been elected party leader during the year, proposed that the Dáil accept the agreement but deplored the fact that more had not been achieved. It was just political posturing. The Opposition seized on the opportunity to take a political swipe at Lemass, who seemed to be undoing much of his own political handiwork, because he was the one who was largely responsible for establishing the tariffs on imports during the 1930s. 'One cannot but reflect that there is no zeal as enthusiastic as that shown by the convert,' Cosgrave remarked.

The task of defending Lemass in the Dáil fell mainly to Lynch, who accused the Opposition of behaving 'as if we were still living in the economy of the 1930s'. Free trade was now 'not only on the horizon, but immediately imminent,' he warned. 'It must be realised that the policies of the 1930s and even of the 1940s must now change,' Lynch continued. 'All around us the nations with which we trade are rapidly approaching free trade in the blocs of which they are members.'

In the early 1960s, during Lynch's period in the Department of Industry and Commerce, emigration virtually ceased and industrial exports climbed above the level of agricultural exports for the first time. But the economic buoyancy gradually incited expectations of substantial improvements in public services as well as personal income, and the expectations began to overrun resources. Facing two critical by-elections in 1964, the government approved a national pay settlement that was well in excess of productivity trends. By the end of 1965 the economy was showing signs of overheating. The expenditure generated by wage increases and liberal bank credit led to an upsurge of imports at a time when exports were handicapped by the British surcharge on industrial imports.

Lynch decided to introduce an exceptionally early budget in 1966. While a deficit could be justified in the budget created during a serious economic depression, in the interests of stimulating the economy, he warned that there could be no justification for 'deficit financing' in the midst of a boom. 'We have outrun our resources and are incurring too big a deficit in our balance of payments,' he warned. This was causing inflation and leading to a balance-of-payments deficit. The estimates behind the previous budget had gone so wrong that they needed to be rectified, and waiting until May, when the next budget was due, would cause serious difficulties, especially with a presidential election scheduled to be held in June. Lynch therefore moved to stabilise public capital expenditure by introducing his budget for 1966 on 9 March, less than ten months after the previous budget. He said that part of the reason for the budget being so early was because Dáil sittings in April would be restricted by the celebrations to commemorate the fiftieth anniversary of the Easter Rising. This might have made sense if the budget was due in April, but it was not due until May. Lynch admitted that there was an element of a supplementary budget about the whole thing, because his previous budget had developed a serious deficit. Revenue did not come up to expect-ations, and expenditure on certain items was greater than had been envisioned. There had been 'errors of estimation' that could not be justified on financial or economic grounds, he explained.

'The enormous deficit on current account is the most obvious of these,' Lynch said. This was 'attributable mainly to the cost of improvement and extension of public services. Increased subsidies on diary products, relief on rates for agricultural land, increased social-welfare payments, an excess of current spending which led to an increase in the cost of servicing the debt, and higher-education costs all contributed to the deficit.

Increases were announced on the price of beer, wine, spirits and tobacco, as well as a 10.5 per cent increase in the income-tax rate. As a result, Gerard Sweetman denounced the measure as 'the harshest budget any Minister for Finance has ever introduced.' Of course, much of the media attention was diverted from the economy by the celebrations commemorating the Easter Rising.

Lynch suggested that even though the growth in the economy had declined, 'it was still two and a half times the rate that obtained in the ten years up to 1958.'

'When I presented my budget in 1965, I made no secret of the fact that certain discouraging trends were emerging. There was evidence that the balance of payments was not going well and that our balance of trade was also moving against us. This was, of course, the result of a combination of adverse factors.' The drop in trade as a result of the British surcharge on imports was com-pounded by the cost of the government coming to the rescue of the exporters. 'One of the main factors in that trend was the decline in cattle exports in the early part of 1965,' he explained. 'Cattle prices were very buoyant, with the result that farmers and cattle-dealers generally were selling whatever cattle they had available to take advantage of these buoyant prices. The result was that the numbers of saleable cattle on the land declined very significantly.' Farmers were encouraged to build up the national herd, but then in early 1966 the EEC was closed to Irish cattle, and the cattle trade was further hit when the British market was effectively cut off by a dock strike in Britain.

'Experts cannot foresee everything and make all assumptions come true,' Lynch told the Dáil. 'If we knew a bit more about contemporary Europe and the problems faced by other countries such as Belgium, Norway and Denmark, we could see our own in better perspective. We should cease making "crises" and "disasters" out of the inevitable and, I might add, the curable vicissitudes of economic life. We have to make adjustments but we are well on the way to recovery, provided we stop moaning and bickering as we have been doing, particularly from the other benches.'

The income of farmers did not increase as estimated because of the bad weather conditions in the winter and spring as well as a drop in cattle prices. This was to lead to considerable farmer unrest in 1966. The Irish Creamery Milk Suppliers Association (ICMSA) exerted pressure for an increase of four pence per gallon in the price of the first 7,000 gallons of milk supplied by the farmer and two pence per gallon on milk supplied above that quota. Lynch insisted that the increase would have to be resisted because its inflationary impact would have a knock-on effect on the price of butter.

'An increase of one penny per gallon of milk would add about 2.33 pence to the price of one pound of butter,' he noted. The scheme would be difficult to implement, Charlie Haughey argued, as Minister for Agriculture, because once a farmer exceeded 7,000 gallons, milk could be brought to the creamery in the name of another family member. As a result, it was likely that the four-pence increase would apply to most milk. 'I believe that the great majority of farmers who send milk to the creameries would qualify for the full value of the four-pence increase,' Lynch explained. He estimated that the whole thing would cost the government around £6 million. 'This proposition would involve substantially increased taxation or, alternatively, on the basis of the rate of increase to which I have just referred, about 1 shilling per pound in the cost of butter. This would certainly not be in the interest of the community at large and, indeed, of many farmers, some of whom do not supply milk to the creameries. Many who do are small farmers with big families and would lose out in the long run. I need not refer to the increase which would occur in the price of delivered loose or bottled milk.'

The farmers put a picket on Leinster House, and the government responded by jailing the picketers. It was Lemass and his Minister for Agriculture, Haughey, who were on the front line on this issue. As the dispute dragged on and more than a hundred picketers were jailed, the government came under electoral pressure, as Éamon de Valera was running for re-election as President in June 1966. He was under great threat from the younger Fine Gael candidate, T. F. O'Higgins. As it turned out, the election was extremely close and the chances were that de Valera would have been defeated if the government had not essentially caved in to the ICMSA's price demand and conceded the farmers a three-pence-per-gallon increase.

After de Valera's re-election, Lynch had to introduce a mini-budget to cover the rise in the price of milk. Some of the cost was passed on to the consumer, and the government sought to recoup the remainder by raising the tax on petrol by two pence a gallon and adding the same amount to the price of twenty cigarettes.

'The people now know what it cost to buy the presidential election,' Gerard Sweetman remarked.

'Why do you not put up with your defeat and shut up talking?' Frank Aiken replied.

The Opposition was naturally critical of Lynch for having got the figures so wrong in his first budget in May 1965 that he had to bring the second budget forward to March 1966, and within fourteen weeks of that he had to introduce a mini-budget, because the government had been thrown off course by the need to win the presidential election. The party essentially bought itself out of the hole by conceding to the farmers.

'There is strong evidence that this government lacks leadership,' T. F. O'Higgins contended. 'They are incapable of planning even for a period of 365 days.'

The Opposition charged that the March budget had been more about the presidential election than the economy. Had the government waited until May to implement the budget, it would have had to implement harsher measures on the eve of the presidential election, but by introducing the budget in early March, the government was able to gloss over the previous miscalculation and tide itself over until after the presidential election.

Even though Lynch was the Minister for Finance, it was others who got the bulk of the blame, such as the Taoiseach and Haughey, who was not only the Minister for Agriculture but de Valera's national director of elections. In the public mind, the whole thing was seen as a concession to farmers in order for Haughey to buy himself out of his political corner and avoid the embarrassment of losing the presidential election. Lynch did not get the blame; instead, Haughey was depicted as the manipulator.

In September the Minister for Education, Donogh O'Malley, stunned the Irish people with his announcement of free secondary education, even though no provisions had been made for this in the financial estimates. Lynch did not even learn about the speech until some time afterwards, as he was out of the country for a financial conference in Athens at the time. The proposal had not been discussed in Cabinet, its financial implications had not been examined, and there had been no consultations with the Department of Finance. T. K. Whitaker, the secretary of the Department of Finance, was particularly critical, as he noted that O'Malley had left the Department of Health 'gravely insolvent' after his stint as minister.

Lemass wrote to O'Malley on the day after his Dun Laoghaire speech, warning that normal procedure would have to be followed and full government approval secured. O'Malley had discussed the idea with Lemass in advance and might well have been authorised to float the idea as a kind of trial balloon.

'It was my understanding that I had your agreement to my outlining these lines of action, particularly in view of the fact that Fine Gael were planning to announce a comprehensive educational policy this week,' O'Malley wrote to Lemass. 'If I was under a misapprehension in believing that I had your support for my announcement, I must apologise.' To what extent the Taoiseach may have approved is unclear.

'What is undeniable is that from this point onwards Lemass watched O'Malley exceptionally closely,' John Horgan noted in his highly acclaimed biography of Lemass. But Lemass announced his retirement less than two months later. On one occasion when Lynch brought up the matter of the unauthorised announcement, O'Malley seemed to be about to cite the Taoiseach, but Lemass cut him off precipitately.

'Don't involve me in this,' he said. 'This is a row between you and the Minister for Finance.'

O'Malley's proposal was a bold initiative that captured the imagination of the public. It was noteworthy that the following year 18,000 extra pupils enrolled in second-level education. But that is getting ahead of the story.

At the time of O'Malley's announcement, the government was already involved in another serious dispute with farmers that was reaching crisis proportions. The Anglo-Irish Free Trade Agreement came into effect on 1 July 1966. Lemass had previously stressed its importance to Irish agricultural development. It was 'all gain' as far as Irish agriculture was concerned, he said. But the Irish government's agricultural policy seemed to backfire in 1966. There had been a planned cutback in cattle exports in order to increase cattle numbers at home so that the government would be in a position to export more at a later date. The cattle numbers increased by 7.5 per cent, but then, as was mentioned earlier, the EEC closed its doors to Irish cattle in January, and the British market was closed as a result of a dockers' strike. When that strike ended, the extra Irish cattle were dumped on the British market and prices fell precipitously, giving rise to a serious unrest among Irish cattle farmers.

Haughey advised farmers to hold on to their cattle for better prices, but Rickard Deasy, the president of the National Farmers' Association (NFA), advised farmers to sell the cattle, and Haughey took exception when the contradictory advice was mentioned on RTÉ news. He protested to RTÉ and the item was dropped from subsequent bulletins – much to the annoyance of some in the news department. The NFA then decided on a massive march to Dublin from various centres around the country.

Over 20,000 people descended on Dublin and, after a protest rally in Merrion Square, the leaders tried to call on Haughey but he refused to meet him. They then announced that they would camp on the minister's doorstep for a month if necessary. They camped out with sleeping bags on the steps of the Department of Agriculture.

In the midst of the ensuing controversy, Seán Lemass announced his decision to step down as Taoiseach and leader of Fianna Fáil. Even though there was an expectation within political circles that he was going to step down before long, his actual announcement came as a real surprise. George Colley, Seán McEntee and Frank Aiken were all out of the country at the time, and Lemass had already indicated to Colley that he was not likely to retire in advance of the forthcoming Fianna Fáil *ard fheis*, which was due to begin on 22 November.

'Before he left for the US, Mr Colley had a conversation with me in which he asked me whether my resignation was likely to take place before the date of the Fianna Fáil *ard fheis*,' Lemass explained to a press conference on 8 November. 'At that time I said I thought this was unlikely.'

'My decision to relinquish office is purely a political decision, uninfluenced by any personal considerations,' he said. 'I am convinced that it is in the interests of the country, the government and the Fianna Fáil Party that responsibility should now pass to a younger man.

'If the next general election takes place in 1970, when it is due, I shall be seventy-one years old. My resignation before this date would be inevitable.' He added that the new man 'should have ample time in which to prove his worth and acquire the experience which will enable him to achieve another victory for the party.'

The government was involved in the serious row with farmers at the time and there were two by-elections coming up in December in Kerry South and Waterford. If Fianna Fáil lost both of those, it would inevitably have a destabilising effect on the Dáil, and this might damage the opportunity for Lemass's successor to establish himself before the next election. With the *ard fheis* coming up, however, there was an opportunity to have a new man selected and formally installed as party leader before the by-elections. 'The one consideration that is important above all others, insofar as I am concerned, is the success of the Fianna Fáil Party at the next and subsequent general elections, and I believe that a change of leaders at this time will help to ensure this,' Lemass explained.

Colley had obviously been thinking on those lines when he asked if Lemass intended to step down before the *ard fheis*. Although Lemass immediately notified Colley of his change of mind, there is a certain amount of confusion about the role the

Taoiseach played in the succession drama. He led some correspondents to believe he was supporting Colley, but it has been
argued that this was a deliberate ploy to help Haughey by
discouraging others from entering the fray.

Colley was seen as the candidate of party traditionalists in the
mould of de Valera, who was more concerned with the revival of
the Gaelic language than with economic matters. Some of the
senior members of Fianna Fáil detested Haughey and were
convinced that he would destroy the party if he became leader.
When he had first been promoted, for instance, he was appointed
parliamentary secretary to the Minister for Justice, Oscar Traynor,
who predicted that Haughey would one day ruin Fianna Fáil.
Traynor said he would have refused to take any parliamentary
secretary if he had known he would be saddled with Haughey, who
was a constituency colleague of his. At the end of the term, Traynor
retired from the Dáil.

Other senior party figures shared Traynor's suspicions of
Haughey. Gerry Boland, whose son Harry had been in partnership
with Haughey in an accountancy firm, distrusted him but, like
Traynor, he was now retired from active politics, though he was a
vice-president of Fianna Fáil. Two of the most senior members of
the old guard, Frank Aiken and Seán McEntee, detested Haughey.
Hence they supported George Colley, even though he was one of
the more inexperienced members of the Cabinet, having been a
minister for less than two years.

Describing himself as 'a Special Correspondent', McEntee
wrote a tribute to George Colley which was sent to the press.
'Dublin's political commentators unanimously favour this week, as
the man destined to rule the government, a tall, quiet man of 41,
George Colley,' he wrote. 'Argue as we will, plans, progressions,
schemes, policies, advances in our political life must be left to clever
men, to ambitious men even, provided they can take pride in their
ambitions. But for all our sakes, such cleverness and such drive

must be tempered at all times with a quality we should not be ashamed to acclaim. That quality is patriotism. If George Colley becomes the new Taoiseach, we should be happy that while he excels in other qualities he is, above all things, a patriot.' The implication, of course, was obvious: Haughey was too clever for his own good and he was not a real patriot.

Haughey's support came largely from those interested in a more pragmatic, business-minded approach. He was the epitome of the new breed of urban politician who was changing the face of Fianna Fáil. He hung out at the Russell Hotel in the company of Donogh O'Malley, Brian Lenihan and a coterie of self-made men – speculators, builders and architects – who were substituting the concrete jungle for the pastoral idealism that had inspired de Valera's dream of comely maidens dancing at the crossroads.

Haughey, O'Malley and Lenihan advocated modernising Ireland by encouraging change with industrious zeal. Lenihan had succeeded Haughey at the Department of Justice and made a name for himself by reforming the country's draconian censorship laws, which had become notorious after they had resulted in the banning of many works of some of the country's most famous writers.

Haughey ensured that he was identified with the ideas of economic progress and development that were associated with his father-in-law. He was not afraid to take up a challenge and tackle a task with great energy and dynamism. He had the intellectual grasp of what was required. He worked very hard but he also played hard, and he became the subject of an elaborate mythology of rumours, many ribald and vicious. His bon-vivant lifestyle commanded attention if not always the approval of those he seemed to be imitating. He was often despised for being nouveau riche. He lived well but was secretive about the source of his wealth.

In comparison with the genial Lynch, Haughey was an abrasive individual who got into a whole series of political scrapes. Earlier in 1966 he had been involved in the dispute with the ICMSA in which dozens of farmers were jailed for picketing Leinster House illegally, and since then he had become involved in an equally bitter dispute, not only with the NFA but also with the news department of RTÉ. In the midst of the controversy over dropping the news item on Rickard Deasy's contradictory advice about selling cattle, it became apparent that some members of the news department were annoyed that Haughey had been allowed to pull a political stroke in manipulating the television coverage of the presidential-election campaign.

De Valera, already in his mid-eighties and almost totally blind, was not capable of conducting the same kind of campaign as his much younger opponent. Haughey suggested, however, that as president it would not be proper for de Valera to campaign and that in the interest of balanced coverage, RTÉ should not cover the O'Higgins campaign. Just before the campaign formally began, de Valera received enormous television coverage in connection with the fiftieth anniversary of the Easter Rising, in news footage of commemorative events and in a series of documentary programmes on RTÉ. Moreover, during the campaign proper, several ministers campaigned on de Valera's behalf by making newsworthy announcements at the various rallies. These announcements were covered by RTÉ. De Valera won by a margin of only around 10,000 votes, with the result that many people felt O'Higgins might have reversed the result had he received proper campaign coverage.

Initially it was believed that the leadership contest would be between Colley and Haughey. For some years Haughey had been seen as a likely successor to Lemass, but his chances were seriously hurt by his controversy with the farmers and RTÉ. As a result, Colley was regarded as the likely winner, not on his own merits but on the basis that Haughey was much too controversial at the time.

Thinking that Colley's lack of experience would be a serious handicap, Aiken pleaded with Lemass to hold on for another couple of years. 'As I see it, George would be the most acceptable to the party but he could do with another couple of years' experience,' Aiken wrote. 'He would also need time and opportunity to become better known to the country so that he could lead Fianna Fáil to victory in the next election.'

Lemass, who had never been very close to Aiken, was determined to step down. 'My decision to relinquish office is purely a political decision, uninfluenced by any personal considerations,' he told a press conference. 'I am convinced it is in the interests of the country, the government and the Fianna Fáil Party that responsibility should now pass to a younger man.'

This was only the second time in forty years that a Fianna Fáil leader had stepped down. On the previous occasion, de Valera had prepared the way for Lemass to take over, but now Lemass believed that he should remain aloof, which was particularly understandable when his son-in-law was one of the main contenders. 'The most damaging thing you could do with a party is to give the impression among the members that everything is cut and dried behind closed doors and that they have no choice or say in the matter at all,' Lemass told Michael Mills of the *Irish Press*.

The previous November, John Healy had speculated in his 'Backbencher' column in *The Irish Times* as to who would succeed Lemass. If Frank Aiken ran, Healy felt that he would not be opposed, but if he decided that he was too old, 'then it would be Mr Jack Lynch by a distance,' Healy concluded. For months Healy had been virtually touting the merits of 'the three musketeers' – Charles Haughey, Brian Lenihan and Donogh O'Malley. He had written so much about Haughey that it was even being suggested that Haughey was the anonymous 'Backbencher' – supposedly a member of the Dáil writing with inside knowledge. Even though Healy rarely mentioned Lynch in the column, he still felt that the Corkman had the inside track on the leadership.

'It is suggested in many places in the public prints that it would be "a tight thing" between Mr Lynch and Mr C. J. Haughey for the leadership,' Healy wrote. 'I tell you now it would be no contest . . . Mr Jack Lynch would win pulling up in a party vote tomorrow morning. He does everything right. When every other government minister drives a Mercedes, Jack drives a Cork Ford. He smokes a thinking pipe. He likes the quiet little jar. He doesn't want anything, just does the job. A nice fellow. A hell of a nice fellow.' Healy went on to argue that Lynch had the common touch. He went to the *ard fheis* and made himself available by mixing with the delegates, while Haughey dutifully attended a function at Iveagh House and a Macra na Feirme dinner. He merely appeared on the platform while agriculture was being discussed. Haughey was not a good mixer as far as the ordinary Fianna Fáil punter was concerned. 'Whenever they wanted to see him, sure all they had to do was look in *The Irish Times* and there he was on a horse,' Healy continued. 'Thus I will ask those of my readers who go in for ante-post betting to take the odds, at this time, on Jack Lynch. He's the best bet since Arkle.' That was published on 20 November 1965.

While Colley and Haughey vied to succeed Lemass, Lynch remained aloof. Many of the provincial deputies were uneasy about the choice being offered to the party. Deputies like Tom McEllistrim of Kerry and Eugene Gilbride of Sligo called on Lynch to run, but he expressed no interest in doing so. Although *The Irish Times* described Haughey as 'far and away the strongest candidate,' the political correspondent of the *Cork Examiner* believed that Colley was virtually certain to win a contest, because Haughey was so unpopular at the time.

When Haughey approached Neil Blaney for his support, for instance, he was refused. 'No, Charlie,' Blaney replied, 'you haven't got the background.' Blaney decided to run himself, and Kevin Boland announced on 3 November 1966 that he would be nominating him. This changed everything. Donogh O'Malley, Haughey's campaign manager, promptly threw his support behind Blaney. At that point, Lemass decided to put pressure on Lynch to stand.

Lynch agreed to reconsider and respond after discussing the matter with his wife, Máirín. Once he had said that he would stand, Lemass called in the other candidates and informed them that he would be backing Lynch. He basically wished them to withdraw. Colley told him that he would first have to consult his wife, Mary.

'What kind of people have I got when one man has to get his wife's permission to run and the other has to get his wife's permission to withdraw?' Lemass asked. His own wife told the press at the time that Lemass had not forewarned her about his retirement. He just came home and told her that he had announced his impending resignation. That was his way of doing things.

Haughey's chances had already been undermined by the defection of Donogh O'Malley, so when the Taoiseach talked to him, he immediately agreed to withdraw and even offered to nominate Lynch.

'I'm glad someone can give me a straight answer around here,' Lemass remarked.

The Taoiseach then called in Blaney and asked about his plans.

'What are George and Charlie doing?' Blaney asked.

'Charlie is no problem,' Lemass replied.

'What about George?'

'George is going out to Mary to allow him to withdraw.' With that, Blaney agreed to stand down.

'We were foolishly blinded by the necessity for unity in the party,' Blaney explained afterwards. 'Lynch literally didn't have a Fianna Fáil background at all; it would have been the reverse, if anything.' Both Blaney and Boland were the sons of founder members of Fianna Fáil and both of their fathers had served in the

Dáil. In their sneering arrogance, they essentially questioned Lynch's party pedigree from the outset. 'Look,' Boland said to Blaney, 'let him in so long as he does what we tell him.'

Boland later contended that Blaney would have won the contest, had he stayed in it, but that seemed most unlikely. No one should put much credence in Boland's political judgement in such matters, because his subsequent career demonstrated that while he was a man of honour, he had unreliable political instincts and was a very poor political prophet.

Haughey and Blaney publicly announced that they would be supporting Lynch. But George Colley – who, as the son of a former Fianna Fáil deputy, had an impeccable party pedigree – announced that he would not be withdrawing. There would be a contest, but the outcome was a foregone conclusion, Brian Lenihan told the *Cork Examiner*. Lynch was a virtual certainty to win.

'In American parlance, he has been drafted and in the very moment that his consent was secured the hopes of all other aspirants vanished into the air,' the *Cork Examiner* noted in an editorial. 'Such is the magnet of his personal popularity and dedicated service to the party that there now remains only a formality of selection before Mr Lynch assumes the mantle of his distinguished predecessor.

'Not the least of his many fine qualities is his modest assessment of his own capacity, a modesty which impelled him to declare up to last evening that he was not a candidate for the highest office of all,' the editorial continued. 'It is almost certainly true to say that, had Jack Lynch declared his interest in promotion to Taoiseach at the time Mr Lemass announced his intention of retirement, no other candidate would have been considered seriously.'

'This is the greatest decision I have had to make in my life,' Lynch told a gathering in Waterford on 4 November. 'If I am nominated by the party and elected as Taoiseach, I have no illusion about the magnitude of the task before me. It was a tremendous decision to make and I only allowed my name to go forward after prolonged and insistent pressure.'

Even though the outcome was a foregone conclusion, Colley persisted. 'I am still in the race,' he told a press dinner in Dublin. 'I feel that the members of the party want an opportunity to consult together and [to talk to] their own organisations about the situation. The whole question is going to be decided in a democratic way. Any talk of a split in the party is ridiculous.

'We are both extremely friendly: have been, are still and will continue to be,' he added. 'I think we each understand the other's position very clearly.'

When Lynch was asked in Cork about Colley's continuing challenge, he seemed unperturbed. 'He is doing no more than I am doing in letting his name be put forward for election by the democratic process,' Lynch said.

On the eve of the parliamentary-party meeting to select his successor on 9 November, Lemass patched up a deal ending the dispute with the farmers. He invited the NFA leaders to meet himself and Haughey, and the farmers called off the protest outside the Department of Agriculture. At the ensuing meeting it was agreed that there would be further discussions with the incoming government.

At the outset of the crucial parliamentary-party meeting, Lemass asked that no sympathetic speeches be made about his retirement and that his successor be selected without any long speeches. Although Colley decided to contest the election, he indicated that he would have no problems supporting Lynch if he became leader of the party. All seemed set for an amicable contest, but Seán McEntee threw a spanner in the works with a desperate attempt to prevent the inevitable. There had long been an intense rivalry between himself and Lemass, but they had been able to keep their differences within the Cabinet. Now McEntee attacked the Taoiseach for abandoning the party when it was 'at its lowest ebb'. He said that Lemass 'could not have chosen a worse time' to stand down.

'Responsibility for this situation in my view rests mainly on the Taoiseach,' McEntee declared. 'The devious course which he has pursued, not only in relation to his leadership and on the succession but to other questions as well, has confounded the members of our organisation, so that none of them knows where we stand on any issue.

'It is astonishing and unjustifiable that the Taoiseach, at this precise moment, should propose, by resigning, to wash his hands of responsibility for the country's affairs,' McEntee continued. 'Only reasons of the utmost gravity, on the borderline, so to speak, between life and death, justify such a step on the part of a leader.' De Valera had passed on a great Fianna Fáil heritage, but Lemass had squandered it, in MacEntee's opinion. 'Sometimes in recent years it seemed as if it were being dealt with like a personal possession,' he said. 'The state was tottering towards anarchy.'

What the Taoiseach was doing was tantamount to 'deserting in the face of the enemy,' McEntee contended, as he insisted that Lemass should stay in office for a further two years. 'Is he so weary, so unnerved, that he baulks at the task which he will leave to his successor?'

Members sat in stunned silence. McEntee could hardly have chosen a more inappropriate moment for such attack. After forty years on the front line in Fianna Fáil, Lemass had every right to retire then, without having his patriotism questioned in such a manner. Mac-Entee's contribution was as absurd as it was outrageous. He had accused the Taoiseach of leading the country towards anarchy and was at the same time insisting that he should stay on for two more years. At one point in his speech, he actually invoked the images of the quasi-fascist dictators Francisco Franco of Spain and Antonio Salazar of Portugal as the prototypes of proper leadership. Both of them had shown consistent contempt for democracy.

Although Dick Grogan promptly took issue with MacEntee's contribution, most of those present wished to move on to the business of the day. Tom McEllistrim nominated Lynch and he was seconded by Eugene Gilbride of Sligo.

Frank Aiken then nominated Colley but clearly realised that the outcome was a foregone conclusion, because in the course of his nominating address he denounced the way that Lynch was being selected by the tyranny of consensus. Colley's nomination was seconded by Bobby Molloy, who called for strong leadership rather than that directed by the media. Another veteran, Paddy Smith, also supported Colley, but Seán McEntee announced that he was supporting Lynch. After his untimely tirade against Lemass, his support was more likely to be a liability, which possibly explains why he openly declared himself for Lynch.

It was a secret vote and an old shoebox was used to collect the ballot, prompting Lemass to exclaim: 'A queer receptacle for such a momentous decision.' The vote was a decisive victory for Lynch, by 52 votes to 19. Afterwards Colley pledged his loyalty and support to Lynch and professed that he was happy with his own showing.

'I am satisfied that I have attained two objectives,' he said. 'Firstly, I have succeeded in demonstrating that the party is quite capable of choosing its leaders in a democratic and orderly way, and secondly, I have succeeded in establishing that the new leader is clearly and unequivocally the choice of the party. I think his position is strengthened because this has been demonstrated.'

Lynch's election was widely welcomed, even in opposition circles. His most trenchant critic, Noël Browne, admitted that 'personally Mr Lynch is the nicest politician in Leinster House.' There was also obvious relief among members of the Opposition that Haughey had not succeeded.

Lemass proposed Lynch for Taoiseach on 10 November with just one sentence spoken first in Irish and then repeated in English: 'I recommend to Dáil Éireann Deputy John Lynch for appointment as Taoiseach.' This was seconded by Aiken, who spoke a mere five words.

The outcome was a foregone conclusion and there was no objection from the Opposition. As the proposer, Lemass had the right to wind up the debate, which he did very briefly. 'Before you put the motion,' he said to the Dáil, 'I should like to say a few words. As regards my own work in government, this is a matter of record and I am not going to make any comment on it now. It is finished and the Dáil is now concerned only with the future. The political leadership of the party has passed to Deputy Jack Lynch. It is a great privilege to me to propose Deputy Lynch as Taoiseach. I believe he has the qualities of intelligence and integrity and the capacity to work which will enable him to become a great leader and Taoiseach. Time will prove this to be so.'

The motion was then put 'That Deputy Seán Lynch be nominated as Taoiseach'. He was elected by 71 votes to 64.

Lynch began with some perfunctory words in Irish and immediately translated and expanded on them. 'I should like to express to the Dáil my thanks for having nominated me to be Taoiseach. I deeply appreciate the honour that has been conferred on me. Conscious of the heavy responsibilities that are now mine, I request the cooperation and assistance of deputies on all sides of the House in the discharge of these responsibilities.

'I think this is the appropriate time for me to say on behalf of our party and on my own behalf how sorry we are to see my predecessor leaving the front bench. No man has left a greater mark on the progress of this nation than Seán Lemass. As I said already, he has set the highest of standards because these were the only standards he knew and aspired to. I shall do my best to attain these standards.'

PART TWO

9

THE RELUCTANT TAOISEACH

1966–1969

Taking over in mid-term, without the advantage gained from the normal endorsement of the electorate at a general election, Lynch felt inhibited in his selection of a Cabinet. Lemass had effected the changeover to the younger generation by replacing all but Frank Aiken of the founding leaders of the party. The new Taoiseach therefore felt that his own scope for change was severely limited.

'I had merely to endorse the changes he had made,' Lynch explained. 'While superficially this made life easier for me, it did cause problems, for I was thereby deprived of one major strength every prime minister usually enjoys: the power of Cabinet appointment. Of course, I had that power formally, but in effect most ministers knew that they owed their position to Seán Lemass, not me.'

hen the Dáil reconvened at three o'clock on the afternoon of 10 November 1966, the new Taoiseach announced his Cabinet. Frank Aiken was appointed as both Tánaiste and Minister for External Affairs. The other appointments were: Erskine H. Childers to Transport, Power, Posts and Telegraphs; Neil T. Blaney to Agriculture and Fisheries; Kevin Boland to Local Government; Michael Moran to Lands and the Gaeltacht; Michael Hilliard to Defence; Paddy Hillery to Labour; Charles Haughey to Finance; Brian J. Lenihan to Justice; Joseph Brennan to Social Welfare; Donogh O'Malley to Education; George Colley to Industry and Commerce; and Seán Flanagan to Health.

As usual, members of the Opposition criticised the various appointments. Liam Cosgrave, the Fine Gael leader, referred to Frank Aiken as a 'historical relic', but the bulk of Cosgrave's attack was reserved for Haughey, as one who had to be got out of the Department of Agriculture. 'Not since the days of landlordism has there been such resentment and bitterness in rural Ireland,' Cosgrave said. Haughey had antagonised the farmers to such an extent that he 'not merely nearly upended the government but certainly cost himself the position of future Taoiseach,' the Fine Gael leader argued.

'If there was a need for change in any particular sector of the economy it was in agriculture,' Brendan Corish, the leader of the Labour Party, contended. In a way it was symbolic that the two opposition leaders should concentrate their attack on Haughey, because his shadow was to hang over Lynch for the remainder of his political career, until Haughey replaced him a little over thirteen years later.

In winding up the debate, Lynch dismissed assertions that there was a split within Fianna Fáil and that he was a reluctant Taoiseach. 'I may have been reluctant to let my name go forward for nomination as Taoiseach,' he said. 'I had my personal reasons but these are now irrelevant. I have put them aside. I can assure the deputies opposite that I shall not be a reluctant Taoiseach. On the contrary, I shall be a vigorous and progressive one. Neither am I here in a caretaker capacity. As I told my party, I shall stay as long as I am able to hold down the job.'

Within Fianna Fáil there had never been any doubt about who

should lead the party. De Valera had been leader for thirty-three years, from the foundation of the party until Seán Lemass was chosen to succeed him. Lemass was the youngest of the old guard, so there was no real opposition to him either, but now Lynch had at least five ministers who had openly shown ambitions for his position. They were convinced that they could do a better job and probably believed that they might have got the position if fate had not conspired against them in the timing of the Taoiseach's decision to step down.

James Dillon, the former leader of Fine Gael, felt that those whom he called the Camorra – Haughey, Lenihan, Blaney, Boland and Donogh O'Malley – would relentlessly pursue their own ambitions to succeed Lynch. He was going to be 'as expendable as an old shoe' in their eyes, Dillon said. 'He is too decent a man to be treated in this way,' he argued. 'I do not despair that our people will recoil with loathing from the prospect of replacing a man of integrity, as I believe Deputy Jack Lynch to be, with one of the Camorra, who are now sharpening their knives and whirling their tomahawks, not only for their enemies but for one another.'

To have so many ministers harbouring such naked ambition might well have destabilised another Taoiseach, but Lynch seemed to welcome the ambitions of his colleagues as a healthy political phenomenon. He was quite prepared to allow them to shine, just as he would have welcomed the stellar performances of a team-mate in the hurling championship.

'When a deputy is elected to the Dáil I take it as a natural ambition for him to become a minister and a natural progression of that ambition is that the deputy, having become a minister, would look to the day when he might become Taoiseach,' Lynch told John O'Sullivan during his first year in office. 'I am ten years older than many of my colleagues and it would only be natural, certainly among the younger ones, that they would look to the day when they might become Taoiseach, and therefore they will have the incentive to perform their particular duties well, to make themselves seen to be performing them well, so that when the time for the appointment of a successor to me comes, they will have projected themselves.'

Of course, it suited his more ambitious colleagues to think that he was only an interim Taoiseach, and by his reluctance to stand he contributed to the idea that he was just a caretaker until circumstances were more favourable for somebody like Haughey to take over, but Lynch emphasised that now that he had the job, he was determined to hold on to it.

He went home to Cork and was taken through the city in triumph, sitting on the back of a Cadillac convertible, smiling and waving to the crowd on 12 November 1966. The parade started in Blackpool and paused briefly at the Glen Hall, where his brother Theo was chairman of Glen Rovers Club. By the time the parade reached Grand Parade, the crowd was so large that there was barely room for his car. Lynch contended that it was a healthy sign of democracy that so many supporters of other parties had turned out.

'I would not be human if I did not regard this great honour highly and take pride at being the first Corkman to be elected head of a free Irish government,' Lynch told the crowd. 'I am very glad that some of those who first encouraged me to enter public life are here with me, to share this honour. You know that I pray that God will forgive them because sometimes I feel that I cannot do so.'

The next day, Lynch returned to Dublin for the second replay of the all-Ireland under-21 hurling final between Cork and Wexford, and he was given the honour of presenting the trophy to the winning Cork captain after the game. 'I don't think,' he said, 'I could get a better present for my first visit to Croke Park as Taoiseach than to present this cup to a winning Cork all-Ireland team.'

In the debate on the formation of the government, he outlined his views for his administration. There was still the unfinished business of Donogh O'Malley's announcement of the introduction of free secondary education in September. O'Malley had essentially treated Lynch with contempt by not even consulting him before making the announcement. Lemass had tended to dismiss the whole thing as a dispute between the two ministers.

'There can be no such thing as free education; the community must be prepared to pay one way or the other for whatever improvements are required,' Lynch told the Dáil as he outlined the aims of his administration. 'The important thing is to see that inability to pay whatever cost is involved in such education will not debar any child who can benefit from it from receiving it.'

He spoke highly of his two predecessors in the leadership of Fianna Fáil – Éamon de Valera and Seán Lemass. 'I served under both of them,' he told Marian Finucane in a radio interview. 'I always regarded that they worked very well in tandem – de Valera with the long vision, Lemass with the practical mind.' He liked de Valera's long view of things but also had 'a very high regard for Seán Lemass in being a realist, a very practical man, in every way.' He therefore tried to marry their different approaches to politics.

Over the decades, de Valera had regularly spoken about his twin goals of reviving the Irish language and ending partition. 'The national aim,' he said, was 'to restore the Irish language as a general medium of communication.' His next aim was 'the reunification of the Irish people, north and south', but Lynch consistently emphasised that this unification should be 'based on agreement and mutual toleration and respect and an assurance to all Irish people of full equality of status and opportunity.'

Economically, de Valera espoused a pastoral ideal of a people who would not be materialistic but spiritually contented, living in 'frugal comfort' in 'cosy homesteads'. He was not greatly concerned with economic affairs, whereas his successor Seán Lemass was preoccupied with the economy during his tenure as Taoiseach. Lynch had been the minister most associated with the economic side of the Lemass initiative, having been chosen to succeed Lemass as Minister for Industry and Commerce as well as being appointed the first of the new generation to serve as Minister for Finance.

'In our economic policy, we will be seeking the cooperation of all sections of the community in working for a better living for more families in Ireland,' Lynch told the Dáil in one of his first speeches as Taoiseach. 'Our ideal is more jobs, more families, a rising population and more and better opportunities for all. Progress towards this ideal depends in part on having the right policies, but also in large measure on having a consistently good team spirit among all members of the community, particularly those engaged in production.'

Lynch had always been a team player, whether on the playing pitch or in the political arena. He called for a team effort from his Cabinet for the sake of the party and the people, but opposition deputies had qualms about his ability to unite some of the members of his government team. He dismissed talk of a split in Fianna Fáil as the perennial chatter of Fine Gael deputies. For as long as he had been in the Dáil, he said, James Dillon and company had been predicting a split within Fianna Fáil. As so often happens with people who continuously make such predictions, they eventually get it right. Lynch was to have real problems keeping his team together.

He tended to preside as a chairman over his government, allowing ministers as much leeway as possible within their own portfolios. Lemass had done this to a great extent but there was never any doubt that he was ultimately in control. He had served a political apprenticeship of well over thirty years, many of them spent close to the top of Fianna Fáil, whereas Lynch had been there less than a decade and even in that time had always been overshadowed by colleagues.

One of the main duties of any head of government in terms of foreign policy is meeting the heads of other governments. It was significant that Lynch's first meeting with one of his counterparts was with Harold Wilson, the British Prime Minister, in December 1966. The two pipe-smoking leaders were very similar figures. Both were mild-mannered men with an avuncular image. Although surrounded by more ambitious colleagues who demanded radical action, Lynch and Wilson seemed unflappable. They kept their heads, moving cautiously, while their frustrated colleagues often appeared hysterical in comparison.

At their first meeting as heads of government, Lynch expressed concerns about the religious and political discrimination against Catholics in Northern Ireland, especially the flawed electoral system of local government, which was riddled with discrimination in housing allocation and schooling. 'Anything that can be done to reduce political and religious discrimination in Northern Ireland would considerably help to achieve a relaxation in tension,' Lynch explained. He added that serious efforts had been made to accommodate the sensitivities of the Protestant community in the Republic, where the government's tendency had been to discriminate in favour of the Protestant community when it came to assistance with regard to schools.

Wilson expressed the deep concern held by many Labour backbenchers about the discrimination against the Catholic community in Northern Ireland. He was convinced that Prime Minister Terence O'Neill was trying to implement housing, education and electoral reforms to eliminate that discrimination, but he noted that O'Neill had genuine problems, because if he went ahead too quickly he would face problems from within the Unionist Party. He needed more time, but time for reform was running out as the Catholics were becoming decidedly impatient. This may have been O'Neill's problem initially, but it soon became a problem for both Wilson and Lynch.

During his short spell as Minister for Finance, Lynch had seemed to be on an economic roller coaster. He had inherited a strong economy from his predecessor, Jim Ryan, but things had gone sour over trading difficulties with both the EEC and Britain. Despite the farmer unrest, the economic figures at the end of year were particularly encouraging: the index of retail sales rose by 5 per cent as compared with an increase of only 1 per cent in the first half of the year. The expansion was maintained during 1967. In the first nine months of the year the index of retail sales rose by another 5 per cent. Another positive indicator was the output in volume of transportable industrial goods, which rose by 8 per cent in the second half of 1966, followed by an increase of 9 per cent in the first quarter of 1967 and 14 per cent in the second quarter. These increases were due to the expansion in both domestic demand and exports.

Lynch was also able to report 'a marked recovery in the building and construction industry in 1967'. Housing starts almost doubled over 1966 and the domestic sale of cement rose by 14 per cent. The unemployment figures did not show much improvement until late 1967 but this was largely due to a drop in emigration and even reverse migration as former emigrants returned to take up jobs at home in the booming economy.

Of course, this was largely inherited growth. Up to 1956 the country had a growth rate of about 1 per cent, but this was halted by the decline in 1957. The introduction of the Whitaker Plan led to a dramatic improvement.

'From 1958 to the end of the First Programme for Economic Expansion, the total growth rate was 23 per cent, or over 4 per cent per annum,' Lynch told the Dáil in December 1967. From 1964, the growth rate was estimated at 12 per cent. Thus since 1958 there had been an average annual growth rate of 4 per cent, which was the figure for that year.

His government had inherited many schemes, like the movement of the headquarters of a number of government departments. In 1964 James Ryan, the then Minister for Finance, informed the Dáil that certain government departments would be transferred from Dublin to provincial centres, but none had yet moved. 'The only way in which to achieve progress in this matter was for the government to take a firm decision to send certain departments to named provincial centres,' Lynch commented afterwards. On 16 November 1967, therefore, he announced that the Department of Education was being transferred to Athlone and the Department of Lands to Castlebar.

Lynch fostered a recognisable persona of his own. He was the quiet voice of authority, doing his job in a routine way without trimmings or extravagant postures. There was none of the abrasiveness frequently associated with Haughey. Instead, Lynch adopted a kind of presidential style as he took a greater interest in external affairs and relations with Northern Ireland. Despite his reserve and caution, he had made a serious tactical error in stating publicly at the start of his term of office that one of his priorities was to meet the Northern premier, Captain Terence O'Neill. As he had said that one of his two main goals was to promote the unification of Ireland, it was naturally assumed in the North that Lynch wished to persuade O'Neill to abandon partition. In the circumstances, any meeting between the two men was only likely to fuel unionist fears. O'Neill therefore baulked at an early meeting with Lynch, who turned his attention elsewhere.

In April 1967 Lynch blocked an attempt by RTÉ to send a news team to investigate the war in Vietnam. In the 1930s Éamon de Valera had spoken out against the Japanese invasion of Manchuria and the Italian invasion of Ethiopia. He was not slow in expressing support for the people of Manchuria and Ethiopia, whose rights were being ignored. Nor was he afraid to antagonise the Americans by calling for the League of Nations to intervene in the Chaco War in Latin America. Later, the governments of both de Valera and Seán Lemass further annoyed the Americans by calling for the admission of the People's Republic of China to the UN. It should be remembered that Lynch publicly supported that policy as Minister for Education. 'If we as a nation are to command respect,' he said, 'we must act with some degree of independence of mind in these national assemblies.' Yet in the late 1960s, when American involvement in Vietnam became a major international issue, Lynch was unwilling to take an independent stand. He refused to endorse the call by U Thant – the Secretary General of the UN – for a halt in the American bombing of North Vietnam, despite a petition signed by a number of prominent Irish people. Therefore his decision to thwart RTÉ's proposed investigation was entirely in line with his policy on the matter.

He told the chairman of the RTÉ Authority that 'such a visit would be an embarrassment to the government in relation to its foreign policy'. He later explained that he did not order that the proposed trip be cancelled but merely expressed his views directly to the chairman of the Authority 'on behalf of the government'. Had the chairman decided to go ahead with the idea, Lynch might well have removed the chairman and the whole Authority, as his government would do later, but this was not necessary in April 1967.

'If a team representing Radio Telefís Éireann went to Vietnam, the peculiar character of a semi-state body, as we know it, could well be misinterpreted all over the world,' Lynch told the Dáil. 'It was the intention of RTÉ to sell whatever film or coverage this team might have had on Vietnam, presumably to any customer who would come along and offer to buy it. These customers might well be people who had a particular interest – opposed, perhaps, to one side or the other – and there was a great danger that the people in those countries who might buy that film would present the news or whatever items RTÉ would have given them in a slanted way. As I said, there is a danger of the misinterpretation of the functions of a semi-state body vis-à-vis the governments in other countries in such circumstances.'

Lynch inherited Fianna Fáil's difficulties with RTÉ – difficulties which had surfaced as a result of a series of controversial programmes. Every time the Catholic hierarchy complained about anything that was broadcast, the politicians seemed to run for cover. Eamonn Andrews, the chairman of the RTÉ Authority, noted that Seán Lemass took the complaints to heart, because he seemed to believe that 'television should be an arm of the government'. When the politicians found that attacking RTÉ made good copy, the station was assailed by complaints from all sides. 'We were at once the destroyers of the national heritage, the national music, literature, sport, culture, the enemy of the churches, the breaker of families, the weakeners of morals, the money-grubbers, who buy Mickey Mouse instead of Finn MacCool and Rambo – had he then existed – instead of Cúchulainn,' Andrews wrote.

The Late Late Show was a prime target, especially after the 'Bishop and the Nightie' affair in February 1966. That rumpus emerged after a woman was asked if she could remember what colour nightdress she wore on her wedding night. 'I didn't wear any nightie at all,' she giggled.

The idea of the naked woman sent Bishop Thomas Ryan of Clonfert through the roof. He protested to the *Sunday Press*. The Loughrea town commissioners then denounced *The Late Late Show* as 'a dirty programme that should be abolished altogether'. The Mayo County Board of the GAA and the Committee of Vocational Education in Meath passed similar resolutions. The following month there was another incident on the programme, when Brian Trevaskis, a student at Trinity College, provoked a furore by calling Bishop Michael Browne of Galway a 'moron' for squandering so much money on building new churches, such as a cathedral in Galway, while unmarried mothers were being shunned and treated as outcasts in society. Trevaskis, who was brought back the following week to apologise, then compounded the insult. 'I must ask whether the Bishop of Galway knows the meaning of the word "moron",' he said. 'I doubt very much whether he knows the meaning of the word "Christianity".'

This provoked outrage. One man in the audience told Gay Byrne 'to stop characters coming up here to slag the clergy.'

'Wait a minute,' Byrne replied. 'I did not bring people in here to slag the clergy. We have a programme and we are proud of it as a programme on which you are allowed to say what you want.'

'If the programme is allowed to develop along the lines on which it has been moving in recent times, it would be better if it were taken off the air,' Joe Brennan, the Minister for Posts and Telegraphs, wrote to Eamonn Andrews. 'I must take exception to the view expressed last Saturday night by the compère when he implied, or indeed explicitly stated, that anybody is free to say anything they like on this programme.' Andrews defended *The Late Late Show*'s freedom of expression. The programme survived but Andrews quit as chairman of the RTÉ Authority little over a fortnight later. 'I am afraid the authority as now constituted is too susceptible to outside pressures,' he wrote to Lemass. 'I have tried to compromise to the point beyond which honesty will not permit me to go.'

Other controversies followed when RTÉ was persuaded not to cover the presidential-election campaign of 1966, and over RTÉ news coverage of Charles Haughey's difficulties with the National Farmers' Association. When Lynch took over as Taoiseach in 1966, Erskine Childers advised him that television was 'going to play an ever more important part in political life in the coming year. It is absolutely essential for about ten to twenty government supporters, TDs and ministers to be trained on TV in the right way,' Childers noted. 'There is a dearth of effective talent.' But Lynch showed little interest in this idea.

On 1 November 1967 Gay Byrne telephoned the Taoiseach's office to request approval for ministerial participation in an edition of *The Late Late Show*. He had already discussed the idea with Charles Haughey, George Colley and Donogh O'Malley, and they were willing to participate, if the Taoiseach approved. But Lynch did not like the idea. 'He didn't approve of ministers going on *The Late Late Show*,' an aide noted. 'There was already provision for political discussion; there wasn't any need for Gay Byrne to call on him to discuss the matter.'

The essence of any Taoiseach's power is the ability to influence people from what one American president called 'the bully pulpit'. But Lynch was showing a distinct reluctance to use the powers of his office to influence others. He passed up the opportunity of exploiting *The Late Late Show*, which was consistently the most popular programme on television. Moreover, his stance on RTÉ's plans for coverage of the Vietnam War revealed that he feared the power of television.

In June 1968, Lynch went to Washington for the funeral of Senator Bobby Kennedy, who had been assassinated while running for the presidency. After the funeral, the Taoiseach met President Lyndon Johnson and his main advisers, Secretary of State Dean Rusk and National Security Council Adviser Walt Rostow. Here was a golden opportunity to speak out about what was happening in Vietnam. Instead, they talked about the proposed amalgamation of Trinity College and UCD. Lynch never dared to raise the thorny issue of Vietnam. The record of the meeting noted that he deliberately avoided discussion of any issue of political importance, either in the international or domestic field.

On another issue of foreign policy, however, Lynch showed more decisiveness. Although initial Irish efforts to join the EEC had come to nothing, the Lemass and Lynch governments had continued to prepare the country for eventual membership, and this issue came very much to the fore on the day that Lemass announced his decision to resign, because it coincided with Prime Minister Harold Wilson's announcement of Britain's intention to apply for membership in the near future. Lynch personally took charge of the European negotiations, which he initiated by formally applying for membership on behalf of the country on 11 May 1967. Britain, Denmark and Norway applied on the same day.

An Irish delegation was selected to visit the various EEC capitals to discuss the application with members of the different governments. The delegation was composed of Lynch and Haughey, together with two senior civil servants, T. K. Whitaker, secretary of the Department of Finance, and Hugh J. McCann, secretary of the Department of External Affairs.

A round of bilateral talks with Dutch premier Petrus de Jong began in the Hague on 21 June 1967. Six days later, the Irish delegation met with Federal German Chancellor Kurt Kiesinger and Foreign Minister Franz Josef Strauss in Bonn. The Dutch and German leaders expressed support for Irish membership but warned that Britain's application posed real problems, because of the likely opposition of President Charles de Gaulle of France. Italian Prime Minister Aldo Moro and his Foreign Minister, Amintore Fanfani, expressed basically the same views when the Irish delegation met them in Rome on 21 July.

The fate of the Irish application was inevitably bound up with that of the British request. If Britain joined the EEC, Ireland could not afford to stay out, and vice versa, because the Irish economy was still heavily dependent on trade with Britain. When the Dáil debated the government's decision to apply for EEC membership the following week, Lynch explained that membership would mean subscribing to the Treaty of Rome, and he said that 'the ultimate goal of the Treaty is, essentially, to bring about a united Europe through the fusion of national economies.'

'We recognise that membership of the EEC would inevitably

have political implications for us,' Lynch added. 'It would entail certain limitations of our national sovereignty. Every international agreement, such as the Charter of the United Nations or the Statute of the Council of Europe, entails such limitations and imposes certain duties on the participating states.'

Lynch returned to the Continent while Haughey wound up the debate on behalf of the government. Ireland had no choice economically. 'We are now at a turning point in our history,' Haughey said. 'Either we go on and give our people, and especially our young people, access to new horizons and give them the chance to live and work in the stimulating climate of the new Europe, or we decide to remain isolated, with very little prospect of progress or opportunity for development.'

Membership of the EEC would afford budgetary freedom that would relieve the national exchequer 'of the burden of supplementing the export of agricultural surpluses'. Over 26 per cent of the agricultural budget was being spent on export subsidies, with the result that their removal would provide 'very great scope for the development of social services, health services and education services to European levels,' according to Haughey.

'It offers us an opportunity to take part in the building of a new Europe,' he added. 'Inside that new Europe I think we could feel a great deal more secure in this troubled world because this new united Europe would be a potent influence in world affairs, in the promotion of international peace in our time.' He left no doubt that the country's avowed policy of neutrality should not be allowed to prevent involvement in the military alignment which seemed an inevitable aspect of EEC membership. The Taoiseach had already explained that the EEC aimed at eventually becoming a political union, and Haughey argued that such a union 'would be utterly meaningless' without a common defence policy. He therefore favoured 'the working-out of common defence arrangements.'

Meanwhile, Lynch was in Brussels for talks with Belgian Prime

Minister Paul van den Boeynants, who voiced misgivings about Ireland's neutrality. He noted that all six members of the EEC were part of the North Atlantic Treaty Organisation (NATO) and he said that they were anxious that all new members of the EEC should also be in NATO.

The question of Irish neutrality was raised again the following day when the Irish delegation met with members of the European Commission in Brussels. Lynch explained that his government had no reservations about the political union envisaged in the Treaty of Rome. And Haughey, who by this time had rejoined the delegation, supplemented the Taoiseach's remarks by summarising his own comments made in the Dáil the previous day. Commission President Jean Rey described the assurances as 'very important' and the commissioners were favourably disposed towards admitting Ireland to the EEC, as was Prime Minister Pierre Werner of Luxembourg the following day.

'It is now clear that all six governments and the Commission have no objection in principle to Ireland's application,' Lynch told the Dáil. 'For them it presents no major problems. Moreover, they all accept the importance for Ireland of becoming a member at the same time as Britain.' But none of them was optimistic about the chances of early membership, because of the attitude of the French government towards Britain's application.

On 29 September 1967 the European Commission unanimously recommended the opening of negotiations with the Irish and other governments seeking to join the EEC. The next step was to discuss the matter with the French.

The Irish delegation went to Paris in early November for talks with President Charles de Gaulle, Premier Georges Pompidou and Foreign Minister Maurice Couve de Murville. In a private discussion with the Taoiseach, de Gaulle explained that France had no objections in principle to Ireland joining the EEC but he had strong reservations about admitting Britain at that time.

'In Paris,' Lynch said, 'all assured me that there is no objection in principle to Ireland's accession to the European Communities and that France looks forward to the day when it will be possible for this country to become a member. President de Gaulle and his ministers adverted to the problems posed by the British application, and in this context mentioned the close trading arrangements which exist between this country and Britain.'

De Gaulle suggested that Britain might accept some form of association with the EEC short of actual membership, and he asked if the Irish government had considered such an approach. 'I explained why Ireland's application was for membership and the importance for Ireland of simultaneous accession with Britain,' Lynch said. 'The President stated that, in the event of progress not being possible for a considerable time on the British application for membership, it might be helpful for us to have an interim arrangement with the communities, pending full membership. I expressed appreciation of his offer of support and goodwill in this connection but emphasised that our application, which is at present before the Council, is for full membership and that we hoped for an early favourable response to this.'

French reservations about Britain's admission could only have been strengthened within the fortnight, when the British decided to devalue sterling by 14.3 per cent, on 14 November 1967. The Dublin government announced a similar devaluation simultaneously, because not doing so would mean placing an effective tariff of 16.7 per cent on all Irish exports to Britain. De Gaulle effectively vetoed Britain's application to the EEC and the Irish application had to be postponed until after de Gaulle departed the political scene in 1969.

Lynch had been in office more than a year before he finally managed to arrange a meeting with Prime Minister Terence O'Neill of Northern Ireland, at Stormont on 11 December 1967. O'Neill was criticised for the secrecy that had surrounded his first meeting with Lemass, so he decided to announce Lynch's visit as the Taoiseach crossed the border. Word was promptly passed on to the Reverend Ian Paisley, who exploited the visit by going to the Carson statue near Stormont and getting himself filmed throwing snowballs at Lynch's car as it passed around Carson's statue.

'We'll have no Pope here!' Paisley shouted.

'Just which one of us does he think is the Pope?' Lynch asked T. K. Whitaker, who was accompanying him.

O'Neill returned the visit a few weeks later in January 1968. 'Once again we announced the visit as I crossed the border and once again extremists were given time to act,' O'Neill noted. As the discussions were drawing to a close in Iveagh House, a worried official advised that O'Neill should return to Belfast by a circuitous route because if they went back through County Down they would run the risk of being attacked. The Prime Minister therefore returned via County Armagh and he was then criticised for sneaking home and not having the courage to return by the main road. Even the normally supportive *Belfast Telegraph* turned on O'Neill over the affair.

10

RETAINING POWER

1966–1969

On the home front, ministers like Haughey, Donogh O'Malley and Brian Lenihan were changing the face of Fianna Fáil. They projected a liberal, modern approach. O'Malley pushed ahead with plans to build nine regional technical colleges in Cork, Limerick, Galway, Waterford, Carlow, Dundalk, Athlone, Sligo and Letterkenny. Building work on six of the colleges was due to begin in the spring of 1968 and it was hoped to have them in operation by September 1969. This was evidence of O'Malley's great drive and initiative, but there was a mutual dislike between him and the Taoiseach. After all, O'Malley had demonstrated political contempt for Lynch by essentially ignoring him before announcing the 'free education' scheme in 1966.

O'Malley sprung another initiative on an unsuspecting public in April 1967 when he announced plans to amalgamate Trinity College and University College Dublin. This idea had been shot down a decade earlier by John Cardinal D'Alton while Lynch was Minister for Education.

Cardinal D'Alton was now gone, but John Charles McQuaid was still the Archbishop of Dublin. He had been one of the most outspoken proponents of the ban on Catholics attending Trinity College, so the whole thing evoked memories of the mother-and-child controversy, especially as Lynch had a comparatively similar style of leadership to John A. Costello, and both had to cope with a Cabinet of particularly headstrong ministers.

In announcing his latest plan, O'Malley described the dual-university set-up as 'a most insidious form of partition on our own doorstep' because it segregated Catholics and Protestants. He added that he foresaw that the new university would be 'inter-denominational'. When he was asked what Archbishop McQuaid thought of the proposed merger, O'Malley replied rather nonchalantly that he had not asked him. It was an exquisite touch, which highlighted the fact that it was really none of McQuaid's business, so why would he ask him? It was as if he was inviting another confrontation with the hierarchy, which had clearly won out in the mother-and-child controversy. This time the hierarchy quickly backed off. William Cardinal Conway said that the plan 'contained a number of good ideas' and the hierarchy itself welcomed the proposal at its next meeting, but O'Malley was to die suddenly soon afterwards. His successor, Brian Lenihan, was unable to overcome the objections of the academic powers within the two institutions.

Lenihan had made a name for himself as Minister for Justice when he sought to modernise the country's censorship laws. He appointed a new film-censorship board. He was the kind of politician who liked to get on with journalists and never seemed to take umbrage at even the most trenchant criticism. He obliged the media and facilitated them when it came to having his picture taken, even in the most ridiculous of circumstances, such as closely examining a lavatory bowl at the opening of a new building. He was not above playing the clown, with the result that he was often underestimated. His indiscretions were the product of an affable nature and a desire to please just about everyone and anyone.

Haughey, O'Malley and Lenihan were urban realists with no time for the pastoral idealism of the de Valera era. Haughey was secretive about his business dealings and was the subject of widespread speculation and constant rumours – most of which went unpublished, in view of the country's strong libel laws, which Haughey had helped to strengthen as Minister for Justice. The rumours were transmitted by the political bush telegraph and frequently elaborated on by the so-called Fine Gael rumour machine, with the result that the gossip was repeated and further embellished in virtually every bar and public house in the country.

Haughey was seen as the most important of Lynch's ministers, because he was a dynamic individual who worked even harder than he played. Unlike Lynch, he was always acutely conscious of the value of publicity and had hired his own public-relations man even when he was a mere backbencher. But some of the people with whom he associated provoked strong hostility within sections of the party. The old guard was deeply suspicious of Haughey, but then he was trying to change Fianna Fáil by modernising the party, reforming it into a professional structure, and it was natural enough that older politicians would see this as a kind of criticism of the way they had handled things. In the circumstances, many of their objections were inevitably dismissed as pique at having a youngster like Haughey questioning their judgements.

Although he had undoubtedly seen himself as the best choice for Taoiseach, Haughey was realistic enough to realise that he could not win a contest in November 1966, and hence he backed Lynch. He was rewarded with a prestigious promotion to Minister for Finance, which was generally seen as the second most powerful post in the government. Haughey softened his hard, capitalist image with imaginative social giveaways in his budgets.

In his first budget as Minister for Finance, he announced welfare increases that more than compensated for the inflation resulting from the devaluation of the Irish pound in line with sterling. The welfare increases were to be financed by raising the duty on drink, tobacco and petrol. Such increases were typical of Haughey's budgets but he cloaked them with strokes of political genius that involved innovative yet comparatively cheap giveaways, such as a hundred free units of electricity for the old-age pensioners every two months. They were also to be allowed to travel free on public transport at off-peak hours. The exchequer then compensated the ESB and CIÉ.

He also introduced tax-free exemptions for artists and creative writers, which received considerable international publicity, especially after some high-profile writers like Frederick Forsyth took up residence in Ireland. Haughey told Forsyth that the scheme had not been designed to attract foreign writers to Ireland but to encourage native ones to remain there. Many of the country's most famous writers – including Oscar Wilde, James Joyce, William Butler Yeats and Samuel Beckett – lived and died in exile. In short, the tax exemption was a measure to ensure that the country's most talented people could earn a proper living at home.

As Minister for Agriculture, Haughey said that he had been appalled by the poverty he witnessed on small farms, especially in the west of Ireland. The government therefore took steps to help the less well-off among the farming community by announcing a complete derogation from rates on holdings of agricultural land valued at less than £20 under the poor-law valuation system, and there was scaled-down relief for those whose land was valued at between £20 and £33 under the same system. In addition, some 10,000 farmers, who were barred from drawing unemployment assistance from March until October, were henceforth allowed to draw 'the farmer's dole' throughout the year.

Haughey also sought to turn around Fianna Fáil's financial position by adopting American fund-raising techniques. In 1966 he helped draw up the blueprint for a supporting organisation that was made up mostly of businessmen. The organisation was called *Taca*, the Irish for 'support'. People were invited to join at £100 per year. The money was then deposited in a bank until election time, and the interest was used to fund lavish dinners at which members of *Taca* could mix with Cabinet ministers.

Taca was 'a fairly innocent concept', according to Haughey. 'Insofar as it had any particular motivation it was to make the party independent of big business and try to spread the level of financial support right across a much wider spectrum of the community,' he said. Some individuals would previously have subscribed 'substantially more' to the party at election time than the £500 that would accumulate in *Taca* subscriptions, if there were five full years between elections.

Although Haughey was the politician most associated with *Taca* in the public mind, the original idea had come from somebody else and the funds were controlled by the Taoiseach, Kevin Boland and Neil Blaney. But Haughey embraced the scheme with enthusiasm and took over much of the organisation of the first dinner, which was a particularly lavish affair, with the whole Cabinet in attendance. 'We were all organised by Haughey and sent to different tables around the room,' Kevin Boland recalled. 'The extraordinary thing about my table was that everybody at it was somehow or other connected with the construction industry.'

Lynch publicly defended *Taca* from the outset. 'In order to maintain our system of democracy, we have to have political parties,' he said. 'Political parties can't run without funds and these funds can only be provided voluntarily.

'Traditionally our means of accumulating funds were first, the national collection, and second, the special collections that are made at election time,' he added. 'With the increasing cost of running elections, the increasing cost of maintaining party headquarters and the necessity to increase the services at party headquarters, we find that the existing means of collecting funds have not been sufficient, even though we have been stepping up our national collection.' Hence it was necessary to turn to new methods.

'The criticism levelled against *Taca* was that those who became members of it could expect some favour from the government,' Lynch noted. 'Well, I can say now that if any member has joined *Taca* for that purpose, he has been, or will be, gravely disappointed.' Maybe he believed that himself, but if so, he must have been one of the few people in the country who did. Opposition deputies certainly questioned the propriety of the cosy relationship between the property developers and members of the government. In particular, there were questions about the selection of the property rented by government departments and agencies as they mush-roomed in the midst of the unprecedented economic growth.

Boland insisted that he 'never did a thing' within his department for any member of *Taca*, but he admitted that other ministers might have been 'susceptible'. A cloud of suspicion was cast over the operations of *Taca* and it 'unfortunately provided a basis for political attack which,' Haughey said, 'did us a lot of damage at the time.'

'Our people will get the government they voted for,' James Dillon declared. 'If it is *Animal Farm* they want, they should vote for Fianna Fáil, but if it is democracy and decency they want, I suggest they will have to look elsewhere. I think the acceptance of corruption as the norm in public life is shocking.'

'Is it not another form of corruption to take people's character away, to spread false rumours about them?' Haughey asked. Fine Gael was vilifying and slandering him with malicious rumours, he said. 'That is all you are good for, the lot of you.'

But the questions about Haughey's methods were by no means confined to the opponents of Fianna Fáil. The snide insinuations were widespread, and they were fuelled in May 1967 when George Colley urged those attending a Fianna Fáil youth conference in Galway not to be 'dispirited if some people in high places appear to have low standards.'

It was widely assumed that Colley was alluding to Haughey in particular, in view of the intensity of their rivalry over the party leadership some months earlier. Lynch reportedly gave Colley a severe dressing-down over the remark, and the Opposition naturally sought to make political capital out of the divisions within Fianna Fáil. At the Fine Gael *ard fheis* a few days later, Liam Cosgrave tied the whole thing to *Taca* and challenged Colley to identify those with low standards.

Colley rather disingenuously suggested that he was really referring to Fine Gael members of the last Inter-Party Government. But there was no real doubt that he was alluding to Haughey, nor that the latter was referring to Colley when he said that he looked with suspicion on those politicians who put themselves forward as men of virtue.

Colley and Haughey were seen as rivals within the Cabinet. Representatives of the new generation in Fianna Fáil, they were the same age and had been classmates in school. In fact, Colley had been largely instrumental in bringing Haughey into Fianna Fáil. Colley's father, Harry, was a Fianna Fáil deputy in the Dáil from 1944 until 1957, when he lost his seat to Haughey. Not long afterwards, the intense rivalry began with George Colley, who was closer to the values of the old guard and was associated with de Valera rather than Lemass. Frank Aiken was Colley's chief mentor.

Openly ambitious and convinced that he represented what was good and pure in Irish public life, Colley liked to think of himself as being motivated by a conviction that government should be run by upright men who would put the public good before either their own personal interests or those of business colleagues. His support came primarily from those elements of Fianna Fáil who were ashamed of the Tammany Hall methods of some of the party hierarchy. He therefore offered an alternative image.

Lemass had appointed Colley as chairman of a committee to draw up recommendations for constitutional reform, and this committee continued to sit after Lynch took over. Shortly before Christmas 1967 the committee published an interim report. It was a workmanlike document with three potentially controversial recommendations. It called for the deletion from the Constitution of the controversial Article 44, which recognised the 'special position' of the Catholic Church. The other two main recommendations were for the introduction of civil divorce, and an amendment to Article 3 of the Constitution in relation to the reintegration of the national territory.

Little came of the committee's recommendations, because Fianna Fáil disrupted the spirit of cross-party cooperation by forcing a referendum on the contentious abolition of the system of proportional representation. Kevin Boland, the Minister for Local Government, was the minister most associated with that initiative.

He had become a Cabinet minister on the same day as Lynch in 1957, but in Boland's case it was his first day in the Dáil. He obviously owed his position to his father, Gerry Boland, who along with Seán Lemass had been one of de Valera's main lieutenants in the formation and development of Fianna Fáil. Gerry Boland had come out against the inclusion of a clause in the 1937 Constitution that would have recognised the Catholic Church as the one true church of Christ. During the war years he had served as Minister for Justice: internment without trial was implemented, while six members of the IRA were executed and four others were allowed to die on hunger strike.

De Valera eased Gerry Boland out of his Cabinet in 1957 by appointing his son Kevin as Minister for Defence instead. As dour and dull as he was determined, the younger Boland had an even more wooden approach than many of the geriatric ministers around him. He was fanatical about the use of the Irish language, even though he tended to speak it badly himself.

'He was adamant that he would force it on whoever happened to be in a subordinate position to him,' according to a profile in

Hibernia magazine. 'In a bullying, unimaginative and roughshod manner, he attempted to impose Irish upon the officer corps, many members of which spoke it better than he did. He met with resentment and barely concealed hostility and was a particularly unpopular minister as far as the Army was concerned.

Described as 'one of the most tortuous personalities in the Cabinet', Kevin Boland had a volatile streak to his nature. He neither smoked tobacco nor drank alcohol, and he was prone to lose his temper. As Minister for Local Government, he was responsible for the periodical redrawing of the constituency boundaries, and he was accused of doing this in a way which was likely to favour Fianna Fáil. At the time it was called 'Boland's Gerrymander'.

He was determined to reverse Fianna Fáil's failure to abolish the multi-seat constituencies in favour of the British first-past-the-post system of voting. He took the 1959 referendum defeat badly and was determined to have another crack at a referendum in 1968. Liam Cosgrave, the leader of Fine Gael, personally favoured the change also. If he had been able to carry his party with him, the referendum would undoubtedly have passed, but most members of Fine Gael were more determined to embarrass Fianna Fáil.

In neither of his two general elections as Taoiseach had Seán Lemass been able to lead Fianna Fáil to an overall majority, and those elections had been held in the most favourable of political circumstances. Under Lynch's leadership, Fianna Fáil had managed to secure an overall majority by winning four consecutive by-elections in his first year of office, but there was a genuine sense that the days of majority government were numbered. It was felt that PR would eventually lead to an almost permanent need for coalition government.

Charles Haughey was appointed national director of the Fianna Fáil referendum campaign. If Lynch had been seen as a principal exponent of the constitutional amendment, it might have been possible to sell the idea as something that was in the national interest, but in the hands of people like Boland and Haughey, it was seen as a cynical attempt by Fianna Fáil to preserve its own hold on power. As a result, the party suffered a humiliating setback at the polls.

Haughey managed to evade political responsibility for the setback, as he was in hospital during the final part of the campaign, following a road accident on 20 September 1968. He was seriously injured in a car accident in County Wicklow while driving home following a referendum rally. Thereafter ministerial drivers were ordered not to allow anyone else – even their respective ministers – to drive their cars. The circumstances of the crash were never explained publicly. As Haughey was seriously injured, the Opposition did not press the matter on this occasion.

Following the referendum debacle, Fianna Fáil's days in power looked distinctly numbered, as the Northern troubles burst onto the unsuspecting public on 5 October 1968 when a civil-rights march in Derry turned ugly before a television camera. The march had been banned for fear that loyalists would provoke trouble, but the marchers were essentially attacked by the Royal Ulster Constabulary (RUC). It was like a mini-rerun of the police riot in Chicago at the National Convention of the Democratic Party some weeks earlier. The trouble in Derry began when an RUC inspector struck one of the peaceful marchers in the groin with his baton. The resulting cry of anguish was heard around the world. People were appalled at the sight of the inspector hitting an unsuspecting man on the back of the head with his baton and frantically flailing at just about anyone he could hit.

Lynch deplored the scenes of violence and expressed the hope that their root cause would be eliminated so that people of differing religious beliefs and political convictions could live together as equals in mutual respect and harmony. Eddie McAteer, the Nationalist leader at Stormont, urged the Taoiseach to call for the intervention of the United Nations in Northern Ireland. When Lynch discussed the Derry march with Prime Minister Harold Wilson in London on 30 October, neither of them seemed particularly well informed. Lynch blamed the whole thing on partition, while Wilson warned that 'banging the drum' would only make conditions worse. Even though he was apparently referring to the vociferous Catholic demand for civil rights, Wilson's allusion to drums was particularly apt. The Lambeg drum used by the loyalists was a symbol of their domination, and a major element of the ensuing strife was not so much the demand by Catholics for civil rights as the loyalist resistance, often with the surreptitious help of the police or police reserves, such as at Burntollet Bridge, when a student march from Belfast to Derry was attacked.

Terence O'Neill tried to stop the drift towards disorder by calling a general election in February 1969. Ian Paisley ran against him in Antrim. Although O'Neill won, he did not win by as much as some commentators expected. Unionists supporting O'Neill took 44 per cent of the overall vote, while the anti-O'Neill unionists took 17.1 per cent of the vote. In other words, O'Neill's supporters won over 72 per cent of the overall unionists' vote, yet the media somehow depicted him as the loser, because Paisley claimed a moral victory. O'Neill's days were numbered.

The overwhelming sympathy of the Republic was with the Catholics of the North who were demanding their civil rights. In March Lynch tried to modify the tone by talking about promoting reunification of the island 'by fostering a spirit of brotherhood'. But the violence continued, much of it actually orchestrated by the loyalists. On 28 April 1969 O'Neill was compelled to resign after bombing attacks on Belfast's water supply. These were represented as being the work of the IRA, but the bombs were set off by the Ulster Volunteer Force to destabilise the O'Neill government.

In the midst of all the gloomy news from Northern Ireland, the Republic got a great psychological boost in May 1969 when the former French President Charles de Gaulle visited for an extended holiday. He had resigned as President on 28 April, fulfilling a threat to step down if a referendum that he had proposed was not passed. He arrived at Cork Airport on 10 May and planned to stay for six weeks – the duration of the campaign to elect his successor in France. Lynch, his wife, Mairín, and Frank Aiken, the Minister for Foreign Affairs, were at the airport to meet de Gaulle.

'All Ireland is honoured by your visit,' the Taoiseach said in greeting him.

It was de Gaulle's first visit to Ireland and he surprised many people by announcing that he was happy to be here in the country of his maternal ancestors, the MacCartans. His great-grandmother's great-grandmother was a MacCartan from County Down. Her father or perhaps her grandfather had in fact been killed in the Battle of the Boyne. De Gaulle intended to spend much of his time in south Kerry, though plans had been made for him to visit Connemara for a short stay. He had no intention of going to County Down, because he considered it to be occupied by the British.

Shortly after de Gaulle's arrival, Lynch had President de Valera dissolve the Dáil and call a general election for 18 June 1969. It was a brilliant piece of political timing. The civil-rights campaign had begun in Northern Ireland and civil unrest was growing in the area; this would soon explode into widespread violence, but not until after the general election.

The opposition parties were confident of doing well. The plethora of small parties from the 1940s and 1950s had disappeared and the Labour Party had persuaded a number of high-profile candidates to stand in the election. These included intellectuals like Conor Cruise O'Brien, the former Irish and UN diplomat who was lecturing at the University of New York at the time; Dr Justin Keating of UCD; Dr David Thornley of Trinity College, who was also a presenter of current-affairs programmes on RTÉ television; and Dr Noël Browne, of mother-and-child-controversy fame. In addition, Rickard Deasy, the former head of the NFA, was selected to stand as a Labour candidate in Tipperary, and the party was endorsed by the former general Michael J. Costello, the managing director of the highly successful Irish Sugar Company.

Labour was standing on a strong socialist platform with Brendan Corish, the leader of the party, proudly proclaiming that 'Ireland will be socialist in the 'seventies.' The party nominated the greatest number of candidates in its history, as did Fine Gael, which nominated even more candidates than Fianna Fáil. The Labour Party, which refused to conclude any kind of pre-election pact with Fine Gael, had no intention of going into government with anyone. Instead the party indicated that it would back a minority government, provided it implemented Labour's policies.

During the campaign, Lynch cleverly exploited the divisions between Fine Gael and Labour. The two previous coalitions had ended in political grief, and the Taoiseach warned that 'a captive minority government would be even worse' if it was constantly faced with the danger of the Labour Party pulling the political rug from under it. 'Such an exercise of power without responsibility could only mean the end of any effective leadership in the country's effort to achieve economic and social betterment,' Lynch warned.

Pat Norton, the son of the former leader of the Labour Party, William Norton, was particularly upset that Noël Browne was being allowed to run as a Labour candidate. He said that his father had voted against Browne's admission to the party.

'My father did this,' he explained, 'because he believed in the Christian principles of social justice which, under his leadership, were the base of Labour policies, and he did not accept and would not forward the brand of alien and godless socialism which he believed that Dr Noël Browne purveyed.' He added that the Labour Party were proposing 'nakedly the alien doctrines and theories of Dr Noël Browne and his disciples.'

Some of Lynch's Cabinet colleagues were even more critical of some of the Labour personalities, whom Neil Blaney denounced as 'the new Irish Marxists'. He rather hysterically accused them of promoting the false doctrines that had preceded the downfall of democracy in Russia, Cuba, North Korea and North Vietnam. He did not bother to explain the kind of 'democracy' that was supposedly in those countries before the communists took power. Instead he said that Brendan Corish was being driven along the road of self-destruction by merry Marxists with their pseudo-intellectual sham talk.

'He tells us about Nero fiddling while Rome burns, but he fiddles with dangerous imported doctrines while a triumvirate battles over control of agriculture,' Blaney said. 'It used to be honest Mickey Pat Murphy from West Cork who spoke for the party on agriculture. Now the newcomer Dr Keating is catching the headlines, while the irrepressible Mr Deasy, the new Mussolini of the rural scene, aspires to the same post.'

Haughey, who had been appointed National Director of Elections, became the subject of some particularly strong opposition criticism in relation to both his own finances and his fundraising tactics for the party, especially after a sensational report in the *Evening Herald* on the sale of his Raheny home, which was sold to his developer friend, Matt Gallagher, for over £200,000.

'I object to my private affairs being used in this way,' Haughey declared. None of the figures could be given with certainty, because he did not give details to any reporter. 'It is a private matter between myself and the purchaser.' The controversy became a national issue when Gerard Sweetman of Fine Gael charged that Haughey might have acted improperly by benefiting personally from legislation that he had introduced himself, without explaining the situation to the Dáil. It was suggested that he might have been liable for income tax on the sale of his land, if part of the 1965 Finance Act had not been repealed recently.

As Minister for Finance, Haughey referred the matter to the

Revenue Commissioners, who promptly reported that Haughey would have had 'no liability to income tax or surtax' under any provision of the 1965 act. Although this should have killed the issue, one of his opponents in his Dublin North-Central constituency – the Labour Party candidate, Conor Cruise O'Brien – raked up the issue repeatedly during the campaign in an effort to expose what he described as 'the Fianna Fáil speculator-oriented oligarchy'.

Lynch engaged in a kind of presidential campaign, visiting each constituency in the country. At one point he travelled from Donegal to Dublin by helicopter for a television appearance and then flew on to Ballina afterwards. It was the first time a party leader had used a helicopter for a campaign in the Republic. His rallies were well attended and the party engaged in an extensive advertising campaign in the press, with full-page advertisements in national newspapers using scare tactics, stating that there were really two Labour Parties. 'One is made up of the traditional Labour supporters,' the advertisement explained. 'The other is a group of extreme left-wing socialists who are preaching class warfare and who want state control and all that goes with it.'

Fianna Fáil ended the campaign with a massive eve-of-election rally in Cork. This began with a motor cavalcade from Blackpool to the city centre. Four bands headed the parade, with Lynch being carried in triumph like a hero of Roman times. Flaming tar barrels and bonfires lined the route. The bonfire beside the Glen Rovers Club was so enthusiastic that the local fire brigade had to be called to dampen the flames as it threatened to get out of control. Many thousands of people turned out, either to observe or lend their support.

About a hundred people marched down Patrick's Street carrying republican banners and chanting slogans. They then lined up in front of the speaking platform. An egg was thrown at the Taoiseach and the republican element gave the Nazi salute, shouting 'Sieg

Heil!' All of this played neatly into the hands of the moderate Lynch, who had been emphasising his opposition to the alien philosophies supposedly embraced by Fianna Fáil's opponents, especially the Labour Party, as he sought to highlight the differences between that party and Fine Gael.

'One of the more striking features of the election campaign now ending has been the fact that we have been witnessing a contest between Fine Gael and Labour,' Lynch told the Cork gathering. He challenged Corish to define what the Labour Party meant by calling for a new republic. 'Will it involve the confiscation of industrial firms such as Guinness and Waterford Glass, in which many workers have shares?' the Taoiseach asked. 'Who will compensate these shareholders? Will Labour take over the banks and building societies?'

Although Labour 'had reasonable expectations of gaining some seats', the party actually lost four seats. Conor Cruise O'Brien, who was one of the successful candidates, complained that the underhand campaign tactics of Lynch and his henchmen had undermined the Labour Party. He actually accused the Taoiseach of 'making use of Catholicism for party-political purposes, similar to the use by the Northern Unionist Party of Protestantism.'

The key to this aspect of Lynch's campaign was supposedly 'a tour of the convent parlours', where he and his people made snide suggestions that Labour was tainted with communism, and the reverend mothers then spread the word among the mothers of the children in their schools. 'The press and media were not present for that series of convent chats,' Cruise O'Brien added, 'but the word came through all the same.'

In the 1930s Fine Gael had enlisted the Catholic hierarchy and used the media to smear Fianna Fáil with the taint of communism, but those Red smear-tactics had failed dismally. Lynch was therefore much more subtle in his approach in 1969, according to Cruise O'Brien. He used a whispering campaign, not loud accusations to smother the Labour challenge in June 1969. 'In the wider and more barren parts of the country, where a whisper would not have carried, a ruder tone prevailed among Mr Lynch's henchmen,' Cruise O'Brien added, 'but Mr Lynch managed to be adequately uninformed about this.'

'Lynch is one of the most sanctimonious politicians alive,' Cruise O'Brien contended. As a hurler, he suggested, Lynch got away with foul play because he had an acute sense of knowing when the referee was not looking. Cruise O'Brien would probably not have claimed to know much about hurling, and in this instance his political analysis was as faulty as the suggestion about Lynch's sportsmanship as a player. Playing the demanding position of centre-field, Lynch would have known how to look after himself, but he always had a reputation as a clean player, among both his team-mates and opponents. It was Cruise O'Brien who was guilty of the smear tactics in this instance. Indeed, his overall analysis hinted of seeking a scapegoat for the Labour Party's own failings. It was absurd to suggest that Labour lost due to a whispering campaign in the convents. Fianna Fáil campaigned openly against some of the more radical people in the Labour Party – those who had been loudly proclaiming that 'the 'seventies will be socialist'.

Labour lost ground due to its own campaign tactics. The party had never had much support 'in the wider and more barren parts of the country', and there were no grounds to suggest that they were likely to have much support in those areas in 1969. Cruise O'Brien believed that he was the 'prime target of the offensive against "communism"' himself, but of course he played into the hands of his critics when, at the Labour Party convention in January 1969, he suggested that the Irish embassy in Portugal, a Catholic country under the neo-fascist rule of Antonio Salazar, should be closed and an embassy should be opened in communist Cuba. Yet he noted that he 'was elected easily for Dublin North-East'. The Labour Party's first-preference vote was 17 per cent nationally, which was more than 1 per cent higher than it had ever achieved in any elections since the foundation of the state. So much for Red smear-tactics!

Labour did lose four seats but this probably had a lot to do with the party's faulty campaign tactics, which were part of a long-term strategy. Labour ran on the platform that it would not go into coalition with either Fianna Fáil or Fine Gael but would seek to force the two main parties to get together. If they could be compelled to form a government, this would leave the Labour Party as the main opposition, and it would thus be in a position to make major gains in the following general election. The Labour message, therefore, emphasised the differences that existed between Labour and both Fianna Fáil and Fine Gael, parties which were socially conservative, with similar economic outlooks. Was Cruise O'Brien so naive as to believe that Labour could get the same level of support from Fine Gael as when the two parties were offering to form a coalition?

Previously the Civil-War animosities had been so strong that there was little chance of Fianna Fáil or Fine Gael votes transferring to each other, but Lynch represented a new generation in Fianna Fáil, untainted by Civil-War bitterness. For the first time, both Fianna Fáil and Fine Gael were being led by men who had played no part in that war. There was an inevitable decline in past hostility.

Lynch exploited the Labour strategy by emphasising the differences of approach among the opposition parties, thereby highlighting the fact that Fianna Fáil was the only party likely to be able to form a cohesive government. Some of the opposition claimed that Kevin Boland had been responsible for a partisan redrawing of the constituencies to give Fianna Fáil an advantage, but there is little doubt that the main contributory factor was the lack of cooperation between the opposition parties. In previous general elections, going back to the 1940s, Labour or Fine Gael had tended to transfer votes to each other, but in 1969 rivalry between the two parties had minimised the level of transfer. Labour politicians attacked Fine Gael, which they characterised as being the same as Fianna Fáil, and were then surprised when Fine Gael voters did not transfer to Labour in the same proportion as previously.

In the general election of 1973 the Labour Party lost 19.4 per cent of its 1969 vote but it actually gained a seat, because it had concluded a pre-election pact with Fine Gael. Had there been such a pact in 1969, the outcome would probably have been very different. In the 1969 election, Fianna Fáil's first-preference vote dropped by 2 per cent nationally from its level of four years earlier, but the party still gained two seats, to win an overall majority. Lynch became the first party leader since independence to lead his party to an overall majority in his first general election as leader.

On the eve of the election, de Gaulle arrived in Dublin for a two-day stay with President de Valera. Many people were taken by the similarities between the two tall, bony old men, each of whom was seen by supporters as the virtual personification of his country. De Gaulle had unquestionably been one of the giants of twentieth-century Europe, while de Valera was probably the most influential Irish politician of the century. He led Fianna Fáil to power in 1957 and the party had been there continuously since then. It certainly did not harm Fianna Fáil's chances in the election to have de Gaulle and de Valera splashed on the front pages of the national newspapers on election day.

As the election count was concluding, Lynch and his government colleagues were attending a state dinner at Dublin Castle in honour of de Gaulle, who was returning home to France the following day. He had clearly enjoyed his stay. 'At this point in my long life,' he wrote privately, 'I have found here what I was looking for: to be face to face with myself. Ireland has given me this, in the most delicate, the most friendly way.'

At the dinner Lynch said that 'the meeting between General de Gaulle and President de Valera has been a historic moment for all Irish people.' The former French President was gracious in his response. 'It was a sort of instinct that led me towards Ireland, perhaps because of the Irish blood that courses in my veins,' he said. 'One always goes back to one's source.' Then suddenly he added, 'I raise my glass to a united Ireland.' It was an explosive declaration, reminiscent of his infamous remark the previous year in French Canada when he declared, *'Vive le Québec libre!'* His biographer, Jean Lacouture, suggested that somebody in Dublin may have expected something similar because there was a mysterious technical fault with his microphone as he was proposing his toast, with the result that only those close to him heard what he actually said. It was probably just as well, because Northern Ireland was about to explode that summer.

11

'WE WON'T STAND BY'

1969–1970

When the new Dáil met for the first time, on 2 July 1969, Lynch was nominated for Taoiseach by Frank Aiken and he was easily elected, without rancour. He announced a Cabinet, which was most remarkable for the fact that Aiken – the last of the original Fianna Fáil government – was being excluded. Erskine Childers, who was put in charge of Health, replaced Aiken as Tánaiste. The other ministers were Neil Blaney in Agriculture and Fisheries, Kevin Boland in Local Government and Social Welfare, Michael Moran in Justice, Charles Haughey in Finance, Paddy Hillery in External Affairs, Brian Lenihan in Transport and Power, George Colley in Industry and Commerce, Joe Brennan in Labour, Seán Flanagan in Lands, Pádraig Faulkner in Education, Jim Gibbons in Defence and P. J. Lalor in Posts and Telegraphs.

The Chief Whip was young Des O'Malley, who was appointed parliamentary secretary to both the Taoiseach and Minister for Defence. He had succeeded his uncle, Donogh O'Malley, on his untimely death. Lynch had great faith in him. He described him to the young businessman Tony O'Reilly as 'a great bit of stuff'. From an early stage, Lynch saw O'Malley as a future Taoiseach.

The Cabinet represented the broad spectrum of the party. On one side there were the republicans, Kevin Boland and Neil Blaney, and on the other side there were the urban realists like Haughey and Brian Lenihan. Haughey was much more interested in the economic and business side of things. Blaney, Boland and Haughey were all ambitious and had little real respect for Lynch. They believed he was being manipulated by the new breed of civil servant, who had come very much to the fore with the advent of T. K. Whitaker. The civil servants were not only implementing, but essentially formulating policy, the ministers believed.

Lynch was already showing a certain weakness in his un-willingness to take on his critics within Fianna Fáil. During the debate on the nomination of his government on 2 July 1969, for instance, Kevin Boland broke with tradition and delivered a long personal speech, defending his own record and baiting the Labour Party. As this turned into a kind of slanging match, Lynch sent a note to Boland, who crumpled it up in his hand and threw it on the floor, in what those on the other side of the House considered a display of contempt.

The new government would soon become preoccupied with the growing unrest in Northern Ireland. Lynch warned the Dáil that the Apprentice Boys' parade in Derry could provoke serious trouble because there were reports that loyalist elements planned to bring in people from outside and have as many as seventy marching bands, instead of the usual seventeen. 'The holding of this parade at all could well have serious consequences,' Lynch warned, 'but to enlarge participation in it threefold or fourfold, as we were reliably informed would be the case, we are convinced would be highly provocative, to say the least.'

This might have seemed like a good opportunity for the Taoiseach and British Prime Minister to get together, but the civil servants at the Department of the Taoiseach did not want this kind of summit meeting, for fear that the Taoiseach would be manoeuvred 'into appearing to have asked for, or approved of, the use of British troops in the North. This could lead to an adverse reaction from extremist groups in the South.' Lynch therefore decided to stay in the background.

Paddy Hillery went to London instead, on 1 August, to plead with Michael Stewart, the British Foreign Secretary, to block the Apprentice Boys' parade in Derry. He warned that it was likely to have cataclysmic results. It would inevitably be seen as a clear provocation of the majority nationalist population of the city of Derry, especially if the dreaded B-Specials were allowed to participate, but Hillery's appeal was contemptuously rebuffed.

'You expect the situation will not get out of hand?' he asked.

'Yes,' Stewart replied firmly.

'You want to handle this yourselves. Is the position then that we cannot discuss this further?'

'Yes.'

'You realise our concern?'

'Yes,' said Stewart. 'I must say to you that there is a limit to the extent to which we can discuss with outsiders – even our nearest neighbours – this internal matter.' In blunt diplomatic terms, Hillery was told to butt out and mind his own business!

As Dublin feared, nationalists attacked the Apprentice Boys' parade on 12 August 1969 and serious violence ensued. The police, supported by unionist thugs, then besieged the nationalist area, giving rise to what became known as the Battle of the Bogside. This quickly spread to other nationalist areas of Northern Ireland, which seemed on the brink of a full-scale civil war.

Appeals were made to Dublin to intervene militarily. Young Bernadette Devlin telephoned the Department of Defence in Dublin the day after the parade. She said that the Catholics were fighting a combined force of police and Paisleyites and needed assistance in the form of 'fresh men inside two hours, either officially or unofficially', as well as a supply of tear gas and gas masks.

Lynch arrived for an emergency Cabinet meeting with the draft of a speech that he intended to deliver on television that evening. It had been prepared by civil servants. He had said in a St Patrick's Day speech earlier that year that it was 'the aim of the government to promote the reunification of Ireland by fostering a spirit of brotherhood among all sections of the people.' Now Haughey, Blaney and Boland were calling for a stronger approach, and they were supported by Jim Gibbons, Brian Lenihan and Seán Flanagan. A different address was therefore prepared for Lynch at the Cabinet meeting.

'That speech was composed word for word – every comma, every iota – as a collective Cabinet speech,' Blaney later contended. 'It was not Jack Lynch's speech, made on behalf of his government. It was a Cabinet speech, made by Jack Lynch.'

This was part of a pragmatic line that he would take in the following months as he fluctuated between a hardline republican stance and a more conciliatory approach towards the unionists, depending on the circumstances. When passions were strained, he tended to take a hard line, but when things were calmer, he would be more conciliatory.

When the Taoiseach arrived at RTÉ's studios in Donnybrook, Desmond Fisher, the senior journalist on duty, gave him a bottle of whiskey to calm his nerves. Fisher noticed that Lynch's script had alterations 'scrawled all over it'. At one point he asked for a telephone and consulted his wife, Mairín, about some further changes. 'He asked me what I thought would happen if he were to order the Army into the North, as some of his advisers counselled,' Fisher noted. 'I said I thought they would go about twenty miles into Down or Derry before they would be massacred in a fight with the British. He smiled wanly at my answer and said he had come to the same conclusion himself.'

By then the script of the speech was in such a mess that Fisher had it retyped in large type with double spacing to facilitate Lynch in his delivery. 'The Stormont government evidently is no longer in control of the situation, which is the inevitable outcome of policies pursued for decades by them,' Lynch told the nation that evening. 'The government of Ireland can no longer stand by and see innocent people injured and perhaps worse. It is obvious that the RUC is no longer accepted as an impartial police force. Neither would the employment of British troops be acceptable, nor would they be likely to restore peaceful conditions – certainly not in the long term. The Irish government have, therefore, requested the British government to apply immediately to the United Nations for the urgent dispatch of a peacekeeping force to the Six Counties of Northern Ireland and have instructed the Permanent Representative to the United Nations to inform the Secretary General of this request.

'Very many people have been injured and some seriously,' the Taoiseach continued. 'We know that many of these do not wish to be treated in Six-County hospitals. We have, therefore, directed Irish Army authorities to have field hospitals in County Donegal adjacent to Derry and at other points along the border where they may be necessary.'

Blaney thought, for instance, that the Irish Army would inevitably move into Derry city, where they would be welcomed by the nationalist population. 'Most of us believed the army would cross over, particularly into Derry, which was already coming under attack,' he later explained. 'That would have precipitated UN intervention immediately. And I don't have any doubt that, had that happened, the international scene would have been set.'

Lynch did not believe that his government had the authority to send troops across the border. 'It would have been an act of war,' he later told Raymond Smith of the *Irish Independent*. 'Under the Constitution, only the Oireachtas has the power to declare war.' People might have backed the idea of the Army moving into the Bogside at the time, because emotions were running so high, but he believed that history would ultimately condemn this as a mistake. 'It is from moments like that,' Lynch added, 'that you realise later what leadership is all about. The destiny of people and the nation is in your hands. It is then one must keep one's head and not be swayed by emotionalism and one must examine coldly the consequences of any hasty action one might take.'

He knew that the Army could have been sent in to the Bogside area of Derry 'simply and solely as a protective measure' and an appeal could then have been made to the United Nations to intervene. This was what Blaney desired, but he had a simplistic view of the situation. The United Nations could not intervene without the approval of the British government, because Britain could veto any move at the Security Council. In 1982, when Argentina invaded the Falkland Islands, the British decided to retake the area. Logistically, moving into Northern Ireland would have been infinitely easier, especially as there was a general perception among the British that Northern Ireland had supported them against the Nazis while the rest of Ireland had remained neutral. Winston Churchill had stressed that sense of debt at the end of the war, and the British would undoubtedly come to the aid of their unionist brethren. Moreover, it was naive to think that the Protestant population in Northern Ireland would have waited meekly for the United Nations to intervene.

'That would have been overlooking entirely what would have been happening elsewhere in the Six Counties and forgetting how many Catholics might have died before assistance could be rushed to them,' Lynch argued. 'Once our troops had been sent in, one could not control the situation.'

Kevin Boland, one of the Cabinet's most outspoken proponents of assisting nationalists in the North, concurred with that assessment of the situation. 'I, certainly, had enough common sense to see that interference by the Irish Army would be disastrous,' Boland wrote. 'Places contiguous to the border could obviously be assisted effectively, but to do so would mean the wholesale slaughter of nationalists (or Catholics) in other areas where there was no defence available. I feel reasonably certain that the others also saw this and that none of them visualised an actual incursion.'

Even if the Republic had had the military might to take the North, Lynch felt it would have been political lunacy to attempt this. 'We would have had a situation where a million people in Northern Ireland would have been prepared to take up arms against the new institutions and it would have been the reverse of the earlier position, perpetuating the internal strife which the IRA mounted in the North,' he argued.

Back in March, Lynch had talked about promoting reunification of the island 'by fostering a spirit of brotherhood' but now he spoke about requesting 'the British government to enter into early negotiations with the Irish government to review the present constitutional position of the Six Counties of Northern Ireland.' Although the speech was really little more than emotional posturing, it had an electrifying impact on the situation in the North, where besieged nationalists in the Bogside thought Irish forces were going to come to their aid, while the unionist population feared an imminent invasion of Northern Ireland from the Republic.

'We must and we will treat the government which seeks to wound us in our darkest hour as an unfriendly and implacable government, dedicated to the overthrow by any means of the statutes which enjoy the support of the majority of our electorate,' Terence O'Neill declared. James Chichester-Clark, the Minister for Agriculture, was just as intense a few days later. 'In this grave situation the behaviour of the Dublin government has been deplorable, and tailor-made to inflame opinion on both sides,' he said. 'The moving of the Army units, the calling up of reserves, the absurd approaches for United Nations intervention have all been moves of almost incredible clumsiness and ineptitude.'

Of course, Lynch had no actual plans to do anything in the North itself, much less invade the area with an army that was totally unprepared and woefully under-equipped. Conor Cruise O'Brien later criticised the speech as 'inflammatory' but he defended the Taoiseach against British accusations of inflaming the situation at the time. 'I said that the British public and parliament would do better to examine their own responsibilities, through their collusion with an oppressive sectarian system, over nearly fifty years,' Cruise O'Brien noted.

Defence Committees were being established in nationalist areas of the North and their representatives came to Dublin for help. They pleaded for arms to protect themselves, because they felt extremely vulnerable in the face of the irrational frenzy of the armed unionist community. The nationalists had few weapons, while the unionists frequently had guns, as they were often members of gun clubs. They also had the armed RUC and the dreaded paramilitary police reserve, the B-Specials, at their disposal. People who were later renowned as moderates were among those asking for guns to protect themselves. There were not enough British troops to protect them, and anyway, many felt that it would be naive to depend on the British for protection because they had done nothing about the discrimination against nationalists over the years. Cruise O'Brien personally felt that seeking arms was only increasing the danger, but he had no answer when the nationalists asked him: 'What would you do if your own house was attacked?' Although people would later claim that talk of a Protestant backlash was only a bluff, he believed that there was a very real danger of it at the time.

'The Catholics of Belfast in August 1969 had only too good reason to know that there was no bluff about it,' he wrote. 'In the circumstances the Dublin government, understandably, was under pressure to help the Catholics get guns for self-defence, and some of its members saw that they did get guns.'

'We asked for guns and no one from Taoiseach Lynch down refused that request or told us that this was contrary to government policy,' John Kelly, one of the young Belfast activists, later stated.

'I want to say categorically that I did not promise . . . arms to people who came to me from the North,' Lynch insisted, but he did not take issue with Neil Blaney's interruption that he had not refused them, either.

Kevin Boland was annoyed that the Northern delegations 'were being fooled by almost being promised the type of help they were seeking.' He was not impressed by the Cabinet decision to establish five field hospitals at the border, nor by plans for an international propaganda campaign, which he considered little more than idle talk. He saw the occasion as a great moment in history.

'I felt that surely now it would be seen that this was the opportunity for which the Warriors of Destiny [an obvious reference to Fianna Fáil, which literally means 'warriors' or 'soldiers of destiny'] had been waiting all these years,' Boland noted. 'For the first time, the oppressed community was standing out unitedly against oppression and saying they would have no more of it and they were insisting on their right to be Irishmen and Irishwomen.' At another Cabinet meeting on 15 August he called for Irish soldiers on UN duty to be recalled to the country immediately. 'I had gone to the Cabinet meeting intending to resign unless the Cabinet was prepared to give a real indication to the United Nations of the seriousness of the position in the country by the recall of our troops from Cyprus and by calling up the second-line reserve.'

Boland was more influenced by emotion than logic. He had ruled out an Army incursion, because it would invite the slaughter of nationalists, yet he did not seem to see the danger of threatening an invasion by recalling the troops in such a public way. This would undoubtedly have heightened the tensions that had already been inflamed by the Taoiseach's television address a couple of nights earlier. In the circumstances, ministers like Erskine Childers, Paddy Hillery and George Colley considered Boland's approach 'appalling'.

'I looked around the Cabinet table and saw a no-good pathetic lot,' Boland later explained. He promptly announced his resignation and walked out of the meeting, but he made no public statement to that effect. Blaney and Haughey tried unsuccessfully to talk him into withdrawing his resignation. President de Valera was then asked to use his influence. This was not only irregular, but also highly improper, because the President would seem to have been acting for party-political motives in inviting Boland to meet him at Áras an Uachtaráin.

'The President talked of the constitutional crisis – particularly on this issue,' Boland recalled. 'He foresaw a change to a Fine Gael-controlled government and pointed out the seriousness of this in the circumstances. I agreed that I did not want to change the government and, while I did not agree to withdraw my resignation, I said I would attend the next government meeting of which I was notified.' He was behaving like a spoiled child. 'I made a mental resolution that for the remainder of my time in government I would speak no word about the Six Counties at government meetings,' he explained. 'I admit, however, that I often helped (or endeavoured to help) Blaney out with scribbled notes.'

Although Boland liked to think of himself as helping the beleaguered nationalists in the North, he was providing no help at all, pouting within the Cabinet. Others of whom he was so highly critical felt that all Dublin could really do was provide moral support and financial help to relieve the distress.

'There was a feeling among the government, and among the community as a whole, that we could not do a great deal to help the people of the North,' Haughey explained. 'We knew that a lot of people were suffering very severe hardship and distress, and the government decided to be generous in coming to their aid. I was appointed as the person to see that this aid was given as freely and generously as possible.' The actual terms of the Cabinet decision were that 'a sum of money – the amount and the channel of disbursement of which would be determined by the Minister for Finance – should be made available from the Exchequer to provide aid for the victims of unrest in the Six Counties.'

'There was no sum of money specified,' according to Haughey. 'I was instructed by the government to make money available on a generous scale to whatever extent we required.' In short, he was given virtual carte blanche to help the nationalists financially. 'I have never seen a government decision that was drafted in such wide terms,' commented Charles H. Murray, the secretary of the Department of Finance.

A Cabinet committee, consisting of Haughey, Blaney, Pádraig Faulkner and Joe Brennan, was set up to deal with the government's lack of reliable information about what was actually happening in Northern Ireland. 'We were given the instruction that we should develop the maximum possible contacts with persons inside the Six Counties and try to inform ourselves as fully as possible on events and on political and other types of developments in the Six-County area,' Haughey later testified, but that committee never really functioned. Some of the ministers did their bit within their own department or just acted off their own bat.

Defence Minister Jim Gibbons was instructed to have the Army draw up contingency plans in case the government decided to intervene militarily in the North. As the Army had been starved of money for years, Haughey and Gibbons were told to ensure that the forces were properly prepared with the best equipment the State could afford.

'It was an amazingly irresponsible thing to do,' Kevin Boland noted. Haughey and Gibbons had been advocating a hardline policy with which Lynch did not agree, but he was giving them a virtual free hand. Part of their overall design was to ensure that people in the North were as prepared as possible in the event of what Gibbons called a 'doomsday' situation developing. They arranged for young men from Derry to join the Army reserve (FCA) in Donegal to receive training in the use of arms at Fort Dunree. As a natural corollary it was also decided that weapons would be made available to the people in the North to protect themselves.

In the coming months, Blaney and Haughey went their own way, with Lynch appearing to ignore their activities. He should have seen the danger signs within days.

On 20 August 1969 Peter Berry, the secretary of the Department of Justice, gave Michael Moran, the Minister for Justice, a seven-page document which, among other things, outlined details of a meeting between a Cabinet minister and Cathal Goulding, the chief of staff of the IRA. According to the report, an unidentified minister had promised that the government would not interfere with IRA operations in Northern Ireland if the IRA called off all its activities in the Republic. Moran related this at the next Cabinet meeting.

'That could have been me,' Haughey volunteered. He had been asked to see somebody and it turned out to be Goulding. 'There was nothing to it,' Haughey added. 'It was entirely casual.'

Berry 'was completely reassured', because Haughey had a good record in dealing with the IRA. As Minister for Justice, he had taken a resolute stand and played a major part in compelling the IRA to end the border campaign in 1962. It was therefore virtually inconceivable to Berry that Haughey would act in the irresponsible way described in the report, but the security people were not reassured.

'They repeated that their sources had proved reliable in the past,' Berry noted. They added that Haughey had actually promised £50,000 to Goulding. The Special Branch also reported that while in Britain recently, as part of a deputation sent by the Minister for

Finance to galvanise sympathetic support in Britain for nationalists suffering distress in Northern Ireland, Haughey's younger brother, Pádraig – better known as 'Jock' – had been involved with a northern Republican, John Kelly, who would play a major role in the unfolding drama. They were attempting to purchase arms, but this was called off when they realised that they had been rumbled by the British authorities.

The British Cabinet papers for 1969 clearly show that Harold Wilson's administration feared Northern Ireland was in danger of anarchy and saw the possibility that Irish troops would cross into Derry to defend Bogside Catholics. The British Ambassador to Ireland, Sir Andrew Gilchrist, reported that feelings in Dublin were violent and confused. People felt that something had to be done. Initially they were influenced by hardliners like Blaney and Boland. Gilchrist thought that they were looking for military intervention. 'I believe,' he reported, 'that the Irish Army was sounded out with a view to ascertaining what fulfillable orders should be issued to them over intervention designed to succour the Bogside Catholics.'

James Callaghan, the British Home Secretary, had previously found Lynch 'to be a cool, level-headed person' who was unlikely to get carried away in the heat of the emotions of the time. 'I really did not believe that he would involve the South in an invasion of the North,' he added. 'Nevertheless, the talk of opening hospitals on the border might conceivably be a blind for further troop movements, and it would have been imprudent to have ignored it.' The British responded by sending troops to Northern Ireland.

The introduction of these troops on 15 August 1969 lessened the demand for Irish intervention in two ways. The Catholics in troubled areas like Belfast welcomed the British soldiers as defenders, and this moderated the demands on Dublin for help. It also reduced the danger that the IRA would gain real credibility in the Twenty-six Counties by taking some kind of spectacular stand to defend the nationalist people in the Bogside area of Derry. 'Unless the [British] government took immediate and conspicuous action,' Gilchrist noted, 'the IRA would move first and attract widespread public support for violent policies.

'Very probably,' he continued, 'Lynch allowed some of his hotheads to believe this might happen, but I am reasonably sure he himself would not have permitted it, so long as he remained in charge.' In short, the ambassador did not think that Lynch would allow the Irish Army to intervene, but he pretended that he would in order to placate the likes of Haughey, Blaney and Boland.

Lynch's government was reacting to the crisis in a number of ways. In addition to his hardline speech, he launched a massive propaganda campaign to generate international sympathy for the nationalist position. The Government Information Bureau under Eoin Neeson seconded a number of public-relations people from the various government agencies and semi-state companies, such as Bart Cronin of the Department of Industry and Commerce, Colonel Jim Brennan of the Army, Jack Millar of Aer Lingus, Aidan O'Hanlon of Bord Fáilte, Frank Nealis of British and Irish Shipping, Tim Dennehy of CIÉ, and Percy Lovegrove and Martin Sheridan of Córas Tráchtála Teo. Other public-relations people drafted in included Don Brennan, Pat Comyn, Richard O'Farrell and John O'Sullivan, along with journalists like Lochlynn Mc-Glynn, John Ross and Seamus Brady. Most of these were then assigned to Irish embassies and consulates in London, Birmingham, Washington, Boston, New York, Paris, Bonn, Brussels, Rome, Madrid, Stockholm, Copenhagen and Canberra to explain what was happening in Northern Ireland, from Dublin's perspective at any rate. The Government Information Service wished to promote the idea of a federal solution, but this was deemed a non-runner by officials in External Affairs. Both hoped, however, that international publicity about discrimination and police brutality would embarrass the British into providing the Dublin government with some practical input into the government of Northern Ireland. It was also supposed to create a receptive climate for the Irish government's call for the United Nations to intervene in Northern Ireland, but this was really only posturing for Irish consumption.

After receiving what the British described as 'a courteous brush-off' at the Foreign Office in London, Paddy Hillery went to the United States, ostensibly to call on the Security Council of the United Nations to intervene in Northern Ireland. The British could have stopped any discussion of the matter, as it was a British domestic issue, but they went along with Hillery's little stunt. He was just posturing for the domestic audience, as there was never any real possibility that the United Nations would intervene, because even if there had been the remotest chance that a majority of the Security Council could be persuaded to support such a move, the British would have used their veto to kill the matter. The British representative, Lord Caradon, allowed Hillery to raise the issue, and then had the Zambian representative propose the matter be adjourned – and that was the end of it.

'Hillery said afterwards that he knew there was no prospect of a UN peacekeeping force,' British Home Secretary James Callaghan explained. 'But Lord Caradon's approach avoided giving him a personal rebuff while adhering firmly to the British position, and Lynch was able to show his fellow countrymen that he had taken the matter to the Security Council and done as much as he could.'

Eoin Neeson later claimed that the results of the propaganda campaign were 'rapid and rewarding', in the form of more balanced coverage of the Northern troubles in the foreign press, radio and television. This undoubtedly helped to temper the demand for action in Dublin, but Neeson was largely deluding himself about the situation abroad, because outside the Republic, the whole thing merely fuelled the paranoia of the Northern unionists and aroused the nationalist sympathies and emotions of some Irish-Americans.

Even though the Taoiseach specifically renounced the use of force, the British felt that he had upped the political temperature both by sending troops to the border and by launching the international propaganda campaign. In addition, the Irish diplomats abroad had engaged in anti-partition rhetoric, and Hillery further inflamed unionist opinion with his stunt at the United Nations.

Why did Lynch decide to send the field hospitals to the border? Some years later he wrote to the journalist Bruce Arnold that Dublin had been 'reliably informed that some Northern nationalists, many of them non-participants, having been injured in various incidents involving the security forces, were reluctant to seek treatment in Northern hospitals.' These Army field hospitals could provide some medical assistance, but the personnel had another brief, Lynch explained in his 1992 letter: 'At the time there were stories of some people in the South with ideas of assembling arms for use in the Six Counties either by themselves or for the IRA.' He said that he had therefore ordered the Army Chief of Staff to have the units on the border keep a lookout for gun-running and stop it wherever possible.

The Taoiseach's explanation that he sent medical units to do intelligence work is absolutely mind-boggling. Having heard rumours of gun-running, he sent medical units to investigate! Just who was advising the Taoiseach? He apparently could not trust about half of his Cabinet, and the Government Information Bureau was more interested in generating propaganda than in providing a balanced assessment of what was happening.

Ken Whitaker, who had grown up in Northern Ireland, had given Lynch some particularly astute advice the previous November. Force had long been ruled out, he noted. 'We were, therefore, left with only one choice: a policy of seeking unity in Ireland by agreement in Ireland between Irishmen,' he wrote to the Taoiseach on 11 November 1968. 'Of its nature, this is a long-term policy, requiring patience, understanding and forbearance and resolute resistance to emotionalism and opportunism. It is none the less patriotic for that. This is the policy enunciated and followed by Mr Lemass as Taoiseach and it underlies the contact made by him and by the present Taoiseach with Captain O'Neill and the members of his government.'

On 21 April 1969 Whitaker wrote a memorandum to Charles Haughey arguing that Articles 2 and 3 of the Constitution should be amended to take account of the extremely volatile situation in the North, as it 'might easily spread to the whole of this partitioned island'. This should be part of a broad policy of moderation in which Southern politicians should 'do nothing to inflame the situation further, but aim to impress the moderates on both sides, Catholic and Protestant'. He advocated a policy of deploring the turn of events in the North, while emphasising the desirability of the kind of social reforms which had sparked the civil-rights movement, and calling for a period of restraint, with no public demonstrations by either side for a few weeks. 'Avoid playing into the hands of extremists who are manipulating the civil-rights movement and who wish to stir up trouble and disorder. Civil war, or anything near it, would make real North–South unity impossible by destroying goodwill and creating fierce new enmities and divisions.'

Unfortunately, Whitaker was not available to advise the Taoiseach on the night of 13 August 1969, when he delivered his RTÉ address. Whitaker was on holiday in Carna, County Galway, and had no telephone in his cottage. Through the gardaí, Lynch did get word to him to telephone him a couple of days later.

Whitaker was horrified by the 'teenage hooliganism and anarchy' and he warned Lynch on 15 August that no government could benefit from appearing to support such behaviour. He gave a particularly perceptive warning against the 'terrible temptation to be opportunist – to cash in on political emotionalism – at a time like this.

'It should never be forgotten that a genuine united Ireland must be based on a free union of those living in Ireland, on mutual tolerance, and on the belief that the ultimate governmental authority will be equitable and unprejudiced,' Whitaker continued. 'Every effort should be made' to avoid identifying only with the Catholic side and 'a special effort' was needed to reassure moderate Protestants who might otherwise be driven into the arms of their own extremists by the fear of 'losing their "freedom, religion and laws".' Thus he cautioned Lynch against the appearance of the government as being 'driven before the emotional winds fanned by utterly unrepresentative organisations such as Sinn Féin', as well as the 'quite disproportionate publicity' that those elements had been given by RTÉ.

Unfortunately, Lynch had succumbed to both emotionalism and opportunism in his broadcast of 13 August 1969. He clearly realised that it had been a mistake, and he turned to Whitaker to draft a speech returning unambiguously to the old line of seeking 'the reunification of the country by peaceful means', emphasising repeatedly 'that we have no intention whatever of using force to realise this desire.' On Lynch's specific instructions, Whitaker included an insistence that the Dublin government had a right to be consulted about what was happening in Northern Ireland: 'Our views on how peace and justice can be assured in this small island are relevant and entitled to be heard. We have always believed, and recent events have in our view confirmed, that there can be no lasting solution which does not envisage the eventual reunification of Ireland.'

It was a carefully crafted speech, which not only echoed the advice that Whitaker had given to Lynch the previous November, but also stressed both the desire for unity and the determination to use only peaceful means to achieve that aim. 'This unity we seek is not something forced but a free and genuine union of those living in Ireland, based on mutual respect and tolerance,' Lynch

The young hurler: Lynch *circa* 1939

Courtesy *Irish Examiner*

Lynch leading the Cork team in a parade before the all-Ireland final against Kilkenny, September 1939

Courtesy *Irish Examiner*

Lynch with the McCarthy Cup after captaining Cork to an all-Ireland win in September 1942

Courtesy *Irish Examiner*

Lynch visits his old school, North Monastery, as Minster for Education, May 1957

Courtesy *Irish Examiner*

H. J. McCann, Seán Lemass, T. K. Whitaker and Lynch at Dublin Airport

Courtesy Lensmen

A private moment for George Colley, Seán Lemass and Lynch in Lemass's office on 9 November 1966. Lynch is telephoning his wife with the news that he is to succeed Lemass.

Courtesy Colman Doyle

Lemass formally congratulates Lynch on his victory in the leadership contest, as Colley looks on

Courtesy *Irish Examiner*

Lynch with British Prime Minister James Callaghan

Des O'Malley, former British Prime Minister Edward Heath and Lynch in 1990

Lynch meets President Lyndon B. Johnson at the White House, June 1968
Courtesy LBJ Library, Austin, Texas

Lynch and his wife, Máirín, greet President Richard Nixon, October 1970
Courtesy *Irish Examiner*

Lynch with
Jackie Kennedy

Courtesy
Colman Doyle

Pope John Paul II shaking hands with President Paddy Hillery, with
Cardinal Tomás Ó Fiaich, Lynch and Michael O'Kennedy, September
1979

Courtesy *Irish Examiner*

Lynch demonstrating the art of hurling to some young players

Courtesy Colman Doyle

President de Valera, Lynch and King Baudouin of Belgium at Áras an Uachtaráin. Lynch is explaining the rules of hurling to the King.

Courtesy Colman Doyle

President Erskine Childers welcomes Lynch to Áras an Uachtaráin, 1973
Courtesy *Irish Examiner*

Inauguration of President Patrick Hillery, November 1976. From left: H. Percy Dockrell, former president Cearbhall Ó Dálaigh, Garret FitzGerald, Paddy Hillery, Frank Aiken, Tom O'Donnell, Seán MacEntee, Tom Fitzpatrick and Lynch.
Courtesy *Irish Examiner*

Lynch with Patrick Hillery and Noel Lemass, on the occasion of Ireland's entry into the EEC

Courtesy Colman Doyle

Lynch presiding at an EEC summit conference in Dublin Castle, November 1979

Courtesy Lensmen

Lynch campaigning in the 1977 general election

Courtesy Colman Doyle

Lynch speaking at a victory rally at Grand Parade, Cork, following the 1977 general election

Courtesy Irish Examiner

Irish Times cartoon commenting on Lynch's return from the United States, November 1979

Courtesy Martyn Turner

Irish Times cartoon commenting on Lynch's announcement of his impending resignation, December 1979

Courtesy Martyn Turner

Lynch shakes hands with his successor, Charles J. Haughey

Courtesy Colman Doyle

Lynch in Tralee on 20 September 1969 after delivering his famous address outlining his Northern policy, with, from left, Tom McEllistrim Jr, Tom McEllistrim Sr and Tom McEllistrim III

Courtesy Tom McEllistrim Jr

Lynch and his wife, Máirín

Lynch and Máirín in Buncrana, County Donegal

Lynch being welcomed back to Cork following the 1977 general election victory

Courtesy Colman Doyle

Lynch receives thunderous applause as he takes the field as a member of the 'Team of the Century' on all-Ireland final day in Thurles, September 1984

Courtesy *Irish Examiner*

Jack Lynch
1917–1999

Courtesy Colman Doyle

declared on delivering the speech in Tralee on 20 September 1969. 'We are not seeking to overthrow by violence the Stormont Parliament or government but rather to win the agreement of a sufficient number of people in the North to an acceptable form of reunification.'

The *Irish Independent* welcomed 'the conciliatory tone' of Lynch's remarks and contrasted them in an editorial with the 'vituperative crudity' of Neil Blaney. 'We are left, however, to wonder who speaks the government's mind: a perilous and improper situation for a country whose political system boasts the cornerstone of collective responsibility,' the paper noted.

'I am glad your speech got such a good reception (though it was somewhat less conciliatory than I would have liked),' Whitaker wrote to the Taoiseach the following day. 'If only public speaking on this extremely delicate matter could be reserved to yourself and subject to your approval, to the Minister for External Affairs.' But it would be some time yet before Lynch would try to muzzle the Blaney element.

If force was being ruled out, James Callaghan reasoned that it would be necessary for the Taoiseach to win over the unionists by persuasion. 'If he really wants a united Ireland, he must conciliate Protestant opinion,' Callaghan noted. Lynch's response was to move towards amending the controversial Article 44 of the Irish Constitution, which recognised 'the special position of the Catholic Church'.

Lynch had a secret discussion with a representative of the British government who was unnamed in the Cabinet papers. The emissary described the Taoiseach as conciliatory but uncompromising at the same time. Lynch was remarkably straightforward and friendly throughout the interview. He warned, for instance, that Harold Wilson and his colleagues should 'not imagine that the Irish government could be told by the Northern Ireland Prime Minister, Major Chichester-Clark, by the British Foreign Minister or the Home Office Minister, Lord Chalfont, to keep its nose out of affairs in Northern Ireland.' Lynch said that he approved and admired the way Callaghan had handled things in the North. If that was the case, the emissary asked, why did the Irish blackguard him at the United Nations on civil-rights issues?

'Lynch professed to be offended and was shocked by the word "blackguard" and then dodged my questions by a long, uneasy and not always plausible defence of this sabre-rattling, arguing that he had done the least possible which would suffice to contain public opinion and prevent IRA propaganda successes,' according to the report. The Taoiseach argued that his strong public reaction to trouble in the North had been justified by results, in the sense that it had defused the situation in the IRA and enabled him to restrain the more warlike members of his Cabinet.

Irish policy was designed to embarrass not the British but Stormont, for its fifty years of injustice towards the nationalist minority in Northern Ireland, Lynch explained. 'In his own opinion,' Lynch said, according to the emissary, 'the South was quite incapable of taking over the North in the foreseeable future,' because of the financial and social adjustments that would first be necessary before there would be any possibility of the two societies coming together. He dismissed the idea of Catholic police for Catholic areas as an absurdity but he wondered if a beginning of a united Ireland might be made with cross-posting of police between North and South. Irish unity was not something that he thought could be arranged overnight; it would be a long-drawn-out process that would take seven to fifteen years.

'Mr Lynch asked me to assure Harold Wilson and James Callaghan that he and his Cabinet were sincere in wishing for a truce to rioting and anarchy in the North and that the genuine settlement of social justice in the North would be welcomed,' the emissary noted. But the Taoiseach was making no apologies for his government's behaviour at the UN. He bluntly warned Gilchrist that he would continue to take a close and public interest in Northern Ireland and the British should have 'no illusions about that'. He defended his own policy as restrained and said that the proposals made at the UN were 'moderate, forward-looking and not condemnatory.'

There was a tremendous ignorance in Dublin about what was really happening in the North. The situation had developed 'like a thunderclap on top of everybody,' according to Colonel Michael Hefferon, the Director of Military Intelligence. His deputy, Captain James J. Kelly, happened to be in Derry on holiday in August 1969 when the Battle of the Bogside began. A twenty-year Army veteran who had spent the previous ten years in Military Intelligence, Kelly reported his impression of events when he got back to Dublin.

'I was very glad of any information,' Hefferon said. 'I had to run around and try to find out the people that would give me the most because you had a whole lot of rumours going which had no foundation to them.' He instructed Captain Kelly to maintain his Northern contacts, and the captain made another visit to the North in September, this time accompanied by Seamus Brady, a journalist working on the government's propaganda campaign.

While in Belfast, Captain Kelly met with John Kelly (no relation), who had recently been in London with Jock Haughey attempting to purchase arms. John Kelly had joined the IRA back in the early 1950s and had been arrested in 1956 during the border campaign, spending seven years in jail. During the rioting of 1969, when Catholic and Protestant families were being burned out of their homes, many of the Catholics turned to the older members of the IRA for help. 'Remember, this was perceived as a doomsday situation,' John Kelly later explained. 'We were looking at the ethnic cleansing of Catholics to end all ethnic cleansings. And because I came from an old republican family, respectable nationalists who would never countenance violence were coming to the likes of me asking us to defend the Catholic areas. There was a lot of fear and ambiguity.'

Citizens' Defence committees were formed and people like John Kelly and his brother Billy looked to Dublin for weapons to defend their community. 'What we need are guns to protect the Catholics,' John told Captain Kelly. The Kelly brothers brought Captain Kelly to the home of a prominent nationalist who pleaded for weapons without delay. At the time, Northern nationalists were highly critical of the inactivity of the IRA, which seemed more concerned with lofty considerations of socialist dogma than with what was happening on the ground.

On the other hand, Cathal Goulding, the existing chief of staff of the IRA, felt that the young hotheads did not know what they were doing. 'I and others felt that the movement as a whole had never given a thought to winning a war,' he argued. 'They had only thought of starting one.'

Seamus Brady and John Kelly later discussed their visit with Brady's friend Neil Blaney, who was a member of the Cabinet committee charged with finding out what was happening in the North. Blaney arranged for them to meet Haughey.

Brady suggested to Haughey the possibility of establishing a newspaper and a pirate radio station to direct propaganda at Northern Ireland in order 'to maintain the newfound morale of the minority and to keep pressure up against the unionist authorities.' Government information and propaganda came under the aegis of the Taoiseach's Department, but Brady had a high regard for Haughey, so he was anxious to sound him out. 'As director of elections for the Fianna Fáil Party in two successive general elections, he had acquired, in my opinion, considerable expertise in regard to publicity and propaganda work,' Brady explained.

Haughey endorsed the idea of establishing the newspaper and even suggested that it be called the *Voice of Ireland* – an idea which was partially adopted when Brady launched the *Voice of the North* a few weeks later. The Taoiseach had not even been consulted. Haughey had essentially expanded his own remit with a certain contempt for Lynch and for the bulk of the Cabinet, because the idea was never presented to the government for approval. Therefore the Government Information Bureau refused to provide financial support for the project, and Brady turned to Haughey for help.

'He came to me,' Haughey said, 'and indicated that he had put £650 of his own money into the publication and he was now in difficulty with the Government Information Bureau because they were not prepared to pay up.' Haughey therefore agreed to talk to Lynch. 'I went to the Taoiseach on the matter,' he later recalled. 'The Taoiseach gave me a direction and a ruling that public moneys were not to be used for this publication.'

Haughey said that he told Brady to suspend publication of *Voice of the North*. 'I myself will see you all right with what you have spent if it comes to that,' he added. But then, with blatant disregard for the Taoiseach's instructions, the Department of Finance secretly financed Brady's newspaper by paying him over £5,000 from the money earmarked for relief of distress in Northern Ireland.

It was initially envisioned that the relief money for the North would be distributed by the Irish Red Cross, but it could not function in Northern Ireland, and Haughey was not about to give the money to the British Red Cross. He therefore turned to Military Intelligence for help.

'About the end of September,' Colonel Hefferon recalled, 'I was asked by Mr Haughey to see him at his residence and to bring Captain Kelly along.' Haughey was looking for advice in order to establish a committee of reputable individuals who would oversee the distribution of financial relief. Captain Kelly therefore briefed him on the position in the North.

At this point Haughey was particularly interested in the backgrounds of various individuals who had been coming down to Dublin to meet different ministers and part of secret delegations seeking help. 'Primarily the conversation was about the members of these delegations – any of them I had met – what information

I had concerning them and so on,' Captain Kelly noted. He told Haughey that he had arranged to meet between fifteen and twenty representatives from the various Defence Committees in nine days' time at a hotel in Bailieboro, County Cavan, but he needed money to cover his expenses. Haughey promptly instructed the Department of Finance to provide £500.

Captain Kelly's activities had already aroused the suspicion of the Garda Special Branch, which was disturbed that he had been meeting with known members of the IRA. Peter Berry, the secretary of the Department of Justice, was in hospital for tests when he learned that Kelly was in Bailieboro for a meeting with Cathal Goulding and other leading members of the IRA. Berry immediately tried to notify the Minister for Justice, but he was unavailable. He then tried to get Lynch, but he was not at home either, so he telephoned Haughey, who promptly called to the hospital.

'I told him of Captain Kelly's goings-on and of the visit planned for Bailieboro,' Berry noted. 'He did not seem unduly perturbed about Captain Kelly but was quite inquisitive about what I knew of Goulding. I felt reassured.'

Of course, Berry did not know that Haughey was providing the money to finance the Bailieboro meeting, and Haughey did not enlighten him. Berry had taken Haughey into his confidence, but the minister had not reciprocated. It was only a matter of time before the Special Branch learned of Haughey's involvement, and Berry naturally felt a sense of betrayal.

12

STANDING BY

1969–1970

When Peter Berry learned what had happened at the Bailieboro meeting from his sources, he was undergoing tests in hospital. He could not contact Moran, so he telephoned Lynch, who called to the hospital on the morning of 17 October 1969. Berry, who was sedated, tried to explain the situation with a tube going from one of his nostrils that was drawing fluid from his stomach. Two nurses and two doctors repeatedly entered the room to deal with the fluid. Lynch became exasperated at holding the conversation in such circumstances.

'This is hopeless,' he said. 'I will get in touch with you again.'

Although Berry later admitted to being 'a bit muzzy' at the time, he was certain he told the Taoiseach about Captain Kelly's activities. 'I told him of Captain Kelly's prominent part in the Bailieboro meeting with known members of the IRA, of his possession of a wad of money, of his standing drinks and of the sum of money – £50,000 – that would be available for the purchase of arms,' Berry wrote.

'Where would they get that money?' Lynch asked. Although they were planning to get it from the Department of Finance,

Berry did not know that. 'Two millionaires of the *Taca* group might put up the money,' he suggested.

'Those boys don't give it up that easily,' Lynch replied.

Little over ten years later Lynch told a rather different story. 'Berry had made no mention whatever of the alleged conspiracy,' Lynch noted. 'He did mention that there were, from time to time, a number of attempts to import arms with some success, as they had monitored them and in at least one case they knew where the arms were being delivered. It was a small consignment. I asked him why the Guards had not "pounced". He said it was not possible because the Guards felt it more prudent not to do it at that stage, as they felt that their source of information would be in danger.'

Lynch insisted that Berry had not told him at this meeting about the conspiracy to import the arms that were subsequently the subject of the arms crisis some months later. That whole matter was at a preliminary stage at the time, and it would have been clear only in hindsight that Berry should have mentioned it. All that Berry could have known in October 1969 was that Captain Kelly had merely passed on the promise to provide the money to procure arms. Indeed, that was what he said he told Lynch.

There is no doubt that Berry did tell the Taoiseach about the Bailieboro meeting, because a few days later Lynch questioned Jim Gibbons about Captain Kelly's involvement in Bailieboro. The Taoiseach told Gibbons that Berry was his source of information. In turn, Gibbons told Colonel Hefferon that Lynch had questioned him as a result of the meeting with Berry. In this way the story made the full circle. Later Gibbons stated that he 'did pass on information to the Taoiseach at that time in 1969 that there were questionable activities on the part of certain members of the government making contact with people they should not make contact with, certainly without the sanction of the government and the Taoiseach.'

'No person with a scrap of intelligence could doubt that the Taoiseach was made aware by me,' Berry insisted. Yet Lynch did not make 'any more than a cursory inquiry' about the Bailieboro meeting. This was seen as an indication that he did not wish to be informed about these matters, because he could not be seen to condone such conduct, but had no intention of interfering. Berry, who formed the distinct impression that the Taoiseach 'was not thankful to me for bringing awkward facts to his notice, suspected that Lynch actually wished to be able to turn a blind eye to the planned gun-running.' This assessment was shared by more than one member of the Cabinet.

There had already been rumours regarding an earlier importation of a quantity of small arms destined for Northern Ireland. Members of the government were certain that there had been gun-running, and Lynch admitted that Berry had informed him of this. Kevin Boland concluded that the Taoiseach privately approved of smuggling arms. 'As far as I could see,' Boland explained, 'everyone assumed everyone else knew and the matter was spoken of as if it was a case of the government assisting in the only way a government could assist without a diplomatic breach.' But Boland was convinced that Lynch would veto any gun-running, if someone brought it up at a Cabinet meeting. 'I felt sure this importation would not be agreed to by the Taoiseach if it came up for specific government decision,' he noted.

The Bailieboro meeting had nothing to do with providing arms for the Provisional IRA as such, because that organisation had not yet been established. Those who attended the meeting saw themselves as representatives of the Defence Committees from the North, rather than the IRA. Dublin preferred to finance them rather than Cathal Goulding's Marxist IRA, because Fianna Fáil had no truck with communists. Hence Captain Kelly favoured the defence groups.

On 30 October 1969 the *United Irishman*, the organ of Sinn

Féin and the IRA at the time, reported that Haughey, Blaney and Boland were trying to buy over Northern nationalists to Fianna Fáil. 'The party was cynically stumbling about trying to get in on the act in the North, but only to keep itself in power in the South,' wrote Seán Mac Stiofáin, who was shortly to become chief of staff of the breakaway Provisional IRA. 'Fianna Fáil has been running a propaganda sheet called *Voice of the North*. It has been providing some degree of aid to the Citizens' Defence Committee.'

Neil Blaney later claimed that he had a hand in the formation of the Provisional IRA. Although this was disputed by Mac Stiofáin, there was undoubtedly an element of truth in the statement, inasmuch as the offer of arms to the Defence Committee helped exacerbate the rift in republican circles, and the Provisional IRA was established within a matter of weeks of the Bailieboro meeting. Nonetheless, it would be a gross exaggeration to suggest that Blaney or the Dublin government created the Provisional IRA.

A relief committee of three Northern republicans was selected to administer the government's relief funds. They opened a bank account under their joint control in Clones, County Monaghan. Haughey personally telephoned the Secretary General of the Irish Red Cross to deposit £5,000 in the account. Thereafter Haughey's personal secretary, Anthony Fagan, would transfer money to the Red Cross with instructions that it should be forwarded to the relief account in Clones.

The Irish Red Cross was basically being used to launder the money in order to hide the involvement of the Department of Finance. Of course, this was also to protect the men from the North, as there would be hell to pay in the Six Counties if people knew the Irish government was funding their activities. Haughey instructed his staff to ensure 'that no communication should go north of the border which indicates that we are interested in helping out these people.' Captain Kelly acted as an unofficial liaison between the Minister for Finance and the Northern republicans. Whenever Haughey wanted information or to pass on a message to the Northern republicans, he would get Kelly to do it.

Sir Andrew Gilchrist, the British ambassador in Dublin, was naturally keeping a close eye on developments. Even at a very early stage, he believed that Haughey was very active behind the scenes. On 10 November 1969, for example, he reported to the Foreign Office that he had been trying to probe for some time a report linking Haughey with a small organisation in Monaghan devoted to cross-border activities. He noted that the organisation had been set up by Haughey with party funds and it contained an intelligence unit involving Irish Army Intelligence officers who briefed visitors to and from the North. There was also a propaganda unit in the organisation for liaison with civil-rights workers in the North, principally in the field of journalism, and funds were readily available for suitable contacts. Gilchrist had no doubt about these things, but he had to rely on conflicting rumours on other matters. He concluded, for instance, that Haughey had a greater passion for Irish unity than either Lynch or Hillery and was more convinced than either of them that the British government could not hold their position in the North. 'Hence his Monaghan organisation, which he would no doubt describe as an essential contingency plan to secure control of Northern Ireland through the civil-rights movement in a quicker time than Hillery's line of approach,' Gilchrist added.

The ambassador sought to determine to what extent the civil-rights movement in the North was looking to Dublin and away from loyalty and participation in a Northern administration, even a reformed one. Conor Cruise O'Brien explained to Gilchrist that Haughey's activities were not part of a subversive plan to pose an effective military threat. Instead, he argued that they were intended to come to public knowledge in order to bolster the image of

Fianna Fáil as the patriotic party, still striving for Irish unity.

The Monaghan organisation which the ambassador mentioned obviously referred to Haughey's funding of the group being organised by Captain Kelly and the *Voice of the North* newspaper that the Department of Finance was secretly funding.

The money deposited in Monaghan was transferred to Dublin, where two bank accounts were opened in the fictitious names of George Dixon and Ann O'Brien. Relief money allocated by the Department of Finance was then sent to the Red Cross with instructions that it should be forwarded to the relief account at a branch of the Munster and Leinster Bank in Baggot Street. Some of this money was then transferred to the George Dixon account to finance the purchase of arms, while some £5,000 of the relief money was transferred to the Ann O'Brien account, from which payments were made to Brady in support of his publication of *Voice of the North*, in blatant disregard of Lynch's instructions.

John Kelly was sent to the United States with the veteran republican Seán Keenan in November 1969. The trip was apparently funded out of the money voted for Northern relief, and Kelly believed that they went at the government's behest. 'We were sent by Jim Kelly with Neil Blaney's approval,' John Kelly later explained. 'We met the nucleus of what was to become Noraid. They were very reluctant to deal with us at first.'

'What are you doing taking money from the Free State government?' they asked.

John Kelly explained that Dublin was putting up the money for the guns. 'In the end we had everything arranged,' Kelly noted. 'The guns would go out through New York Port without any customs check and would come into Dublin Port the same way. We had the unions on both sides organised.' But Blaney scuppered that plan. He preferred instead to organise the importation through the Continent with the help of a business friend of his, Albert Luykx, who had been in jail after the Second World War in his native Belgium for collaborating with the Germans. Kelly thought that Blaney was afraid of the Irish-American connection, because the government would have no control over the guns coming in.

There is little doubt that Blaney was playing a major role in machinations in Dublin. He delivered a speech in Letterkenny, County Donegal, on 8 December 1969, at a celebration to commemorate his twenty-one years in the Dáil. 'The ideal way of ending partition is by peaceful means, but no one has a right to assert that force is irrevocably out,' he said. 'The Fianna Fáil Party has never taken a decision to rule out the use of force, if the circumstances in the Six Counties so demand.' He added that if the nationalist people were under 'sustained and murderous assault, as the Taoiseach said on 13 August, we "cannot stand idly by".'

This was not some off-the-cuff remark. It was a carefully prepared speech that Blaney took the unusual step of reading, and he also circulated it to the press. It was a challenge to the approach announced by Lynch in Tralee less than three months earlier. Although John Hume denounced the address as 'totally irresponsible', the Taoiseach behaved as if there was no challenge at all.

'While Mr Blaney's feelings on the partition issue are very deeply felt – and he occasionally finds it difficult not to give public expression to them – he knows and endorses government policy on this issue, as he did in his speech in Letterkenny,' Lynch said.

By this stage Blaney really held Lynch in contempt. 'Jack was a weakling,' he would say afterwards. 'I resent very much Jack Lynch's whole performance. I think he played silly, subtle games. And I had been a part of some of those games during that critical time.'

Blaney was openly defying the Taoiseach's announced policy and putting forward a policy of his own, while Lynch was acting as if such behaviour was perfectly proper. Blaney actually seemed to be gearing up for a leadership challenge. During October, in his feature column on the back page of *Hibernia*, Proinsias Mac Aonghusa was touting Blaney as a possible replacement Taoiseach.

'Blaney is the one major figure who has emerged well from the crisis so far,' Mac Aonghusa wrote. 'Inside the Cabinet he has demanded a tough, uncompromising approach. Most ministers will gladly go along with the Lynch line while it appears to give Dublin a voice in the issue and also keeps people in the Twenty-six Counties happy. But when the Northern crisis comes, Neil Blaney will be in a position to dictate what line is taken. With his close friend, Kevin Boland, he dominates the party organisation.'

After the Letterkenny speech, Blaney was asked on RTÉ's *This Week* programme if he would be interested in the position of Taoiseach. He pointedly refused to rule out the possibility. 'If there was a situation in which there was a Taoiseach being sought for the party and that the party wished to consider me, well then, in all possibility, I would have to consider very seriously the implications of that and leave it to the party's best judgement.'

Some of his ministers treated Lynch with contempt, but he ignored their behaviour. His style was one of consensus leadership. He was a team player who never tried to hog the limelight for himself, but he did not mind others going on solo runs. Cabinet colleagues like Neil Blaney, Kevin Boland and Charles Haughey held him in contempt, because he did not throw his weight around. Yet that was one of the reasons why people loved him.

Berry was passing on his information to the Minister for Justice, who said that he was informing the Taoiseach, but nothing was happening. In the last week of December 1969, Lynch did tell Moran that he wished 'to throw the book' at republicans from Derry who were arrested with weapons near the border in County Donegal.

On learning that the men had been arrested and charged with criminal activity, Haughey asked Berry who had given the gardaí 'the stupid direction'.

'I told him that the decision came from the very top,' Berry noted.

'Do you mean the Taoiseach?' Haughey asked.

'Yes.'

Berry explained that the charges would probably be dismissed, if the men recognised the court. Otherwise, he said, they would be committed for contempt. Haughey, who responded that he would ensure that there would be no contempt, remained furious. 'His language was not the kind usually heard in church,' according to Berry.

Blaney appeared to orchestrate an overt challenge to Lynch's leadership at the Fianna Fáil *ard fheis* on 17 January 1970. This was the biggest *ard fheis* in the party's history as it was held over a weekend rather than in midweek, as previously. The first four speeches in the debate on the Taoiseach's Department were made by delegates from Blaney's own Donegal constituency. They eulogised Blaney as the one member of the Cabinet to whom the beleaguered people of the Bogside had been able to turn during their crisis in August.

Kevin Boland waded in with a strong speech of his own denouncing partition. He said that there should be no concession 'whether directly or by implication of any legitimate British interest in any part of our country.' This was an overt attack on the Taoiseach's policy.

'I was criticising in public and to the Taoiseach's face his slavish acceptance, by his silence, of Callaghan's and Wilson's jingoism and his failure to comment on the deployment of the British Army as being useful in the circumstances created by them but entirely unacceptable in principle,' Boland wrote. 'The Taoiseach knew exactly what I was doing. He knew it was mainly to him I was talking in my speech and that I was castigating him in public.'

Lynch promptly confronted this challenge, departing from his prepared script in his presidential address to the party. James Doyle, the political correspondent of the *Cork Examiner*, reminded readers afterwards that in 1966 he had warned that those who thought that Lynch 'would be no more than a caretaker occupant of the office would be making the mistake of their lives about Jack Lynch, that they were forgetting the steel that lies behind that mild exterior.' The Taoiseach now demonstrated that he was not about to be brushed aside easily.

Those who advocated the use of force to eliminate the border might be advocating what appeared to be a romantic and heroic master stroke, but it would be wrong, Lynch warned. 'We may feel with our hearts,' he said, 'but we must think with our heads, for when the heart rules the head the voice of wisdom goes unheard.' It was patently obvious to all that the country did not have the military strength to end partition by force, but even if it did, that would be the wrong approach, because it would not secure unity. A sizeable minority would be aggrieved and left feverishly nursing grievances and secretly plotting revenge.

'The answer is surely clear, and because it is clear the government are determined to explore every peaceful means to remove the injustice of partition,' he declared. 'If anybody wants this policy to change, this is the place to do it and now is the time,' he said, throwing down the gauntlet. 'If people want this traditional Fianna Fáil policy to be pursued by me as leader of the government and the party, now is the time to say it.' At the end of the address the Taoiseach received a standing ovation that lasted for a full minute, with delegates chanting, 'We back Jack!'

Blaney promptly backed off and denied any intention of challenging the Taoiseach. 'No matter what inference may be given, there is no anxiety on my part: wherever I might be placed during the year,' Blaney said, 'one place I have no ambition to get into is his seat.'

Boland also backed off, and he seethed when his own speech was depicted by the media as a 'defence of the Taoiseach against the pro-Blaney flood tide.' Boland was particularly caustic about 'the superficiality of the political correspondents', who suggested that he had deliberately defused the challenge. 'They couldn't have been more wrong,' he wrote. 'I didn't set out to defuse the situation and my speech did not defuse it. If the situation was defused, this was done by the totally dishonest speech of the Taoiseach later in the evening. What I had done was to state as party policy the ideas which he was rejecting by his inaction.'

Lynch had clearly seen off the first challenge with some aplomb. He had won the support of the overwhelming majority of the *ard fheis* while Blaney found himself humiliated – compelled to protest his own loyalty and renounce the challenge launched in his name by his own supporters. At the same time Boland was reduced to silence in his own blind, seething indignation.

In early February 1970 Blaney summoned a couple of nationalist activists from Derry to meet him in Dublin. Paddy Doherty has recalled what happened in his memoir, *Paddy Bogside*, which provides an insightful glimpse into government divisions at the time. Doherty went to Dublin with Seán Keenan, who had been chairman of the Derry Defence Association and was a leading member of the breakaway Provisional IRA. Blaney told them that some .303 rifles that were being discarded by the Irish Army – as it had been equipped with more modern equipment – had almost fallen into the hands of loyalists in the North. By law, the weapons could only be sold outside the country and they were being sold off to a dealer in Liverpool. At Blaney's suggestion the dealer was checked out and intelligence sources learned that the man was acting on behalf of Northern loyalists. That scuppered the plan, but if the weapons could have been supplied to loyalists so easily, Blaney saw no reason why they should not be provided for the nationalist population. He was thinking of a scheme to get Haughey to supply the nationalist Defence Associations with the money to buy the decommissioned arms.

Blaney summoned Haughey to their meeting and he, in turn, suggested that Jim Gibbons should be invited. Two others were also considered, but Kevin Boland was not available and Michael Moran was indisposed.

'We were most exercised by the attempt by Protestant extremists to accumulate arms,' Doherty recalled. 'We also discussed the gun clubs set up by the disbanded B-Specials and the support they were receiving from Unionist MPs. We knew that the loyalists had about 100,000 legally held guns.' They feared that another 'pogrom against the Catholic population in Northern Ireland was on the cards'.

'Let's take the North,' Haughey said to Blaney and Gibbons. 'We should not apologise for what is our right.'

'We couldn't,' Gibbons replied. 'The Army is 3,500 under establishment figures.' A recruitment drive was already under way 'and I am preparing for a doomsday situation in Northern Ireland,' he added. 'If the fears expressed here become a reality, we will have to become involved.'

'I pressed him to explain why the training of Northern Irishmen by the Irish Army had been terminated,' Doherty continued. Gibbons explained that he called off the training after the press got wind of the story, but this would begin again as soon as possible.

'These men need to make their case to Lynch,' Blaney said. 'It's about time he did something.' But Blaney was not going to approach the Taoiseach. 'You'd better ring him,' Blaney said to Haughey. 'I can't stand the man.'

Haughey telephoned Lynch on the spot and made an appointment for Keenan and Doherty to meet him the following morning. Keenan suggested that the Taoiseach should be told in no uncertain terms what he should do.

'You can't walk in on the leader of a country and make demands, no matter how important or how just those demands might be,' Doherty warned. Gibbons agreed. He cautioned that such an approach would be counterproductive. Doherty argued that they should just present the facts of the situation to Lynch and hope that he would turn for advice to his Cabinet colleagues. Blaney, Haughey, Gibbons, Boland and Moran could then use their influence. Blaney suggested that they should get some kind of commitment from the Taoiseach and should press for the rifles which were being discarded to be given to the Defence Associations.

'We will ask that the weapons be held close by the Irish Army, close to Derry, so that we can be quickly armed in the event of an attack and play the rest by ear,' Doherty said.

'A commitment from the Taoiseach is essential,' Blaney insisted. 'If he won't deal with the .303s, ask him for gas masks. That's the least he can do.'

That night Doherty and Keenan stayed at the home of Captain Jim Kelly. Next morning they were accompanied to the Taoiseach's office by Billy Kelly, as a spokesman for the Defence Association in Belfast. He was a brother of John Kelly.

Lynch seemed shy as he invited them into his office. 'Some people had told me he was weak, but I didn't believe them,' Paddy Doherty noted. Lynch was still being dogged by the suggestion that he had been a compromise Taoiseach – a man with little support of his own, selected to hold the party together in the face of the more popular Haughey and Colley. This was absurd. Lynch had had much more support than either of them. He had routed Colley, and Haughey had withdrawn because his chances of winning had already vanished. But the tag of a compromise Taoiseach continued to plague Lynch, weakening the general perception of his political position.

'I noticed what I thought was a sad look on his face and I felt sympathy for the man who had to shoulder so much responsibility at this moment in Irish history,' Doherty wrote. The Taoiseach seemed worried that the Scarman Tribunal investigating the troubles in Derry would blame him for sparking the unionist backlash by declaring that the Dublin government would not 'stand by'. But he felt that his speech in Tralee had helped to mollify the situation.

'I became worried and wondered if the look of sadness was really one of guilt,' Doherty recalled. 'If it was, then it would be difficult to persuade him to respond positively to our request.' Keenan urged Lynch to be prepared for the inevitable confrontation. Reading the situation, Doherty suggested that guns were not necessary. Keenan followed his lead and merely suggested that the weapons should be stored so as to be accessible for ready distribution, near the border in County Donegal. At that point, however, Billy Kelly waded in. He demanded guns to protect the nationalist population of Belfast.

'I watched the Taoiseach flinch under the demands,' Doherty recalled. 'I tried to calm Kelly down by returning to the situation in Derry, which was much more manageable. I asked Lynch to provide gas masks.'

'Gas masks I can give you, even for humanitarian reasons, but guns I will have to think about,' the Taoiseach said.

Lynch then turned the discussion to partition and stunned his visitors by suggesting that a speedy end to partition was out of the question. 'If we were given a gift of Northern Ireland tomorrow, we could not accept it,' he said. The British were spending £150 million annually on social services in Northern Ireland, and Dublin would have to provide that to sustain the existing standard of living in the North. If it provided it for one part of the country, it would have to provide the same services elsewhere and a multiple of the £150 million would be needed. The country simply did not have that kind of money, but he suggested that with the current rate of economic growth, the Republic would be able to afford unification in about a decade.

Although Doherty was despondent on leaving the Taoiseach's office, he was surprised to find that Keenan and Kelly were jubilant. They thought that Lynch had given them a commitment to provide weapons. 'We blew it,' Doherty told them. 'That man has no intention of getting involved in Northern Ireland.' Too many people were hearing only what they wanted to hear.

On 6 February Jim Gibbons informed Colonel Hefferon that delegations from the North had been making urgent demands on the Taoiseach and other ministers for 'respirators, weapons and ammunition, the provision of which the government agreed.' The Minister for Defence specifically ordered the Director of Intelligence 'to prepare the Army for incursions into Northern Ireland.' Lynch later confirmed for the Army chief of staff that this order was a Cabinet decision, though it would seem that it was just another order to prepare contingency plans.

At the time, Army planners concluded that they could send 800 soldiers across the border as far as Newry, but they would not be able to keep them there for twenty-four hours. Even then, they would take heavy casualties. As a result it would seem that Conor Cruise O'Brien's allegation that the Irish Army could not hold a good-sized town in Armagh was justified.

During the following weeks and months, Captain Kelly visited Germany on a number of occasions to purchase a variety of weapons, including machine-guns, grenades, rifles and pistols, as well as flak jackets and ammunition. It was initially planned to ship the arms from Antwerp on the *City of Dublin*, which set sail on 19 March and docked in Dublin six days later.

As Minister for Finance, Haughey used his authority to instruct customs to authorise entry of the cargo without inspecting it. Captain Kelly and John Kelly were at the Dublin docks with a lorry to take the arms to a hiding place, but the weapons had not been loaded because the papers for them were not in order. Apparently British intelligence had put a figurative spanner in the works.

There was uneasiness within the Cabinet in Dublin. Boland urged Haughey to secure government approval for the plan to arm the nationalists. Although an honest and honourable politician, Boland was not one of the more perceptive members of Dáil Éireann. Haughey had no intention of confronting the Taoiseach as Blaney had done – with such embarrassing consequences – at the recent *ard fheis*.

The money for the North was being handled in a highly secretive way throughout all of this. 'We administered this particular money more or less along the same lines as we would administer the Secret Service Vote,' Haughey explained. On 2 March 1970, when he sought formal Dáil approval for the expenditure of £100,000, the whole thing was passed without any difficulty. 'Nobody asked me questions,' he noted. 'It went through without any discussion whatsoever.'

Captain Kelly made a further trip to the Continent, and brought Albert Luykx to act as his interpreter. At first the captain planned to have the cargo transferred to Trieste for shipment to Ireland, but while it was en route it was off-loaded in Vienna when the Lufthansa personnel became suspicious. It was initially hoped to fly the consignment directly to Ireland on an Aer Lingus plane on 7 April, but this had to be cancelled because it was against the law to transport explosives on a commercial flight. This was not just a consignment of small arms for mere defensive purposes. There were 200 sub-machine guns, 84 light machine-guns, 50 general-purpose machine-guns, 50 rifles, 200 grenades, 200 pistols and 250,000 rounds of ammunition.

Captain Kelly returned to the Continent the following week and arranged the charter of a cargo plane, owned by an Aer Lingus subsidiary, to fly the weapons from Vienna to Dublin. He was in Vienna supervising arrangements on Friday 17 April when Brian Lenihan, the Minister for Transport and Power, tipped off Colonel Hefferon (who had retired from the Army the previous week) that Dublin Airport had been staked out by the Special Branch, whose aim was to seize the arms and arrest Captain Kelly on arrival.

On learning of this, Haughey telephoned Peter Berry.

'You know about the cargo that is coming into Dublin Airport on Sunday?' Haughey asked.

'Yes, Minister.'

'Can it be let through on a guarantee that it will go direct to the North?'

'No.'

'I think that is a bad decision,' Haughey said. 'Does the man from Mayo know?'

'Yes.'

'What will happen to it when it arrives?'

'It will be grabbed,' replied Berry.

'I had better have it called off,' Haughey said, and then hung up. The following morning Haughey's office instructed Captain Kelly to call off the operation.

Berry was particularly reassured by Haughey's question about 'the man from Mayo', which was an obvious reference to Moran. If Haughey did not know whether Moran was aware of the whole operation, it meant that Moran was not in on the whole thing. Until that conversation, Berry had not been able to decide whether Moran was also involved in the planned gun-running.

Moran had a serious drink problem at the time, with the result that Berry was not sure that he was actually passing on the warnings to the Taoiseach. The Special Branch had been on top of matters for the past few months but the government had done nothing about its warnings. Moran did complain to at least one colleague that he had been trying to get Lynch to act on the matter, but the Taoiseach would do nothing.

Berry had been harbouring his own doubts about Lynch after nothing had happened following his warning about Captain Kelly's activities back in October. 'I had some lingering doubt that all this could not have gone on for several months without the knowledge of the Taoiseach, unless he was wilfully turning the blind eye,'

Berry wrote. The time had come to force Lynch's hand.

Berry went to President Éamon de Valera on the pretext of seeking advice about what to do if he was not sure the Minister for Justice was passing on information 'of national concern' to the Taoiseach. As he had confidently expected, de Valera told him to go directly to the Taoiseach. Berry then went to Lynch and told him that President de Valera had advised him to tell the Taoiseach what was happening.

'By consulting the President, and telling the Taoiseach that I had consulted the President,' Berry wrote, 'I would be pushing the Taoiseach towards an enforcement of the rule of law.'

Berry told the Taoiseach about the planned gun-running. Lynch immediately instructed him to have the whole matter investigated thoroughly and to report again the following morning, when Berry confirmed that Haughey and Blaney had been involved in the plot.

Lynch decided to interview Blaney and Haughey on 22 April 1970, but Haughey had a riding accident that morning. Returning from his morning ride at about 8.30, he reportedly tried to lift himself off the horse by grabbing the guttering above the stable door, but it gave way with a loud crack that frightened the horse, which shied. Haughey was thrown heavily to the ground and suffered fractured ribs, a ruptured eardrum, a broken right collarbone and a fracture to the tip of one of the bones in his back. He was due to deliver the budget address that day.

'Before leaving his home this morning the Minister for Finance met with an accident which has resulted in concussion,' Lynch told the Dáil. 'He is now in hospital and has been ordered to remain under medical observation for some days. Therefore I will introduce the financial statement myself.'

There were the usual speeches in support of and against the budget. Very few had any idea of what was going on behind the scenes. But one person who knew a little more than others was Neil Blaney, who concluded his long speech by stressing the need for government unity. This probably puzzled most people, but in the light of subsequent events, it was obviously a coded warning to Lynch.

'We should also keep in mind that this government will be here, bar some strange and extraordinary happening – and there could be one that comes to mind – but bar that,' Blaney said.

'An earthquake?' Michael O'Leary of the Labour Party interjected.

'No, but the next thing to it,' Blaney remarked.

That evening there was an incident at the Gresham Hotel during a reception for visiting members of the Canadian Bar Association. As Minister for Justice, Michael Moran was invited. He was seated next to the president of the Canadian bar, who delivered an address during which he made some reference to Serjeant A. M. Sullivan, who had been a distinguished member of the Irish bar. Sullivan had defended Roger Casement during his treason trial in 1916, but later apparently sided with Dublin Castle during the Black and Tan conflict. Moran took exception to the mention of Sullivan's name.

'Don't you dare mention that man's name!' Moran snapped. He was apparently drunk. When the speaker ignored him and referred to Sullivan again, Moran rose to his feet and shouted that he was leaving in protest against the repeated references to a man whom he held in contempt. He then stormed out of the room, but he was apparently so disorientated that he actually stumbled through the hotel kitchen, leaving his fellow guests and the hotel staff as dumbfounded as his Canadian hosts. It was a staggering perform-ance of extraordinary bad manners.

Moran subsequently checked himself into hospital for treatment. The Chief Justice of the Supreme Court, Cearbhall Ó Dálaigh, was so incensed by Moran's insulting behaviour that he privately called on Lynch to dismiss the Minister for Justice. For Lynch it must have seemed like his government was crumbling. Two of his ministers were in hospital, and he was facing the biggest political crisis since the Civil

War. He could not even get in to visit Haughey.

'I sought permission from his doctor to interview him in hospital but he refused to give it for several days because of the serious condition of his client, who, he told me, had a fractured skull,' Lynch explained. It seemed strange that Blaney and Boland were able to visit Haughey, but not the Taoiseach.

All kinds of rumours were already circulating by then. Berry told Lynch that the Garda Commissioner had reported a rumour that 'Haughey's accident occurred in a licensed premises on the previous night.' It was suggested that he had been upstairs in a public house, in bed with a young woman, and was caught by the woman's father and brother, who supposedly almost beat him to death.

'Oh no,' Lynch exclaimed. 'Not that too!'

Lynch was emphatic that there should be no garda inquiries into the matter. But that did not stop the speculation. 'Within a couple of days there were all sorts of rumours in golf clubs, in political circles, etc, as to how the accident occurred, with various husbands, fathers, brothers or lovers having struck the blow in any one of dozens of pubs around Dublin,' Berry noted.

'I ultimately got the doctor's permission and I decided to interview Deputy Haughey in hospital on Wednesday 29 April,' Lynch explained. Before the meeting the Taoiseach was very agitated. 'What will I do? What will I do?' he kept muttering as he paced about his office.

'Well, if I were you,' Berry said, 'I'd sack the pair of them and I would tell the British immediately, making a virtue of necessity, as the British are bound to know all that is going on anyway.' Lynch had not been looking for advice, however. He had just been talking to himself and he abused Berry for having the impertinence to advise him.

The Taoiseach spoke first to Blaney, who denied any involvement in smuggling arms and flatly refused to resign. 'Nothing doing,' Blaney said. 'Forget about it, I'm not resigning. I've done nothing. Why should I resign?'

Lynch let the matter stand and then went to the hospital to speak to Haughey, who also denied that 'he instigated in any way the attempted importation of arms'.

'They asked me for time to consider their position,' Lynch told the Dáil. 'I agreed to do so.'

Back in August, when Boland resigned, the Taoiseach had just ignored him and the whole thing blew over. Now it was the other way around – the two ministers were refusing to resign – and Lynch apparently decided to forget about the whole thing, hoping that it could be swept under the carpet. He sent for Berry on 30 April and told him that he had talked to the two ministers and that the matter was therefore ended, as there would be no repetition of the attempted gun-running. Berry was stunned.

'Does that mean Mr Haughey remains Minister for Finance?' he asked incredulously. 'What will my position be? He knows that I have told you of his conversation with me on 18 April and of the earlier police information.'

'I will protect you,' replied Lynch.

The Taoiseach also held what amounted to a conference with the Attorney General, Jim Gibbons, Berry, Chief Superintendent John P. Fleming and the new head of Military Intelligence, Colonel Patrick Delaney. Lynch later told the Dáil that this meeting was necessary because the Minister for Justice was in hospital and he called the conference 'to coordinate as well as I could the evidence that was available from both of the special sources and also to receive guidance from the Attorney General.' Yet throughout the meeting he never asked either Fleming or Delaney any questions. He obviously knew all he wished to know, and he became annoyed afterwards when Berry remarked that Fleming and Delaney were puzzled about why they had been asked to attend and were then ignored.

Lynch was not looking for information. He was just trying to contain the situation.

13

THE ARMS CRISIS

1970

On 1 May 1970 the Taoiseach told his Cabinet that he had decided to accept the denials of Blaney and Haughey that they had been involved in attempted gun-running. But he warned, according to Boland, 'that henceforth no minister should take any action in regard to requests for assistance from the Six Counties without approval.'

That same day the Special Branch arrested James Kelly, who had retired from the Army the day before. He was taken to the Bridewell but refused to answer any questions. He demanded to talk to Jim Gibbons, who explained that the whole thing was an investigation for the Taoiseach. The detectives would not leave Gibbons and Kelly alone together, so Kelly refused to talk again. But he did indicate that he would answer questions for the Taoiseach, as it was his investigation. Kelly was therefore taken to the Taoiseach's office by Chief Superintendent Fleming, who agreed to leave Kelly with the Taoiseach. There was a secretary present. Lynch explained that the secretary was needed to take Kelly's statement.

'But I'm not making a statement, Taoiseach,' Kelly said.

Lynch became impatient. He was a busy man with a lot of important work to do, he said. He had been led to believe that Kelly had asked to see him and agreed to make a statement to him if the Taoiseach would meet him.

'No, I'm sorry Taoiseach, I don't agree. When the suggestion was put to me that I talk to you, I agreed to do so, nothing more; there was no question of a formal statement.' Kelly would not answer any questions about the involvement of ministers in the whole affair, either. 'It's out of my sphere,' he argued. 'It's a question for the Cabinet, a matter between you and your Cabinet colleagues.'

Lynch explained that the whole thing had serious international implications. 'Too many people know about it – departments of state, various individual functionaries – it cannot be swept under the carpet,' he said. Lynch then asked if members of the Cabinet were involved.

'Possibly.'

'Two members?'

'Yes, possibly.'

'Names?'

'It is not my business to name people in this situation.'

Lynch said that he knew them anyway.

'Then you should approach them yourself, Taoiseach,' Kelly said.

'But I have approached them, they won't talk to me.'

'I'm sorry, Taoiseach, I'm afraid I can't help.'

Lynch realised that he had to remove Moran as Minister for Justice. He was still in hospital at the time, drying out. The Taoiseach visited him and they had a brief meeting at which Moran essentially told Lynch that he could have his resignation without any argument. He then ordered the Taoiseach to get out of his room.

'He will go quietly,' Lynch told Berry.

'As Taoiseach,' he told the Dáil, 'I should like to announce, for the information of the Dáil, that Deputy Michael Moran yesterday tendered his resignation to me as a member of the government. I have advised the President, and he has accepted the resignation with effect from today.' It was a cold statement that pointedly contained no expression of regret, or any of the usual expressions of appreciation for the work done. Moran had been a member of the Dáil since 1938, and he had entered the Cabinet at the same time as Lynch, with the result that he was one of the most senior members of the government.

'Can the Taoiseach say if this is the only resignation we can expect?' Liam Cosgrave asked.

'I do not know what the deputy is referring to.'

'Is it only the tip of the iceberg?'

'Would the deputy like to enlarge on what he has in mind?' Lynch asked. However, the Dáil then moved on to its regular business. Most of the press had no idea what was behind the exchange, or that Cosgrave had already got wind of the trouble within Fianna Fáil. A few days earlier he had received an anonymous note which read:

> A plot to bring in arms from Germany worth £80,000 for the North under the guise of Dept. of Defence has been discovered. Those involved are Captain James Kelly I.O., Col. Hefferon, Director of Intelligence (both held over the weekend in the Bridewell), Gibbons, Haughey, Blaney and the Jones brothers of Rathmines Road and Rosapena Hotel in Donegal.
>
> See that this Scandal is not hushed up.
>
> Garda

This was then confirmed for Cosgrave by another source. According to Stephen Collins, political correspondent of the *Sunday Tribune*, one of the tips came from Phil McMahon, a retired head of the Special Branch. Cosgrave shared the information with Ned

Murphy, the political correspondent of the *Sunday Independent*, but Hector Legge, the newspaper's editor, decided not to run the story. This may have been either in the national interest, as he contended, or to avoid the danger of expensive complications with the country's draconian libel laws.

When Lynch was asked in the Dáil by Michael Pat Murphy of the Labour Party if Moran's resignation had been requested, he seemed to prevaricate. 'The resignation was tendered,' he replied. But the opposition deputies pressed for a direct answer. 'His resignation was tendered to me on grounds of ill-health,' the Taoiseach explained, as he tried to avoid admitting the truth. Later, when Kevin Boland openly stated that Moran's resignation was demanded, Lynch expanded on his explanation a little further. 'I was conscious too of his physical condition, and frankly,' he said, 'I did suggest to him that he should resign because of that condition.' By then, however, the issue had been swamped by other events.

Following the announcement of Moran's resignation, Cosgrave informed some trusted colleagues about the anonymous warning that he had received. They advised him to go to the Taoiseach with his information.

'Deputy Cosgrave approached me and showed me an anonymously typewritten note allegedly involving the two ministers in an attempt to illegally import arms,' Lynch recalled later. He told Cosgrave that the note was true. 'I decided then that I could no longer await the recovery of one of the ministers before requesting them to tender their resignations.'

Cosgrave returned to tell his colleagues. 'It's all true,' he told them.

At 9.45 p.m. Blaney was chairing a meeting of the Fianna Fáil National Organisation Committee at Leinster House when he received a note summoning him to the Taoiseach's office. About a quarter of an hour later, Boland was in the parliamentary secretaries' dining room with Paudge Brennan when Blaney came in to say that the Taoiseach had demanded his resignation and had warned him that if it was not tendered immediately, the President would be instructed to dismiss him.

Boland was incensed. He immediately wrote a letter of resignation to the Taoiseach. 'As you know, I have found myself in disagreement with your handling of the Six-County situation for some time,' he wrote. 'Apart from this, I find the present method of government intolerable. I accordingly submit to you, herewith, my resignation as a member of the government.' Paudge Brennan, his parliamentary secretary, also submitted his resignation.

At about two o'clock the following morning, Lynch telephoned Peter Berry to inform him that Cosgrave was aware of the story and that he was insisting on the resignations of Haughey and Blaney from the Cabinet. At 2.50 a.m., he issued a statement to the press that was to cause a political earthquake:

> I have requested the resignation of members of the government Mr Neil T. Blaney, Minister for Agriculture, and Mr C. J. Haughey, Minister for Finance, because I am satisfied that they do not subscribe fully to government policy in relation to the present situation in the Six Counties as stated by me at the Fianna Fáil *ard fheis* in January last.

Among those Lynch consulted was Frank Aiken, who was still a member of the Dáil, having retired to the backbenches after the last general election. 'You are the leader of the Irish people – not just the Fianna Fáil Party,' Aiken told him. 'The Irish people come first, the party second and individuals third. If you are asking me what I would do, the whip would be off these two men as from now.' In short, he felt that they should not only be dismissed as ministers but should be expelled from the Fianna Fáil parliamentary party.

As people woke up, later that morning, the country was awash with rumours that the Taoiseach had discovered plans for a *coup d'état*. At 10 a.m. Lynch led members of his government, as well as the dismissed ministers, at the annual commemoration at Arbour Hill. Afterwards the Dáil met briefly at 11.30 a.m. and the Taoiseach confirmed that the resignations of Haughey and Blaney had not been received, but added that he was entitled to have them removed under the Constitution.

'The country has been in the throes of a crisis greater in magnitude than anything experienced since those stormy, far-off days of the Treaty debates, which were but a prelude to the darkest chapter in the sad history of this island, the Civil War,' the *Cork Examiner* proclaimed.

The Dáil reconvened at 10 p.m. that night and the Taoiseach announced the appointment of Desmond O'Malley as Minister for Justice. He explained that he had had Haughey and Blaney removed because the security forces had informed him 'about an alleged attempt to unlawfully import arms from the Continent.' As Haughey and Blaney were reportedly involved, he said that he asked them to resign, on the basis that 'not even the slightest suspicion should attach to any member of the government in a matter of this nature.' A highly charged debate ensued throughout the night and the following day, and only ended with a formal vote on O'Malley's nomination at around 2.30 the next morning. During the vote, scuffles took place in the voting lobby: a couple of pictures were knocked off the wall and a bust of one of the 1916 leaders toppled.

During his speech, Lynch read from the anonymous Garda note, as did Liam Cosgrave, the leader of the Opposition, but neither of them mentioned that Jim Gibbons had been named in the note. If he had been involved in this plot, it would have been legal, because as Minister for Defence, he had the authority to import arms. Gibbons later testified under oath that he had been fully informed about the gun-running plans. Although he was never asked on the stand what he told the Taoiseach, he subsequently said that he had kept him fully informed. If he had not informed him, why did Lynch not demand his resignation along with those of Moran, Blaney and Haughey?

One suggestion that some would later make was that Lynch knew that Blaney and Haughey could never be prosecuted if Gibbons was involved, because of his right to authorise the importation of arms. Of course, this would have involved a whole different conspiracy – a conspiracy to set up both Blaney and Haughey on felony charges. It would have been 'felon setting', as Kevin Boland later charged. But if Gibbons had been conspiring with them behind the Taoiseach's back, it would have been utterly reckless of Lynch to rely on Gibbons to turn around and engage in a different conspiracy against them. The much more logical explanation was that Gibbons had indeed informed Lynch, who had been turning the blind eye, as Peter Berry suspected.

Lynch sought to play down the sense of crisis at a dinner on 7 May, referring to the former ministers as 'able, brilliant and dedicated men'. The following day he announced one of the most extensive Cabinet reshuffles in the history of the state. Except for himself, Minister for Foreign Affairs Paddy Hillery and the newly appointed Minister for Justice, virtually every other minister was moved.

Colley became Minister for Finance and the Gaeltacht, Gibbons was moved from Defence to Agriculture and Fisheries, Joseph Brennan was transferred from Labour to Social Welfare, Paddy Lalor went to Industry and Commerce, and Bobby Molloy, Gerry Cronin and Gerald Collins were promoted from parliamentary secretaries to the respective ministries for Local Government, Defence, and Posts and Telegraph. David Andrews was appointed parliamentary secretary to both the Taoiseach and Minister for Defence, as well as Fianna Fáil Chief Whip.

The debate on these appointments turned into a marathon affair lasting some thirty-six hours straight. Captain Kelly had told the press that his actions were sanctioned by Gibbons, who denied this in the Dáil. 'I wish to deny emphatically any such knowledge or consent,' Gibbons said. 'I was aware through the Director of Intelligence that there was a danger of attempted illegal importation of arms and at all times these activities were kept under closest observation. I discharged my duty to the full extent of my knowledge of the situation.' This was a lie, as he would have to acknowledge some months later.

Kevin Boland said that he did not resign over the Taoiseach's dismissal of Haughey and Blaney, but because he found 'the conditions under which the government has to operate as intolerable, and inconsistent with the dignity of free men.' He resented that the security forces could pass on information about ministers. He specifically named Peter Berry, contrary to the rules of the Dáil. Instead of keeping ministers under surveillance, he said, the gardaí should have been trying to find the person who had murdered Garda Richard Fallon some weeks earlier. That was particularly ironic, because gardaí suspected that Neil Blaney had helped the murderer to escape across the border. That rumour was so strong that Blaney actually mentioned it in the Dáil.

On 14 May 1970 the government had to face a formal vote of confidence. The Taoiseach claimed that he could not be specific about some of the charges against the ministers because those involved might yet be prosecuted. 'If the Attorney General takes no action, that will not be the end of the matter, and I am not afraid to give to the country what information, what evidence I have about this whole transaction,' he told the Dáil. 'This, however, is not the time.'

The confidence vote was won easily, by 72 to 64, with Haughey, Blaney, Boland and Paudge Brennan voting with the government. Moran abstained, as he was still in hospital. If the five of them had voted against the government, it would have fallen, but none of them was ever able to bring himself to vote against the Fianna Fáil government.

On 27 May 1970 Captain Kelly, John Kelly from Belfast and Albert Luykx were arrested and charged with conspiring to import arms illegally. The following day, Haughey and Blaney were arrested, charged, and promptly released on bail. Although the media as a whole had been slow to question Lynch's motives in dismissing his two ministers, there could be little doubt that political considerations played a major part in the timing of their arrest.

Both still enjoyed support within the parliamentary party, so there was a danger that their supporters might react emotionally to the arrests and bring down the government in a fit of pique. Haughey and Blaney were not arrested with the others. Their arrest took place the day after the Dáil broke up for the long weekend. It was not due to reassemble until the following Wednesday. This gave deputies a chance to get over their initial shock and time to ponder the consequences of bringing down the government.

Kevin Boland was, as usual, outraged. He accused Lynch of 'felon-setting' and 'unparalleled treachery' and he called for a special party *ard fheis*. 'There is certainly a leadership crisis,' Boland declared at a press conference called by Seamus Brady. But Lynch responded that there would be no election and no *ard fheis*. To call a special *ard fheis*, Boland needed the backing of one third of the party's branches, and this would take at least three weeks to gather.

As it turned out, however, Boland had nothing like that kind of support in the party. When the Fianna Fáil parliamentary party met on Wednesday 3 June, he was told to withdraw his accusations against the Taoiseach, but he refused and was expelled from the parliamentary party, by 60 votes to 11. A fortnight later, he resigned from the National Executive of Fianna Fáil, and his father, Gerry, one of the leading founding members of Fianna Fáil, resigned as a national vice-president of the party.

Yet when it came to voting in the Dáil, Kevin Boland still

dutifully trooped into the government lobby rather than risk bringing the government down. A public-opinion poll conducted by Irish Marketing Surveys found that Lynch was the choice for Taoiseach of a staggering 89 per cent of those who had voted for Fianna Fáil at the last general election. In the circumstances, Boland's challenge had even less chance than Blaney's, earlier in the year.

The dissidents again voted with the government in the adjournment debate before the summer recess on 31 July. It was not planned to meet again until 28 October 1970. Lynch played the party-unity card with some finesse. 'So long as I have the support, the strength and the confidence – and I have – I will let no organisation, no opposition, no clique – I repeat, no clique, person or persons, wherever they come from – assail the unity and strength of the Fianna Fáil party.'

Notwithstanding Lynch's enormous popularity in the polls, there was considerable political uneasiness during the summer. On 5 July senior Cabinet ministers and the security chiefs held an emergency meeting as a result of some unfounded rumours of a possible *coup d'état*. The gardaí placed an armed guard on Berry's home and began escorting him to and from work in a police car. He was also given a pistol and instructed in its use. Ever since the book of evidence for the forthcoming arms trial had been circulated on 17 June, he and his family had become the target for particular abuse. With the marching season reaching its peak in the North on 12 July, there was a massive exodus of nationalists, especially from the Catholic areas of Belfast, as some 1,600 refugees fled to Army camps in the Republic.

Lynch made an appeal to the Catholic population on 11 July not to interfere with the Orange parades on the following day. He essentially called for a new attitude towards the partition problem. 'Let us not appeal to past gods as if past generations had said the last word about Ireland,' he declared. 'We have our opportunity to say for our generation what is in our hearts and minds.'

Erskine Childers was appointed to replace Gerry Boland as vice-president of Fianna Fáil, and Patrick Hillery replaced Kevin Boland as a joint honorary secretary on 12 July. Lynch had cleared another political hurdle with some panache.

Throughout the summer, the Special Branch kept Haughey and his home under surveillance, but he kept a low profile, avoiding public contact with Blaney or any of his co-defendants. Peter Berry reported to the Minister for Justice, Des O'Malley, that Haughey had been seen at Tralee Races with Brian Lenihan, the Minister for Transport and Power. With the arms trial due to begin in September, Berry commented on the inadvisability of ministers consorting with Haughey before the trial, because Special Branch officers had the former minister under surveillance and might get the wrong impression. This was a subtle admonishment of O'Malley himself, who had also been seen with Haughey in Tralee.

Their meeting lasted only about a minute and a half, according to O'Malley, who explained that Haughey had asked to meet him. O'Malley had agreed to call out to Haughey's Kinsealy home when he got back to Dublin the following week. Berry objected strongly to such a meeting in Kinsealy, because Special Branch would inevitably learn about it. If O'Malley was determined to go ahead with the meeting, Berry said, it should be in the minister's own office in Leinster House, beyond the gaze of the Special Branch.

Following a half-hour meeting with Haughey in Leinster House on 9 September, O'Malley told Berry that their conversation had centred on Berry's statement in the book of evidence and the testimony he was likely to give at the trial. 'He said that Mr Haughey's principal worry was over my evidence and that he had asked if I could be "induced", "directed" or "intimidated" into not giving evidence or changing my evidence,' Berry recalled. Berry asked if 'induced' meant bribed, but O'Malley did not answer him.

'The whole nature of the meeting,' Berry added, 'left me in no doubt that he [O'Malley] was pretending to Mr Haughey that he was a friend. It gave me a touch of nausea.'

'I suppose, in retrospect, I would not have met him,' O'Malley noted more than a decade later, 'but it is easy to say that many years after the event.' In September 1969, he saw nothing wrong with such a meeting. 'I thought it quite appropriate at the time,' he contended. 'I had told Mr Berry beforehand that I was meeting Mr Haughey and I told him afterwards what had transpired. But unfortunately the connotation is put on it that I made some kind of request to him, which I certainly didn't. I factually reported what had happened because I thought it was appropriate that he should know.'

The trial began on 22 September 1970. The defendants were charged with having 'conspired together and with other persons unknown to import arms and ammunition illegally into the State' between 1 March and 24 April 1970. The real issue was not whether they had sought to import arms – that was essentially admitted – but whether the planned importation would have been legal or not.

As Minister for Finance, Haughey had used his authority to instruct Customs to admit the unspecified consignment without inspection. Michael Moran testified that from his perspective the entire government was aware of Captain Kelly's activities and that he remembered John Kelly being discussed in Cabinet, but he was hazy as to specific dates, because, he said, he had been denied access to notes he had made on files at the Department of Justice.

Gibbons admitted on the witness stand that Captain Kelly had told him at their first private meeting that he intended to help the Northern people in looking for guns. He further admitted that the captain had given him details of a botched attempt to import the guns on a ship from Belgium in March, and had also told him that he intended to try to ship them from southern Europe.

'I seem to have a recollection of Captain Kelly mentioning the possibility of having them shipped through a port in the Adriatic because I suggested to him would that port possibly be Trieste,' Gibbons told the court. He admitted that he had not even suggested that Captain Kelly should have nothing to do with the gun-running.

By the time Gibbons left the stand on the fifth day of the trial, the prosecution's case was in trouble. It received a further damaging blow when Colonel Michael Hefferon testified as a state witness. He had retired from the Army just before the arms crisis, after almost eight years as Director of Military Intelligence. He testified that Captain Kelly had always acted with the knowledge and approval of Hefferon himself, though not under his orders. There was an obvious break in the chain of military command. While Captain Kelly was reporting to Colonel Hefferon, he was apparently taking his orders from one of the members of the government. As Director of Military Intelligence, Hefferon had reported directly to the Minister for Defence on a regular basis, and he kept Gibbons fully briefed on Captain Kelly's activities. He testified, for instance, that he had told Gibbons that Kelly was going to Frankfurt in February 1970 to make inquiries about purchasing weapons.

'Were you satisfied at that time that the Minister for Defence had full knowledge of the activities of Captain Kelly?' Hefferon was asked.

'Yes,' he replied emphatically.

The prosecution seemed surprised at this evidence. There was no indication in the book of evidence that Hefferon was going to take that line, but this was because his original statement to the gardaí had been selectively edited to remove all pertinent references to Mr Gibbons. Des O'Malley, the Minister for Justice, later contended that 'the bits that were excluded were inadmissible in evidence, because they related to expressions of opinion, or they related to details of conversations that did not take place in the presence of any of the accused and, as a result, would not have been admissible in evidence against any of the accused.' The evidence was clearly admissible, as demonstrated by the fact that it was given in evidence not just once, but on two separate occasions before two different judges.

After Hefferon left the stand, the prosecution case was in tatters, but the judge declared a mistrial after one of the defence barristers accused him of conducting the trial in an unfair manner. Haughey was livid.

'Get off the bench, Ó Caoimh,' he shouted. 'You're a disgrace.'

A member of the jury said immediately afterwards that the defence 'had the case won' without even presenting their side of the story. 'It was not a guilty verdict, even at this stage,' the juror told Captain Kelly. 'As the trial went on,' *Private Eye*, the satirical British magazine noted, 'it became clear that if Mr Haughey and his co-defendants were guilty of importing arms into Ireland, so was the entire Irish Cabinet.'

There was a lot of speculation about the judge's motives in declaring a mistrial. 'Was it that, having heard the critical evidence, he did not want to have to direct the jury?' Kevin Boland later asked. Some people thought the judge was simply giving the state an opportunity to drop the case without having to suffer the indignity of losing it in open court.

A new trial began on 6 October 1970 with Seamus Henchy of the High Court presiding. Gibbons again admitted not only that Captain Kelly had told him about the plan to bring in the arms but also that he himself had made no effort to indicate any degree of disapproval of the plan. In addition, there was the testimony of Captain Kelly and the invaluable corroboration of Colonel Hefferon that Gibbons had been fully informed of the whole operation and the Minister for Defence had never disapproved of it. In fact, they had been convinced that he was authorising it.

The two army officers had been very effective witnesses. 'No one in Dublin with whom I discussed the case – and I discussed it with many people of widely different views,' Conor Cruise O'Brien wrote, 'had any hesitation in believing Captain Kelly and Colonel Hefferon.'

Haughey testified that he only knew that the cargo contained items 'needed by the Army to fulfil the contingency plans', and so he authorised its clearance through Customs. He said that he did not know, or for that matter care, about the actual contents. It would have made no difference if he had been told that guns were involved. He added that he called off the shipment on 18 April in order to avoid bad publicity.

'It was made clear to me,' he explained, 'that the Special Branch wished this cargo to come, and wished to seize it. I was quite certain in my mind that evening that something had gone wrong, and that Army Intelligence was clearly at cross purposes with the Special Branch, and there was a grave danger of an unfortunate incident occurring at Dublin Airport with, as I said, all the attendant publicity.' But throughout all this he maintained that he did not know for sure that a consignment of arms was actually involved. Peter Berry, Captain Kelly and Jim Gibbons had known when Haughey talked to them about controversial consignments, but he contended that he never knew himself what they were really talking about, and he never asked them.

'Do you tell us that a conversation took place with your colleague, the Minister for Defence, in the privacy of your office – with nobody else present – and you decided between you to call off the importation of a certain consignment, and that that conversation began and ended without you knowing what the consignment was?' Haughey was asked.

'Yes,' he replied. 'Nor did he mention what the consignment was.'

'Did you not ask him what it was?'

'No. It did not arise. In my mind was present the fact that this was a consignment being brought in by Army Intelligence in pursuance of their own operations.'

'As a matter of simple curiosity, were you not interested at that stage in finding out what the cargo was that all the hullabaloo was about?'

'No,' replied Haughey, 'the important thing was that the Army and Special Branch were at cross purposes, and that it had better be stopped. I don't rule out the possibility that it could well have been in my mind that it could have been arms and ammunition – but it could have been a lot of other things.'

His contention that he did not know if the consignment contained arms certainly stretched credulity. Kevin Boland later stated that Haughey did talk to him about the arms, but Boland was not called as a witness.

John Kelly was allowed to make an unsworn statement to the jury. In the course of his remarks he quoted from Paddy Hillery's speech at the United Nations, but when he referred to what he called Lynch's 'we will not stand idly by' speech, the judge intervened to rule that Kelly could not quote extracts from speeches. This prompted Conor Cruise O'Brien to observe that the judge 'seemed more interested in keeping out references to the Taoiseach than he was in eliminating other supposed irrelevancies.'

'You are entitled to say anything you wish to say to the jury which bears on your own defence, within reason,' the judge told John Kelly.

'My lord, this would bear on my own attitude. This is part of the reason why I stand in this court today; these are the reasons why I stand here.'

'It is not normal for people making statements, sworn or unsworn, to quote from political speeches,' the judge insisted.

'Specifically, this is the situation in Belfast and what circumstances that I first met Captain Kelly,' John Kelly argued.

'If you would kindly pass on to that.'

'Well,' said John Kelly, 'I reluctantly pass on, my lord, because I think what Taoiseach Lynch said is very, very significant as far as I am concerned, but I will pass on reluctantly.'

'Please do.'

'Everything that happened within that time leaves me in no doubt whatsoever but that what was being done was being done with the full knowledge and consent not only of Mr Gibbons, but of the government as a whole,' John Kelly added in his statement to the jury. 'It is my conviction that I stand here and those who stand with me, that we are here as a matter of political expediency, and not from any desire that the course of justice be impartially administered.

'My lord,' he continued, 'I find it a very sad occasion indeed, that these institutions for which so much was sacrificed, which had been gained by such nobility, should be abused in this manner. There is no victory for anyone in these proceedings, my lord. There is only an echo of sadness from the graves of the dead generations. I thank you, gentlemen, I thank you, my lord.' This was virtually theatre. The public gallery burst into applause, and one member of the jury was seen to join in the clapping.

In his closing statement Haughey's counsel contended that Gibbons was posturing when he claimed to have been opposed to importing the arms, as he had never even suggested to Captain Kelly that the whole thing should be called off. 'If Mr Gibbons's attitude to what was happening was as he now declares it to be, surely he would there and then have said, "Captain Kelly, you cannot go on with this – this must stop." But Gibbons did nothing. He let the captain go out of his office without a reprimand, a rebuke or a warning.

Delivering his summation to the jury, the prosecutor challenged Haughey's testimony. 'For the purpose of establishing the case made by Mr Haughey in his defence, it is necessary,' he said, 'to disbelieve the evidence of four other witnesses: Captain

Kelly, Mr Fagan, Mr Berry and Mr Gibbons.'

For one thing, Captain Kelly had testified that he had told Haughey of the nature of the consignment, which flatly contradicted an integral part of Haughey's defence. Moreover, there was 'one piece of evidence which is crucial to the case, crucial in the sense that a verdict in favour of Mr Haughey cannot be reconciled with this piece of evidence,' the prosecutor continued. 'Mr Berry said that Mr Haughey said on the telephone: could the consignment be let through if a guarantee was given that it would go direct to the North?

'Gentlemen,' he added, 'if it was just Mr Haughey and just Mr Berry, or just Mr Haughey and just Mr Fagan, or just Mr Haughey and just Mr Gibbons, or just Mr Haughey and just Captain Kelly, nobody could quarrel with the decision that you are not prepared to reject Mr Haughey's account. But I think you have to consider the cumulative effect of the evidence: is he right, and all they wrong? Because you, gentlemen, have got to hold that they are all wrong.'

In his charge to the jury on the final day of the trial, 23 October 1970, the judge directed that 'in fairness to Mr Haughey' the whole question of the financing of the guns should be ignored. He then spent some time on the conflict of testimony between Gibbons and Haughey, content that one of them had committed perjury. 'There does not seem to me to be any way of avoiding a total conflict on this issue between Mr Haughey and Mr Gibbons,' Henchy stated. The discrepancies were so great that he did not think they could be attributed to a simple lapse of memory by one of the participants. 'I would like to be able to suggest some way you can avoid holding that there is perjury in this case.'

The crucial issue was whether Gibbons had authorised the importation. If he had, then the operation was legal. Mr Justice Henchy told the jury that they could conclude that when Gibbons 'got information about the attempted importation into the port of

Dublin, and the projected importation from Vienna, and when he did not say no, in categorical terms, Captain Kelly was entitled to presume that Mr Gibbons was saying yes. That is a view that is open to you.'

The verdict was a foregone conclusion. What Kevin Boland called the 'establishment representatives who had attended each other day of the case' were conspicuous by their absence from the court on the last day. 'Everyone had come to cheer the inevitable result,' he wrote.

Lynch was not even in the country, but he was making news himself in New York, where he had gone to speak at the United Nations. While there, he had his first ever meeting with British Prime Minister Ted Heath. He said afterwards that he pressed Heath on the need for reform in Northern Ireland. On the final day of the arms trial, the lead story in the newspapers at home was Lynch's address to the General Assembly of the United Nations, in which he emphasised his belief that the future of Northern Ireland lay with the rest of the island, but he called this 'an historic problem which we are determined to solve peacefully'. It was a strong speech, somewhat on the lines of Éamon de Valera's famous radio address in reply to Churchill at the end of the Second World War in Europe, but of course it lacked the sense of occasion.

'Mine is a country which has suffered much from war – repeated again and again through hundreds of years,' Lynch said. 'There was no recognised Irish state when I was born. But there was an Irish nation which had survived a war of conquest forced upon it long ago by ambitious rulers of another state. Our country was regularly made into a cockpit of war and its life was warped by human misery.' It was all gloriously irrelevant but it was enough to capture the headlines at home.

It took the jury only forty-eight minutes to reach a verdict at the Four Courts. The four defendants were found 'not guilty' on all counts. 'Immediately, the court erupted into a wild scene of cheering and shaking hands,' Captain Kelly recalled. 'People jumped for joy and I pushed through the exuberant crowd to arrive on the street, battered and in disarray.'

Haughey was surrounded by a force of gardaí, who escorted him out of the courtroom. Outside in the foyer, his supporters were ecstatic. 'We want Charlie,' they shouted. 'Lynch must go.'

In the Four Courts Hotel immediately afterwards, Haughey was in defiant mood. 'I was never in any doubt that it was a political trial,' he told the press.

'The whole prosecution was born out of politics,' Michael Moran told a reporter. 'There is a leadership crisis in our party,' he added. 'This is something that will have to be solved in the first instance by the parliamentary party.'

'I think those who were responsible for this debacle have no alternative but to take the honourable course that is open to them,' Haughey told the press conference.

'What is that?'

'I think that is pretty evident,' he replied. 'There is some dissatisfaction with the Taoiseach at the moment.' He was clearly challenging Lynch to resign. When asked if he would be a candidate for Taoiseach himself, Haughey replied that he was 'not ruling out anything'. His remarks were 'unanimously interpreted by the media as a dramatic throwing down of the gauntlet to the Taoiseach,' according to Kevin Boland. 'After a long silence, Mr Haughey was exploding into action and coming out with all guns blazing.'

But Lynch was in a confident mood in New York. There was no doubt of an attempt to smuggle arms and that those acquitted were involved, he said. Even though Haughey was acquitted in court, he had misbehaved, as far as Lynch was concerned. 'He certainly did not keep me informed of a vital matter,' Lynch told Sean Duignan of RTÉ in New York. 'I think that a government must exist on complete mutual trust and confidence. That was certainly absent on this occasion.' He added that Blaney was similarly involved. 'He clearly knew of this attempt to import arms for some period.'

Lynch seemed confident of coping with any challenge to his leadership. 'If the issue is raised,' he said, 'I look forward to the outcome with confidence.'

It was expected that he would meet a barrage of questions from journalists at Dublin Airport, as his former ministers – Haughey, Blaney, Boland and Moran – were all calling for his removal. But Lynch's supporters were ready for a showdown. They called on all members of the party to be at Dublin Airport on 26 October to welcome the Taoiseach home and thereby show solidarity. Forty-four Fianna Fáil deputies showed up, which was a comfortable majority of the parliamentary party. The twenty-seven who stayed away included the four former ministers, as well as people like Paudge Brennan, Flor Crowley, Bill Loughnane, Ben Briscoe, Vivion de Valera, Noël Lemass, Chub O'Connor and Ray Mac-Sharry. The turnout at the airport dealt a devastating blow to Haughey's challenge.

The Taoiseach was lifted by the turnout. Any member of the party was free to table a motion challenging for the leadership of Fianna Fáil, and Lynch seemed to dare his opponents to challenge him. 'If they want to do that, then I'll face that motion, and face it with confidence,' he said. 'If that's what they want to do, they ought to do it.'

The call to be at the airport 'looked like a light left lead rather than a knockout punch, but Mr Haughey has a glass chin, because that was the end of the fight,' Boland later stated. Unlike Boland, who was as naive as he was politically irrational, Haughey was a realist with no stomach for a fight that he could not win. He was prepared to bide his time. He did not press his challenge at the parliamentary party the next day, but Lynch insisted on an open vote of confidence in his own leadership.

Five members – Blaney, Geoffrey Timmons, Des Foley, Seán

Sherwin and Paudge Brennan – indicated initially that they would not support the Taoiseach, but after more discussion and the realisation that Haughey's challenge was not going to materialise, Brennan and Sherwin reversed their decisions. The final vote was 70 to 3. The dissidents had been routed.

Having already been expelled from the parliamentary party, Boland was not at the meeting. He was particularly critical of the outcome. 'The hat thrown into the ring was the wrong hat,' he wrote, 'because it was taken out again at the first sign of resistance and the government survived.'

The Taoiseach was really in an unassailable position within Fianna Fáil. Haughey recognised this and waited nine years for his opportunity, while Kevin Boland impetuously led the assault against Lynch from outside the parliamentary party, with disastrous political consequences for himself. Lynch could not have selected a more appropriate foil, because the rash, hard-headed Boland lacked both the political skill and judgement to overcome the wily Corkman.

14

THE BITTER AFTERMATH

1970–1971

When things go wrong domestically, a Taoiseach can often turn the spotlight onto international affairs by taking a stand on high-profile issues. Just before the start of the second arms trial, in October 1970, Richard M. Nixon became only the second sitting American President to visit Ireland. The Taoiseach was advised about what he should and should not say to Nixon. 'We do not think that it would be appropriate to touch on the Vietnam situation,' he was told by the Department of Foreign Affairs. 'We are not directly involved in any way in the Vietnam situation and publicly to give advice on the subject in such a speech might be resented and perhaps even evoke a reply.'

Thus, Lynch passed up another opportunity to express an opinion on one of the greatest crises of the cold-war period. This was in marked contrast to the earlier policy of Éamon de Valera, who took strong independent positions on the major crises of the 1930s and 1940s. The tradition was continued by the government of Seán Lemass, which took a strong stand in favour of the admission of communist China to the United Nations – much to the chagrin of the United States.

The Nixon visit was somewhat marred by an incident that occurred when a protester threw an egg at his car as he drove by. The egg splattered on the President's suit.

During a brief private meeting with Nixon, the Taoiseach outlined the Northern situation. He suggested that James Chichester-Clark, the Prime Minister of Northern Ireland, 'may not last under extremist right-wing pressure. A successor who would not put through real reforms would mean great trouble for the minority in the North and for Dublin.

'Direct rule from Westminster is a possibility,' the Taoiseach said, 'but, although we would object, it might be preferable to a hardline government, as we could press Westminster to put through reforms. We are worried about the pace and pattern of reforms, especially the vital housing and local government ones.' The Taoiseach mentioned that 'an expression of US friendly concern to the British would be appreciated.'

The two men were joined by John Moore, the US ambassador to Ireland, and Hugh McCann, the secretary of the Department of Foreign Affairs. Nixon played down the Vietnam situation. He said that 'the Middle East and Europe are now much more important than Vietnam.'

The day that Nixon left Ireland, a major crisis was developing in Canada. The British trade commissioner, James Cross, was kidnapped by the Front de Libération du Québec (FLQ), the militant Québecois counterpart to the IRA. Five days later Pierre La Porte, the Minister for Labour in the Quebec provincial government, was kidnapped. His body was found in the trunk of a car on 18 October. Lynch was about to leave for New York, where he was due to address the United Nations.

As with Nixon and Vietnam, the Department of Foreign Affairs advised Lynch not to be become involved in the La Porte affair. 'I suggested to the T[aoiseach] that we had some reservations about the matter, as a provincial minister and internal Canadian security and policies were involved,' Hugh McCann of the Department of Foreign Affairs noted, 'but he wished to issue a strong statement nevertheless.'

A statement was drafted and Lynch 'made some changes'. The statement was then handed to the Canadian Ambassador and to RTÉ for the 6 p.m. news. 'On behalf of the government of Ireland, I deplore and wish to express our horror at the cold-blooded murder of Mr Pierre La Porte, the Minister for Labour of the Provincial Government of Quebec. The killing of this man, democratically elected to promote the well-being of all his people, is a crime which merits the condemnation of the entire civilised world.' Lynch also expressed the hope for the safe release of James Cross, who was eventually freed unharmed some weeks later.

As has been mentioned, Lynch was in New York when the arms trial ground to its inevitable conclusion, and while there he had his first meeting with the new British Conservative Prime Minister, Edward Heath. Even though Britain and Ireland were very close geographically and had so many common interests, the two leaders would not meet again for more than ten months. When Haughey issued his challenge in the immediate aftermath of his acquittal at the arms trial, the Taoiseach was able to make his grand return.

Little over a week later, Charles de Gaulle died in France. Although he had not endeared himself to Ireland by the manner in which he effectively blocked Irish membership of the EEC, he did redeem himself by coming to Ireland for his extended holiday while the campaign to select his successor was being fought out in May and June of 1969. Attending de Gaulle's funeral in France allowed the Taoiseach to secure a further respite from domestic politics.

Many people who met Lynch were impressed by his un-assuming modesty, a quality that is rare among leading politicians. One could not conceive of Lynch saying, as de Gaulle had done during an address at a dinner given in his honour by the French ambassador to Ireland, Emmanuel d'Harcourt, in Dublin on 18

June 1969: 'I, de Gaulle, am honoured to be here because you are d'Harcourt. And you, d'Harcourt, are honoured to have me here, because I am de Gaulle.'

Lynch's unassuming demeanour had a great appeal for people at home, but it apparently made little impression on world leaders. Over the years he had private meetings with a whole range of international leaders – American presidents Lyndon Johnson, Richard Nixon and Jimmy Carter; French presidents Charles de Gaulle, Georges Pompidou and Valerie Giscard d'Estaing; German chancellors Kurt Kiesinger and Helmut Schmidt; and British Prime Ministers Harold Macmillan, Alex Douglas-Home, Harold Wilson, Edward Heath, James Callaghan and Margaret Thatcher – but one finds few mentions of Lynch in any of their auto-biographies or biographies.

Richard Nixon's only reference to Lynch was a passing mention to having met him at the White House on 16 March 1971, which was the First Lady's birthday and also the day that the couple's daughter Tricia informed them of her intention to marry. One sensed that the meeting with the Taoiseach that day was memorable only because it disrupted the family occasion.

Even though Lynch's government had overcome the arms crisis and the political threat posed by Charles Haughey's challenge to the leadership, the Taoiseach was still faced with a whole series of crises during the remainder of the Dáil term. In late November, Peter Berry learned that a hard core of about fifteen activists in the republican splinter group Saor Éire were planning to kidnap him and hold him for ransom against the extradition of one of their members who had been arrested in Britain. The following day, Des O'Malley, the Minister for Justice, instructed Berry to prepare the documents necessary for the government to invoke internment without trial of the Saor Éire activists. Berry was told that the decision would be taken at a Cabinet meeting the following Tuesday, 2 December 1970.

Berry suspected that the decision had essentially been taken by a kind of cabal within the Cabinet, and he later accused the government of using the kidnap threat as a pretext for internment in order to win the popular support of the large Protestant population in a Donegal by-election that was taking place on 2 December. But if that had been their aim, surely they would not have held off the decision until the exact day. If they had waited until after the Cabinet meeting to make the announcement, more than half the day would have passed by the time word got out, and most people would probably have voted before they even heard the news.

The whole thing was badly handled, because the government left itself open to the charge of being prepared to resort to naked political opportunism against the recommendations of the security authorities. No facilities had been prepared for internees. One of the biggest objections was that it would open the way for Stormont to introduce a similar measure in the North that would probably be directed solely against nationalists. Berry decided to resign as secretary of the Department of Justice. He had had enough, as his family was under intense pressure. His daughter had to have armed protection, and his wife had been hospitalised on three different occasions with heart trouble as a result of stress.

On Friday 4 December, the government issued a statement indicating that it intended to reactivate the internment provisions of the Offences Against the State Act. This led to uproar in the Dáil the following week. 'Let it be perfectly clear at the outset that the government has interned nobody,' the Taoiseach said, going on to explain that the announcement was really intended as a warning to certain individuals that if they did not abandon their illegal intentions, they would be interned. He did not specify what they were planning but he did say that the government did not want to see 'kidnapping and things of that kind happen in this country.'

'The government considered all the repercussions, North and

South, that might flow from the warning given,' Lynch explained. 'The warning should have no repercussions in terms of similar action in the North, as it is directed against a specific plot here.'

About a thousand people gathered outside the Dáil to protest. Speakers included Eamonn McCann, Bernadette Devlin, Sinn Féin Secretary Mairín de Búrca, and Mick O'Riordan of the Irish Communist Party. 'This is a matter of politics and class and has to be fought as a class war,' Bernadette Devlin told the crowd.

The Taoiseach was in defiant mood inside Leinster House. 'The government intend to protect and defend the lawful rights and liberty of our people, no matter how unpopular we may become in doing so,' he declared. 'That is the least that any government worthy of the name can do.' He was not seeking the permission of the Dáil, he was merely informing the assembly that the government was invoking the powers it already had under the Offences Against the State Act, which had never been repealed since the Emergency period of the Second World War. Lynch then left the chamber as other business was called. There was going to be no debate on the issue – much to the annoyance of the Labour Party.

Brendan Corish, the Labour leader, refused to accept the ruling of the chair. 'We had time to talk for days and hours about the accusations, unsubstantiated, which Jack Lynch made against Haughey, Blaney and the two Kellys, but we have no time now to talk about the Offences Against the State Act,' Corish complained. 'What I want to do now is to make the people of this country and the members of this House who have not read the act aware of what the government's proposal really means.'

He then proceeded to talk about the act, despite repeated calls from the chair for him to sit down. There were cries from the Fine Gael benches of 'Where is the Taoiseach hiding?' Corish was then 'named' and the Ceann Comhairle asked for his suspension for four days.

'Is it a police state you want?' Corish shouted as the vote was being taken. He was suspended by 69 votes to 21. Noël Browne then began reading the Offences Against the State Act. Lynch had returned for the vote, and when Browne refused to take his seat, the Taoiseach 'named' him and he was suspended by a vote of 69 to 14. Still Browne persisted. 'I see no difference between the Taoiseach setting aside the institutions of this House and the Young Maoists . . . '

At that point the Captain of the House approached Browne to escort him from the chamber. 'I know, and the Taoiseach knows, where this is going to end: in hunger strikes and Civil War,' Steve Coughlan of the Labour Party declared. 'Be it on the Taoiseach's head.' This provoked uproar in the chamber. Coughlan was then 'named' and he was suspended on a vote of 69 to 13.

Conor Cruise O'Brien was on his feet next. 'Your ruling that this is not a matter of public importance is probably the most scandalous ruling that has ever been given here,' he said.

The Ceann Comhairle had had enough, and he suspended the sitting until the following morning. The whole issue turned out to be little more than a storm in a teacup, because internment was never introduced.

The Fianna Fáil *ard fheis* the following month turned into a raucous affair when Boland and Blaney supporters tried to take over proceedings. As Paddy Hillery was speaking, Boland's supporters were heckling and trying to drown him out with cries of 'We want Kevin Boland.'

Hillery responded with the immortal line captured by the television camera: 'You can have Kevin Boland,' he shouted at the hecklers, 'but you can't have Fianna Fáil!' Fighting broke out at the back of the hall and Boland was then carried out of the hall on the shoulders of his supporters. Yet there was no doubt that Hillery was the hero of the hour. Lynch emerged from the *ard fheis* unscathed, with his supporters in firm control of the party.

The Dáil Committee of Public Accounts began hearings in January into whether money allocated for relief of distress in the North had been misappropriated. Legislation was passed by the Oireachtas allowing a select twelve-man committee to subpoena witnesses to testify under oath. Members of the committee included Ray MacSharry, Jim Tunney, Ben Briscoe, Sylvester Barrett, Hugh Gibbons and Thomas Nolan of Fianna Fáil; Garret FitzGerald, Dick Burke, Eddie Collins and Patrick Hogan of Fine Gael; and Justin Keating and Seán Tracy of the Labour Party.

Most of the witnesses at the Arms Trial were called, and the hearings inevitably covered much of the same ground. Some of the witnesses were actually cross-examined on the testimony they had given at the trial, though witnesses like Gibbons, Haughey and Blaney treated the committee with disdain – even a certain amount of contempt. Court rules did not apply during the committee hearings, so witnesses were able to give hearsay testimony that would have been inadmissible in court. Chief Superintendent Fleming of the Special Branch admitted at the outset that all his pertinent information was second-hand 'from confidential sources' whom he was not at liberty to name. He said that Haughey had promised a leading member of the IRA £50,000 for the North.

The chief superintendent explained he was 'not sure of the date or the place' of the meeting. All he could say was that it took place somewhere in Dublin in either August or September 1969. When asked if he thought Haughey had had any further meetings with the IRA, Fleming replied that he did not know but that his brother Jock 'was deeply involved'. In fact, the chief superintendent said that he believed Jock Haughey was George Dixon, the person who controlled the bank account used to purchase the arms.

Charlie Haughey vehemently denied either meeting the IRA leader or having promised to pay him money. 'No such meeting ever took place, and no such promise was ever made by me,' Haughey declared in an open letter to the committee chairman.

Haughey testified before the committee on 2 March 1971. This was inevitably going to be the big news of the week, but Lynch subtly reminded people of who was in charge by giving an interview to the BBC's *Panorama* programme on the eve of Haughey's appearance before the committee. The Taoiseach was adopting de Valera's old tactic of playing the Green card to distract political attention from other matters. He essentially denounced partition as an aberration of democracy. All of the people of the island were Irish, even the unionists in the North, he argued.

'They claim to be British, but nevertheless they claim also to be Irish and the Irish are one nation and as one nation they should be able to live together,' Lynch said. 'There cannot be two nations. We are the one. I can assure them that we could accommodate their affiliation to Britain in some way.' But he admitted that he could not say that partition was likely to end during his lifetime.

'I know it is going to be a difficult process,' he said. 'Nobody ever envisaged it otherwise than as such. It has been in existence for fifty years and it has not produced the kind of society in the North that any normal democracy would like to see. I do not think as long as it continues that it can produce reasonable society – normal living. You cannot continue to have armies in the street maintaining peace. That is not democracy and the development of no state can go on in a meaningful way as long as this is necessary.'

Although the Taoiseach was speaking in comparatively moderate terms about willingness to accommodate the desire of unionists to be British, he was not prepared to try to modify the Republic's constitutional claim to the Six Counties. Chichester-Clark had said that such a move would alter things greatly. He was a comparative moderate in unionist terms, but he was already in deep political trouble. Yet Lynch could see no room for manoeuvre on the issue of the constitutional claim. 'This is fundamental to our thinking. We are one nation and we regard in our constitution that the Irish territory is Ireland as a whole and its territorial seas,' he said. 'Therefore, when

I speak for the majority of our people, even if I were so inclined, I could not abandon that claim. Personally, I would not want to.'

Before the Dáil committee the following day, Haughey testified that the money voted for relief of distress in Northern Ireland went through the Dáil 'without any discussion whatsoever'. A good case could probably have been made for arguing that certain propaganda activities – or the provision of arms – were methods of relieving mental distress, but Haughey accepted that using money for such purposes was 'absolutely' out of order and irregular. 'Public funds were misappropriated,' he declared. 'That is a criminal offence.'

The main doubts about the validity of expenditures were in relation to the state funds used to finance *Voice of the North* and to purchase the arms. Haughey had thought that the Taoiseach's Department should have paid for *Voice of the North*, but Lynch disagreed.

'The Taoiseach gave me a direction and a ruling that public moneys were not to be used for the publication,' Haughey explained. Yet the money to finance it came from the Department of Finance, and Haughey's denial that he was aware of this seemed rather implausible.

Chief Superintendent Fleming of the Special Branch had testified to his belief that Haughey's brother, Pádraig (Jock), was George Dixon, the man in whose name the money was deposited to fund the purchase of guns. Jock denied that, but otherwise he refused to answer questions, for fear of incriminating himself. He was cited for contempt and was sentenced to six months in jail by the High Court, but that decision was overturned in June by the Supreme Court on the grounds that he could not be compelled to incriminate himself.

'This judgement deprived the committee,' reported the Public Accounts Committee, 'of any effective powers in the event of a witness refusing to attend, to produce documents or to answer questions.' The Opposition wished to ask the Oireachtas to give the committee the necessary powers, but this was blocked by Fianna Fáil members, with the result that the hearings came to a rather ineffective conclusion with the presentation of the committee's final report on 13 July 1972.

The committee concluded that a little over £29,000 was definitely 'expended on or in connection with the relief of distress' in Northern Ireland. A further £31,150 may have been spent in the same way, but over £39,000 was, in effect, misappropriated. There was no definitive finding as to who was directly responsible for the misappropriations, but the committee concluded that Haughey's action in providing the £500 given to Captain Kelly for the Bailieboro meeting was not justified and that 'the misappropriation' of the money used to purchase the arms 'might have been avoided' if either Haughey, Blaney or Gibbons had 'passed on to the Taoiseach their suspicion or knowledge of the proposed arms importation.'

That was a most extraordinary conclusion, because Lynch was never called to testify, and no effort was made to compel the three ministers to testify about what they had told the Taoiseach. On 14 May 1970 Lynch had told the Dáil that he did not know how the guns were financed. 'I made specific inquiries as to whether any moneys could have been devoted or could have been paid out of the exchequer funds or out of public funds in respect of a consignment of arms of the size we have been dealing with and I am assured that there was not nor could there have been.'

Charles H. Murray, the Secretary of the Department of Finance, had given that information to Lynch. He testified that he actually wrote out a draft reply for the Taoiseach stipulating that 'every penny of state funds had been spent for the purpose for which it was voted by the Dáil.' Gibbons testified that he did not know how the guns were being financed until Captain Kelly told him on 30 April, which meant that he knew the truth when Lynch misled the Dáil two weeks later.

'Had you informed the Taoiseach at that stage?' he was asked.

'The Taoiseach had not asked that question, as far as I can recall,' Gibbons replied.

When Gibbons was asked what he had told the Taoiseach, he refused to answer. 'The communications between me, as a member of the government, and the Taoiseach is a matter of privilege,' Gibbons insisted, but he did add categorically that 'at no time did I consciously conceal from the Taoiseach or anybody else any relevant information. In fact, I can demonstrate this. I can prove this.' He was testifying under oath at that point. He later said outside that he actually kept the Taoiseach informed. Peter Berry was the person who is reputed to have first told Lynch about the planned gun-running, but he was never asked any questions regarding what he told the Taoiseach. When Charles Murray was first asked about his advice to the Taoiseach in relation to the money that was used to purchase the guns, he replied that he would need Lynch's permission to talk about the advice he had given. The Taoiseach authorised him to speak and he explained what had happened to the committee at a subsequent meeting. But nobody bothered to ask Berry. It would not be until ten years after the arms crisis that the public would learn that Berry had told Lynch in October 1969 of the plans hatched at Bailieboro to bring in guns.

When Vincent Browne asked Lynch about this in a private interview on 6 May 1980, the tenth anniversary of the arms crisis, Lynch not only denied that Berry had told him but threatened to sue if the story was published. He also denied that Gibbons had informed him.

'This I said was unbelievable,' Lynch noted in his record of the conversation with Browne, 'and I asked him who had told him so. He said a colleague of his did. He could take it from me that he had never informed me about any conspiracy to import arms.' Browne then mentioned that Michael Moran had brought the matter to Lynch's attention 'on a number of occasions'.

'I told him that that was entirely untrue,' Lynch noted. 'If he attempted to publish anything of that nature, I would take my own remedy, no matter what that might be. I assured him that Mr Moran never once brought any such thing to my attention . . . I suggested to him that he was acting on information which he ought to be careful about, that if he published any allegation against me that would in any way reflect on my integrity then I would have to consider my situation.' Browne did publish this information in a famous series of articles in *Magill* magazine, but Lynch never tried to sue him.

Lynch wrote this report and then had it typed up, so he would have had an opportunity to consider it more carefully than if he were just speaking off the cuff. It is interesting to note that he did not deny that Gibbons had actually told him, as in the case of Moran. He used the word 'unbelievable' rather than 'untrue'. What he denied was that Gibbons had ever informed him 'about any conspiracy to import arms'. The use of the word 'conspiracy' suggested something illegal, but if Gibbons was actively involved, the whole thing was legal and he would only have been telling the Taoiseach about legitimate plans, not a conspiracy. This was what the Americans called 'a non-denial denial' during the Watergate scandal. Lawyers and politicians are masters of this kind of wordplay, and Lynch was both a lawyer and a very able politician.

If Gibbons did not tell Lynch what was happening, why was he not dismissed or asked to resign, like Moran, Haughey and Blaney? When Lynch fired Blaney and Haughey, he said there could not be 'the slightest suspicion' against them as ministers. Now that the trial was over, Lynch justified his actions on the grounds that the ministers had not kept him 'informed on a vital matter'. If he had no suspicions about Gibbons and he was not blaming him for failure to pass on information, it must have been because Gibbons had briefed him about what was happening.

'Poor Mr Gibbons was the anti-star of the trial; from his evidence it is hard to avoid drawing a number of inferences, all unflattering: he seems to have been foolish to the point of idiocy,' the British ambassador, Sir John Peck, reported on 10 November 1970. 'Mr Lynch, before he went to New York and while the trial was still in progress, told me privately that he was furious with Mr Gibbons for his performance as a witness, and that he seems to be getting into an impossible position. I thought it very likely that his resignation would be ready to be put into the Taoiseach's hand when he returned.' But instead Lynch held on to Gibbons and gave him his full support.

Members of the Public Accounts Committee never questioned the Taoiseach, and they never really tried to find out what anybody else had told him either. In many ways it was like investigating the Watergate scandal without asking any questions about what Richard Nixon knew and when he knew it!

Garret FitzGerald, one of the Fine Gael members of the committee, later indicated that he believed that Lynch did know about the attempt to import the arms but felt unable to act at the time, because he did not think he was strong enough to take on Blaney. 'You have to understand, the atmosphere of Blaney taking over underlaid everything,' according to FitzGerald. What Fitz-Gerald was really saying was that Fine Gael did not seek the truth for fear of exposing the Taoiseach and thus clearing the way for Blaney to take over. Was Lynch really that vulnerable? After all, he had routed Blaney at the party *ard fheis* in January 1970 and he subsequently ousted him from the party with little difficulty. In the circumstances, it would seem that Lynch lacked the will rather than the necessary power to deal with Blaney, but he was such a nice man that his Fine Gael opponents were taking no chances on toppling him and being saddled with Blaney, Boland or Haughey.

People like Boland and Blaney were still members of the national organisation and they were causing problems by sniping at the Taoiseach. Speaking to the Trinity College Historical Society in early March, Boland accused Lynch of breaching the collective responsibility of the Cabinet when he did not stand by Blaney and

Haughey. The following month Blaney was obviously referring to
Lynch when he denounced the 'peaceful-means hypocrites' during
a speech at Arklow. He said that he could name twenty-five people
at Leinster House who gave weapons to be sent to the North in
August 1969. He added that the government had ordered the
gardaí to turn a blind eye to men crossing the border with arms.
That was certainly not a formal government decision. We have
already seen that Boland was privately complaining in early 1970
that Lynch would block such a decision if it was brought up in
Cabinet.

Although Lynch was in firm control of Fianna Fáil by the
beginning of 1971, he was in a somewhat precarious position in
the Dáil, because the handful of disgruntled Fianna Fáil deputies
could bring the government down. The Taoiseach's critics believed
he was showing weak leadership within his Cabinet, and the
government appeared to dither. On 6 April 1971, for instance,
Joseph Brennan, the Minister for Social Welfare, issued an order
withholding unemployment assistance from men with no depend-
ants from 14 April until 16 November 1971. Such an order had
not been invoked since 1966, but when it had last been applied,
it had referred only to rural unemployment. Brennan's order
initially applied to single men in both rural and urban areas, but
next day he issued a new order stipulating that it should only apply
to single men in rural areas. Then, before the end of the month,
the Minister for Finance, George Colley, restored the benefits to
all affected by Brennan's order as part of that year's budget.

Two Fianna Fáil deputies, Des Foley of Dublin and Timothy
'Chub' O'Connor of Kerry, defied the Fianna Fáil whip by
abstaining during a Dáil vote in April, while Joe Leneghan of
Mayo actually voted against the government and was expelled from
the parliamentary party. Kevin Boland resigned his membership of
the Fianna Fáil organisation on 1 May 1971. But Lynch did get
a boost when he was invited to deliver the funeral oration at the

grave of the late Taoiseach Seán Lemass a couple of weeks later. This amounted to a posthumous endorsement from Lemass, which was particularly significant as he was Charles Haughey's father-in-law. In June Boland set up a new party, Aontacht Éireann, with himself as president and Captain James J. Kelly as vice-president.

There was little real flexibility anywhere. Lynch was being hounded by the republican wing of Fianna Fáil, while Heath was preoccupied with other matters, like the quest for admission to the EEC and coping with industrial strife in Britain. He preferred to leave the unionist government at Stormont to manage its own affairs, subject to London's overall control of the security forces. In Belfast, Chichester-Clark's remedy was to call for more and more troops. On average two bombs were going off each day in Northern Ireland, but the casualties were comparatively light in the midst of such bombings. In the four months from April to August, for instance, four soldiers and four civilians were killed. Of course, that level of violence was unacceptable.

On 1 May 1971 Chichester-Clark resigned as Prime Minister of Northern Ireland and was replaced by Brian Faulkner, who could be described as the first professional politician to lead the Unionist Party, after a succession of landowners and gentleman farmers – Sir James Craig, Sir John Andrews, Sir Basil Brook, Captain Terence O'Neill and Major James Chichester-Clark. Faulkner's remedy for the violence in the North was to look for internment without trial of suspected IRA members, but he was warned that this would be counterproductive unless the Dublin government also introduced internment in the Republic. If Lynch had wished to do so, he might have been able to bring it in the previous December, but at this stage his position was so precarious, with so many disgruntled deputies in his party, that he did not have the political capability to do so. He would have needed cross-party support. He might have been able to depend on Liam Cosgrave to do the patriotic thing and put the national interest first, but it would soon become all too apparent that in those circumstances Cosgrave would have been unlikely to retain the support of members of his own party. In order to shore up his own political position, the Taoiseach repeatedly made use of nationalistic rhetoric.

During ceremonies in the Garden of Remembrance on 11 July 1971, Lynch called on the British government to declare an interest in reuniting Ireland, and he denounced the so-called 'British guarantee' given to Northern Ireland after the Republic was declared in 1949. The British had regularised the declaration of the Republic with a bill that contained a proviso guaranteeing that Northern Ireland could not be detached from the United Kingdom without the consent of the Stormont legislature.

'Its principal result, in its present form, is to encourage infamous conduct, represented again and again on the streets of Derry and Belfast, and elsewhere throughout the North,' the Taoiseach said. On the eve of the Orange Day marches throughout Northern Ireland, his remarks could be seen as an expression of solidarity with the beleaguered Catholic community, but, of course, Faulkner saw it as naked provocation of his fellow unionists.

'It is quite extraordinary that Mr Lynch should choose to make a speech in these terms at this particular time,' Faulkner declared. The British subsequently complained, in diplomatic terms, that parts of Lynch's Garden of Remembrance speech were unhelpful, while Kevin Boland attacked the Taoiseach and called for a policy of 'resistance to British acts of war on Irish territory.'

Kevin Boland's aim in creating a new political party was to take a strong stand against the British. 'There is no voice in Dáil Éireann to make it clear that the British Army is at present engaged in aggressive imperialistic action against the Irish people,' he explained on 5 August. He seemed to be advocating a policy that was little short of going to war with Britain. 'I wish to say on behalf of those who are now organising a truly republican party that, if this new British aggression is persisted in, it must inevitably produce determined resistance and further bitterness between the two nations involved,' he said. 'If the British Army is at war in Ireland, where it has no right to be, the only possible stand to be taken by any true Irishman is of opposition to the "real invader" in our country.'

The following day the Dáil rose for the summer recess. Sir John Peck was instructed to find out where Lynch would be over the weekend, as it might be necessary to get in touch with him. There were already rumours that internment would be introduced in the North, so the ambassador surmised what was about to happen, and he suspected that Lynch also realised.

15

KEEPING HIS HEAD

1971–1972

Internment was introduced in Northern Ireland in the early hours of 9 August 1971, when 337 suspected republicans were rounded up. The intention had been to arrest 450 but the more active republicans had realised that internment was imminent, and they took precautions to avoid arrest. Many of those rounded up had not been active since the border campaign of the 1950s, and even earlier in some cases.

In *The RUC*, his history of the organisation, Chris Ryder noted that the faulty intelligence on which the round-up was based 'reflected the poor performance of the police and the absolute ignorance of the Army'. The whole thing was done in a highly selective manner, with only suspected republicans being arrested. Loyalists had been responsible for much of the strife in Northern Ireland, including all of the early murders. Indeed, James Callaghan had noted that the troubles 'were caused by the demands for civil rights and the attacks by Protestants on Catholics'. Just before Parliament went into recess for the summer, Callaghan realised that internment was being seriously considered and he warned the House of Commons 'that action should also be taken against those

Protestants who held guns'. But no effort was made to detain even a token handful of the loyalist troublemakers. 'The last pretence of an even-handed security policy had been abandoned,' according to Chris Ryder. As a result, the nationalist sense of grievance was inflamed.

On informing Lynch, the British ambassador Sir John Peck asked if the Dublin government would introduce internment in the South, as it had previously been used to contain republican violence at the same time in both jurisdictions during the 1920s, 1940s, 1950s and early 1960s. The British Army had warned that internment would only work if it was introduced simultaneously in the Republic, but no effort was made to consult Dublin in advance. Peck was instructed to speak to Lynch only after the round-up in the North had begun.

'He not only stated most emphatically that there was not the remotest possibility of internment being introduced in the Republic,' Peck wrote, 'but he gave me the most serious and solemn warning that the consequences in the North would be catastrophic: for every man put behind the wire, a hundred would volunteer. Of course, I reported this urgently and earnestly, but without seriously expecting that it could affect decisions that had obviously already been taken.'

In the circumstances, it was obvious that nobody expected Lynch's government to bring in internment immediately, so the British government should have realised that the practice was doomed from the outset. 'Those who thought it an appalling error in August 1971 were absolutely right,' Peck wrote a few years later.

'The Provisional IRA did not cause the civil-rights movement; the movement gave birth to the Provisional IRA,' the British ambassador explained. 'Internment therefore attacked the Catholic community as a whole. What was worse, it was directed solely against the Catholics, although there were many Protestants who provided just as strong grounds for internment, if internment there had to be. So their reactions, and Mr Lynch's warning, were entirely predictable.'

There had been an average of two deaths a month over the previous four months in the North, but in the days following the introduction of internment, twenty-two people were killed in rioting, including Father Hugh Martin, the first priest to be killed in the Troubles. He was shot while administering the last rites during the rioting in Belfast. In the final twenty weeks of the year, 140 people died. There was also considerable social upheaval, as Protestants were burned out of their homes in enclaves within Catholic areas and Catholics were burned out of Protestants areas.

Anglo-Irish relations plumbed depths not reached since the dark days of the Black and Tans in the early 1920s. Had Lynch not kept his head while some of those around him were losing theirs, Ireland could very easily have found herself not only in a Civil War, but also at war with Britain at the same time. Throughout the crisis, Lynch was firm yet restrained.

'The introduction of internment without trial is deplorable evidence of the political poverty of the policies which have been pursued for some time,' he warned. 'Even if it succeeds in damping down the current wave of violence, it does nothing to forward the necessary long-term solutions. The sympathies of the government and of the vast majority of Irish people, North and South, go to the nationalist minority in the North, who are again victimised by an attempt to maintain a regime which has long since shown itself incapable of just government and contemptuous of the norms of the British democracy to which they pretend allegiance.' It was imperative, he added, that 'a conference of all the interested parties take place in order to obtain a new form of administration for Northern Ireland.'

With all the modern technology at their disposal and the availability of swift methods of transportation, it was amazing that Heath and Lynch did not talk to each other or even have trusted advisers meet to discuss the situation. The two of them had still met only once, at the United Nations headquarters the previous October. Plans were made for a further meeting in London in October, which was more than two months away.

When Heath summoned Faulkner to London to meet him on 12 August, Lynch used that opportunity to send the following telegram to the British Prime Minister:

> The events since the introduction of internment without trial on Monday 9 August clearly indicate the failure of intern-ment and of current military operations as a solution to the problems of Northern Ireland. It must now be obvious to you that solutions require to be found through political means and should be based on the principle of immediate and full equality of treatment for everyone in Northern Ireland irre-spective of political views or religion.
>
> In the event of the continuation of existing policies of attempting military solutions, I intend to support the policy of passive resistance now being pursued by the non-unionist population.
>
> In the event of agreement to a policy of finding solutions by political means, I am prepared to come to a meeting of all the interested parties designed to find ways and means of promoting the economic, social and political well-being of all the Irish people, North and South, without prejudice to the aspiration of the great majority of the Irish people to the reunification of Ireland.

The Taoiseach undoubtedly had good grounds for complaint given the way the whole internment issue was being handled, but the second paragraph, warning that he was going to support resistance – albeit passive resistance – in another jurisdiction was extraordin-arily undiplomatic. Moreover, this telegram was not transmitted through Donal O'Sullivan, the Irish ambassador in London, or even handed to Peck for delivery. Instead it was sent outside the normal diplomatic channels by the ordinary commercial route, through the Irish and British postal services. Obviously if it had been sent under the auspices of anyone who knew anything about diplomacy, the Taoiseach would have run the risk of being warned against putting his views in such a blunt, undiplomatic fashion. He certainly knew better himself, so one must conclude that the telegram was sent via the commercial route in order to save the diplomats from embarrassment. They would have to continue working with the British, and it would be easier for them if they were seen to have had no part in Lynch's telegram.

Faulkner was with Heath, Foreign Secretary Sir Alec Douglas-Home, Home Secretary Reginald Maudling and Defence Secretary Lord Carrington when Lynch's telegram arrived. The Prime Minister informed them of the contents and 'a few unprintable comments were volunteered all round,' according to Faulkner.

Without waiting for Health's reply, Lynch read a prepared statement to the media. 'The violent reactions to the introduction of internment without trial in the North, which is seen to be a deliberate decision by the Stormont administration to attempt the outright repression of the minority, is not surprising,' he said. 'The main victims of violence are the people in areas that have been consistently victimised by the Stormont system.' He emphasised that he was not condoning the violence or the escalation in the 'armed activity which will inevitably cause further suffering and death.'

'The case can be simply stated,' he added. 'There exists in Northern Ireland a government whose main concern appears to be to meet the wishes and demands of the most extreme elements within the unionist community.' He called for the current Stormont regime to be replaced with a power-sharing executive that would include unionist and non-unionist parties.

About fifteen minutes later, the British ambassador was

instructed to deliver the Prime Minister's reply to Lynch's telegram. 'It will be on the News at Ten, and you've got to get it to him before then,' the Downing Street official instructed. The embassy staff had already finished for the day, so Peck had to get his son to type up the telegram and then drive him to Lynch's home in the Rathgar area of Dublin.

Although Peck described the reply as 'a fair stinker', he still thought it 'predictable, and in the circumstances perfectly reasonable.' It read:

1   Your telegram of today is unjustifiable in its contents, unacceptable in its attempt to interfere in the affairs of the United Kingdom and can in no way contribute to the solution of the problems of Northern Ireland.

2   You should know that the principle of equality of treatment for everyone in Northern Ireland irrespective of political views or religion is the accepted policy of the government of the United Kingdom and of Northern Ireland and is being fully implemented. By seeking to obscure this fact, you do no service to any of the people of Northern Ireland.

3   The military operations to which you refer are designed solely for the defence of the people against armed terrorists whose activities, many of which originate in or are supported from the Republic, I hope you would deplore and join me in suppressing. These operations are thus a necessary prelude to the restoration of greatest harmony between the communities in Northern Ireland.

4   While I naturally welcome contacts with you as the head of a friendly government, and while Mr Faulkner and I have often made clear our desire to see greater cooperation between all governments concerned in promoting mutual prosperity and well-being of the people of

Northern Ireland and the Republic, I cannot accept that anyone outside the United Kingdom can participate in meetings designed to promote the political development of any part of the United Kingdom.

5 I find your reference to supporting the policy of passive resistance now being pursued by certain elements in Northern Ireland calculated to do maximum damage to the cooperation between the communities in Northern Ireland which it is our purpose, and I would hope would be your purpose, to achieve.

6 I deeply regret the fact that, when a meeting has already been arranged between us to discuss the whole range of matters of common interest to our two countries, you should have publicly taken up a position so calculated not only to increase the tension in Northern Ireland but also to impair our effort to maintain good relations between the United Kingdom and the Irish Republic.

7 Since the text of your telegram was given to the Irish press before it was received here, I am also releasing the text of this message to the press.

The Taoiseach read the telegram in silence. 'I could not draw Mr Lynch out on this one,' Peck wrote. 'I doubt if the reply surprised him.'

'We had better have a drink,' was all Lynch said. Peck's son, Nicholas, was then invited into the room and 'had a charming and relaxed chat with the Taoiseach.' Lynch's reaction to Heath's reply came in the form of another prepared statement to the press. The two governments were engaging in a blatant form of microphone diplomacy. Lynch's statement was:

It is regrettable that the British Prime Minister should have interpreted my message in the way he did. I had hoped that he would have accepted my offer to participate in discussions among all those concerned to find an amicable solution to the problems of Northern Ireland. My message was solely intended to try to bring the present unrest to an end and to begin again the promotion of economic, social and political progress for all the people of Ireland and the ensuring of peace and harmony among them.

No one who has examined the situation could accept that the troubles in Northern Ireland originate in any measure from here. Of all the hundreds of people who have been arrested in Northern Ireland in situations of public unrest in the past three years, charged and convicted under the ordinary law, and of the hundreds who have now been interned without trial, no more than a handful came from outside Northern Ireland.

Mr Heath states that current military operations are a necessary prelude to the restoring of harmony between the communities in Northern Ireland. I believe on the contrary that these operations are driving them further apart. Evidence for this can be found in what is becoming the mass resignation of non-unionist appointees from public office in which they have given remarkable service in recent years. Mr Heath also suggests that these military operations are designed solely for the defence of the people against armed terrorists. I would point out that we have received here in the past twelve days many thousands of refugee women and children, mainly from Catholic ghettos in Belfast, who have described the situation otherwise.

We should all be happy to believe that the principle of equality of treatment for everyone in Northern Ireland, irrespective of political views or religion, is the accepted policy of the government of the UK and of Northern Ireland and is being fully implemented. However, the fact that internment without trial is so patently directed at the non-unionist community only does not encourage that belief.

So far as any question of impairing the good relations between Ireland and Britain is concerned, I have spoken on this subject many times, in particular during the past fifteen months, and have attempted to set these relations on a path which promised hope, progress and an ultimate final settlement, by agreement and through peaceful means only, of the age-old 'Irish Question'. The record speaks for itself.

Mr Heath's assertion that what is happening in Northern Ireland is no concern of mine is not acceptable. The division of Ireland has never been, and is not now, acceptable to the great majority of the Irish people, who were not consulted in the matter when that division was made fifty years ago. No generation of Irishmen has ever willingly acquiesced in that division – nor can this problem remain forever in its present situation.

Apart from this statement of principle, however, a situation where the destiny, the well-being and even the lives of Irish people are involved must affect us deeply. I remain convinced that the time has arrived for all those who can contribute to the peaceful solution of current problems in Northern Ireland to come together to discuss how this can be achieved.

'It is hard to imagine the heads of government of any two other states brawling publicly in this fashion,' Peck noted.

On 15 August the nationalist opposition at Stormont announced a campaign of civil disobedience. The following week sixteen opposition MPs and senators from Stormont – people like Gerry Fitt, John Hume, Austin Currie and Paddy O'Hanlon – met with Lynch at Leinster House. Afterwards they issued a joint statement saying that 'the great majority of the Irish people' wanted to achieve the national unification of Ireland, and they agreed that this goal should be achieved by 'non-violent political means'. In the context of the campaign of civil disobedience already announced by the Stormont opposition, this amounted to an open endorsement of their campaign by Lynch, and that was the way it was seen abroad. The *Toronto Globe and Mail* newspaper reported the following day, for instance, that 'Prime Minister Jack Lynch of the Irish Republic and opposition members of Northern Ireland's parliament had announced a campaign of civil disobedience to bring about the unification of Ireland.'

In the circumstances, Stormont Prime Minister Brian Faulkner was predictably critical. He accused the Taoiseach of committing 'himself and his government to support by political means what the IRA seek to achieve by violent means – the overthrow of the Northern Ireland government.' When the North was in difficulty, Lynch tended 'to exploit the situation in an irresponsible and opportunist way,' according to Faulkner. 'All of us in the North remember his intervention in 1969 when the vague but threatening tone of his television broadcast undoubtedly contributed to the general rise in tension and thus to the death and injuries which occurred here.'

Although Faulkner was complaining about 'the cant and hypocrisy of the attitude of Mr Lynch's government,' his remarks were likely only to popularise the Taoiseach's policy in the Republic, especially when Lynch seemed to be standing up to the British Prime Minister, who had appeared to put himself at the disposal of Faulkner in implementing internment in a sectarian way that was both crude and cruel.

'No further attempt by us to deal constructively with the present Dublin government is possible,' Faulkner argued. The people could hardly blame Lynch for not achieving more in the North, except those like Kevin Boland who seemed to be trying to drag the Republic into the conflict. Even though Lynch had denounced internment in terms that led to a distinct strain with the British,

Boland criticised him for being much too weak. In fact, he denounced the Taoiseach's statement as the most insane ever issued by a government leader at a time of national crisis. The following week, seven active members of Fianna Fáil resigned from the party in Cork and announced that they were joining Boland's new party. This was clearly intended to embarrass Lynch in his own political stronghold.

The situation was rapidly becoming precarious and threatening to get completely out of hand with a series of dramatic border incidents. On Sunday 31 August, Corporal Ian Armstrong was killed after he and some British Army colleagues strayed across the unmarked border. The soldiers were blocked in by a minivan and some cars. A growing crowd of youths poured buckets of water over the armoured cars, attempting to soak the engines. They let the air out of the tyres and finally began setting fire to the vehicles. The British troops were rescued by colleagues from the North and managed to make it back across the border, but Armstrong, a married man with a young daughter, was shot dead and a colleague was seriously wounded. They were only yards inside the Northern side of the border. The British Army complained that Armstrong had been shot by men firing from the Republic while Irish soldiers watched.

Lynch was expected to make a conciliatory statement, but instead his response was terse and tough, with no expression of regret for the death of the young soldier. 'During the past two years, the British Army has made some thirty incursions into the Twenty-six Counties,' he complained. 'They were brought to the attention of the British authorities at the time of the occurrences and assurances were received that they were accidental and that stringent instructions had been reissued to the troops to avoid such infringements.

'At about 1.30 p.m. on Sunday,' Lynch continued, 'a further infringement occurred when a British patrol consisting of two

Ferret armoured scout cars penetrated about one mile into the Twenty-six Counties.' Some twenty government officials had conducted an on-the-spot investigation and concluded that there was 'ample evidence' that the two soldiers were shot from within the Six Counties. 'This information has been conveyed to the British authorities, together with a strong complaint about their failure to control movements of their troops in border areas which could be prejudicial to the peace,' Lynch stated. While all that he said might well have been true, his statement seemed extraordinarily insensitive in the circumstances.

Some strong reservations were being expressed in unlikely quarters about his handling of affairs. Seán McEntee wrote to Lynch on 2 September about the treatment accorded to Joe Cahill, a recognised leader of the Provisional IRA. A native of Belfast, Cahill had been one of five IRA men sentenced to death for the murder of a Catholic RUC officer at Easter in 1942. Due largely to the diplomatic pressure exerted by the United States, the death sentences of four of the men had been commuted, and following his release Cahill played a leading role in the formation of the Provisional IRA.

McEntee was indignant that Cahill was 'accorded a quasi-ambassadorial send-off from Dublin Airport' on his departure for the United States the previous day. Aer Rianta and Aer Lingus had arranged a special room for him to hold a press conference at the airport. 'This is the sort of facility accorded to a minister travelling on important public business,' McEntee wrote to Lynch the following day. 'Far from being a minister, Mr Cahill is a gentleman who denies the legitimacy of the constitution and government of our state; and yet he is treated by the officers of Aer Rianta as though he were one travelling on a mission from the government, even though he has openly stated that his purpose is to procure arms and money to further a campaign of violence which has been repudiated by all parties in the Dáil and which you as Taoiseach have declared to be positively

271

harmful to the cause of a united Ireland.'

'I cannot think of anything more calculated to embarrass you in your talks with Heath or indeed [to] lessen public regard for the government than this occurrence,' McEntee continued. 'It was a disgraceful manifestation of laxity and loose thinking – if not indeed open disloyalty – on the part of responsible officers of two statutory companies which are owned and controlled by the state.'

Lynch was not supposed to meet Heath until 21 October, but this meeting was brought forward to 6 September. Before they could meet, however, the Provisional IRA bombed the Unionist Party headquarters in Belfast, injuring thirty-nine people. Lynch promptly denounced the outrage. 'No Irishman with the least shred of Christianity or sanity can justify or condone the maiming or the killing of innocent people,' he declared.

His talks with Heath lasted eleven hours, extending over two days. There was little personal rapport between the two men. 'It was not quite a dialogue of the deaf, but caught in the middle as I was, I sometimes felt that a pair of powerful hearing aids would come in handy,' Peck wrote afterwards. Heath had invited the Taoiseach to stay at Chequers, but Lynch 'rather curtly refused,' according to the Prime Minister.

Shortly before six o'clock on the first day, Lynch left the room with his advisers and said they would be back in about ten minutes and would decide whether to continue the discussions.

'Prime Minister, do you know why he stepped out?' Peck asked.

'I presume it was for the usual reason, a call of nature,' Heath replied.

'Not at all,' Peck explained. 'The time has come when he wants a drink of his usual Paddy.'

Peck had brought two bottles over from Dublin with him and given them to the housekeeper, so a bottle of Paddy whiskey was summoned. 'When Lynch returned I told him, before he could say anything, that it was customary for us all to have a little refreshment at six o'clock,' Heath noted. He asked if the Taoiseach would like a sherry, gin or even a glass of Paddy.

'The Taoiseach looked as pleased as he was surprised,' Heath wrote. The discussion continued for another ninety minutes before they broke up for the evening, with Lynch agreeing to return in the morning.

'Mr Heath said I did not have the right to be involved in discussions of constitutional change,' Lynch told a packed news conference at the Irish embassy after the talks. 'I insisted I had such a right and I maintain that right because I am the elected head of the government of Ireland and I represent the mass opinion of the Irish people.'

The whiskey may have thawed some of the chill in the relationship between the two leaders, but there was still a gulf between them. Heath would later suggest that 'one of the main purposes of these talks was to obtain Lynch's agreement to a tripartite meeting between himself, myself and Brian Faulkner.' This should not have required much effort, because suggesting such a meeting had actually been one of the main aims of Lynch's controversial telegram a couple of weeks earlier.

'Ireland is one country, one nation, one people, and I think we are both small enough and big enough to live together,' Lynch told the press conference at the Irish embassy. 'We have been one for centuries and only divided in the last fifty years.' He said that he emphasised in his conversation with Heath that he was looking for 'unification by agreement without exacerbating the situation.' He proposed immediate four-way talks involving the Dublin and London governments and both nationalist and unionist representatives from Northern Ireland.

While Heath agreed that Dublin was entitled to aspire to Irish unity, he said that he could not have the Republic interfering in the affairs of Northern Ireland. He therefore ruled out four-party talks. Lynch was trying to ensure the inclusion of the Northern nationalists, who had been almost totally polarised by the fact that only people from the nationalist community had been interned. 'There are men of violence on the other side too,' Lynch explained.

The internment controversy was further exacerbated by reports that the internees had been abused and even tortured in custody. John Hume called for an inquiry into the treatment of internees as early as 19 August. A committee of inquiry was established under Sir Edmund Compton, and it reported six weeks later that there had, indeed, been 'ill-treatment'. In an introduction to the report, however, Home Secretary Reginald Maudling wrote that the committee 'found no evidence of physical brutality, still less of torture or brainwashing.'

The Lynch government was able to demonstrate its concern for the victims by appealing to the European Commission on Human Rights, which concluded in September 1976 that the interrogation techniques breached the European Convention on Human Rights 'in the form not only of inhuman and degrading treatment but also of torture.' The Commission's finding in relation to torture was subsequently rejected by the European Court of Human Rights in January 1978. The Court concluded that the in-terrogation techniques 'did not occasion suffering of the particular intensity and cruelty implied by the word "torture".' But the Court agreed with the Commission's conclusion that the internees had suffered 'inhuman and degrading treatment'.

The three-way meeting between Lynch, Heath and Faulkner was held at Chequers on 27 and 28 September 1971. 'This was one of the historic events of my premiership,' Heath recorded. 'Lynch had to be persuaded to recognise Faulkner as the Prime Minister of a separate territory.' Of course, this was absurd. Lynch – and Lemass before him – had already met Faulkner's predecessor, Terence O'Neill. It was the Northern unionists who were alarmed at the thought of such a meeting, fearing that it could be represented as 'acceptance of Dublin's right to interfere in the internal affairs of Northern Ireland.' Faulkner therefore announced that, while he would meet with Lynch, he would not discuss constitutional issues with him.

The two of them got on well together, according to Heath. 'From the beginning, I felt slightly peripheral to the exchanges between my two guests, and pretty soon I was left out of the conversation altogether as they talked about their island and current events,' he wrote. But it seemed to him that they were avoiding thorny issues as they felt their way through the conversation. 'Look, we really must get down to some of our problems,' Heath reminded them.

'We discussed Lynch's failure to deal with the IRA in the Republic. I pressed Lynch on border security and IRA training camps,' Faulkner wrote. He also asked him not only to stop the theft from Irish quarries of gelignite that was being used to make bombs in the North, but to hand over the forty or so 'known terrorists' who were sheltering in the Republic, and to introduce internment. Lynch responded by expressing concern about internment and the failure of the reform programme in the North. He did agree to try to do something about the training camps and gelignite, but he insisted that extradition and internment were out of the question.

'Reassurances were exchanged all round,' Heath noted. 'The long-term future of the island was not on the agenda, but the summit did bring about what we had set out to achieve. I got the two men, and the two parts of Ireland, talking to one another, establishing a foundation of mutual trust upon which a lasting settlement might one day be built.' This was the start of the tedious process that would eventually lead to the Sunningdale agreement.

In the interim, however, things were to get much worse. Lynch had to cope with the arrogance of Heath and at the same time watch his own political position at home. He was being criticised by Kevin Boland and company for not doing enough to help the

Northern nationalists. Boland was enjoying a high profile with the formation of his new party, Aontacht Éireann. Over a thousand people attended a conference to launch the party formally in Dublin in late September. Boland was joined by Deputy Seán Sherwin, who defected from Fianna Fáil, and by both Captain James J. Kelly and Colonel Michael Hefferon. Haughey and Blaney refused to join the new party.

On 1 October 1971 the government decided to invoke Section 31 of the Broadcasting Act to ban the broadcasting of interviews with members of the Provisional IRA. This was the first time that any government had invoked that section of the 1960 act. It provided that broadcasting could be banned of 'any matter that could be calculated to promote the aims or activities of any organisations who engage in, promote, encourage or advocate the attaining of any political objective by violent means.' *Seven Days*, a current-affairs programme on RTÉ television, had included a number of prominent members of the Provisional IRA the previous week.

This was 'one of the worst examples of the propagandising of the activities of illegal military organisations,' Lynch said. 'If we had acted otherwise, we would have failed in our duty to the public and, though some might consider it an act of censorship, totalitarianism or autocracy, it was in fact done as insurance against tyranny by a minority.'

The Opposition seized on the opportunity to try to bring Lynch down by reopening the wounds of the arms crisis. Paddy Kennedy, a republican socialist member of Stormont, stated in an RTÉ interview at the time of the arms crisis that Captain Kelly could only have been involved with the knowledge and approval of the then Minister of Defence, Jim Gibbons, who promptly refuted this in the Dáil. 'I wish emphatically to deny any such knowledge or consent,' he said. 'If it could be shown to me that at any time I deliberately either misled the Dáil or told untruths, I would have no hesitation in tendering my seal of office to the President and my letter of resignation to the Ceann Comhairle.'

At the arms trial it became apparent that he had lied to the Dáil. He admitted on the witness stand that he was aware of Captain Kelly's activities, and he lamely tried to excuse his deceit of the Dáil by implying that a different degree of veracity was required in Leinster House.

A decade earlier British politics had been rocked by the biggest sex scandal of the century, involving Christine Keeler, who had simultaneous affairs with the Soviet military attaché and Jack Profumo, the British Minister for War. Profumo initially lied about the affair in Parliament. When the truth came out, he was not only expelled from the Cabinet but forced to give up his seat at Westminster. Mindful of what had happened to Profumo, the Opposition smelled blood in the Dáil.

A motion of no confidence was tabled in Gibbons, who had been moved to the Department of Agriculture in the Cabinet reshuffle following the outbreak of the arms crisis. Under the concept of collective Cabinet responsibility, all of the Cabinet ministers were equally responsible for his lying. Yet this line of action was essentially endorsed by Lynch's failure to sack him.

Why did Lynch not drop Gibbons? Was it because Gibbons knew something that could do even more damage to the Taoiseach?

In a sense it was symbolically fitting that Gibbons should not be ousted for lying, because the government as a whole was essentially sustaining a monstrous lie about its supposed ignorance of the scheme to bring in the guns. Even though the judge at the arms trial had concluded that either Gibbons or Haughey had given perjured testimony, Haughey now announced that he would be supporting the government. Fifteen minutes before the vote of confidence on 4 November 1971, Kevin Boland announced that since voting for Lynch and Gibbons would amount to repudiating the decision of the jury in the arms trial, he was therefore resigning his Dáil seat. He was forty-seven years old at the time and was, in effect, committing political suicide, though he did not know it. His gesture was essentially futile, as the government prevailed by 70 votes to 67, while Blaney and Paudge Brennan abstained.

This, in turn, led to another mini-crisis within the government. In order to preserve discipline within the party, Lynch proposed the expulsion of Blaney and Brennan at the next meeting of the Fianna Fáil parliamentary party on 16 November. He insisted on a roll-call vote on the motion, which was passed by 58 votes to 8. The eight who voted against the motion were the two deputies themselves, along with Haughey, Eugene Timmons, Tim 'Chub' O'Connor, Lorcan Allen, Dickie Cogan and Jim Gallagher.

The expulsion meant that the Fianna Fáil government was in a minority situation within the Dáil. Fianna Fáil had seventy deputies, while Fine Gael and Labour had a combined total of sixty-eight, with the result that the government was dependent on five independents, four of whom had either been expelled or had resigned from Fianna Fáil that year. Blaney, Paudge Brennan and Des Foley announced that they were forming a loose parliamentary group. They said they would back the government on all issues other than those relating to the Northern crisis. Blaney said that he would be taking a more active part 'now that the inhibitions of the past eighteen months have been removed.'

Lynch was therefore under more pressure than ever to make some progress with the British government. The former British Prime Minister Harold Wilson visited Dublin the following week as leader of the British Labour Party. He had talks with Lynch and other interested parties. Upon his return to London the following week, he caused a sensation by suggesting that a constitution be drawn up which would envisage a united Ireland within fifteen years. In return, he suggested that the Republic should agree to rejoin the Commonwealth of Nations and recognise the British Crown as the head of the Commonwealth.

The Heath government denounced his proposals and they never amounted to much, because Labour never pursued them. In any event, Heath and the Conservatives were in power in 1971. Through Peck, Lynch tried to get Heath to acknowledge that Britain would not stand in the way of Irish unity, if the majority of people in Northern Ireland supported the idea. He was asking only for a democratic assertion that Britain would recognise the right of the majority of the people of Northern Ireland to unite with the rest of the island, but Heath was unwilling to make an unequivocal declaration. Peck noted that the Prime Minister would 'not go beyond saying that if they ever did, "I do not believe any British government would stand in the way".'

Although Peck had thought the September agreement to hold tripartite talks between London, Belfast and Dublin had provided a glimmer of hope, that glimmer was extinguished by the end of the year. 'The Taoiseach had held his Fianna Fáil Party together on a policy of denouncing both violence and violent intervention in the North, working with the British government for a just and peaceful settlement, and showing his electorate that he was keeping up all the pressure he could upon Westminster,' Peck wrote. 'After eighteen months he had precious little to show for it, and I knew that he and his government were depressed and frustrated.

'By the end of January 1972 I was tortured officially by doubts about the policy of the government I was serving as the Queen's representative,' Peck added. He was also personally tortured 'by doubts about the impact of the reports, analyses, opinions that I and my embassy were sending to the Foreign Office.' Realising that no real progress was likely to be made through Stormont, he clearly thought that Lynch was Britain's best hope, but he was being shabbily treated. In his annual review Peck bluntly informed the Foreign Office that '1971 had been a bad year for Jack Lynch's "peaceful approach and working through the British".'

Ever since the introduction of internment in August 1971, the situation in Northern Ireland had degenerated alarmingly. Yet Ted Heath wrote in his autobiography that 'by the end of 1971, I was much more optimistic than I had been a year previously. Although a total of 174 people had been killed that year, the most since the troubles began, proper dialogue was at last under way.' His groundless optimism was fuelled by his own frightening ignorance of what was really happening in Ireland, together with his natural arrogance.

Internment had set in train a series of events that were to have disastrous consequences. On Sunday 30 January 1972 a march was held in Derry to protest against internment. The march had been banned, but the organisers went ahead anyway. The march was fired on by troops of the British Parachute Regiment in Derry, killing thirteen people outright and wounding seventeen others, one of whom subsequently died of his wounds. The troops claimed that they were fired on first, and the general in charge stated that around 300 shots were fired at the troops. Yet not one of them was hit. Very few – if any – nationalists, North or South, believed that the troops were fired at first. Moreover, there was no evidence that any of those shot had been carrying any weapons.

That night, the Taoiseach telephoned Heath but was distinctly defensive throughout the conversation. 'I am sorry to ring you at this hour,' he began. 'I am told the British troops reacted rather beyond what a disciplined force might be expected to.' In fact, he said that he had heard that a British newspaper was going to describe the troops as having gone 'berserk'.

'When the funerals take place on Tuesday or Wednesday, I hate to think of what could happen,' he added. For the past couple of years he had been arguing against the marches in the North. Stormont had banned the Bloody Sunday march in Derry, but the marchers defied the law. Yet now the Taoiseach advocated that Westminster should take over full control of security from Stormont.

'It is very difficult for me to accept a condemnation of Stormont for doing something which you yourself have requested, you have constantly requested,' Heath replied. 'You spoke to me last summer that marches should be banned.'

Lynch had already announced that he would be contacting Heath and he now felt that he would have to say something about their conversation afterwards. 'I will say that I have asked you to take very firm political steps, to the point of taking over security and making some alternative arrangement as far as Stormont is concerned,' he said.

'Will you tell me how taking over security and changing Stormont is going to make people obey the law and not challenge it with marches?' Heath asked.

'Well I think it will certainly avoid situations like this arising again,' Lynch argued. It seemed ironic that he was asking for the British to take full control of security when it was actually British troops who had done the shooting in Derry. For the time being, however, Lynch's main problem was going to be coping with the reaction at home. 'Repercussions south of the border are, as I see it myself, going to be so serious that we will both have a much more difficult situation on hand as a result of this unless Westminster takes firm action at this stage,' he warned.

'Perhaps,' said Heath, 'if you had condemned people beforehand who were going to challenge the law, the march might not have taken place.'

'I do not believe that would have happened anyway,' Lynch contended. 'Words would come easily from me but people are not going to obey or accord to what I think might be done in certain circumstances.' He was essentially arguing that he was powerless in the situation, but Heath was critical that Dublin had not done enough previously to contain the IRA.

'I cannot tell people not to support them,' Lynch explained. He was going to say something else but Heath interrupted: 'Well, you could deal very thoroughly with those who are using the South as their refuge and I have always told you this for many months.'

'I know you have. Yes. But on the other hand within the limits of our own law – '

'If you had dealt with them this would have been over long ago,' Heath interrupted again.

'I do not believe it would,' Lynch insisted. 'No, I say it would have been much worse. We know what happened as a result of internment in the North and in fact the suggestion you have been making that we should intern them in the South would have been worse.'

They had come full circle and were back arguing over internment. There was no point in continuing until they knew more details about what had happened in Derry. Lynch suggested that they might talk or meet later and they hung up, with Lynch politely thanking the Prime Minister for talking to him, but there were no reciprocal thanks from the other side. 'This was hardly a time for small talk,' Heath later wrote.

Passions were roused further in the following days. 'Nobody shot at the paratroopers, but somebody soon will,' said Bernadette Devlin, the independent member of the Westminster Parliament from mid-Ulster, in one of the most unparliamentary outbursts ever witnessed at Westminster. 'I have a right, as the only representative in this House who was an eyewitness, to ask a question of that murdering hypocrite.' She was alluding to the Home Secretary, Reginald Maudling, who had just tried to defend the troops. Suddenly Devlin raced across the floor of the House, pulled Maudling's hair and slapped and scratched his face. In the eyes of most nationalists, the shootings were murders, and the flimsy British claims about the soldiers having been fired upon added further insult to the injury.

Paddy Hillery was again dispatched in another purported attempt to secure the intervention of the United Nations. But for the first time since its establishment, the Security Council was not sitting in New York; it was in Addis Ababa. There was no point in going to Ethiopia to secure an international spotlight, so Hillery went to New York anyway. At the airport there he told a press conference that Britain was 'provoking war against a nation which, to large extent, is unarmed.' Therefore, his mission was to 'seek help wherever I can get it' in order 'to end the reign of terror which Britain is perpetrating on our people.

'What was done in Ireland by the British is an affront to justice in the world,' Hillery added. 'If they can get away with it this time, we can have little hope for justice. We would hope that these friendly nations would turn Britain away from the lunatic policies she is pursuing.' He described the IRA as 'a response to Britain's policy' of locking up adults, harassing children and denouncing opponents as terrorists. 'We regard what has been done as an act of war,' he added. 'From now on, our aim is to get the British out of Ireland. We had war declared on the minority population in the name of doing it on the IRA.'

'The atmosphere had grown more poisonous than ever and I feared that we might, for the first time, be on the threshold of complete anarchy,' Heath wrote. In Dublin a huge crowd gathered outside the British embassy to protest on 2 February. It was obvious that the angry crowd was likely to burn down the embassy. A large force of unarmed gardaí was drafted in to protect the building, but they were no match for the frenzied crowd. Defending the place properly would have entailed calling out the army and probably even firing on the people, which would have made a bad situation much worse.

'The potential for the greatest danger in a single moment probably was on that night,' Des O'Malley, the Minister for Justice, concluded. 'We decided that we could not move in to defend the embassy.'

Army leaders 'were not prepared to go in with lead,' O'Malley explained. The government therefore decided to stand aside and allow the mob to burn the building. This had a cathartic effect. On reflection the following day, people realised that emotions had got out of control and it was a miracle that nobody had been killed in Dublin. This was to have a sobering effect.

'The thing defused itself,' O'Malley later argued. 'The sacrifice was made. A burning took place. The emotions of the time spent themselves in the flames of that building.' Thereafter the pull towards involvement in the North began to wane perceptibly. The danger that the Twenty-six Counties would become actively involved essentially dissipated.

A case could undoubtedly be made for suggesting that Lynch could have done more to control, if not stop, the violence in Northern Ireland, but the question of whether such actions would have been effective is one of the imponderables of history. Yet there is no doubt that once the situation threatened to get out of hand, he provided real leadership. It is often said that Éamon de Valera's finest achievement was keeping the Twenty-six Counties out of the Second World War. Jack Lynch's greatest achievement was in keeping the Twenty-six Counties out of the North – and out of what could have been another Civil War.

16

LOSING OUT

1969–1973

Following the resignation of Charles de Gaulle as President of France in 1969, the opposition to British membership of the EEC virtually evaporated. The Irish application had never been withdrawn, so it was simply renewed that year.

In April 1970 the government published a white paper: *Membership of the European Communities – Implications for Ireland.* The Taoiseach initiated a Dáil debate on the white paper on 23 June 1970. Lynch explained that at the end of the process it would be necessary to hold a constitutional referendum before Ireland could formally agree to membership. The country had been preparing for membership for the past ten years, and he was able to explain that its economic obligations would not be dissimilar to those being assumed under the Anglo-Irish Free Trade Agreement. From the political standpoint it was obvious at the outset that there was going to be little difficulty from the legislature, because both Fianna Fáil and Fine Gael favoured EEC membership.

The actual negotiations opened the following week in Luxembourg, on 30 June 1970. The Minister for External Affairs, Paddy Hillery, was primarily responsible for the talks. He was supported by a team of civil servants, predominantly the assistant secretaries of the government departments most involved – External Affairs, Finance, Agriculture, and Industry and Commerce. The main area of negotiation related to the issue of adjustment and involved the agreement of transitional measures to ease the country into the Common Market.

The main transitional measures to be negotiated were those covering industry and agriculture and Ireland's contribution to the community budget. On the issue of the customs union, the Irish delegation sought to have all duties eliminated over a six-year period which would end by 1978. This would have involved introducing a reduction of 20 per cent in each of two years and 15 per cent in the other four years. However, in the end the agreement called for the total elimination of duties in five years, not six, with a 20 per cent reduction each year until their final elimination in January 1977. A similar five-year transition period was agreed for both the full alignment of agricultural prices and the country's complete integration into the EEC's financial arrangements. Quantitative restrictions were agreed on Irish import quotas to secure the elimination of all restrictions by July 1975. Those negotiations were finalised on 19 October 1971. It was envisaged that the ratification process would take a further year and then Ireland, Britain, Denmark and Norway would join the original six member countries of the EEC simultaneously.

It was envisaged that industrial output would grow by 8.5 per cent annually up to 1978 and that industrial employment would increase by about 50,000, which was an annual growth rate of 6,000 jobs as compared to an average of 4,500 during the 1960s. It was also estimated that farm income would double by 1978 and the rate of agricultural employment, which had been falling by 10,000 annually in the 1960s, would decline by 7,000 a year until 1978. The rapid rise in income would have the effect of generating new jobs in the economy, especially in the building and service industries, with the result that a further 50,000 jobs would be created, excluding industrial employment, by 1978. Thus when redundancies and the drop in agricultural employment were factored in, there would still be a net annual increase of over 6,000 jobs, which compared very favourably with the little over 1,000 extra jobs generated annually during what had been seen as the booming 1960s.

In November 1971 the government introduced a bill to provide for a constitutional referendum on what would be the third amendment to the Constitution. It passed the second stage in the Dáil by a majority of 117 to 17 and passed all other stages by the end of January without difficulty.

A further white paper, *The Accession of Ireland to the European Communities*, was published in January 1972, outlining the various implications of joining the EEC. It posed the question of whether there was an alternative to membership of the EEC. The conclusion reached was that 'there is no realistic alternative to membership of an enlarged Community which is compatible with the national objectives of increasing employment and improving the standard of living.'

'Today we stand at a most important crossroads in our history,' Lynch told the Dáil in opening the debate on the latest white paper on 21 March 1972. 'The road we take will determine not only the future of our country for generations to come, but also the contribution we make to the creation of a Europe that will measure up to the ideals of the founders of the Community. I am confident that the decision we take will reflect our people's faith and their capacity to help fashion for themselves and for future generations of Irishmen and women a better Ireland in a better Europe.'

The outcome was a foregone conclusion with Fine Gael supporting the bill, which was passed by 89 votes to 16. The referendum on the constitutional amendment was a spirited enough affair, with the Labour Party and the two Sinn Fein factions opposing membership. All the ministers of the Fianna Fáil government took an active part in the campaign during the final week, while Lynch campaigned in Cork, Kerry, Tipperary, Laois and Offaly. His only fear was that the voters might be apathetic, as the outcome seemed a certainty. Fianna Fáil waged a highly personalised campaign, with banners and stickers declaring: 'Vote Yes. Let's Back Jack.'

Lynch accused the Labour Party of using the 'big lie' technique, trying to scare people into voting against membership of the EEC on the grounds that it would lead to inflation of food prices. He deliberately played down the extent of the inflation. 'The opponents of membership seem to be working in the hope that a falsehood, if repeated often enough and widely enough, is bound to have some effect.' On the Friday before polling, Lynch attended a rally in Cork city. The following day he began in Carrigaline and made speeches in Bandon, Macroom and Mallow. The day after that he was among 30,000 people who watched Cork defeat Limerick in the National Hurling League final.

There was a big voter turnout for the referendum, with just over 71 per cent of the people voting – 83.1 per cent in favour and only 16.9 percent against. Lynch was 'pleased that the people so emphatically endorsed our entry to the European Community.' He paid a particularly warm tribute to the main opposition party: 'The commitment of the Fine Gael Party – especially having regard to their difficulty in supporting the government on any particular issue – of the farmers' organisations and other voluntary groups was of great significance in achieving the overall result.'

This was one of the most important decisions ever taken in Irish history. When a united Europe was being mooted in the aftermath of the Second World War, de Valera had found it necessary to rule out Irish participation. 'I am sure,' he told the Council of Europe at Strasbourg in August 1949, 'you can understand with what a cynical smile an Irish citizen would regard you if you spoke to him about uniting in a huge state the several states of Europe with their diverse national traditions so long as he contemplates his own country kept divided against his will.' It was not from any desire to interfere with or delay the process of European unity that Ireland would not join the new federation. 'It is simply because we know the task that would confront us in persuading our people to proceed by that road,' de Valera emphasised.

People had been reared with the idea that the struggle for Irish independence, which had gone on for over 700 years, was still incomplete. The people had been trying to sever a union with Britain, and de Valera was not about to ask them to go into a much larger union that would include Britain and some of the largest countries in Europe. Much of the credit for the initial impetus to join the EEC should go to Seán Lemass, but over the years the man who did most to promote the idea and prepare the country for eventual membership was Jack Lynch. A little over twenty years after de Valera had ruled out asking the Irish people about joining the rest of Europe, on the grounds that he knew what their response would be, Lynch had secured an overwhelming vote of approval. It was a magnificent tribute to his patient leadership on this issue.

The vote was much closer in Denmark, while the majority of the people of Norway voted against joining the EEC. There was no referendum in Britain – much to the annoyance of the Labour Party – with the result that the issue festered until Labour returned to power in June 1975 and secured popular approval for membership through a referendum. In Ireland the government's adept handling of the issue and the decisive referendum vote killed all further debate on the issue. Henceforth the focus of debate would not be on whether Ireland should be in the EEC, but on how to make the best of the country's membership.

During Lynch's first full term as Taoiseach, the economy deteriorated, but the impact of the downturn was obscured somewhat by foreign investment, which tended to mask the balance-of-payments deficit. Between 1968 and 1972 the balance of payments ran at a deficit of more than double that of the period from 1961 to 1968. T. K. Whitaker stepped down as secretary of the Department of Finance in 1969. He was only fifty-three years old, but he apparently saw the writing on the wall. He had been the young economic guru to whom the old men in government had turned in the late 1950s, but with Lynch's election a new, younger generation began to hold sway within government. Charles Haughey, the new Minister for Finance, was an arrogant young man with limitless confidence in his own ideas and a determination to run the civil servants, rather than allowing them to run him. In 1969, an election year, capital spending was increased, but it was cut back sharply the following year and again in 1971. The government's economic policy was not being dictated by economic necessity but by political considerations.

Whitaker became Governor of the Central Bank, where he had more independence. With the cut in capital spending, unemployment rose, and George Colley sought to spend his way to reducing the unemployment figures. For the first time in the history of the state, a deficit budget was introduced in 1972. Colley aimed at a 1.3 per cent deficit, but he actually ended up with a deficit of just 0.2 per cent, which was less than the unplanned deficits of 1968 and 1970. In the opinion of Professor Joe Lee, however, 'the 1972 budget can stand as a symbol of that breakdown in national discipline.' As Governor of the Central Bank, Whitaker advised strongly against the move. He sensed that 'the fruits of fifteen years' labour were beginning to be frittered away by people who lacked the character and the intelligence to build on the foundations he had been instrumental in laying,' in the opinion of Professor Lee.

In the five years from 1968 to 1972, unemployment rose from 6.7 per cent in 1968 to 8.1 per cent, while the Consumer Price

Index rose by an annual average of 8.3 per cent. This inflation was compounded by trade-union militancy, in the form of intensified strike activity. In 1970 the International Labour Organisation ranked Ireland as third-worst in the world in the number of working days lost per employee to strikes.

The national pay agreements only made things worse, because neither the government nor the unions took much cognisance of economic reality, preferring a short-sighted policy of expediency that fuelled inflation. In 1970, for instance, the wage agreement provided for an 18 per cent pay rise over eighteen months. The next pay agreement, which was to run for a further eighteen months, was apparently drawn up with an eye to winning an early general election. 'The resolve that nothing would stand in the way of electoral victory became even clearer when the government accepted a 21 per cent national pay agreement in the summer of 1972, well above the level of inflation,' Joe Lee wrote. 'The irresponsibility of the government in 1972 can be explained, if not justified, in terms of its consciousness of the price of defeat in purely internal party terms. The really disturbing aspect is that the possibility cannot be entirely ruled out that Colley may have actually believed in the validity, as well as in the expediency, of his policy.'

In the aftermath of internment, Lynch had appealed to Heath to take over security from Stormont and to establish a power-sharing executive in Northern Ireland. Heath had initially reacted rather contemptuously to these suggestions, but by March 1972 he had come around to Lynch's way of thinking. Of course, Heath acted as if these were his own ideas, but then admitting that the Taoiseach had suggested any idea to him was hardly the way to win unionist support. Following the upheaval in the wake of Bloody Sunday, Heath feared that Northern Ireland was on the verge of anarchy. About a hundred bombs were going off every month and forty-nine people had been killed in the first two months of 1972. 'I therefore decided that we had to assume direct control of law and order forthwith,' Heath wrote.

The Foreign Secretary and former Prime Minister Alec Douglas-Home was totally opposed to the idea. He actually wrote to Heath on 13 March 1972 to state that no sustainable framework could be contrived to keep Northern Ireland within the United Kingdom, and London should therefore start pushing the area towards Irish unity. Heath invited Faulkner to London the following week and informed him that London was going to assume control of security in the North, phase out internment and hold a referendum in Northern Ireland on the continuance of the border. The outcome of the referendum was a foregone conclusion but it would afford the people an opportunity of expressing their wishes unambiguously.

'I also put it to him that it was now time for the Northern Ireland government to consider power-sharing with the Catholic minority,' Heath wrote. 'Faulkner refused to do so, on the ground that he could never accept anyone in his Cabinet who was actively seeking unification.' Stormont was therefore prorogued. But the Prime Minister had not given up on the idea of power-sharing in order to isolate the terrorists. 'Everything we did during the latter part of 1972' was intended to promote the idea of power-sharing, according to Heath.

Although the British Prime Minister had come around to accepting the policies advocated by Lynch, there was little personal rapport between the two men. Heath adopted an arrogant and imperious attitude that reeked of superior colonial boorishness, which irritated the polite Lynch, who was a thorough gentleman. They both attended the opening of the Olympic Games in Munich, and seized on the opportunity to meet each other afterwards. Lynch understood their meeting to be confidential and was therefore horrified to learn the following day that the British had issued a rather threatening statement complaining about cross-border incursions from the Republic. 'Unless it were felt both in Great Britain generally and in Northern Ireland in particular that the South is taking action against the IRA,' the official statement read, 'there is little hope of an acceptable solution.'

This did little to improve the personal relationship between the two men, because Lynch was already under pressure from both the Opposition and from within his own party for supposedly being too weak, and not standing up to Heath. The unilateral publication of such a statement to the press only supported the image of the Taoiseach being pushed around. It was as if Heath was acting contemptuously in order to hide the fact that he had completed a political U-turn and adopted as his own the Northern policies advocated by Lynch.

'Whatever arrangements are made for the future administration of Northern Ireland must take account of the province's relationship with the Republic of Ireland,' the Northern Secretary, Willie Whitelaw, told the House of Commons in October 1972. 'The economy and the security of the two areas are to some considerable extent interdependent, and the same is true of both in their relationship with Great Britain. It is therefore clearly desirable that any new arrangements for Northern Ireland should, whilst meeting the wishes of Northern Ireland and Great Britain, be so far as possible acceptable to and accepted by the Republic of Ireland.'

Sir John Peck, the British ambassador, was delighted with Whitelaw's statement. It was what Peck had been advocating for the past couple of years. He felt that this strengthened Lynch's political hand in dealing with the IRA.

Lynch took a particularly strong stand against violence following RTÉ's broadcast of an interview with Seán Mac Stiofáin, the chief of staff of the Provisional IRA, on 19 November 1972. In the course of the interview with Kevin O'Kelly, he had 'unmistakably held himself out as a person in a position of authority in that organisation,' according to Lynch. MacStiofáin was therefore arrested and he protested by going on a hunger and thirst strike.

The Cabinet discussed the matter a couple of days later and Gerard Collins, the Minister for Posts and Telegraphs, issued an ultimatum to RTÉ to accept the government's interpretation of Section 31 of the Broadcasting Act and thus 'refrain from broadcasting any matter that could be calculated to promote the aims and activities of any organisation which engages in, promotes, encourages or advocates the attaining of any particular objective by violent means.'

Lynch had gone to London to take part in the Oxford Union debate which considered the issue of Irish unity. In the course of this speech he argued for an end to partition but stressed that the premature withdrawal of British forces 'would precipitate a disastrous scale of violence and bloodshed. The aim of responsible leadership in all countries must be to avoid such an outcome.' He indicated that Ireland was willing to make constitutional adjustments to win over Northern unionists. 'For our part, we are willing to do everything open to us to work towards such a settlement,' he stated. 'We have no absolute demands or preconditions. I have indicated repeatedly our willingness to adapt in constitutional and other matters to the requirement of a new Ireland. This willingness would quickly become evident if a genuine dialogue developed and a new and definite direction were set for the future.'

The Taoiseach had already indicated that his government was ready to recommend the repeal of Article 44 of the Consitution, which recognised 'the special position of the Roman Catholic Church'. He had also hinted at a willingness to reform the country's legislation banning the sale of contraception. 'I would not like to leave contraception on the long finger too long,' he declared – much to the amusement of more than a few people.

When the RTÉ Authority failed to provide an assurance that the station would respect the government's interpretation of the Broadcasting Act, Collins issued a statement at 10 p.m. on Friday

24 November 1972 announcing that he had dismissed all nine members of the Authority. They included the Chairman, Dónal Ó Moráin of Gael Linn; Matthew Feehan, a former editor of the *Sunday Press*; James Fanning, editor of the *Midland Tribune*; Michael O'Callaghan, editor of the *Roscommon Herald*; Professor T. W. Moody of Trinity College; and Phyllis O'Kelly, widow of former President Seán T. O'Kelly. At the same time he announced that they were being replaced by a new Authority, under the chairmanship of James A. Scannell, a former permanent secretary of the Department of Posts and Telegraphs.

'I have just sacked the RTÉ Authority who supported Kevin O'Kelly,' Lynch told Ulick O'Connor that night. 'I suppose you don't think much of that.'

'I certainly don't,' O'Connor replied. 'It doesn't say much for your views on freedom of speech. You'll rue that.'

Lynch grinned. 'Fuck them,' he said, and walked off.

Mac Stiofáin went on trial at the Central Criminal Court the following day. Kevin O'Kelly was called to identify him as the man that he had interviewed, but O'Kelly refused. A garda did testify, however, that he recognised Mac Stiofáin's voice on the tape, and Mac Stiofáin was therefore convicted and sentenced to six months in jail for membership of an illegal organisation.

'It might as well be six years!' he shouted at the three judges. 'I'm going to die in six days. I have taken no liquids and no food since my arrest. I'll not take liquids or food. I'll see you in hell before I submit. You had no evidence against me. I repeat: I will be dead in six days. Live with that.'

'British traitors!' a young man in the public gallery shouted, as he threw coins at the judges. The coins hit a light fixture, shattering the glass, which crashed to the floor of the court. The twenty-seven-year-old man was arrested and promptly sentenced to three months in jail for contempt of court. Kevin O'Kelly received a similar sentence – much to the dismay of his colleagues, who shut down RTÉ for two days in protest.

The next couple of days, while RTÉ was off the air, were certainly eventful. Mac Stiofáin had been taken from the court to the Mater Hospital. A bomb went off outside a cinema on Burgh Quay in Dublin at about 1.35 a.m. the following morning, injuring some forty people. The day after that, some 7,000 protesters gathered outside the General Post Office and paraded to the hospital to protest at Mac Stiofáin's detention. That night, eight armed men, disguised as priests and hospital workers, tried to rescue Mac Stiofáin at the hospital. Three gardaí were held at gunpoint by the two bogus priests but one of their colleagues managed to radio for help. Special Branch detectives arrived and a shoot-out took place in the hospital corridor. One of the intruders was shot in the fingers, one of the detectives was shot in the hand and two bystanders were injured, but none of the wounds were serious. The would-be rescuers escaped in a waiting taxi that they had hijacked earlier that evening.

Mac Stiofáin was then transferred to St Brichin's Military Hospital, but there was no question of releasing him, as far as Lynch was concerned. 'If a member of such an organisation, and especially a self-confessed leader, could secure his release from prison through resorting to hunger or thirst strike, the inevitable consequence would be that not only he but all his associates would be effectively above the law of the land and free to act as they choose and would be seen to be so,' the Taoiseach warned. 'This is so for the obvious reason that other prisoners, now or in the future, need only adopt the same tactics to ensure that they, too, would be released. Accordingly, the issue in the present case is nothing less than whether parliament, government, the courts and the law are all to surrender to an unlawful organisation. The challenge to the institutions of the state is direct, deliberate and unmistakable. The government have no choice but to meet it.'

Mac Stiofáin would die before the Taoiseach would agree to release him. 'The consequences that may ensue are regretted by the members of the government as they no doubt are regretted by everybody with a normal human concern for human life,' Lynch explained. 'The consequences, however, are not of the government's making.

'Hundreds of people have been killed by bombs and guns and hundreds have been maimed by bombs and guns,' he added. 'Many of these people were innocent women and children. Unfortunately, they had no choice between life and death.' The Taoiseach did not have to spell out the significance of that aspect of his message. Public alarm, he added, would be all the greater 'if this government or any government were to abdicate their authority on an occasion such as this.'

Even though he took a firm stand on the hunger strike, Lynch was careful to project a compassionate and humane attitude. When he learned, for instance, that Mac Stiofáin's wife had been refused permission to see her husband at the hospital late the previous night, the Taoiseach described the refusal as a regrettable decision.

In the midst of this crisis Des O'Malley introduced an amendment to the Offences Against the State Act which would allow a senior garda to give evidence in court as to his belief that an accused was a member of an illegal organisation. Aspects of the 1939 legislation conflicted with the European Convention on Human Rights, so the Offences Against the State Act had to be amended to ensure that what amounted to hearsay evidence from senior gardaí could be admitted in evidence. Many of those previously convicted had already been released by the courts, and few convictions would be secured unless senior gardaí were allowed to give their opinions as evidence. It would then be up to the courts whether or not that evidence was believed. Lynch enthusiastically endorsed 'every word and every sentence' that O'Malley had said in introducing the legislation.

'We do not want to impose internment,' the Taoiseach explained. 'We are not intending to impose internment in this bill, but we want to do something far less and we want the help from the Fine Gael Party that they promised through so many of their speakers.' The Fine Gael leader, Liam Cosgrave, had said on many occasions that he would give the Fianna Fáil government whatever support was needed to deal with the problem. He wished to uphold his promise, but it was likely to cost him his leadership, because too many of his party colleagues were determined to exploit the occasion for party advantage, as there was a real chance of bringing down the government. This use of partisan politics was to have disastrous consequences.

Among those leading the revolt within Fine Gael were the future Taoiseach, Garret FitzGerald, and the future Chief Justice, T. F. O'Higgins. Another future Taoiseach, John Bruton, was among their supporters. The Fine Gael parliamentary party voted by 38 to 8 to oppose the legislation. After that ballot, six of those supporting Cosgrave changed their votes, leaving Cosgrave supported by Paddy Donegan alone.

FitzGerald had said in August 1971 that Fine Gael would back the government in introducing internment as a last resort, if the government first tried the Special Criminal Court and found it wanting. 'This party has always stood by any government, no matter how much it is opposed to it, which, acting properly and with due process, seeks to protect the liberties and lives of our people and the society in which we live,' FitzGerald had said then. But now that there was a political advantage to be gained, he and his colleagues were acting differently.

'We are now looking for that support and it is apparently going to be denied us,' Lynch declared. 'We have indicated and, indeed, we have proved the difficulties we have, difficulties Deputy Garret FitzGerald spelled out so eloquently. We went through everything. Our courts have not been effective. Juries have been intimidated. Witnesses have been intimidated. The Special Criminal Court itself has not been successful because, as I indicated, the rule of evidence prevented that court from bringing in convictions against known leaders of the IRA.'

The Dáil hung in the balance and sat on a Friday night, 30 November 1972, to take the crucial vote. As T. F. O'Higgins was speaking, Noël Davern of Fianna Fáil interrupted him. 'Does the Deputy support the two bombings that occurred a few minutes ago?'

'Don't be a bloody ass,' O'Higgins replied, unaware that two bombs had just gone off in Dublin. At that point FitzGerald whispered to him what had happened. O'Higgins quickly finished his speech. Cosgrave could not be found, so O'Higgins took it upon himself as the party's spokesman on justice to withdraw the Fine Gael amendment. When the vote was taken that night, only two Fine Gael deputies voted against the government.

It was still taken for granted, however, that the missing Cosgrave was finished as party leader, but his colleagues did not know he was actually appearing on television that night, to great effect. 'By Saturday morning he was widely seen as the hero of the hour,' according to FitzGerald. Cosgrave was 'the man who stood firm and had, in tragic circumstances, been proved right.'

Lynch considered going to the country in December 1972 and would have had to do so if the government had been defeated on the Fine Gael amendment. This was the kind of thing that de Valera would have done, but Lynch waited. In hindsight, it was probably a political mistake, but calling an election in the circumstances would have left him open to the damaging charge of using the Northern situation for electoral advantage. On the other hand, most of the Opposition had clearly been playing that game.

Of course, Lynch did leave himself open to the accusation of playing politics with the North, but then political reality dictated that he could not ignore the issue. On 3 February 1973 he noted that the British had claimed the North as part of the United

Kingdom for over fifty years, but they had permitted standards of public behaviour that fell far short of those that applied in Britain. 'Knowing what they now know, and seeing what they have seen, I believe that the British people, and the thinking moderate unionists in the North, are no longer prepared to tolerate this version of "the British way of life" to be perpetuated, nor would they endorse a British government doing so in their name,' the Taoiseach said. 'The faded Orange card will have to be trumped this time.' He was clearly intimating that it should be trumped with his own Green card.

The speech was really the first shot in the forthcoming general-election campaign. The Dáil still had fifteen months to run when Lynch made that major speech on the North, so it was not immediately apparent that it was an election address, but two days later the Taoiseach asked President de Valera to dissolve the Dáil and call a general election.

Fianna Fáil might well have won handsomely had the election been held in December. Since then, Fine Gael and Labour had entered negotiations to fight the election as part of a coalition in order to oust Fianna Fáil, but little progress was being made. 'These talks are getting nowhere,' Cosgrave reportedly told a meeting of the Fine Gael parliamentary party. 'We might as well end them.'

Lynch supposedly heard of this and called a general election on 5 Feburary, to be held on 28 February. This forced the Fine Gael and Labour negotiators to concentrate their efforts and within a couple of days they had drawn up a fourteen-point manifesto on which they would fight the election as a coalition. Fine Gael had negotiated promises on security matters, European affairs and the removal of Irish as a compulsory examination subject, while Labour was more interested in social and economic reforms, such as more public housing, price controls and the removal of VAT from food. This was the first time that the two parties had ever entered into a pre-election pact to promise something to virtually everyone. It was an extraordinary show of unity.

At the same time, the wounds from the arms crisis were still gaping in Fianna Fáil. Frank Aiken notified the Fianna Fáil Director of Elections on 7 February that he intended to stand again for election, but only on condition that Haughey was not ratified by the party as a candidate. 'In view of the shortness of time before nomination day, I wish to give you due warning, as quickly as possible,' Aiken wrote, 'that after much consideration I finally decided this morning that if I am selected as a candidate and Charles Haughey is selected and ratified by the National Executive, I shall withdraw my agreement to stand as a Fianna Fáil candidate.'

When Haughey was duly selected, Lynch refused to intervene and the nomination was ratified by the National Executive. Aiken therefore withdrew his candidacy. in protest on 10 February. He still planned to support the party, and he recommended that he should be replaced on the Fianna Fáil panel by either John Hume or Austin Curry of the Social Democratic and Labour Party in Northern Ireland.

Aiken intended to make a public announcement of his reasons for retiring, but pressure was brought to bear on him to remain quiet. 'It is too late to oust Haughey,' Paddy Smith wrote to Aiken on 12 February. 'That should have been done two years ago.' Haughey had been elected a national vice-president of Fianna Fáil at the most recent *ard fheis*. He had been attending all National Executive meetings and consistently supported the government in the Dáil. Hence the National Executive had no choice but to ratify Haughey's nomination.

'I have no brief for the man. I am not trying to be his case-maker but I know I have no course open to me but to do the only thing left to me, and you are just as guilty as I am and every other member of the party,' Smith continued. 'This man for better or for worse has been functioning in the party ever since he made that speech after the trial.'

President de Valera eventually persuaded Aiken not to go public with his reasons for retiring. The public announcement was made by Lynch at a rally of some 200 party activists at Dundalk Town Hall on 13 February. This was the first stop on Lynch's nationwide pre-election tour. He paid tribute to Aiken for having done Trojan work during his forty-nine years as a Dáil deputy. It was actually Aiken's seventy-fifth birthday and the gathering was told that he was stepping down due to his health. It was further indicated that he had not attended a rally in Navan earlier that day because he was not feeling well. The story about Aiken's health was a deliberate lie.

Lynch initially used the same campaign tactics which had worked so well in 1969. He drew attention to the differences between Fine Gael and Labour, warning that the two could not form a stable government. Campaigning in Sligo, he concentrated on the Labour leader's criticism of Fine Gael during the 1969 campaign. 'What were Mr Corish's views then about a coalition with Fine Gael?' Lynch asked.

When Labour spokesmen said that their party was moving to the left in 1969, Corish admitted that nobody had believed them. 'What's worse,' Lynch said, 'they don't even believe it themselves.'

He had had little trouble exploiting the differences between Fine Gael and Labour in 1969, because Labour was determined then that it would not go into government with any party. This time, Labour and Fine Gael were fighting the election as part of a coalition. They were clearly united in their determination to oust Fianna Fáil. The Taoiseach was trying to exploit the skepticism of left-wing voters, but Fianna Fáil had its own credibility problems, and those seemed to grow during the campaign.

Campaigning in Mayo in June 1973, Lynch shared a platform with Michael Moran and Joe Leneghan, who had been re-admitted to Fianna Fáil only days before nominations closed. They were trying to paper over the cracks in the party. In Ballymote Lynch was introduced as 'the greatest-ever statesman', to his own apparent embarrassment. 'I'm not the greatest statesman,' he told the gathering modestly. 'Far from it. What I am is President of Fianna Fáil, which is the most widely representative organisation in the country. I make no better claim than that. I have the honour to represent the party with the greatest cross-section of Irish people in it.'

'If a local team would be champions year after year, I could understand people wanting another to succeed and win the cup,' Lynch declared at a rally in Swinford Town Hall. 'But there is a big difference between football and politics. Change for change's sake is not good enough. I am convinced that a change of government would be in the worst possible interest of this country.'

A day later in Carrick-on-Shannon, County Leitrim, the volatile nature of Irish politics was apparent as the Taoiseach was met by a hostile group who were protesting against the imprisonment of Ruairí Ó Brádaigh, the president of Provisional Sinn Féin. 'Up the Provos!' they shouted. 'Jack Lynch – traitor!' Two eggs were thrown at him, but both missed. 'You have witnessed here this evening the need for strong government for stability, for a government to take on people who refuse to come before the electorate, but who try to intimidate the rest of us with eggs,' Lynch told the crowd.

Martin O'Donoghue realised that the government would save £30 million on subsidies and he advocated that Fianna Fáil should respond to the coalition manifesto with separate promises to abolish rates on dwelling houses. As Minister for Finance, George Colley rejected the idea, but the coalition's promise to abolish VAT on foodstuffs had so captured the public imagination that Lynch realised something had to be done. Before he could act, however, somebody leaked what was being planned, and Cosgrave got in first with a further package of promises on 21 February, exactly one week before the election. On behalf of the coalition, he promised to spend the £30 million that would be saved on subsidies by increasing social welfare. His plans included £1 a week extra on the old-age pension, the widow's pension and the payment to deserted wives, as well as £1.50 a month extra on the children's allowance, and an increase in social-insurance benefits. The overall cost of these increases would run to £40 million, but he said the extra money could be obtained from the recently announced tax surplus from the previous year.

This stole much of the thunder from Lynch's package the following day. His plan included a sensational promise to abolish the rates on all dwelling houses from 1 April 1974. A government white paper published seven weeks earlier had come out firmly against the abolition of rates, and the Monday before, George Colley had said there was no alternative to the rates, even though they were unfair.

'The coalition have taunted us about not putting forward our programme, and this is our answer to them,' Lynch said. But the promise to abolish the rates brought the credibility of his whole campaign into question.

'There is no point in transferring taxation from one pocket to another,' Brian Lenihan had said in ridiculing the coalition proposals. Now Lynch seemed to be proposing to do just that in order to raise the £35 million needed to pay for the new programme that he had just announced. 'I would not deny that we would have to raise extra taxation,' he said. 'When you think in terms of £35 million, somebody is going to have to pay.' But he refused to say who would have to pay the extra tax. 'It is not the practice of a government to say where it will come from,' he argued.

After ridiculing the coalition proposals, labelling them with all kinds of tags, from 'pie-in-the-sky' to 'pious platitudes', Fianna Fáil had been forced by the public reaction to try to produce better terms. Lynch denied that the proposals were '"a bribe", but to any objective observer they clearly are,' wrote Liam O'Neill, the political correspondent of the *Cork Examiner*. 'It does seem that Fianna Fáil, by the production of their proposals yesterday, have flown in the face of almost everything they had been saying about policies since the election campaign began . . . Certainly the issue now is one of credibility.'

After launching the new proposals, Lynch visited eleven different centres. At Ballymun he shared a platform with Charles Haughey. They shook hands but said little to each other.

There was real embarrassment for Lynch and Fianna Fáil the following day. The *Limerick Leader* came out with a large advertisement in the form of a message to the voters in Limerick West from the Fianna Fáil candidates – Gerry Collins, the Minister for Posts and Telegraphs, and Michael Noonan. 'Jack Lynch has not tried to ensure re-election by trading on the innocence of some of the people. He does not dangle rosy promises of "No VAT on food", "No rates", etc, to win over the unsuspecting,' they asserted. 'The plain people of Ireland know only too well that remission of these taxes will only result in drastic increases in taxes on other essentials, such as electricity, fuel, clothing, household goods and indeed on drink, cigarettes and, yes, income tax.'

The Opposition had a field day with that message. They accused Fianna Fáil of panicking in bringing forward the rates proposal without even discussing it in Cabinet. Cosgrave asked if Lynch's Cabinet colleagues even knew what he was doing.

Lynch's team had a tired look about it, in contrast to the leading figures in the coalition. John Healy actually came out in favour of Cosgrave and the coalition in *The Irish Times*. He admired the patriotic way in which the Fine Gael leader had insisted on putting the national interest before the interests of his party at the time that the Offences Against the State Act was being implemented. But the coalition had a fresh team. 'Starkly put,' Healy wrote, 'it offers more talent, man for man, and under the stern leadership of Liam Cosgrave will give the country good government and make for healthy democracy.'

As usual, Lynch wound up his campaign in his own constituency. In company with his wife and a reporter from the *Cork Examiner*, he toured the constituency. His first stop was at St Anne's Shandon, where he and his wife climbed to the top of the 120-foot-high bell tower. From the parapet, they looked out on the city.

'That's where I played as a little boy,' he said.

'Where?' Máirín asked.

'Down there in that churchyard,' he said, pointing to the graveyard below them. 'Up there is the North Monastery, where I went to school,' he added, pointing in the opposite direction.

'That building up there, is it?' she asked.

'Do you see the Bishop's Palace? Just above that!'

On the way from the church, Lynch pointed out to reporters the house where he was born. He stopped for 'a small one' in The Chimes public house. He then went to Glen Rovers Club, before heading off for the final election rally in Patrick's Street, where an estimated 8,000 people had gathered. Pearse Wyse spoke admiringly, describing the Taoiseach as 'the greatest leader Ireland has ever known. Never in its history was Fianna Fáil so united as it was approaching this election.'

Lynch headed the poll in Cork City North-West with 12,427 votes, 7,800 more than his nearest rival. He was elected on the first count with almost a quota to spare. His running mate Seán French was also easily elected, and Fianna Fáil took two of the three seats in the constituency.

It was a measure of Lynch's popularity that Fianna Fáil actually increased its share of the first-preference vote from 45.7 per cent to 46.2 per cent. He had secured an overall majority and Seán Lemass had twice retained power as Taoiseach with a smaller percentage of the vote, but the vagaries of PR came into play as a result of the unprecedentedly disciplined transfers between Fine Gael and the Labour Party.

In 1969, for instance, in counts where there were only Fianna Fáil and Labour candidates left after the last Fine Gael candidate was eliminated, only 34 per cent of the Fine Gael vote transferred to the Labour candidate. Four years later, some 71 per cent of the vote transferred to Labour candidates. In instances where there was a Fianna Fáil and a Fine Gael candidate left when the last Labour candidate was eliminated, only 36 per cent of the vote transferred to Fine Gael in 1969, but that jumped to 70 per cent in 1973. Consequently, even though the Labour vote declined by almost 20 per cent (from 17 to 13.7 per cent nationally), the party actually gained a seat, while Fine Gael gained four seats with a 1 per cent increase in its national vote in 1973. At the same time, Fianna Fáil lost six seats. Thus the coalition of Fine Gael and Labour secured an overall majority of 73 seats in the 144-seat Dáil.

As the results were coming in, Lynch appeared in the RTÉ television studio to take part in the election programme. He had clearly suffered a defeat, but he was as magnanimous and gracious in defeat as he had earlier been in victory and he made a great impression on viewers. Fianna Fáil were out in the cold after sixteen years in power, but Lynch accepted the setback with style.

17

SPUTTERING IN OPPOSITION

1973–1976

After losing power, some of Lynch's critics within Fianna Fáil hoped that he would run for the presidency of Ireland in 1973 to replace the ninety-one-year-old de Valera, who was constitutionally barred from seeking a third term. Fine Gael were perceived to have a strong candidate in T. F. O'Higgins, who had run de Valera so close in 1966. There is little doubt that Lynch could have had the Fianna Fáil nomination, if he had wished. He was so popular that he would probably have won the election, but he was unwilling to stand. His former Tánaiste, Erskine Childers, was selected instead.

With the trouble in Northern Ireland, Childers afforded the Catholic people of the Republic an opportunity to demonstrate their tolerance by voting for him, a Protestant. Unlike his predecessor, Childers defeated O'Higgins by a comfortable margin of 635,162 votes to 587,577. In the process, Childers gained 77,354 more votes than de Valera had won in 1966.

Although Childers stressed that he ran a 'purely personal' campaign and 'kept entirely to the new presidential role outside the party-political field', the result was seen as a victory for Fianna Fáil. 'It will serve as a much-needed morale-booster to Fianna Fáil,

who have been drifting aimlessly since the general-election defeat,'
Liam O'Neill of the *Cork Examiner* wrote. The Cork vote in the
presidential election undoubtedly provided a boost for Lynch's
leadership in the gloom of the general-election defeat. O'Higgins
won all ten Dublin constituencies, but his margin of victory was
reduced to a little over 1,000 from a margin of over 9,000 in 1966.
Cork city, which more than made up for the deficit, afforded
Childers over 61.5 per cent of the vote. Lynch's own Cork
constituency actually gave Childers his highest percentage vote in
the country, and the 6,366 votes that he had to spare there
comprised the largest numerical surplus that he had in any
constituency. Thus the Childers victory was a great boost for
Lynch, which was just as well, because he made one of the greatest
gaffes of his career soon afterwards.

In August 1973 the British government admitted that two
brothers – Keith and Kenneth Littlejohn, who had been involved
in a Dublin bank robbery the previous October – had actually been
recruited by British intelligence to provide information on the IRA.
When the Dublin government sought the extradition of the
Littlejohns from Britain in January, the British insisted that they
should not be tried for any political offences they might have
committed. Lynch criticised the coalition government for acceding
to the request, but it was his own government which had done so,
back in January. Lynch denied this and Colm Condon, his former
Attorney General, denounced the coalition claim as a 'disreputable
lie'.

Garret FitzGerald, the Minister for Foreign Affairs, instructed
the permanent secretary of his department, Hugh McCann, to
remind Lynch that he had shown him a report on 3 January 1973
in which the British had admitted that they had accepted 'an offer
of information concerning IRA activities' from the Littlejohns. The
British insisted, however, that they had not authorised them to
engage in any illegal activities. Hugh McCann reminded Lynch of

the meeting and recalled that the then Taoiseach had asked him to pass on the information to the Minister for Justice, Des O'Malley.

After talking with McCann, the former Taoiseach admitted that he had indeed been informed but had forgotten the whole thing. 'I did not remember the details of it until Mr McCann called,' Lynch explained. 'It is impossible to remember all the scores of messages and interviews the Taoiseach gets each day.'

The Littlejohn incident had been extremely embarrassing for the British government, but Lynch found himself in the spotlight over his gaffe. On 14 August he met with three journalists from RTÉ, the *Daily Mail* and the *Cork Examiner* in the garden of the Eldon Hotel in Skibbereen. He explained that McCann had informed him about the Littlejohn affair while he was busy with preparations for a promotional trip to the United States for the IDA. Hence he had forgotten their meeting.

'My loss of memory was responsible for the confusion of the past week,' he admitted. 'I regarded it as serious and in the circumstances I will have to consider my position of continuing leadership of the opposition party.'

Larry Lyons of the *Cork Examiner* was so surprised by these remarks that he asked the former Taoiseach to repeat what he had said. The report caused a political sensation. George Colley told the media in Dublin that 'the Fianna Fáil Party and organisation would not consider for an instant the question of Jack Lynch resigning.' Des O'Malley told RTÉ that he was taking the blame for what had happened. If he had not been on holidays, he said, he would have helped to refresh Lynch's memory. He was insistent that there was no reason whatsoever for Lynch to resign.

Other prominent members of the party, such as Paddy Smith, Joseph Brennan and Brian Lenihan, urged Lynch not to resign. Lenihan, who was joint National Secretary of Fianna Fáil, said that there was no question of a 'mere lapse in recollection being regarded in Fianna Fáil as a reason why he should resign.' (It was ironic that some of Lynch's strongest backers would later insist on Lenihan's resignation as Tánaiste following a fairly similar lapse of memory over a much less significant issue.)

Garret FitzGerald was curious about the documents that Lynch had forgotten. He asked Hugh McCann to let him see them.

'I showed them to you in May,' McCann responded.

'My sympathy for Jack Lynch went up immeasurably,' Fitz-Gerald wrote. Under the pressure of routine official business, FitzGerald had forgotten that he had seen them himself. He had no difficulty in understanding what had happened to Lynch, especially when the latter had the added burden of the American trip followed soon after by the general-election campaign. 'It is all too easy to forget an episode in the busy life of a government member,' FitzGerald wrote. 'Jack Lynch's reputation suffered thereafter and a degree of fun was poked at him for having forgotten what he had known about this curious incident.'

The comedian Niall Tóibín had a routine in which he played the part of a forgetful singer at a Cork wedding. His punchline in the sketch was, 'Jack can forget; I can forget, too!'

Lynch came under further pressure on the issue of the presidency when Erskine Childers died suddenly of a heart attack on 17 November 1974. The search for a successor became a very messy affair. Media speculation about his successor had begun almost immediately.

'On the night of November 17, I watched the search for the successor described, on a television screen carrying the very emblem of the presidency, as a cat-and-mouse game between the parties,' the late President's widow, Rita Childers, explained. There had even been reports that 'hackles were up' over seating at the funeral. 'I decided immediately that I must intervene. Someone had to expose the political cynicism that was gripping Leinster House.' She issued a statement to the press.

'Let us pledge never again to allow such corrosive, destructive cynicism about politics to contaminate that high office so that the children and youth in whom our whole future depends may at least have this one above-politics focus to inspire them,' she declared. Four days later, on 21 November, Cosgrave suggested to Lynch during a function at Iveagh House that Rita Childers should be named as President by agreement. The coalition government, which obviously wished to avoid a contest, having lost to Childers only the previous year, was prepared to support her nomination as an agreed candidate. Lynch agreed to sound out Fianna Fáil.

The following day, however, a Fine Gael member of Skibbereen Urban Council, acting on his own initiative, suggested at a council meeting that Rita Childers should succeed her husband. This was reported on 23 November in the *Cork Examiner* under the headline, 'Mrs Childers for President: Skibbereen Call'. As a result, Noël Smith of the *Irish Independent* asked the Minister for the Gaeltacht, Tom O'Donnell, about the possibility of Mrs Childers being nominated. O'Donnell mistakenly thought the word of the government decision was already out, so he explained to Smith that the government was prepared to back her. The following day the *Sunday Independent* carried the story under the headline: 'Mrs Childers for President'. Smith quoted a government source as saying that Mrs Childers could have the nomination, if she wished.

Lynch was furious. He considered this a breach of confidentiality, as it looked like the coalition was using her candidacy to upstage Fianna Fáil. That killed the possibility of having her as an agreed candidate as far as Lynch was concerned. He felt that the party would not agree to a woman candidate in the circumstances and he sent David Andrews and Michael O'Kennedy to explain the situation to her.

She took the visit badly. She had never been approached by either side, but insult was added to injury when it was suggested at the time that her name had only been put forward as a political ruse. Nobody bothered to deny the suggestion that floating her name had been a stunt. She therefore announced on 27 November that she was ready to run, even as a non-party candidate.

Lynch flatly ruled out standing for the office himself that day, thereby further enhancing his image as the reluctant politician, as well as someone who was acting for the public good, rather than feathering his own nest. He said that those being considered included T. K. Whitaker, Donal Keenan, the President of the GAA, and Cearbhall Ó Dálaigh, then a judge of the European Court of Justice in Luxembourg.

Lynch decided on Ó Dálaigh and he asked Paddy Hillery, the Irish member of the European Commission, to do the needful in approaching the judge. 'Any chance you'd get hold of Cearbhall Ó Dálaigh and see how he'd react?' Lynch asked.

Ó Dálaigh was not only a former Attorney General but a former Chief Justice, and as such, he seemed eminently qualified. He accepted. Although Rita Childers said that she welcomed his selection, she still expressed horror at the degradation of the presidency and the shabby way in which she, as a woman, had been treated.

While all this was going on, there was a power struggle developing within Fianna Fáil, as pressure was mounting on Lynch to bring Charles Haughey back to the front bench of the party. The pressure became so intense that Lynch issued a statement on 8 December that there was no animosity between them. He had nominated Haughey to the chairmanship of the Dáil Committee on EEC Affairs. 'I don't bear malice towards people and harbour grudges,' he explained. 'I think it's best these things are forgotten.' He said that the criminal charges had been brought against Haughey by the Attorney General. 'As far as I am concerned, it's over.'

Two days later, the government concluded the Sunningdale agreement with the British government and representatives of both communities in Northern Ireland. This was the kind of conference that Lynch had advocated in 1971 and there is little doubt that a great deal of the credit for the agreement should have gone to him, as he had done the groundwork. But now, in opposition, he had to move carefully. The main features of the agreement were that it would set up a power-sharing executive in Northern Ireland with a Council of Ireland to take over agreed functions on an all-Ireland basis. Such a council had been part of the initial Government of Ireland Act, 1920, which had established partition.

To satisfy the demands of unionists, Dublin agreed to recognise that the status of Northern Ireland could not change without the approval of the majority of the people. This had been the reality of the situation for many years, going back to Éamon de Valera's tenure as Taoiseach and before. The unionists were seeking a change to Articles 2 and 3 of the Irish Constitution, but the Cosgrave government feared that any referendum to secure the desired amendments would be defeated.

'If we had tried and failed to amend Articles 2 and 3, we would thereby have destroyed the Sunningdale settlement,' Garret FitzGerald wrote. Even though they thought that Lynch might have wished to facilitate them in this, the coalition government was afraid that he was too vulnerable within Fianna Fáil, given that the party's defeat in the general election had been followed shortly afterwards by the embarrassment of the Littlejohn affair. The republican element within the party might have 'brought him down and replaced him with someone else, who, whatever his own convictions, would have been likely in the circumstances to have been a prisoner of extreme elements in his own party,' FitzGerald argued.

In January 1975 Lynch's line on Northern Ireland seemed to come into question when Michael O'Kennedy, his spokesman on foreign affairs, called on the British to make a declaration of their intention to withdraw from the Six Counties in order 'to concentrate the minds' of the people there. Rather than confront his spokesman, Lynch just backed down and restored Haughey to the front bench as spokesman for health a few days later. The appointment was generally seen as a kind of republican rebellion within Fianna Fáil.

Lynch sought to make a virtue of necessity. 'If we preach reconciliation in the North between people who have clear differences, there is no reason not to practise it ourselves,' he explained. 'Charlie Haughey had, in my opinion, purged whatever indiscretion he was involved in. I felt that I was doing the right thing, the Christian thing and the fair thing in giving him a chance again.'

But when it came to Christian forgiveness, Rita Childers clearly had a different perspective. She rejected an invitation to attend a Mass being organised by Fianna Fáil for the repose of her late husband's soul. 'There will be no representative of the Childers family present,' she replied. 'The late President would not benefit from the prayers of such a party. Happily for him, he is now closer to God and will be able to ask His intercession that his much-loved country will never again be governed by these people.'

Lynch was convinced that her action was the result of her disappointment in being passed over for President. The wounds within Fianna Fáil were still so deep, however, that many people believed she was reacting to Haughey's front-bench appointment.

Gradually Lynch gathered a young, energetic team about him. Martin O'Donoghue, a professor of economics from Trinity College who had joined his staff during the arms crisis, became the economic strategist. Séamus Brennan replaced the retired Tommy Mullins as general secretary of the party, and twenty-five-year-old Frank Dunlop was appointed press secretary.

The coalition government fared well during its first few years of office, but things began to go horribly wrong in 1976. On 21 July of that year, the IRA murdered the British ambassador,

Christopher Ewart-Biggs, as he was driving from his residence to the embassy in Dublin. The government reacted by calling a special session of the Oireachtas to pass a new Emergency Powers Bill. The emergency declared in September 1939, at the start of the Second World War, had never actually been revoked, so the coalition government decided to revoke it now and declare a new emergency as a means of emphasising their determination to end the IRA's murder campaign.

The proposals introduced in the bill included an increase in the maximum sentence for membership of an illegal organisation, to seven years' imprisonment, and it became a new offence to incite people to join an illegal organisation. This would carry a sentence of up to ten years in jail. Certain powers of arrest were being accorded to the army, and the gardaí were accorded the right to hold suspects for seven days without charge.

Lynch denounced the legislation as unnecessary and dangerous. He warned that it could lead to a police state. The effect of declaring an emergency meant that legislation to cope with the security situation could not be challenged in the courts on constitutional grounds. This had essentially been the situation since 1939, so if the government really did not intend to implement drastically different measures, it was legitimate to question why they were declaring a new emergency when those powers already existed. The gardaí already had the right to hold suspects for up to forty-eight hours, and permitting suspects to be held for a further five days would amount to a form of internment, according to Lynch.

Although he opposed the legislation, he was at pains to emphasise that he had no sympathy for members of the IRA. 'We denounced and reject them as the enemy of the Irish people, and the enemies of the progress of our people politically, socially and economically,' he emphasised. 'We denounce them as enemies of cooperation between the people of Northern Ireland within the

North and between the North and South, and the enemies of the genuinely held national aspirations of the great majority of the Irish people towards the unity of our people.'

The legislation was passed by the Dáil without much difficulty the following day, by 70 votes to 64. But this sparked a sequence of events that did enormous political damage to the government. President Cearbhall Ó Dálaigh had doubts about the constitutionality of the legislation and he called the Council of State into session to advise him. He then exercised his power to refer the bill to the Supreme Court before it could become law. This was only the fifth time in history that a President had exercised this power.

Don Lavery, a cub reporter with the *Westmeath Examiner*, was the only journalist present at the army barracks in Mullingar on 18 October when Patrick Sarsfield Donegan, the Minister for Defence, denounced the President's decision. There had been no shortage of alcohol at the function and Donegan had imbibed rather too much for his own good when he addressed the soldiers.

'It is amazing that the President sent the Emergency Powers Bill to the Supreme Court,' he said in an off-the-cuff remark. 'In my opinion, he is a thundering disgrace.'

The remark was seen as grossly offensive on a number of counts. For one thing, the President had an obligation to refer the bill to the Council of State and the Supreme Court when he had doubts about the constitutionality of the legislation. Donegan's criticism therefore amounted to an attack not just on Ó Dálaigh, but on his office and, thus, an institution of the state. The fact that the Minister was addressing soldiers at the time compounded the insult, because the President is commander-in-chief of the army.

After the incident was reported on RTÉ News, the Minister for Defence promptly expressed regret for his remarks and said that he would apologise to the President personally, but Ó Dálaigh refused to meet him. Donegan then wrote a formal letter of apology. He also privately tendered his resignation to the Cabinet, but Cosgrave declined to accept it.

Lynch denounced 'the gross insult offered to the President and the grave reflection on his integrity, capacity and constitutional status as head of state by the Minister for Defence.' He pressed the Taoiseach to say what he intended to do about the matter.

'I regret that the minister should have made any remarks which slighted the President,' Cosgrave replied. 'The minister has offered a full and unreserved apology to the President.'

'Does the Taoiseach intend to ask for the resignation of the minister or, alternatively, to dismiss him?' Lynch asked.

'I have nothing to add to the reply,' Cosgrave responded in his taciturn way.

'Apologies are not enough,' *The Irish Times* thundered in an editorial. 'Until Mr Donegan resigns, the government's own respect for the institutions of the state must be questioned.'

Lynch pressed the matter to a vote of confidence. 'If we permit an attack on the President from ourselves to be treated lightly, are we not undermining the very institutions of the state that we exhort people to uphold?' he asked in the ensuing debate. 'Any attempt to do so could serve to undermine democracy, and therefore we must, in defence of our institutions and democracy, demand that the most serious form of censure must follow any attempt to so undermine our institutions.'

From the political perspective, Lynch scored heavily. Donegan was the only colleague who had stood with Cosgrave against the majority of Fine Gael in refusing to attack Fianna Fáil's introduction of the Offences Against the State Act in December 1972, so there was something admirable in the Taoiseach's defiant support of his colleague on this occasion, but it was politically damaging. 'One might charitably praise his loyalty to a colleague,' *The Irish Times* noted in an editorial the following day, 'but that virtue cannot be justified at the expense of the government's appearing to be less than wholehearted about the institutions of the state.'

By refusing even to move Donegan to another Cabinet post, Cosgrave left himself open to the accusation of endorsing the insult. His government won the confidence vote in the Dáil on 22 October, but that was not the end of the problem. Ó Dálaigh resigned as President the day after the vote, thereby causing a further constitutional crisis and keeping the spotlight on Donegan.

'The real thundering disgrace this weekend is that this man remains a minister, with just a rebuke from his Taoiseach, with no condemnation from any other member of the government, while being given what can only, in all charity, be described as a fool's pardon by the Dáil on Thursday,' the *Sunday Independent* complained in an editorial. 'If Mr Donegan did not know what he was saying last Monday in the cookhouse in Mullingar, then he is a fool, and fools should not be ministers, least of all voluble fools.' This was a remark made in a newspaper that had traditionally been sympathetic to Fine Gael.

When the Fianna Fáil parliamentary party met to select a nominee to replace Ó Dálaigh, a succession of speakers advocated that Lynch should be nominated, either as a reward for his service to the party, or as a means of assuring victory for the party. He listened without a word. He knew that many of them were just trying to kick him upstairs. He wrote out a statement as he listened to one man make an impassioned appeal that had obviously been written by somebody else, advocating that he deserved the presidency as a reward. The meeting broke for lunch at 1 p.m. and Lynch gave Press Secretary Frank Dunlop the statement for transmission to RTÉ for its 1.30 news bulletin.

'The statement was unequivocal,' Dunlop noted. 'Under no circumstances whatever would he be a candidate for the presidency, either on an agreed cross-party basis or as a Fianna Fáil candidate in an election. Having listened to the statement being broadcast on the radio in my office, he then went home to Máirín in Rathgar for lunch.'

The parliamentary-party meeting resumed at 3 p.m., but lasted only a couple of minutes. 'Jack said that having issued his statement he didn't need any further discussion,' Dunlop noted. In one fell swoop he had flushed out those who wanted him to go, albeit allegedly as a reward, and succeeded in frustrating their attempts by issuing his statement during the lunch break.

The coalition government had already informed Paddy Hillery that he would not be re-nominated as Irish Commissioner to the EEC, so he was to return home at the end of the year. Lynch therefore asked him to run for the presidency. 'Would you come yourself?' he asked. As a result, Hillery was nominated by Fianna Fáil to succeed Ó Dálaigh. The coalition did not dare to nominate an opponent and risk probable defeat at the polls. The Minister for Education, Dick Burke, was appointed to replace Hillery as Irish Commissioner in Brussels, and Cosgrave used the occasion to reshuffle his Cabinet. Donegan was moved to the Department of Lands on the eve of the new President's inauguration, and he was subsequently replaced in Defence by Oliver J. Flanagan, whose appointment afforded the Opposition another field day in the Dáil.

When it came to putting his foot in his mouth, Donegan was a mere novice in comparison with Flanagan, who had decades of experience since his first election to the Dáil in 1943. During his first year in Leinster House, he criticised de Valera's government for directing legislation against republicans and 'not against the Jews who crucified Our Saviour nineteen hundred years ago.' He added that 'there's one good thing Hitler's done, and that's to drive the Jews out of Germany.' Four years later, it was largely as a result of charges that he had made that a judicial tribunal was established to investigate the sale of Locke's Distillery. In the subsequent tribunal report Flanagan was not only denounced as 'reckless and irresponsible' but was specifically accused of having lied under oath in his testimony on two different matters. In 1969 Flanagan caused another stir when he called on the Land Commission to repossess land purchased in Ireland by Germans.

'We have no room for Nazis,' he said, 'and we are not going to entertain them. The country is falling too much into the hands of Germans.' He had served for two years and nine months as parliamentary secretary to the Minister for Agriculture in the 1950s, with the result that he was just three months short of securing a ministerial pension. His appointment was seen as a reward for his loyalty, and he was an unabashed advocate of 'jobs for the boys'.

'I am a firm and convinced believer in jobbery,' he had told Gay Byrne during an appearance on *The Late Late Show* in 1968. 'Any time I hear of a Fianna Fáil minister being criticised for putting their friends into jobs, I am angered because I am not in the same position to put my friends into jobs.' Flanagan was a distinct embarrassment to those who had been advocating that Fine Gael offer an alternative to Fianna Fáil.

18

THE REAL TAOISEACH

1976–1977

In early 1976 Professor Martin O'Donoghue commissioned a public-opinion poll of attitudes towards the government. He forwarded the conclusions to Lynch. 'The widespread loss of confidence with the way the government is handling the country's affairs has resulted in the emergence of an exceptionally large body of unsettled voters who are very uncertain about their present political allegiance,' the survey concluded. The coalition government was particularly weak amongst women voters and young people generally, as well as the families of those from skilled working-class backgrounds. People were generally inclined to express dissatisfaction with the coalition.

As far as Lynch was concerned, his main goal in opposition was to prepare for a return to power. He believed that the general election would be held in June 1977.

Senator Eoin Ryan was chosen as national director of elections for Fianna Fáil. The son of the late Dr Jim Ryan, who had been a founder member of Fianna Fáil and a leading member of each of its governments until his retirement in 1965, Eoin Ryan was a good man for the job because he had shown over the years that he was not politically ambitious himself. He was quite content to serve in the Senate. Senator Des Hanafin was selected to take charge of the party's fund-raising. The party's general secretary, Séamus Brennan, was the architect of the campaign strategy which was run on American lines. Brennan had been on a State Department trip to the United States to observe the 1976 presidential race, and he had attached himself to Jimmy Carter's successful campaign.

'It was an incredible exercise in professionalism, scheduling, publicity, press relations, stage management – the lot,' Brennan explained afterwards. 'I came back and said to myself, "If it'll work out there, why won't it work here?" It wasn't easy to persuade people back home that it could work.' Despite a certain amount of resistance to the idea, he managed to persuade the party to have a campaign record, T-shirts printed with the slogan 'Bring Back Jack' and bumper stickers which read 'Put Jack Back'. There were also baseball or jockey caps with 'Get ahead with Fianna Fáil' written on them.

These were distributed at Lynch's rallies around the country to maximise the photo opportunities. The campaign record was played to give a degree of American-election razzmatazz to the campaign rallies that Lynch held in each of the constituencies. The campaign itself was designed to have a particular appeal to young voters, who were especially important in 1977 because this was the first time that eighteen-year-olds were eligible to vote in a general election. As a result, all those aged between eighteen and twenty-five would be voting for the first time. The age profile of the population was such that a quarter of the electorate was voting for the first time in 1977.

The US election also gave Brennan the idea of getting Lynch, a brilliant television performer, to challenge Cosgrave to a televised debate. 'I didn't think for a second Cosgrave would take it up and it had a tremendous effect,' Brennan said. As expected, the Taoiseach declined the challenge, and Fianna Fáil repeatedly denounced him for refusing to defend his performance in government.

Public-opinion polls had indicated that the coalition government was seen as having performed well on matters like the health service, social-welfare benefits, farming, policing and education, but Fianna Fáil had a secret weapon in the form of its election manifesto, which was unveiled on 26 May. It contained a couple of spectacular promises reminiscent of the coalition's 1973 manifesto promising to remove VAT on food. This time Fianna Fáil renewed its promise to exclude private dwellings from rates and to exclude most private cars from road tax. Voters were encouraged to work out for themselves just how much money they would save in a week as a result of the removal of rates and car tax. The focus of the campaign became the promises for the future rather than the performance of the incumbents.

Although the public had a fairly positive view of the government's security policies, there was a distinct degree of uneasiness over its hardline law-and-order stance. Even people who might otherwise have allied themselves with Cosgrave were turned off by reports of garda brutality. There had been well-documented reports of a so-called 'heavy gang' physically abusing suspects in custody. The government was also hurt by the resignation of Cearbhall Ó Dálaigh, who was seen as an honourable man essentially forced out of office because he had taken his presidential duties seriously and questioned the constitutionality of the Emergency Powers legislation in 1976. As a former Chief Justice of the Supreme Court, he was in a better position than any of his predecessors – or, indeed, any member of the government – to evaluate the constitutionality of the legislation.

The government also seemed to adopt a cavalier approach in relation to Section 31 of the Broadcasting Act. The Minister for Posts and Telegraphs, Conor Cruise O'Brien, was not only insistent that no interviews with suspected members of the IRA should be broadcast, but he also intimated in an interview with a correspondent of the

Washington Post that he would favour using the ban to prohibit the playing of some traditional ballads of a militaristic or anti-British nature on air. This was clearly a step too far for many voters.

Liam Cosgrave then blundered just before calling the general election. In his presidential address at the Fine Gael *ard fheis* on 21 May 1977, he attacked the media with some unscripted comments that were to prove particularly controversial.

'There are journals in this country with articles in them week in, week out, vilifying the gardaí and army and vilifying the prison staff,' Cosgrave said. 'And remember, those people who comment so freely and write so freely, some of them aren't even Irish. No doubt many of you are familiar with an expression in some parts of the country where an outsider is considered a "blow-in". Some of these are blow-ins. Now as far as we're concerned they can blow out, or blow up.'

'Did the 2,000 people killed in Northern Ireland or the 20,000 maimed get civil rights?' Cosgrave continued. 'Did they get legal, medical or spiritual advice? The easiest thing for some of these commentators or do-gooders – I don't mind do-gooders operating so long as they don't do any harm – and, I should have mentioned, did Billy Fox get civil rights?' [Billy Fox, a Fine Gael senator, was the only member of the Dáil to be murdered by the IRA in the course of the recent troubles.] The speech went down very well in the hall, but he was speaking to the converted there. The problem was that this was essentially an election address, and he should have been reassuring people, rather than scaring them with his seemingly intemperate language, especially his remarks about blowing people up.

Things augured well for Fianna Fáil. Public opinion surveys indicated that the electorate was most interested in economic matters, with the leadership issue coming next. Throughout the campaign, the surveys bolstered Fianna Fáil's strategy to the point that they were so favourable that strategists had trouble believing the results themselves. Lynch's appeal to young voters was apparently working, because 71 per cent of first-time voters expressed dissatisfaction with Cosgrave's leadership.

In 1969 the Taoiseach's national campaign tour had proved highly successful, so he undertook another tour of all the constituencies this time. Máirín traveled with him, but she stayed in the background. When journalist Stephen O'Byrnes asked her if she was proud of Jack's achievements, she replied shrewdly that 'proud' was not the right word. 'Of course, I am very happy that the people have seen fit to elect him to the various offices he has held,' she replied. 'But politicians are the product of the people, and the values that people hold. And a lot of other people would be equally good at the job. And there is the matter of being the right man at the right corner of the right street at the right time.'

At rallies throughout the country Lynch was regularly introduced as 'The Real Taoiseach'. This was in response to a popular satirical programme on television, *Hall's Pictorial Weekly*. Masterminded by Frank Hall, it had been ridiculing government ministers for months. The Taoiseach, Liam Cosgrave, was depicted as the Minister for Hardship, while the Tánaiste was characterised as a mere skeleton at the Cabinet table. The Minister for Finance, Richie Ryan, was nicknamed 'Richie Ruin', while Conor Cruise O'Brien was lampooned as a kind of ministerial lackey who was ever ready to carry out harsh directives, with comments like, 'Yes, mein Fuhrer.' At the same time, the genial Lynch was portrayed in a favourable light as 'the Real Taoiseach'.

During his campaign tour, Lynch highlighted his party's manifesto promises and also made pronouncements on other issues that were likely to have appeal to local voters. For instance, he promised to appoint more women when deciding the Taoiseach's eleven nominees for the Senate. 'I shall nominate a number of women, and the same will apply to state boards, advisory and others, and to boards of semi-state companies,' he promised. The party's National Executive added six women as Fianna Fáil candidates for the Dáil. Among them were Mary Harney, Síle de Valera and Maureen Quill.

To highlight Fianna Fáil's economic promises, Lynch attacked the economic failings of the coalition parties. They had promised price stability as part of their fourteen-point plan in 1973, 'but prices have almost doubled since,' Lynch told a rally in Tullamore. 'Rather than facing up to the visible consequences of their economic mismanagement, and a four-year-old, fourteen-point failure, the coalition's opening gambit was to urge that everyone else was wrong,' he said. In Galway he returned to the old theme that the policies of Fine Gael and Labour were both socially and economically incompatible. 'There is no way in which the economic and social conservatism of the Fine Gael Party can come together with the social ideology of the urban Labour Party to produce a coherent or effective economic and social platform on a national basis,' Lynch insisted.

Cosgrave fought back by contending that the country could not afford the Fianna Fáil manifesto and that if Lynch were elected, he would either have to break his promises or bankrupt the country. Hence he insisted that the coalition would have no part 'in a demeaning, irresponsible campaign at the end of which the Irish pound would become confetti money.'

The slick professionalism of the Fianna Fáil campaign got its message across best. On the issue of coping with unemployment, Fianna Fáil scored 25 per cent better that the government. This was particularly important because 91 per cent of the first-time voters thought that unemployment was an important issue. Conveniently, a survey of employment was published during the election campaign. It showed that the coalition government had planned to generate 55,000 extra jobs from 1973 to 1977. A total of 71,137 new jobs had indeed been created, but 74,831 jobs had been lost through redundancies from 1973 to 1976, which meant that there was a total loss of 3,694. But it was suggested that even those figures were a distortion, because they did not include the many young people who had come into the job market but had been unable to find first-time employment. Hence economist Richard Keatinge contended that unemployment was up by 55 per cent on the 1973 figure.

'Going by the yardstick of its 1973 manifesto, the only judgement on the coalition's performance on broad economic issues must be that it has been abysmal,' Keatinge wrote. 'The extent to which this was due to factors unforeseen and beyond its control is, of course, one of the hottest issues in this election. Inflation has virtually doubled in the last four years. Job losses are running at three times the 1973 level.'

The coalition blamed the so-called oil shock that resulted from the massive rise in oil prices following conflict in the Middle East, but Lynch ridiculed this. Éamon de Valera and Seán Lemass had not tried to blame other countries for Ireland's economic difficulties during the Second World War. 'When we were arrayed against the world,' he said, 'they got on with the job.' (De Valera had, in fact, blamed the belligerents during a couple of particularly controversial broadcasts to the United States, but nobody bothered to correct Lynch.)

When it came to prices and inflation, 26 per cent more people preferred the Fianna Fáil policies, which had a 27 per cent lead in the area of taxation. A total of 80.7 per cent of the electorate thought that jobs, prices and taxation were the most important issues in the election. On each of these issues Fianna Fáil policies were distinctly more popular than those of the other parties. The coalition's policies scored better than Fianna Fáil's in relation to the Northern Ireland problem and social services, but only 7 per cent thought that either of those topics was the most important issue.

As the campaign was about to enter its final week, Lynch publicly predicted in Ballina that Fianna Fáil would win an overall majority. He based his prediction on 'the reception given by commentators and public alike to the proposals in the Fianna Fáil manifesto, as against the nebulous document of the coalition.'

At a press conference in Dublin on the final weekend of the campaign, Lynch put a figure on his prediction. He said that Fianna Fáil would win an overall majority of 77 seats in the new 148-seat Dáil. The polls seemed too good to be true, because there were some contradictions. For instance, a majority of 52 per cent of the electorate felt that the country could not afford the promises in the manifesto. This view was actually shared by a third of Fianna Fáil, but Cosgrave passed up the opportunity of debating the issue by repeatedly rejecting Lynch's challenge to a television debate. 'We are running our campaign according to a prearranged plan and do not propose to respond to the day-to-day gimmickry of the Opposition,' the Taoiseach said.

Although 54 per cent of voters preferred Lynch for Taoiseach, as opposed to 29 per cent for Cosgrave, 42 per cent of the people thought that the coalition had a better set of prospective ministers, while only 34 per cent preferred the Fianna Fáil front-bench team. Lynch was so well liked that attacking him personally would have been counterproductive, so coalition ministers tried to hit at him by exploiting what became known as 'the Haughey Factor'.

Garret FitzGerald, Tom Fitzpatrick and Conor Cruise O'Brien all cast doubt on Lynch's control of Fianna Fáil. No one could doubt Lynch's desire for peace or his efforts to 'keep extreme forces within Fianna Fáil at bay by remaining at the helm as long as possible,' FitzGerald said, 'but no one can foresee how long Jack Lynch will wish, or be able, to retain the leadership of a party which he has now headed for eleven years.'

Haughey had become the man that so many people loved to hate that the coalition tried to exploit his presence in Fianna Fáil, but Conor Cruise O'Brien had become a kind of public hate figure within the coalition, and Fianna Fáil exploited his presence in much the same way. One public-opinion survey published in *The Irish Times* found that Haughey and Cruise O'Brien were the people that most people would least like to see as Taoiseach. At Lynch's main rally in Cork, the loudest cheer was for Gus Healy when he criticised Conor Cruise O'Brien. 'We will beat the West Britons,' Healy added. 'It's time somebody stood up and told him he's not in the Congo now.'

Lynch had to deal with a number of problems within Fianna Fáil during the campaign. James Gallagher, one of the party's candidates in the Sligo–Leitrim constituency, inserted an advertisement in the *Sligo Champion* promising to try to secure 'the abolition of the Offences Against the State Act, which served to provoke and alienate people from the forces of law and order.' He added that 'our garda force are preservers of peace and order, and should be seen as such, and not as thugs who execute repressive legislation.'

Lynch issued a statement from Fianna Fáil headquarters denouncing Gallagher for 'pandering to a small section of voters' by advocating repeal of the Offences Against the State Act without the authority of the party. Gallagher, who was making a comeback after retiring in 1973, apologised and explained that he had confused the Offences Against the State Act introduced by Fianna Fáil with the Emergency Powers legislation, introduced by the coalition. He had really meant to denounce the Emergency Powers legislation.

In the Longford–Westmeath constituency, the outgoing Fianna Fáil deputy, Frank Carter, had tended to be outspoken in his republican views and had failed to secure selection as a party candidate at the constituency convention. He then sought to be added to the Fianna Fáil ticket, but was rebuffed by the National Executive. He therefore called on his supporters to vote for an independent in the race, instead of the local Fianna Fáil candidate – the future Taoiseach, Albert Reynolds, who would play an important role in a campaign to oust Lynch a couple of years later.

Another who would play a major role in the heave against Lynch was Tom McEllistrim Jr, who defied party rules in Kerry North. McEllistrim inserted a last-minute appeal in the *Kerryman*. 'There is a rumour going around the constituency to the effect that my seat is safe,' he explained. 'Many of my voters might be inclined to vote for one or other of the Fianna Fáil candidates on that account. I think that this is a mistake. My seat could be in danger, due to the fact that we have three candidates this time. I would like to appeal to all my voters to come out and vote for me if they want me elected.' He did not ask for transfers to his running mates, who were irate as a result. The local Fianna Fáil director of elections tried to buy up all copies of the *Kerryman*, but the newspaper baulked at the idea.

Refusing to believe the swing to Fianna Fáil that had been detected in its final MRBI survey, *The Irish Times* decided not to publish the findings. Instead, it predicted a coalition victory. 'Coalition set to take election,' the main front-page headline proclaimed on election day.

Lynch voted in Rathgar and then headed south. As he was caught in traffic in the Gurranebraher area of Cork, a bystander shouted: 'Hey, Jack boy, I hope you have it all sewn up.'

'We had it sewn up long ago,' he shouted back with a friendly wave.

On the morning of the count *The Irish Times* compounded its earlier mistake with a further headline: '75 per cent poll to bring narrow election win for coalition'. The pundits had refused to believe that any swing to Fianna Fáil would offset the effects of the extensive constituency revisions undertaken in Dublin by James Tully, the Minister for Local Government. Previously Dublin had been divided into eight four-seat constituencies and two three-seaters. In both 1969 and 1973 Fianna Fáil had won two seats in seven of the eight four-seat constituencies, but only one seat in the eighth constituency, Dun Laoghaire/Rathdown, and one in each of the two three-seat constituencies. Tully therefore divided Dublin into thirteen different three-seat constituencies and one four-seater, Dun Laoghaire, which contained most of the only four-seat constituency where Fianna Fáil had failed to win two seats in either 1969 or 1973.

Fine Gael and Labour had received a majority of the votes in the Dublin area in both 1969 and 1973. In the previous election, they had received 54.5 per cent of the vote. Anything over 50 per cent would virtually assure the coalition parties of two seats in each of those constituencies. As a result, Fianna Fáil seemed likely to win only about fourteen of the forty-three seats up for grabs throughout Dublin. This 'Tullymander' was a naked response to the previous Fianna Fáil revision before the 1969 general election which had been denounced as 'Boland's Gerrymander'. Lynch promised that if Fianna Fáil won the election, the whole issue of constituency revisions would be taken out of politics and handed over to an independent commission.

'I can assure you of this: there will be no redrawing of electoral boundaries under a Fianna Fáil minister,' Lynch said. 'Fianna Fáil will ensure that the Irish people will no longer be pushed around like political chess pieces.'

To hold their own at the polls, Fianna Fáil would have to win two seats in four of the Dublin constituencies, Liam O'Neill, the political correspondent of the *Cork Examiner,* noted. That seemed unlikely in his view, because the coalition had targeted Dublin, where 43 of 148 deputies would be elected. To boost employment in the area, the coalition announced what amounted to a second manifesto in the week before the election. The revised manifesto aimed at creating 10,000 jobs in Dublin within eighteen months. This was on top of previous plans announced in the budget to generate another 3,000 jobs for young people. An additional 500 extra primary teachers were promised to bring down class sizes in Dublin.

'The most realistic forecast is that the coalition is likely to stay in office,' the newspaper predicted in an editorial on the day of the election. 'The redrawing of the constituencies is likely to prove too big a handicap to Fianna Fáil, although the finish to the election race could be desperately close.'

Political correspondents thought that Tully had outsmarted Fianna Fáil at its own game, but his tactics actually backfired badly when the coalition vote fell below that of Fianna Fáil. Lynch's party took 46.8 per cent of the vote in Dublin, while the combined vote of Fine Gael and Labour amounted to only 42.1 per cent, their lowest share since 1957. As a result, Fianna Fáil won two seats in eight of the three-seat constituencies. Had the old four-seat constituencies been used, the coalition would probably have got two seats in each, as the Fianna Fáil vote was well short of that needed to secure three of the four seats. The coalition members had outsmarted themselves and the 'Tullymander' in Dublin may well have accounted for sixteen of the extra seats won by Fianna Fáil, which also got a significantly higher vote in the remainder of the country, seeing that the party's overall support on the first ballot ran at 50.6 per cent nationally, an increase of 4.4 per cent on 1973. As a result, the party secured a twenty-seat majority, which was the greatest Dáil majority won by any party since 1922.

Lynch personally got the highest vote in the country. His 20,079 first-preference votes was more than twice the quota. Haughey was at the count at the Royal Dublin Society building that evening when it became apparent that Lynch had led Fianna Fáil to the largest majority since the Civil War. An inordinate number of first-time deputies had been elected, including Albert Reynolds, Bertie Ahern, Seán Doherty, Charlie McCreevy, Joe Walsh, Pádraig Flynn, Michael Woods, Síle de Valera, Vincent Brady, Niall Andrews, Liam Lawlor, Martin O'Donoghue, Mark Killilea, Seán Keegan, P. J. Morley, Jim Fitzsimons, Kit Ahern and Terry Lyden. It seemed now that Lynch would be able to stamp his own authority on the party. At the count in Dublin, Geraldine Kennedy of *The Irish Times* was perplexed by the attitude of Haughey, who 'was absolutely thrilled'. She thought that his chances of ever becoming leader were well and truly buried by the Lynch landslide.

'What are you so pleased about?' she asked. 'Sure, this is the biggest electoral victory ever!'

'Yes,' replied Haughey, 'but they're all my people. Now I know I'll be leader.'

Even in the moment of his greatest victory, Lynch was already apprehensive. 'I would have preferred a smaller majority, certainly,' he said during an appearance on RTÉ on the night of the count. 'I will act as if we did have a small majority, because we just can't get our feet off the ground here, and we know exactly what people think, and you just can't alienate yourself from people.' His remarks would prove prophetic a little over two years later.

'Jack is back!' the *Cork Examiner* proclaimed in a bold front-page headline on the morning after the count. 'Jack Lynch must take the lion's share of that credit, because it is true to say that nobody else could have engineered and masterminded as complete a victory,' the newspaper contended in an editorial.

'This is a personal triumph for Mr Lynch, and it is being widely and rightly recognised as being so,' Tim Cramer noted in a front-page report. 'To him and him alone must go the credit for the enormous success of what has been one of the most vigorous and most expensive campaigns ever mounted in a general election. Nobody else could have pulled the party together so well; could so well have represented to the Irish public that the future lay with Fianna Fáil and with nobody else.

'Last night in Blackpool they were gathering the makings of the bonfires, and they were out hunting for tar barrels,' Cramer added. 'For nothing is more certain than the fact that when Jack Lynch comes home to his native city, he will receive a welcome that Parnell himself, the "uncrowned King of Ireland", would have envied.'

On his way to Cork on the Sunday, Lynch stopped off at the Munster hurling semi-final in Thurles between Cork and Waterford. There were some 8,000 people there. 'Never in all his notable playing days on the famous turf,' the *Cork Examiner* noted, 'had Mr Lynch or any other Cork player been given such a prolonged ovation or been greeted by such a spontaneous burst of cheering and hand-clapping as the man who has swept back to power.'

19

THE PERILS OF A LARGE MAJORITY

1977–1979

It was ironic that the magnificent election victory in 1977 actually sowed the seeds of instability that helped to bring about Lynch's own political demise. From the outset it was expected that he would step down midway through the term in order to make way for a younger leader. All the senior figures who had been in government before him had either died or retired from politics, and even the main figures of his own generation were no longer there. Donogh O'Malley and Erskine Childers had died, Paddy Hillery had become President, Neil Blaney had been ousted from the party and Michael Moran and Kevin Boland were no longer in the Dáil. This left just three from his original Cabinet – George Colley, Brian Lenihan and Charlie Haughey – all of whom clearly had ambitions of their own to become Taoiseach.

In his quest for ministerial talent, Lynch offered a Cabinet position to Senator Eoin Ryan, but he declined the offer because he would have had to sever his business connections. Some years earlier, Tony O'Reilly had declined a Cabinet offer on similar grounds.

Lynch was nominated as Taoiseach by Vivion de Valera and

seconded by Kit Ahern, the newly elected deputy from Kerry North. His appointments to the government included many of the old faces. George Colley was Tánaiste and Minister for Finance, but his duties were significantly curtailed by the appointment of Martin O'Donoghue to a newly formed ministry for Economic Planning and Development. As a result, much of the traditional power and influence of the Minister for Finance was transferred to the new department. Brian Lenihan was disappointed at being given Fisheries, while Charles Haughey was surprised to become Minister for Health and Social Welfare. Those two ministries afforded him great political scope, with so many new deputies entering Leinster House for the first time. Of course there were some questions about appointing Haughey to the Cabinet again, but Lynch dismissed those, because Haughey had purged his past indiscretions by behaving himself since the arms trial, both on the backbenches and as the front-bench spokesman in opposition.

Other government appointees were Pádraig Faulkner, who was given Transport and Power as well as Posts and Telegraphs, and Des O'Malley, who was put in charge of Industry and Commerce. Lynch also appointed Bobby Molloy to Defence, Gerard Collins to Justice, Michael O'Kennedy to Foreign Affairs, Denis Gallagher to the Gaeltacht, John Wilson to Education, Gene Fitzgerald to Labour and Sylvester Barrett to Environment, which was a new name for the Department of Local Government. The old post of parliamentary secretary was also being renamed, and the new government announced the appointment of seven junior ministers or ministers of state.

Although Lynch had indicated during the campaign that women would play a greater role, he did not appoint any women to his Cabinet. The only woman appointee was Máire Geoghegan-Quinn, who became a junior minister. In August he named three women – Lady Valerie Goulding, Mary Harney and Eileen Cassidy – in his eleven nominees to the Senate, a list which also included

Séamus Brennan, T. K. Whitaker and Bernard McGlinchy.

From the outset Lynch indicated that economic development would be his government's main priority. 'Our aim will be to improve our economy in the years immediately ahead and to ensure that this progress will have laid the necessary foundations on which successive governments could build and maintain the steady and peaceful advance of our economy and our people's well-being for the remainder of the century and beyond,' he emphasised. Most of the responsibility for the economy fell on Lynch and the three ministers on whom he relied most – Martin O'Donoghue, George Colley and Des O'Malley. They essentially constituted a four-man caucus within the government. Other Cabinet members had to rely on them to get money for their departments, while many of the new backbenchers felt ignored. Lynch walked the streets with the air of the man about town, but he was withdrawn and reserved within the corridors of powers. All leaders find it necessary to restrict access to themselves in order to get their own work done. Otherwise, they would spend all their time listening to the concerns of deputies. The Taoiseach therefore formed a kind of political cocoon around himself with the help of his three most trusted ministers, but this created a problem when they appeared to become particularly aloof. Backbenchers felt that the four were not as concerned as they should be about the problems on the ground.

Meanwhile Haughey was quietly ingratiating himself with the disillusioned backbenchers. Those who sought his assistance found him not only accessible but also helpful in cutting through bureaucratic red tape when it came to facilitating constituents who were looking for medical cards or having problems with welfare payments. In spite of his somewhat waspish reputation, the new deputies found Haughey courteous and charming, often in marked contrast with the seeming indifference of those surrounding Lynch.

The government inherited an economy that was already

improving. It grew by 6 per cent in 1977 and would grow further under O'Donoghue's plan, which envisaged Ireland taking advantage of an expected upturn in world trade. Interest rates and taxation were cut in order to lower inflation so that the country would become more competitive. This was expected to encourage foreign investment and generate employment, which would be further boosted by the government's job-creation programme. The more people were employed, the more money would be collected in income taxes and the less would have to be paid out in welfare payments. Although Jack Lynch described the government's economic design as 'a responsible and realistic programme', time would show that it was in fact far from realistic.

With the generous tax cuts, such as the abolition of domestic rates and car tax, the average worker earned 16 per cent more in 1978 than in 1977, which translated into an increase of 8 per cent in real earnings. Such a high proportion of people worked in the public sector, however, that this naturally fuelled inflation, thereby undermining a vital part of the structure of the economic plan.

Some 30,000 new jobs were created in 1978, which was an unprecedented rise in employment. Lynch was in buoyant form when he spoke in the Dáil just before it went into recess at the end of the year. 'When the House rises at the conclusion of this debate,' he declared, 'it will do so at the end of one of the most successful periods on record for the Irish economy.'

He was on the crest of a wave that was about to break and essentially swallow him up. Had he decided to step down at this time, he could have gone with his popularity and reputation intact, but he hung on for one more year, as 1979 seemed to hold out the promise of an ideal finale. Ireland would have the Presidency of the EEC during the second half of the year, and Lynch planned to preside over the European summit and then step down.

Even allowing for redundancies and the continuing drift from the land, there was still a net gain of 17,000 jobs in the country,

Lynch told the Fianna Fáil *ard fheis* in February 1979. The figures seemed impressive, especially when contrasted with the decline in the number of jobs under the previous government, but 10,487 of the new jobs were in the public service, and another 5,592 were 'actually realised' in the building and construction industry, largely as a result of the government's house-building programme. Thus, of the 17,000 new jobs that the Taoiseach bragged about at the *ard fheis*, only 921 had been generated in the entire agricultural, manufacturing and private-service sectors during 1978.

The success of O'Donoghue's plan was more illusory than real. It was already coming apart. He had envisaged generating jobs in the private sector, which would provide buoyancy in the form of extra tax money for the exchequer. Instead the promised jobs were created in the public sector, which proved a drain on the economy and undermined rather than enhanced the country's competitiveness. Government borrowing, which was £506 million in 1976, the last full year of the coalition, rose to £546 million in 1977, followed by a massive jump to £810 million in 1978, the first full year of the new Fianna Fáil government. This amounted to an increase of more than 60 per cent over the coalition figure.

Plans to set up the European Monetary System (EMS), linking the currencies of the various EEC countries, involved Lynch in a series of talks with EEC leaders. When the issue was considered in some detail at the European summit meeting in Bremen during July, Lynch and the Italian Premier, Mario Andreotti, gave their tentative approval to the EMS on the condition that 'concurrent studies' were carried out to determine what financial help would be needed by weaker member states in order for them to participate. There were suggestions that Ireland would need £650 million in support, in the likely event that Britain stayed out of the EMS and the parity between the punt and sterling was broken. Technically the link with sterling had been broken by the Central Bank Act of 1972, when the Irish punt was aligned with the gold standard, but parity had been maintained. Under the EMS the parity would be severed if the punt and sterling fluctuated by more than 2.5 per cent. This could prove economically damaging to Ireland, because over 50 per cent of the country's trade was still with Britain. In November George Colley, the Minister for Finance, stated that the financial support needed would actually be 'considerably greater' than the £650 million already mentioned, but he reported that the Germans and the French had indicated that they would be generous with their help. He confidently predicted that Ireland would get the £650 million at least.

Ireland already enjoying considerable benefits from the EEC, as the country received much more than it paid into the European coffers. It was estimated at that time that the country was benefiting to the extent of £100 for every man, woman and child, whereas the British exchequer was contributing £2 for every person in Britain.

Plans for the EMS were due to be finalised at the EEC summit in Brussels in December 1978. Lynch held preparatory bilateral discussions in London with Prime Minister Jim Callaghan, with French President Valéry Giscard d'Estaing in Paris, and with German Chancellor Helmut Schmidt in Bonn. It was imperative that Ireland should get a 'reasonable transfer of resources,' Lynch said publicly. 'If we don't get the kind of assistance we are seeking – £650 million – from our partners, it will not be possible for us to live within the system, because the result would be deflationary.'

Following his talks in London, Paris and Bonn, Lynch was particularly upbeat. Helmut Schmidt had been very supportive and, even though Britain intended to remain out of the EMS, at least until after the next general election, Callaghan indicated that his government was ready to support extra financial aid to Ireland. The Taoiseach therefore went to the Brussels summit expressing confidence that he would get the kind of money that Ireland was seeking. Politically this was a bad mistake, because when he did not get that amount of money, he returned home with egg all over his face.

The French president baulked at committing the necessary funds in Brussels, complaining that the Italians and Irish were making exorbitant demands. After much discussion, Ireland was offered a total of £225 million in loans over five years, which one Irish official described as a 'derisory' sum. In each of the first two years the country would be given £70 million in loans, and it would receive a further £45 million in interest subsidies during each of the following three years.

'It simply was not enough to justify my indicating to the council that Ireland would be prepared to enter on that basis,' Lynch explained. Italy and Ireland therefore refused to join the EMS, along with Britain.

'Instead of grants which we had expected, there is nothing,' Tim Cramer of the *Cork Examiner* complained in a front-page comment piece. 'Instead of the "soft" loans at low interest rates which we had hoped for, there is a hardness which we had not anticipated and interest rates at double those which we had hoped to get.' It was a serious setback for Lynch.

Afterwards German Chancellor Helmut Schmidt and Dutch Premier Andreas van Agt indicated that they were still anxious to persuade Ireland to join the system, and some further bilateral talks were held with Irish officials. On 15 December Lynch announced in the Dáil that Ireland would, after all, join the EMS, because he had received an assurance that the money from the Brussels summit would not be wholly restricted to use for infrastructural projects, like roads and telecommunications. It could also be pumped into the capital and current programmes for the following year, enabling the government to avoid the extra-tight strictures on spending that they had been faced with as a result of over-spending that year. 'I am glad to be able to say now that I have an assurance as to the interpretation of the Council resolution which is satisfactory insofar as uses to which the resources may be put,' Lynch told the Dáil. 'They will not be wholly restricted to infrastructure. I have also been assured that there will be sufficient flexibility as to the manner in which the interest subsidies operate to enable us to benefit fully from these arrangements early in the new year.'

He also noted that some of the governments had indicated that, if needed, they would make extra money available on a bilateral basis. 'At this point,' Lynch explained, 'I am satisfied that the new package provides sufficient additonal resource transfers to help us overcome the critical initial two-year period.'

The whole thing had been badly handled politically, especially by George Colley, who had raised unrealistic expectations before the Brussels summit. The government then appeared to dither over the initial decision not to join the EMS, only to reverse that decision ten days later. The concessions received were really a face-saver, as they amounted to little more than a clarification of what had actually been offered at Brussels. It was but the first of a series of bungles involving Colley.

The government simply could not keep borrowing the way it had been without raising taxes, but the ordinary urban workers were already overtaxed. The one place there was scope for extra taxation was among the farmers, who had been doing very well out of the country's membership of the EEC. In 1978, for instance, farmers paid only £16 million in tax and a further £36 million in rates on their land. The combined total came to just 5.5 per cent of total farm income, whereas those in the Pay As You Earn (PAYE) sector were paying a total of 16 per cent of their income in tax. Lynch had indicated in January 1978 that something had to be done about farmer taxation, but nothing happened, though he did state in October that it would be the main priority of his government during 1979. The Irish Congress of Trade Unions responded by insisting that more farmers should be brought into the tax net and that the government should crack down on tax evasion among professional people.

George Colley announced in his budget address on 7 February 1979 that a 2 per cent levy would be charged on the money earned by farmers in selling milk, cattle, pigs, sheep, beet and cereals. Although Lynch strongly supported the budget, it was promptly denounced by Joe Rea, the head of the Irish Farmers' Association, as 'absolutely outrageous'. Even though farmers were still being asked to pay less than half the rate of tax of the PAYE sector, he said that the farmers would not pay the levy, and the beet growers threatened not to grow any beet.

The farming community condemned the levy on the grounds that it took no account of the individual farmer's ability to pay. The poorer farmers would have to pay the same levy as the rich. Traditionally the richer farmers tended to support Fine Gael, which had antagonised its supporters by bringing in income tax for the wealthier farmers during the previous government. Now Fianna Fáil irked its own supporters among the small farmers by trying to tax them.

Amid the ensuing uproar, the government gradually backed down, first by announcing certain exemptions, then by postponing the introduction of the levy, before eventually abandoning it completely. The PAYE taxpayers were naturally aggrieved and they organised a series of protest marches around the country. On 11 March some 50,000 people marched at a rally organised in Dublin by the Irish Transport and General Workers Union, and there were other marches in Ballina, Carlow, Cavan, Galway, Limerick, Sligo and Tralee. A work stoppage was called to take place at the end of the month that would facilitate a further protest march.

George Colley compounded the anger of the taxpayers by stating that he did not think anyone was seriously suggesting that such action would produce a government response. This astounding statement – which amounted to a declaration that the government would not take the legitimate protest seriously, but would ignore the public will – was as arrogant as it was insensitive. Thus on 30 March some 150,000 workers marched in Dublin and a further 40,000 turned out in Cork. The marchers formally demanded a revision of the tax system to 'ease the intolerable burden on the working class' so that 'all would pay their fair share'.

Colley's handling of the whole thing had been incredibly inept. He had antagonised the entire farming community initially and then proceeded to offend all the taxpayers by abandoning the scheme and ridiculing the justifiable sense of grievance of those who clearly bore a disproportionately high share of the tax burden. 'Only a politician of George Colley's insensitivity could proclaim, in advance of the largest protest that Dublin has witnessed in many a year, that the government would not respond to it,' *Hibernia* magazine remarked. The editor wondered whether Colley's conduct was prompted by insensitivity or stupidity.

Much of Martin O'Donoghue's economic plan was dependent on the workforce moderating their wage demands in return for lower taxation. They had enjoyed both major tax cuts and a wage increase that ran ahead of inflation in 1978, but there were already signs in 1979 that they were insisting on more of the same. Lynch warned in January that widespread attempts to win wage increases could cost thousands of jobs. Some 13,000 postal workers, who comprised the largest single sector of the public service, were demanding a 37 per cent pay increase. Colley announced in his budget that the government was aiming for a 5 per cent wage increase, but this was contemptuously rejected by the postal workers, who went on strike a fortnight later. The strike was to become very bitter and last for five months. Within a matter of weeks, the government backed down on the 5 per cent increase and agreed to 8 per cent.

Confidence in the government was being undermined, and it was further damaged when a controversy arose over Charles

Haughey's efforts to legalise the sale of contraceptives. The Family Planning Bill, which was drawn up following exhaustive consultations with the Roman Catholic hierarchy and interested parties, came in for strong criticism in liberal circles. Critics took particular exception to provisions restricting the sale of contraceptives to married people and requiring a doctor's prescription for even non-medical contraceptives like condoms. Haughey described the bill as an Irish solution to an Irish problem, but five Fianna Fáil deputies still thought it was too liberal, and they defied their party's three-line whip by abstaining in the Dáil vote on the second stage of the bill on 25 April 1979. Four of them later apologised, but the fifth, Jim Gibbons, was recalcitrant. As Minister for Agriculture, Gibbons could easily have arranged to be away on business, and his absence would not have been noticed, because his vote was not needed. Instead, he stayed around the Dáil until just before the vote was due to take place and then left. Afterwards he announced defiantly that he would not be supporting any stage of the bill.

This was the first time since the foundation of the state that any minister had publicly defied the government of which he was a member. Gibbons was making a mockery of the constitutional concept of collective Cabinet responsibility, but Lynch ignored what was essentially a challenge to his own authority. John Mulcahy, the editor of *Hibernia*, suggested that Lynch was afraid to act against Gibbons for fear of being put 'in bad odour on the Reverend Mother circuit', with the European elections less than two months away.

This would be Fianna Fáil's first major electoral test since the 1977 general election. It was also the first time that members of the European Parliament were to be elected directly by the people. Lynch addressed each of the four Fianna Fáil selection conventions in Dublin city, Leinster, Munster and Connaught/Ulster. Then during the campaign he toured the country, speaking in the major urban centres in each constituency.

On the afternoon of 30 May, the party's first political broadcast for RTÉ was taped, and he anchored it as leader of the party. Nothing was left to chance. His advisers prescribed even what clothes he should wear. They decided that he was to wear a dove-grey suit with a blue pinstripe, a white shirt with long collar points and a red tie with white dots and a red motif in dots. Even though he was not running for election himself, he was seen as the party's main electoral draw.

He sought to emphasise his government's economic achievements since coming to power, but the economy was turning sour and he was compelled to defend himself and his colleagues. 'The government cannot allow the record growth and increased prosperity achieved in the economy in 1978 to be eroded in one fell swoop by the unreasonable pay claims of any one sector,' he warned a rally in Sligo that evening.

'When Fianna Fáil campaigned in the last general election, on the issue of lowering income tax and abolishing certain other taxes, they said at the time that it couldn't be done,' he told rallies in Carlow, Athy and Portlaoise on 2 June. 'Now, driven by the pressures of seeking electoral support, they [the Opposition] are trying to masquerade as being in the vanguard of the tax-reduction movement.' He contended that the Opposition's attitude to farmer taxation was 'the most blatant example of political hypocrisy'. While the coalition was in government, Garret FitzGerald had advocated a 12 per cent levy on all farm output, which far outstripped the 2 per cent levy proposed by George Colley, but the Opposition still hammered the 2 per cent levy during the European election campaign.

'Leadership in political life must be open and above board, and it must be based on fundamental conviction on where one should go and the road one should follow,' the Taoiseach argued. 'Duplicity on major issues such as we are seeing from the opposition parties is not a good indicator of their aspirations in the longer term. If you don't know where you are going, any road will take you there. At present, the coalition parties seem to be in confusion about their destination and their roads.'

There were four main planks to the Fianna Fáil campaign. They promised to prevent the European Parliament from threatening Irish national interests, to defend the economy against socialist attack, and to ensure that Ireland had a strong voice at home and abroad. Finally, the party was running on its economic record at home in bringing down inflation, creating jobs and raising the living standard by a greater proportion than any other country in the EEC.

Although Lynch initially had a very high profile, he backed off somewhat as the campaign continued. He had the indignity of getting some hostile receptions from striking postal workers, especially in Galway, towards the end of the campaign. He did not go on his usual rounds of convents, where he was apparently no longer so welcome, as a result of the Family Planning Bill. It was noteworthy, for example, that he was not invited to the Vatican for the elevation of the Archbishop of Armagh, Tomás Ó Fiaich, to the College of Cardinals. This was a pointed snub. Lynch declined to take part in some current-affairs programmes on RTÉ television during the campaign and he took four days out to attend the European summit in Greece. In addition, Michael O'Kennedy, the Minister for Foreign Affairs, fronted the party's final election broadcast.

The most damaging challenge to Lynch came from the independent candidacy of Neil Blaney in the Connaught/Ulster constituency. As it was only a three-seat constituency, he needed over 25 per cent of the vote to secure a quota to get elected. Hence he had a mammoth task, but that would make Blaney's success all the more spectacular.

Throughout the campaign Blaney played down his differences with Fianna Fáil, suggesting that they amounted to little more than a personality clash with Lynch. 'It's an obstacle but not an insuperable one,' Blaney said. He sought to tap into the growing disillusionment with the Taoiseach's performance by playing the Green card. 'There is no other republican voice, North or South, in this election,' he contended.

Blaney headed the poll with a massive 81,522 votes, some 5,000 votes above the quota. It was a tremendous personal triumph, which he hyped as a vindication of his own republican policies, as opposed to the more moderate line taken by Lynch and his supporters. 'The vote that I got shows them that I was more right than they were,' Blaney declared. 'It was the first time that committed people really got a chance to vote for a solidly republican position.' His elated supporters celebrated by singing, 'He's got Fianna Fáil in his hands' to the tune of the song 'He's got the whole world in his hands'. This was almost as great a political setback for Lynch as it was a personal triumph for Blaney, whose biographer, Kevin Rafter, concluded that 'many Fianna Fáil supporters had deserted the party and cast their votes for Blaney in protest at Lynch's leadership.'

The overall results were a disaster for Lynch. Fianna Fáil won only five of the fifteen seats, with 34.68 per cent of the vote, which was the party's poorest showing in history. Lynch dismissed the result as a traditional mid-term rebuke for the government. It was obvious that some remedial action needed to be taken, but his options were limited, as Ireland was about to assume the presidency of the EEC during the second half of 1979. His various ministers would be taking over the presidency of the different councils discussing the various aspects of EEC policy, with the result that a Cabinet reshuffle was out of the question at the time, but he did indicate that there would be a reshuffle once the presidency had passed on to the Italians in January 1980.

Lynch's reasons for fearing such a large majority on the night of the last general-election count now began to become apparent. The party was holding an inordinately high number of the marginal seats, with the result that the slump in the party's popularity had many backbenchers fearing for their seats. If the vote in the European elections was replicated in a general election, Fianna Fáil would lose up to thirty seats.

One of those who had become disillusioned with Lynch was Tom McEllistrim Jr, whose late father had not only been one of the provincial deputies who had urged Lynch to enter the Fianna Fáil leadership race in 1966 but, even more significantly, was the person that Lynch chose to nominate him at the crucial party meeting. Now McEllistrim's son would initiate a heave to force Lynch out.

While in Dublin, McEllistrim would stay at Jury's Hotel, which had a special rate for members of the Oireachtas. He and Jackie Fahey used to meet at the hotel at night and talk a lot about politics. Fahey had first been elected to the Dáil in 1965 and had served as a parliamentary secretary from 1970 to 1973 following the arms-crisis upheaval. He was now annoyed at not being reappointed in 1977. McEllistrim had succeeded his father in 1969, and since his father had proposed Lynch for the Fianna Fáil leadership, he might have expected some kind of preferment. He had headed the poll in Kerry North in each of his three general elections and in 1977 Fianna Fáil had taken two seats for the first time since the constituency had become a three-seater in 1961. But he had blotted his copybook in that election by violating party rules with his personal advertisement in the *Kerryman*, announcing that he might be in trouble and asking voters to support him without any reference to his two running mates, Kit Ahern and Denis Foley.

McEllistrim and Fahey believed that Lynch would support George Colley in the race to succeed him, and they were determined to do what they could to prevent this. For one thing, neither had much chance of preferment under Colley, so they decided to back Charles Haughey. Ever since his acquittal at the arms trial,

Haughey had been going around the country to local party functions, building up grass-roots support as part of his preparation to run for the leadership whenever the position became vacant. Earlier that year he had gone to a function in McEllistrim's constituency. The function was very well attended – 'a fierce crowd' turned out, according to McEllistrim. It afforded McEllistrim the opportunity of hitching his political star to Haughey's bandwagon.

McEllistrim and Fahey began discussing Haughey's leadership prospects with other backbenchers. 'We started to have meetings in Jury's,' McEllistrim explained. 'Fahey and myself had the meetings first. We initiated the thing. And then we invited different people to our meetings.' These people included deputies elected to the Dáil for the first time in 1977 – Seán Doherty, Mark Killilea and Albert Reynolds. The five of them were later dubbed 'the gang of five' by Vincent Browne. Although Reynolds was with them, he did not play a major role. 'Albert was very much in the background,' McEllistrim said. 'We knew that Albert would vote for Haughey when the time came. But he did not do very much in the organising of a group to try and get Haughey into power as leader of Fianna Fáil.'

They formed little groups in different sections of the Fianna Fáil Party to discuss the next election. It all remained very informal. 'We invited a lot of those people to meetings and all those meetings took place in one or other of our rooms,' McEllistrim explained. 'We might invite Paddy Power and Ray MacSharry tonight, and we might invite Seán Keegan and Seán Doherty the next night. And the way we got the big group together was by inviting them to small meetings first, getting their feelings as to how they felt about what we felt about the change of leader in Fianna Fáil.'

They relied on people like Tom Meany, Paddy Power, Seán Keegan and Ray MacSharry, who stayed in the background, as he was a minister of state in George Colley's department at the time.

Fahey involved Síle de Valera, who was disillusioned with Lynch over his Northern policy. She brought in Eileen Lemass, Vincent Brady and Charlie McCreevy.

It was subsequently reported that these meetings began in the Coffee Dock of Jury's Hotel, but they did not really talk there. 'The Coffee Dock was too open,' McEllistrim explained. All the meetings were held in somebody's bedroom, because they were anxious not to be overheard by the general public. 'You wouldn't know who would be listening inside in the Coffee Dock,' he said.

They also spoke to other TDs in their offices, usually between eight o'clock and ten o'clock at night when things were rather quiet around Leinster House. 'We did it very gradually,' he said. 'No one suspected there was anything going on because most of the fellows we had recruited were trustworthy. And they never spoke too much about it, except that one of their colleagues would like to join us. It was a secret for a long time and nobody knew what was happening and we kept it nice and quiet, except for trying to recruit people in.

'Some of the people at the top level in Fianna Fáil weren't so much republican at all and that was worrying a lot of TDs at the time and that stirred up the desire as well to get somebody in as leader who would have republican ideals. Jack kind of forgot about republican ideals but a lot of us were very anxious for that.'

During the four years that Lynch had been out of power there had been major changes on the British political scene. Ted Heath's government had lost power and he had been replaced as leader of the Conservative Party by Margaret Thatcher. Harold Wilson had returned to power but he stepped down in March 1976 to be replaced by James Callaghan. But the Labour Party quickly lost its paper-thin majority in the House of Commons. As a result the government became largely dependent on the support of the Liberal Party, which was ideologically closer to Labour than to the right-wing views being expressed by the Conservatives under

Margaret Thatcher. The Liberals therefore agreed to support the government in line with a rather loose agreement dubbed the Lib–Lab Pact.

Callaghan had also approached the unionists from Northern Ireland in March 1977. Labour was doing so poorly in the public-opinion polls that the party had little chance of winning an early general election. He was trying to turn the British economy around, but he needed more time for his reforms to work in order to give himself a realistic chance of securing an electoral mandate of his own at the next general election.

The unionists' main interest was in securing a return of devolved government and obtaining extra representation for Northern Ireland at Westminster. At the time the population of Northern Ireland was under-represented in comparison with England, Scotland or Wales. Callaghan agreed to have the issue investigated as a matter of course, and he listened to their views on devolution. 'I told them the Cabinet would naturally need to know the reactions of the minority in considering the matter, and I could therefore give no pledge, but I saw enough of their proposals to warrant the government examining them seriously, and we would do so,' Callaghan noted in his memoirs.

When Lynch went to London for his first talks with Callaghan as Prime Minister in September 1977, he made it clear that he was going to Downing Street mainly to listen and try to learn what proposals, if any, Callaghan and his government had for the North's short-term future. He was worried that the British intended to integrate Northern Ireland further into the United Kingdom, but from Callaghan's memoirs it would appear that the pressure was in the opposite direction. The unionists were looking for a return to devolved government in Northern Ireland, and the Prime Minister was determined that this would not take place without power-sharing between the unionists and nationalists. If there was a general desire, the British government would be ready to 'devolve a range of powers to a locally elected body under arrangements acceptable to both sides of the community,' Callaghan explained. He sought to put Lynch on the back foot by complaining about border security.

'I was not satisfied that he was taking sufficiently seriously the vital need for close border cooperation if the IRA threat was to be contained, and I employed the argument that this threat was potentially as grave for the Republic as for the North,' Callaghan noted. Of course, Lynch insisted that his government was doing all that it could do. In essence both men wished that the other would do more, but each recognised the other's difficulties. Lynch said afterwards, for instance, that he was satisfied that the British government would like to take a political initiative but felt that this was not the time to do it. It was noteworthy that no date was fixed for another meeting.

They did meet together during European summits 'to exchange views', according to Callaghan, but nothing came of those meetings. Callaghan was obviously preoccupied with his own economic problems and the difficulties of keeping his government in power. He was relatively happy with the way things were going in Northern Ireland. He noted with some satisfaction that the total of 111 violent deaths in 1977 was not only down dramatically on the 297 of the year before but was also the lowest death toll since 1970.

The United Kingdom had been going through a kind of financial crisis and Lynch contended during a radio interview on 8 January 1978 that the British people had no stomach for continuing their subsidy of Northern Ireland, which amounted to £700 million annually. He suggested that the British should declare an intention to withdraw from Northern Ireland in order to concentrate the minds of both communities so that they would get together to do what was best for themselves. Lynch said that this was being hampered by the 'steel wall' of the constitutional guarantee that until there was a majority in the North in favour of changing the constitutional position, there would be no change. Any intransigent unionist could put their backs against the wall 'and nothing will shift them,' the Taoiseach argued.

Lynch was assailed for expressing those views. Roy Mason, the Northern Secretary, not only denounced the suggestions but also reaffirmed the constitutional guarantee by emphasising that Northern Ireland would remain part of the United Kingdom as long as the majority of the area wished. Airey Neave, the Conservative spokesman on Northern Ireland, criticised the Taoiseach for even mentioning the words 'power sharing', while Conor Cruise O'Brien accused Lynch of using 'poisoned rhetoric'.

Lynch was taken aback by the response. 'The reaction to the straightforward and factual answers I gave to questions on Northern Ireland that were put to me in a radio interview on RTÉ's *This Week* programme last Sunday was surprising and unexpected,' he said. He had merely been following what had been the official Fianna Fáil line since 1975, but ironically it was also in line with Callaghan's thinking.

The Prime Minister was under no illusion that he could do anything effective to resolve the problems of Northern Ireland. 'At no time did I feel we were doing more than breasting the tide,' he wrote. 'The cardinal aim of our policy must be to influence Northern Ireland to solve its own problems.'

Callaghan did not outline his private views to the public at the time, but when he did outline them to the House of Commons after he was ousted as prime minister, they were very similar to what Lynch had been advocating. 'Britain should bring forward no further solutions, but must continue to fulfil to the limit its responsibilities for law and order for a predetermined, fixed number of years,' Callaghan explained. During that period the leaders of the two communities should determine where their future lay and they should enter the appropriate constitutional relationship.

'When the interim period came to an end, Britain would offer continued British citizenship to all those who wished to exercise that right so that there might be many dual citizens, but would withdraw from the Province, which would at that time become an independent state,' Callaghan concluded.

He was in no position to press those views while he was prime minister, as he only had a minority government. His government finally fell in March 1979 and he was ousted as prime minister when Margaret Thatcher was returned with an overall majority in the ensuing general election. Lynch had shown no hurry to meet her, and McEllistrim and the more republican-minded members of Fianna Fáil were uneasy.

The 'gang of five' organised a meeting of the party's back-benchers in Leinster House on 26 June 1979. It was all very informal. Their technique was to approach deputies and say: 'There's a meeting of the Fianna Fáil backbenchers on the fifth floor; you should be there.' Nobody said what would be discussed, and they even changed the starting time of the meeting a couple of times while they spread the word. About thirty deputies showed up. In addition to the gang of five, the group included people like Bernard Cowen, Síle de Valera, Brendan Daly, Noël Davern, Pádraig Flynn, Liam Lawlor, Charlie McCreevy, Rory O'Hanlon, Paddy Power, Michael Smith and Joe Walsh.

Jackie Fahey chaired the proceedings and there was a free-ranging discussion in contrast with the more structured procedure of the parliamentary-party meetings. 'There was a discussion about the dissatisfaction in the country with Fianna Fáil and that we wouldn't succeed in the next election, the way things were going,' McEllistrim recalled. 'I remember saying that day that there was an awful lot of dissatisfaction with Jack Lynch as Taoiseach and that he had got stale and that he wasn't as active as he was and that he should be replaced. A lot of them didn't kind of want me to say that, but I said it anyway.'

The following day at the regular parliamentary-party meeting, the first since the European elections, Pádraig Flynn proposed a special meeting to discuss the election results and their implications. Lynch replied that a sub-committee of the national executive was carrying out a complete analysis and that he hoped to have the report soon. The parliamentary-party meetings had previously tended to be casual and amicable affairs, with backbenchers being allowed to ramble on about local issues, but Lynch had recently been showing impatience. He would bang the table in frustration and insist that the discussions be confined to issues of national importance as he tried to force the day's agenda through to a speedy conclusion so that he could attend to his more important ministerial duties.

Lynch clearly did not want a discussion on the election performance, but he was compelled to relent and agree to the arrangement of a special parliamentary meeting on 11 July. He had already heard of the caucus meeting the previous day and he wished to know who had taken part. All sat in embarrassed silence, with the exception of Pádraig Flynn, who alone admitted attending the meeting. Ben Briscoe was subsequently credited with contrasting a caucus and a cactus. All 'the pricks' were on the outside of a cactus, he said, while they were inside a caucus.

At the meeting on 11 July an amount of disquiet was expressed at the way backbenchers had been treated. There was some blunt speaking, and Lynch promised new procedures to provide greater consultation between ministers and backbenchers.

20

The Unkindest Cut

1979

One of Lynch's first functions as president of the Council of Ministers of the EEC was to deliver an address to the new European Parliament on 17 July 1970. As this was the first European parliament elected directly by the people, it was a momentous occasion.

The parliament had opened the previous day with an address by the oldest member, eighty-six-year-old Madame Weiss, a French Gaullist representative. In the course of her address she referred to Pope Urban II and noted the presence in the assembly of Síle de Valera, a granddaughter of 'the illustrious' Éamon de Valera. This was too much for Ian Paisley, who was making his first appearance in the parliament, having been elected in Northern Ireland with over 170,000 votes, the highest tally in the whole community. He was determined to make his presence felt as soon as possible. He protested against the address of Madame Weiss on the grounds that she did not make any reference to the Protestant Reformation, and also kicked up a rumpus because the Union flag was flying upside down outside the building.

As soon as Lynch began speaking the following day, Ian Paisley again interrupted the proceedings. 'In the name of Ulster's dead,' he shouted, 'I indict you as harbouring their murderers.' The parliament had already had enough of Paisley's outrageous antics. He was drowned out by the boos and jeers of fellow members. He then stormed out of the meeting and told the media outside that this was the first opportunity for an Ulster politician to attack Lynch for allowing Irish territory 'to be used to launch IRA attacks upon my people'.

During August, Lynch went to Spain on holidays and was there when he learned that Earl Mountbatten had been killed by an IRA bomb while boating off Mullaghmore, County Sligo. Mountbatten was not only a British war hero, but an uncle of Prince Philip and something of a favourite with the royal household.

The Taoiseach did not suspend his holiday immediately, but did return home to attend the ceremony at Baldonnel Airport on the removal of Lord Mountbatten's body by air to London. Two days later Lynch represented the Irish government at the funeral service in Westminster Abbey.

Afterwards he met Prime Minister Margaret Thatcher, who demanded concessions in the area of security. 'Mr Lynch had no positive suggestions of his own to make at all,' Thatcher noted. 'When I stressed the importance of extradition of terrorists from the Republic, he said that the Irish Constitution made it very difficult.' Those whom the British suspected could be tried in Ireland under the Criminal Law Jurisdiction Act for offences committed in the United Kingdom, the Taoiseach explained. Thatcher called for more effective liaison between the gardaí and the RUC, and she suggested allowing the RUC to sit in on the questioning of suspects by the gardaí. Lynch agreed to consider this.

'I asked that we extend the existing arrangements by which our helicopters could overfly the borders across which terrorists seemed able to come and go almost at will,' Thatcher continued. 'He said they would study that as well.' She was annoyed that he was not prepared to make any concessions on the spot. 'At one point I became so exasperated that I asked whether the Irish government was willing to do anything at all,' she continued. He was prepared to authorise further meetings between ministers and officials of the two countries.

'I was disappointed, though not altogether surprised,' Thatcher explained. 'However, I was determined to keep up the pressure on the Republic.'

Lynch was in a difficult position. The Mountbatten murder was one of the most cowardly acts of the whole troubles. He was in his seventies and was out fishing with his daughter and young grandchildren when their boat was blown up by a bomb. In addition to Mountbatten, those killed included his daughter's eighty-two-year-old mother-in-law, his fourteen-year-old grandson and a fifteen-year-old local boy who was piloting the boat.

The Irish authorities had to bear some responsibility for what had happened. In the early 'seventies an attempt had been made on Mountbatten's life when his boat was holed, but he was late that morning and by the time he arrived it was already apparent that the vessel was taking on water. Thereafter special garda protection was put on the boat, but by 1979 he was no longer considered a likely target for some reason, and the protection was removed.

In an RTÉ interview on the Sunday before the Mountbatten funeral, Lynch insisted that there could be no question of the extradition of Irish citizens to either Britain or Northern Ireland for political offences, nor could British forces cross the border in 'hot pursuit'. Under pressure from Thatcher, however, he agreed that British or Irish helicopters or aircraft could overfly the border in an air corridor extending five kilometres on either side of the border while in pursuit of suspected terrorists.

Rumours of the arrangement circulated in political circles, but there was no official word to explain the increased security activity along the border. Michael Mills, the political correspondent of the *Irish Press*, asked a senior civil servant about it.

'My God, where did you hear that?' the civil servant replied. He confirmed the story but then promptly changed the subject. That was enough for Mills to break the story in the *Irish Press*, but he made the mistake of describing the extent of the corridor as ten miles wide, rather than ten kilometres. This allowed the government to deny the story instantly, a denial which turned out to be an error of judgement on the government's part. Lynch was acting as if they had something to hide, instead of boldly stating his determination to root out the kind of terrorism which would target old men, women and children.

During the Second World War one of the main British air bases for the protection of North Atlantic shipping was a flying boat based on Lough Erne. Éamon de Valera's government authorised the British to fly in and out of the base from Lough Erne to the Atlantic through an air corridor over County Donegal. It was ironic now that one of Lynch's main critics would be de Valera's granddaughter, Síle de Valera.

She was invited to deliver the commemoration address at the grave of Liam Lynch, the IRA leader during the Civil War. It was he more than anybody else who frustrated her grandfather's efforts to end the war. Síle de Valera agreed to deliver an oration near Fermoy on Sunday 9 September 1979. Her remarks were prepared and circulated to the media well in advance.

The Taoiseach learned of the speech on the Thursday evening and summoned her to his office the following morning. He told her to bring a copy of the address.

'I read it in her presence and it was immediately apparent to me that its contents were likely to raise difficulties for the party and cause us embarrassment,' he told the next parliamentary-party meeting. At the time all speeches by members in relation to 'fundamental policy' and partition were supposed to be cleared by the party whip, but de Valera had not bothered to submit her address.

'So many nowadays who only have material interests at heart would tempt to us to dilute our political aims and goal – namely the achievement of a united Ireland,' de Valera declared. 'Those opponents are dangerous, as they so often cloak their views under such guises as reconciliation and peace.' She not only lauded the militant republicanism of Liam Lynch, but did it in such a way as to suggest that the Provisional IRA could be compared with those who had fought for independence in the 1920s. She then essentially went on to insist that Jack Lynch should provide republican leadership and refuse to cooperate with the British in the fight against those who were striving to end partition.

'At no time must we allow our leaders to succumb to British pressure,' she continued. 'They have the effrontery to ask our permission for their army to operate a mile or so over the border. It must be pointed out to the British government in no uncertain terms that they were the cause of partition and that we at no time would wish to cooperate in any scheme of theirs which would attempt to keep the border in existence.' She explained that this would entail refusing to permit extradition or to allow the RUC to enter the Twenty-six Counties 'in any capacity', addressing the suggestion that the RUC should be allowed to sit in on garda interrogations in Dublin.

'If our political leaders are not seen to be furthering our republican aspirations through constitutional means, the idealistic young members of our community will become disillusioned and discontented with the politicians,' she continued. 'So as a young person whose one wish is to further the task which such young men as Liam Lynch have set before us, I look to our party and particularly our leader to demonstrate his republicanism and bring these beliefs to fruition in our people.'

Jack Lynch promptly criticised her address. 'I regret the tone and tenor of Deputy de Valera's remarks, especially at this time,' he said. If she wished to make such statements, she should do so within the confines of the party. He was particularly critical of the way she had left her remarks open to the interpretation that she identified the Provisional IRA with the freedom fighters of sixty years earlier. 'I know that Deputy de Valera did not intend such a comparison,' Lynch added. 'The atrocities of the Provisional IRA would have been as abhorrent to these men as they are now to all of us.' Hence his government was determined to stop them. 'To this end our security forces fully cooperate with their counterparts in the North and elsewhere,' he explained. 'As agreed in London last Wednesday, this cooperation will be improved where possible and to the fullest extent possible within the law.'

Although Lynch was quite positive that day about his willingness to cooperate with others to stamp out IRA violence, he still found it necessary to defend his republican credentials when the parliamentary party discussed the issue on 28 September 1979. De Valera told the meeting that the Taoiseach had not indicated to her that he objected so strongly to her speech on the Friday before she delivered it. The speech had already been circulated to the media, so it was obvious that she had had no intention of changing it.

Lynch arrived at the meeting with a speech carefully prepared and written out on a series of cards. This was not an attack on Síle de Valera but a defence of his own approach to the partition question. He explained that he had stressed the need for equality for nationalists in the North during his first meeting with Prime Minister Harold Wilson, and he made the same point with his successor, Edward Heath. He noted that the invitation to the talks at Chequers with Heath and Brian Faulkner in September 1971 was tantamount to 'the first overt acknowledgment by the British regime of our entitlement to be involved in whatever negotiations would take place about the future of the North.' This ultimately led to the Sunningdale agreement, which involved the establishment of a power-sharing executive in Northern Ireland and a Council of Ireland for the whole island when it was signed in December 1973. In the way that he referred to Sunningdale, he seemed to be suggesting that he approved of that agreement, which was ironic because he had opposed it in the Dáil. However, by then most people realised that Lynch had only been going through the motions for political purposes. His speech to the parliamentary party would certainly seem to confirm this. He concluded his prepared speech by reaffirming his determination to secure Irish unity by peaceful means. 'The sort of Ireland which the Irish government seeks is one based not on domination by one tradition or another but on the recognition that peace can only come through arrangements which accommodate the full richness and diversity of both traditions, the republican and the unionist,' he said.

The whole tenor of his carefully prepared address showed that he was very much on the defensive. He could easily have chosen to be assertive at the time. This was the eve of Pope John Paul II's visit to Ireland. It was going to afford the Taoiseach the kind of exposure of which most Catholic leaders could only dream.

On his way to meet the Pope, Lynch was stopped by a senior garda and informed that an English newspaper was on the verge of breaking a story suggesting that President Paddy Hillery was going to resign as President because he was having an extramarital affair. The Taoiseach, fearing a major sex scandal while the Pope was in Ireland, immediately telephoned Hillery.

'What's going on?' Lynch asked.

'I don't know.'

'There are all sorts of rumours.'

'It's my duty to tell you as a friend, and as Taoiseach and your President, that these rumours are going all about me and I don't know what to do about them,' Hillery said. 'If I had a woman I could easily put her away from me, but I haven't anybody to put away from me. What do you advise me to do?'

'I'm told that the story is going to break in a couple of days and

I advise you to talk to the editors of the four national dailies and discuss it with them,' Lynch advised. 'They're reasonable men.'

Hillery invited the editors of the three Dublin-based national newspapers – Douglas Gageby of *The Irish Times*, Aidan Pender of the *Irish Independent* and Tim Pat Coogan of the *Irish Press*, together with Wesley Boyd, the head of news at RTÉ – to Áras an Uachtaráin and asked for their advice on how to respond to an unfounded story that was about to appear in *Hibernia*, suggesting that he was on the point of resigning.

They advised him to talk to their political correspondents, so a further briefing was arranged for that evening, at which the President read them a brief statement. 'In recent days it has come to my attention that there are rumours circulating as to the possibility of my resigning as President,' he began. 'There is absolutely no foundation for such rumours. I am not resigning.' He also told them that there was no truth to the rumour that he was having an affair.

'Why are you doing this?' Seán Duignan, RTÉ's political correspondent, asked. It seemed amazing to him that the President would bother denying something that had never been reported.

'Because I'm advised by the government,' the President replied.

It was already getting close to his deadline for the nine o'clock news, so Duignan had to leave early. As he departed, one of the President's aides asked what Hillery had said.

'He said he wasn't involved with another woman,' Duignan replied.

'Oh, Jesus!' was the last thing Duignan heard as he left the Áras. That probably typified the response around the country when he reported the story on the evening news. Most people were perplexed at the President's denial of a rumour that they had never even heard.

There was a great deal of speculation about who was responsible for the rumour. Hillery believed it was spread by some of

Haughey's supporters to ensure the President did not resign in order to run for Taoiseach. To qualify himself for this, Hillery would have been required to stand in one of the forthcoming by-elections in Cork or one of the Taoiseach's nominees would have had to stand down in the Senate so that Lynch could appoint Hillery to the vacancy. But no senator had ever been elected Taoiseach. The whole idea seemed fanciful in the extreme.

Another theory was that Haughey's supporters were trying to create a vacancy in the presidency so that Jack Lynch could be kicked upstairs. Haughey's critics seemed ready to believe just about anything of his supporters – that they were trying to get Hillery to resign and not to resign at the same time. It seemed particularly ludicrous that they should try to exploit rumours of an affair, because Haughey himself had been having an affair with the journalist Terry Keane for several years, and this was one of the worst-kept secrets in Ireland.

There were also some other theories which were even more bizarre. The author Gordon Thomas suggested that the whole thing was a plot by the Soviet secret service to stop Ireland joining NATO. The Soviets supposedly feared that the Pope was somehow going to arrange a deal to end partition in return for Ireland joining NATO. It really took some imagination to think that the Pope, of all people, was going to persuade Ian Paisley and company to agree to Irish unity.

Another idea suggested later was that British intelligence, either MI5 or MI6, was behind the whole thing as a dirty-tricks operation to embarrass the Irish government while the Pope was in Ireland, in retaliation for failing to afford Earl Mountbatten proper protection. All the theories were indicative of the volatile state of Irish politics at the time.

During October 1979 Lynch took a very active part in two by-election campaigns in Cork. After the debacle of the European election result, it was important that Fianna Fáil should do well in the by-elections, especially as one of them was in Lynch's own Cork City constituency, where Pat Kerrigan, the late Labour Party deputy, was to be replaced. The other by-election was in Cork North-East, to fill the vacancy caused by the death of Fianna Fáil's Seán Brosnan.

Fianna Fail had a comfortable majority in the Dáil, so the outcome was not going to have any influence on the balance of power, but the Taoiseach obviously realised that it could have a profound impact on his own power base. He spoke at the party convention held at the Metropole Hotel to select a candidate in Cork City on 10 October 1979. Although he lived in Dublin, he took an active part in the by-election campaigns, delivering a series of public addresses on each of the four weekends prior to polling. In the process, Lynch staked his own political reputation.

The Fianna Fáil candidate in Cork City was John Dennehy, a factory worker in Irish Steel, while county councillor John Brosnan, a solicitor and son of the late Sean Brosnan, was the party's candidate in Cork North-East. Brosnan was going to have the advantage of the 'sympathy vote', which had traditionally been a significant factor in by-elections. A high-powered local election team was put together in Cork City, with Gene Fitzgerald, the Minister for Labour, as the director of elections. Pearse Wyse, the minister of state at the Department of Finance, was director of canvassing, and his assistant director was Seán French. Both of them had been elected to the Dáil from the Cork City constituency on the ticket with Lynch in 1977.

As far as winning the by-election went, Cork City should have been the safest seat in the whole country for Fianna Fáil, because the party had won three of the five seats in the last general election, with 58.6 per cent of the vote. At the various rallies, Lynch appealed for support by defending his government's record and contrasting it with that of the opposition parties' failures in government. He pointed out that a record 30,000 new jobs had been created since Fianna Fáil's return to power. In addition, the country's population was again on the increase, as more people were returning to Ireland than were emigrating. 'What a contrast with the times when much greater numbers emigrated each year through the port of Cork!' Lynch exclaimed to a party meeting in Cork on 20 October.

'You may wish to cast your minds back to some of the areas in which our predecessors were setting new records,' he added. 'I am thinking of such things as the rate of inflation, which at one stage approached 25 per cent, or the numbers out of work, which in 1976 reached 108,000, or the percentage of GNP represented by the government's borrowings in a single year, which in 1975 closely approached 17 per cent, or the burden of taxation, which in 1976 rose to 46 per cent of national income. Perhaps, on reflection, you may prefer to forget rather than to recall those unhappy days.'

'With the confidence fostered by Fianna Fáil's careful planning and decisive government,' he told a rally in Cork city the following day, 'Ireland today is a country on the move.' Although he was trying to paint a very rosy picture of the economy, emphasising the 30,000 extra jobs created and contrasting those with 20,000 jobs lost during the coalition years, he had to admit the following weekend that things had become quite bumpy lately. He blamed it on external factors.

'This year, difficulties outside our control have prevented us reaching the ambitious targets we set for the economy,' he explained. 'We have had to face increases in the price of oil which by the end of the year may be up by 40 per cent or more on 1978. This inexorably cuts 1 or 2 per cent off our rate of growth, which now appears unlikely to exceed 4 per cent. This will still be among the fastest in the Western world.'

While Lynch was concentrating on the by-elections, Tom McEllistrim decided both to ask a question and simultaneously to put down a motion at the next parliamentary-party meeting. He asked if the Taoiseach and government had given permission to the British to overfly the border, and he moved that if this was so, that the permission should be withdrawn.

This was part of the overall scheme to make way for Haughey, which Lynch must have realised but the media did not. McEllistrim was emphatic that Haughey was not directly involved in the scheming. He and the others informed Haughey about what they were planning, but they never looked to him for directions. Of course, he could have objected, with the result that his silence was tantamount to approving of their actions. He was essentially a silent partner in it all.

The Chief Whip, Michael Woods, telephoned McEllistrim to withdraw the motion.

'No way,' McEllistrim replied.

When he arrived at Leinster House on the eve of the meeting, he found himself the focus of considerable media attention. Lynch was late for the parliamentary-party meeting on 24 October, and the proceedings were delayed for half an hour, which was most unusual. Such meetings normally went ahead without the Taoiseach, but this time Willie Kenneally, the chairman of the parliamentary party, insisted on waiting. There was an unusually heavy agenda for the meeting that day, with five motions on different topics, but when the meeting began, the other four motions was postponed in order to concentrate on McEllistrim's motion.

'I wanted to know as a member of the parliamentary party whether permission was given by our government to the British to overfly the border,' he explained. 'If permission was given, I am proposing that we withdraw it.' His father had taken part in an attack on Gortatlea barracks in April 1918, which was the first attack of its kind since the Easter Rising. 'My father started guerrilla warfare in Ireland after 1916,' he said, adding that twenty-seven men from his locality were killed in the subsequent struggle.

If the British were now allowed to cross the border, he said, 'my father would turn in his grave.' Moreover, he added, Fianna Fail 'would lose thousands of votes' in the next general election.

After four or five other people spoke, the Taoiseach interrupted. 'We'll be here all day,' he said. 'If I reply to this, it might satisfy everyone.' According to McEllistrim, he then said something like, 'As of now, the British have not permission to overfly the border.' The Taoiseach assured them that the issue did not infringe the country's sovereignty.

Bill Loughnane of Clare interrupted the Taoiseach at one point. 'Do you mean when you say there will be no infringement of sovereignty that the Irish government will not allow the British Army to cross the border either on land or in the air?' Loughnane asked.

'The British Army will not be allowed across the border,' Lynch replied.

McEllistrim then asked that his motion be withdrawn. He later said that he was personally convinced that the Taoiseach had given the British permission to overfly but had possibly withdrawn his permission during the delay before the meeting. Although some people wished him to pursue the matter further, McEllistrim decided not to question Lynch's veracity. Nevertheless, he noted with a certain satisfaction that the parliamentary party was distinctly uneasy.

On the final weekend before the by-elections, Lynch delivered two prepared speeches in Cork city, and also spoke in Cobh and Midleton, where he emphasised the government's agricultural performance. He noted that Fianna Fáil had negotiated membership of the Common Market, which he described as 'the mainspring of agricultural development in the 'seventies'. He added that the government looked like exceeding the target of a 25 per cent increase in gross agricultural output for the four-year period. 'This achievement will surely mark this period as the greatest era in Irish farming development,' he argued.

Lynch also anchored the party political broadcast on RTÉ on behalf of Fianna Fáil. In this he highlighted the economic achievements of the government, producing 50,000 new jobs, cutting inflation in half, increasing social-welfare spending by more than a third and abolishing car tax and the rates on private dwellings. Of course, the Opposition was still complaining. 'The Opposition accuse my government of failure,' he said. 'We have not yet succeeded, they say, in repairing the widespread damage they inflicted.' Cattle prices had more than doubled and the price of lamb and pork had already risen appreciably, while the value of agricultural exports had exceeded £1 billion for the first time in history.

'I watched Mr Lynch's final rally in Cork city on the eve of the elections,' Michael Mills recalled. 'It seemed to me his extraordinary personal appeal to voters, which had seen him win the 1977 general election with the biggest majority in the party's history, had lost much of its magnetism. Gone was the old enthusiasm of the crowds; in its place was a dull apathy.' This certainly did not bode well for the Taoiseach.

As people were voting in the Cork by-elections, Lynch set out for the United States on an official eight-day visit. The following morning, he had a formal meeting at the White House with President Jimmy Carter, who was having his own political difficulties. Three days earlier, the American embassy in Tehran had been overrun and the staff taken hostage. 'These have been the worst three days of my presidency,' Carter told Lynch. On top of everything else, Senator Ted Kennedy and Governor Jerry Brown of California had just announced that they were going to oppose Carter for the Democratic Party's nomination for the presidency in 1980.

The prime-time network-news programmes on CBS and NBC highlighted the Taoiseach's ceremonial meeting with the President on the south lawn of the White House, where they stressed their joint opposition to terrorism, whether in Iran or Ireland. Although Lynch was officially visiting as President of the EEC, he and Carter talked mainly about the situation in Northern Ireland, but this was obviously quite low on the President's list of priorities at this stage.

'We will do everything we possibly can to prevent American citizens' assistance to the terrorists in Ireland, who do so much to obstruct the realisation of the hopes and dreams of all the Irish people, no matter what their religious background or convictions,' Carter declared after the two men emerged from a one-hour meeting.

Lynch told the media that Carter had emphasised 'the need that terrorism be put down, no matter where it raises its head, especially in Northern Ireland, and those who support terrorism must be deterred from doing so.' That evening there was a formal dinner hosted by the President and his mother, in the absence of the First Lady, who was abroad. After Carter spoke some warm words in a short toast, Lynch responded by telling the story of the good Catholic Irish woman who had six children. She was asked when she was going to have her seventh. 'Sure,' she replied, 'haven't I heard that every seventh child born in the world today is Chinese.'

That afternoon in Washington, Lynch had heard the devastating political news that Fine Gael had won both by-elections. 'It was obvious at an impromptu press conference for Irish political journalists accompanying him on his US trip that he was profoundly shaken by the results, particularly as they were from his own county, where he would have expected the old loyalties to be maintained,' Michael Mills of the *Irish Press* noted. It was a humiliating political defeat in Lynch's own backyard.

'The outcome in each and both constituencies could not possibly affect the life of the government, so I believe myself that there was a certain degree of non-participation among Fianna Fáil supporters because they felt that the outcome wouldn't matter anyway,' Lynch told the media.

The following morning he was interviewed on the NBC's *Today Show* at 7.15 a.m., and he also hoped to be interviewed on the popular ABC programme *Issues and Answers* at the weekend, but he was informed that ABC had decided instead to feature a former prime minister of Iran. Other similar programmes were taken up with the news that Kennedy and Brown would be opposing Carter in the forthcoming primary elections. Lynch did give a pre-arranged interview to the news magazine *US News & World Report* in which he praised Carter and expressed the hope that the United States 'would use its influence with the United Kingdom to bring forward a political initiative for Northern Ireland.' But he informed *Time* magazine that he did not want American mediation because 'the forum must be between the British and ourselves and the elected representatives of the North.' He added that he did not favour a British withdrawal from the North before there was 'a system of administration established and accepted by both communities.' Even then he stressed that withdrawal 'must be on a gradual scale.'

Did Lynch want a united Ireland at all? Americans asked. 'The Irish government, for internal political reasons, have been evasive on this crucial point,' the *New York Times* commented. 'Mr Lynch can be reasonably pressed to dispel the suspicion.'

The Taoiseach was invited to address the National Press Club in Washington. He had been particularly depressed with the political news from Cork but he drank some wine with his lunch and seemed very relaxed. Although nobody wrote about it at the time, it seems possible that Lynch had developed a problem with drink. The indications were already there when he had to have a break in his meetings with Heath to have a drink back in 1971. While in opposition in the mid-1970s he had a boating accident in which he injured a heel. Even though it was later operated on, it never healed properly. He walked with a limp and he developed a hip problem, possibly as a result of his limp. Hence he was not able to walk off the effects of whiskey as he had in earlier years, and his tolerance for alcohol began to decrease.

At the Washington dinner he said that he would agree to a united Ireland 'with suitable financial arrangements in a transition between the situation that now obtains in the North and South, and I mean, and I say candidly, we could not afford at this time to make available that kind of subvention of $2 billion per annum in the North. But with suitable financial arrangements, certainly we can take on the economic problems that face us at the present time, given a reasonable interim period.' He seemed to be saying that the way things were, Dublin did not want Northern Ireland, at least for the time being, and then his government would only be interested if it was paid enough to take on the problems. Of course, Lynch had said as much many times in recent years, but for the Americans his remarks presented a startling contrast with what Paddy Hillery had said when he went to the United States to rail against partition ten years earlier.

It was the custom at the dinner for members of the National Press Club to submit questions to the top table in writing, and about a half-dozen of these would be read out for the guest of honour to answer. Seán Cronin, the Washington correspondent of *The Irish Times,* submitted a question about the recent security arrangement with the British. Lynch replied that there was a security pact but it was secret as 'there is no point in telling your enemy what you are going to do to offset him or overcome him.' He added that the Air Navigation Act of 1952 remained unchanged 'except in one slight respect'.

According to Elizabeth Shannon, the wife of American ambassador William Shannon, Lynch 'indicated that an air corridor along the border between Ireland and Northern Ireland was part of the improved security arrangements that he had worked out with Mrs Thatcher following the murder of Lord Mountbatten in August.'

'Oh my God!' one of the Irish civil servants was heard to exclaim at the top table. Although British military aircraft could overfly the Republic, the Taoiseach emphasised that British troops did not have the right of 'hot pursuit'.

Michael Mills promptly reported to the *Irish Press* that the Taoiseach had essentially confirmed his original story about the air corridor along the border. A reporter from the *Irish Independent* contacted Bill Loughnane for a comment. The Clare deputy recalled the assurance that Lynch had given the recent parliamentary-party meeting when Tom McEllistrim's motion had been discussed.

'Now, if he said what he is reported to have said in the United States, then that was a false statement to us,' Loughnane said. 'When he returns I am going to demand that he comes clean and tell the truth. Will the British Army be allowed to cross the Border into the Republic or will they not?'

To make matters worse, the report of Loughnane's remarks was followed by word from Dublin the following day that Haughey had delivered what was viewed by some as a coded attack on Lynch when giving an address at a dinner in the Burlington Hotel, Dublin, commemorating the centenary of Pádraic Pearse's birth. 'The idea of partition was totally inconceivable to Pearse and his contemporaries,' Haughey said. 'It was a British-inspired concept that had appeared for the first time during the tangled home-rule negotiations on the eve of the Great War. Pearse would, if he were here today, insist that all the policies and programmes of government should be directed to the welfare of the people. "The end of freedom is human happiness," he said, and so in his Ireland that central republican purpose would certainly take precedence over any other.' Towards the end of the address he quoted the famous lines from Pearse's poem 'The Fool': 'Oh wise men riddle me this: what if the dream came true?'

Haughey may well have been thinking of his own long-cherished dream of becoming Taoiseach that night. He and Lynch were putting a very different emphasis on the partition question on each side of the Atlantic, but it was not a blatant attack on the Taoiseach's policy, as Síle de Valera's oration had been in September. Nevertheless the script of Haughey's speech was faxed to Lynch, who responded by inserting a reference of his own to Pearse into a speech that he delivered in Boston that same evening.

'The paradox of Pearse's message to the Irish nation today is that we must live and work for Ireland, not die, and most certainly not kill for it,' the Taoiseach told the Boston gathering. 'We are not concerned now with legitimacy or nationhood, for we are fully accepted in the brotherhood of nations throughout the world.' The sacrifice of past generations had already guaranteed that nationhood. 'We are concerned with the moral, cultural and material well-being of the Irish people; and that can be advanced not by killing, not by death or hatred or destruction, but by life,' Lynch stated.

This went down well with the Boston gathering, according to Dick Walsh, the political correspondent of *The Irish Times*. 'If Mr Lynch is fighting a rearguard action across the Atlantic, invoking the heroes of party and state,' Walsh reported, 'he is meeting with some popular success in the US.'

Frank Dunlop, the government press secretary, circulated a copy of Haughey's Dublin speech to the journalists accompanying the official party on the American Air Force plane put at the Taoiseach's disposal. 'None of them thought it amounted to much,' according to Walsh. But Lynch's response indicated that he certainly thought it was part of the unrest within the party.

'You have to know the code,' Seán Duignan, RTÉ's political correspondent, observed. 'They're sending semaphore messages to each other across the Atlantic. The people in the back know what it means and they don't like it.'

Politics at home was obviously playing heavily on the Taoiseach's mind and he was clearly upset by Loughnane's comments. The following night in Chicago he told some of the reporters accompanying him that he had been in touch with George Colley by telephone and that Loughnane's accusation would be dealt with firmly at the parliamentary-party meeting the day after. 'This sort of thing has gone on too long,' Lynch said. 'It must be stopped now.'

Things picked up for the Irish delegation the following day in New Orleans, where a crowd of nearly a thousand people waited to greet Lynch, who was mobbed. Of course, in a kind of perverse way this highlighted the lack of enthusiasm elsewhere, especially in the strong Irish-American centres like Boston and Chicago. But the news that Lynch received from the parliamentary-party meeting in Dublin was not good.

As deputy leader of the party, Colley had demanded the removal of the party whip from Loughnane. 'Sure he couldn't even get it as far as a vote,' McEllistrim recalled. 'There was consternation.'

Jackie Fahey proposed as an amendment that the matter should be deferred until the Taoiseach's return. Timothy 'Chub' O'Connor seconded this, but Colley insisted his motion should be put to the floor. Several deputies spoke in favour of Fahey's amendment. Vivion de Valera, Éamon de Valera's eldest son, opposed the removal of the whip on the grounds that Loughnane's original question about cross-border overflights had not been answered properly.

After several attempts to get Loughnane to explain himself, he eventually responded with a story about the singer Father Sydney McEwan going to John McCormack for an audition. As McEwan waited nervously, McCormack burst into the room and invited him out to lunch, as he could not sing on an empty stomach. The meeting broke for lunch and intense efforts were made to persuade

Colley to back off. Martin O'Donoghue pleaded with him, because he was sure that Colley would be defeated on the issue.

Ray MacSharry suggested that some of the leaders should talk with Loughnane privately to try to resolve their differences. Colley, Brian Lenihan and the parliamentary-party chairman Willie Kenneally left the room with Loughnane for a discussion outside. A compromise was hammered out. Loughnane withdrew his criticism of the Taoiseach and denied that he had called him a 'liar', which was technically true, because he had not used that word, but he had certainly implied it. Colley had suffered another humiliating defeat, but he did not have the political savvy to realise it.

Following the debacle at the parliamentary-party meeting, Haughey was convinced that Lynch was finished. 'What the fuck are you doing over there?' Haughey said to Press Secretary Frank Dunlop on the telephone. 'Don't you know Lynch is on the way out? Get back, the man is finished.'

Lynch went to New York on 15 November. At a reception in his honour at the Hilton Hotel, he delivered a short speech which went down very well with the gathering. But the Loughnane affair, taken in conjunction with the Cork by-election defeats, had 'tended to spoil what should have been a very happy visit by the Taoiseach and Mrs Lynch,' Liam O'Neill of the *Cork Examiner* noted at the time.

'They really love you in New York,' Elizabeth Shannon remarked to Lynch after his address.

'They haven't heard the result of the Cork by-elections,' he replied.

The next day Ambassador Shannon and his wife went out to Kennedy Airport to see the Lynches off. They would see them again in Dublin shortly, but a sense of foreboding hung over their departure. 'There is an air of sadness and anticlimax in the air, and we all bade each other goodbye as if it were final,' Elizabeth Shannon noted in her diary.

Lynch was welcomed at Dublin Airport the following morning by some thirty-five deputies and senators. Those included all but three members of the government. Sylvester Barrett, the Minister for the Environment, was in Geneva, and Jim Gibbons was in Rome. The airport gathering was reminiscent of Lynch's return from New York after the arms trial. But then the turnout was to get behind him; this time it seemed that they were just jockeying for position.

The *Cork Examiner* seemed to attach more importance to the news of Haughey's absence than to the presence of all of the others, since the newspaper led off its front-page report of the events at Dublin Airport with the observation that 'Mr Haughey was conspicuous by his absence.' A spokesman explained that he had 'a personal family commitment at 8 a.m. and could not make it to the airport.'

But the same report included an observation by Eddie Collins, the Fine Gael spokesman on education, that 'it was well known' that Haughey was in conflict with Lynch 'and was openly pursuing a policy of divide and conquer within the Fianna Fáil Party.' Even more ominously, however, Collins added that George Colley too was waiting 'to stab Jack in the back'.

McEllistrim and company moved in for the political kill at this stage by drawing up a petition calling on Lynch to step down. There were two parts to this. The cover sheet contained the demand, and the second page had the list of names in support, but this was folded so that those signing could not see the other names until they signed themselves. It was agreed that the organisers would bury their names in the list. McEllistrim, who retained the document, signed fifth. Fahey, Killilea and Doherty also signed. It was a measure of the extent to which Albert Reynolds kept himself in the background that he never actually signed the document. Of course, the whole thing was supposed to be secret, but the word was already out. When the Chief Whip, Michael Woods, was asked about it, he replied that he was not aware officially that backbenchers were circulating a petition for Lynch to stand down.

As the parliamentary party was about to meet on 22 November, the lead story in the *Cork Examiner* suggested that Lynch was likely to come under attack from two fronts within the party. 'Mr Lynch's ability to lead the party has been under serious question privately since the shattering defeats in Cork City and Cork North-East two weeks ago,' Liam O'Neill wrote. 'The questioning is believed to have come not only from the Haughey camp, which is traditionally seen as waiting to challenge Lynch's leadership, but also from a faction led by Mr George Colley, who unsuccessfully fought for the leadership with Mr Lynch thirteen years ago.'

A spokesman for Mr Colley telephoned the newspaper to 'deny emphatically' that he had ever had any intention of attacking Mr Lynch's leadership. 'There is not a scintilla of truth in such a suggestion. The Tánaiste's stand has been one of unswerving loyalty to Mr Lynch since he was appointed leader of the party in 1966.'

The parliamentary-party meeting turned out to be something of a damp squib. Lynch gave a report on his visit to the USA and they then spent an hour discussing bog development. This was not the time to question his leadership openly, as he was due to preside at the European summit meeting in Dublin Castle the following week. An attempt was made to stifle any further debate on the by-election results, but Síle de Valera and others strenuously objected. It was therefore decided to postpone the debate until the next parliamentary-party meeting after the European summit.

In all probability Lynch would have had little difficulty in beating off a challenge from Haughey, but he was a political lame duck, as he had already indicated that he intended to step down before the next election. He had actually told his wife and Martin O'Donoghue that he would resign in early January after Ireland's presidency of the EEC was completed. O'Donoghue now warned him, however, that the party was in danger of splitting itself, so he decided to bring the date forward to early in December, after the EEC summit meeting.

As the Fianna Fáil parliamentary party was about to discuss recent events, on Wednesday 5 December 1979 Lynch made an announcement to the assembled press and television cameras. 'During my absence on an official visit last month to the United States, the results of the Cork by-elections came through and these, associated with other recent events, created some uncertainty among members of my party,' he explained. 'But I was especially concerned that doubts as to my intentions about my continued leadership of the government were creating uncertainty in the minds of the public as well, and I felt that this was not good for our country. Therefore I have decided in the national interest that instead of waiting for a further three or four more weeks, I should remove any further uncertainty by announcing my resignation forthwith.'

At the parliamentary-party meeting he read a prepared, detailed speech:

> I have decided to resign as Taoiseach. I am today asking you, the Fianna Fáil members of Dáil Éireann, to convene a meeting within the next few days to select my successor so that I can as early as possible next week present my resignation to President Hillery.
>
> I had already decided, irrespective of the outcome of the 1977 general election, that I would resign the leadership of Fianna Fáil during the lifetime of the present Dáil. I discussed this with my wife and she agreed with this course.
>
> Shortly after the change of government in 1977 I stated in an interview with the political correspondents of the Irish news media that the time of my resignation would leave about two years to the ensuing general election, during which pe-

riod my successor could establish himself as leader. Given the possible date of the next general election as likely to be late in 1981 or early in 1982, I had decided therefore that I would resign at the end of Ireland's presidency of the EEC, that is, early in January 1980.

Following the result of the European parliamentary elections and the local elections in June last, I was asked on a television programme about possible Cabinet changes. I replied that there would be a Cabinet reshuffle early in the New Year. I said that this would not be done sooner, as our presidency of the EEC was about to start and I did not wish then to change ministers who had already built up knowledge and experience in their respective areas of administration which would be important for them in handling EEC matters, especially the various EEC councils over which they would be presiding during the ensuing six months.

I had in mind, of course, that these Cabinet changes would involve my own resignation. During my absence last month on an official visit to the United States, the results of the Cork City by-elections came through and these, associated with other recent events, created some uncertainty among members of the party, but I was especially concerned that doubts about my intentions as to my continued leadership of the government were creating uncertainty among the public and this was not good for the country.

Therefore I have decided that instead of waiting for three or four weeks more I should remove any further uncertainty by announcing my resignation forthwith – especially now that the European summit has concluded quite satisfactorily from Ireland's point of view, and the terms of office as president of the various ministerial councils have almost come to an end for the other members of the government.

I am now in my sixty-third year and having spent about

thirty-two years in political life, during which I occupied a number of ministries, including nine years as Taoiseach and thirteen years as leader of Fianna Fáil, it is obvious to me that the time has come when someone with a new approach and fresh thinking should take over the leadership of the government, a leader who will carry on the traditions established by the founders and successive leaders of Fianna Fáil, a leader who will, with new vigour, continue to strive for the further economic progress of our country, and a leader who will continue to encourage the coming together of all the peoples and traditions on this island, without confrontation or violence, but in peace, with mutual respect and understanding . . .

O'Donoghue and Colley had persuaded Lynch that Colley would win in a contest. They thought that Haughey would be caught on the hop if the Taoiseach stood down early, but Haughey had been preparing for this day for years. Colley thought he could count on the support of nearly all the twenty-five members of the government. It came as quite a shock when two eventually came out openly for Haughey. Neither Colley nor his main backers had bothered to canvass the backbenchers before assuring Lynch that Colley had the contest locked up.

'The advice was bad, however, as any of the political correspondents could have told him at any time in the preceding months,' Michael Mills noted. 'For more than a year we had been conducting regular polls among ourselves as to the likely outcome of a leadership contest between Mr Colley and Charles Haughey. In every one of them, Mr Haughey came out on top.

'The only person who ever asked me for an opinion on the outcome was Mr Haughey himself,' Mills explained. 'I told him that our estimates gave him forty-five or forty-six votes. He was somewhat disappointed, as he told me his own estimate put him at more than fifty votes, but then, he said, forty-five votes would be a victory in any case. Up to the end, Mr Colley's supporters continued to express absolute confidence in the outcome. I tried to explain to one of his aides that they were being misled and that some deputies were obviously promising their votes to both men, but they were not prepared to listen and, in any case, it was too late.'

Haughey discussed with McEllistrim and some of the others how people were likely to vote in a leadership contest, but they found him much too optimistic. He had worked assiduously in helping out deputies who came to him for assistance over the years, and he expected them to return the compliment now. Sitting in his office on the eve of the vote with his campaign team, he totted up his likely support and concluded that he would get fifty-eight votes to Colley's twenty-four.

'Do you know,' Seán Doherty exclaimed, 'you're the worst fucking judge of people I ever met.'

It was going to be much tighter, but most of the backbench deputies obviously supported Haughey. Many were terrified by the party's poor showings in the recent European elections, and especially in the Cork by-elections. If those showings were repeated in a general election, Fianna Fáil would be lucky not to be annihilated. In the circumstances, a change was needed. The government was being blamed by the people for its handling of industrial unrest and inflation, and its failure to deal with the inequitable system of taxation. Colley had antagonised rural and urban voters with his budget debacle, as well as women voters with a highly publicised, dismissive comment about well-heeled, articulate women. In a public-opinion poll earlier in the year he ranked as the poorest performer other than Pádraig Faulkner, who was plagued by a postal strike at the time.

Des O'Malley, Brian Lenihan and Michael O'Kennedy were mentioned as outsiders who might come into the reckoning in the event that the party could not decide between the other two. O'Malley would have been Lynch's first choice, but he firmly ruled himself out and publicly pledged his support to Colley, while Lenihan kept his own counsel. Lenihan was asked to nominate Haughey but refused to do so.

'I felt duty-bound to support Mr Haughey during this period,' he later wrote in his book, *For the Record*. He realised the time was not right for himself, so he twice tried to persuade Lynch to hold on longer, but the Taoiseach had obviously had enough and wanted out. Lenihan privately admitted to his family that he considered the choice between Haughey and Colley as being a choice between a knave and a fool.

Haughey's people cleverly set his bandwagon rolling with some announcements timed to give him a boost at the right moments psychologically. After Lenihan refused to nominate him, Haughey turned to Vivion de Valera, the former President's eldest son, but he also refused. He then turned to Colley's parliamentary secretary, Ray MacSharry, who agreed to do the needful. With reporters waiting outside Leinster House to pick up scraps of news, MacSharry went out and announced rather stiffly, 'I will be proposing Haughey for leader tomorrow.'

Colley was caught completely by surprise. Suddenly his colleagues realised that he was in trouble. They made frantic efforts to persuade deputies to support him by threatening to cut off funds already allocated for local projects.

Garret FitzGerald later related an extraordinary story in his memoirs about some backbench deputies who said they were being intimidated by Haughey's supporters and wished to know if Fine Gael could 'do anything to ensure a genuine secret ballot'. It was decided to use booths so that deputies could vote in private.

Next morning the Colley camp was to get another shock. 'Michael O'Kennedy is voting for me,' Haughey telephoned Frank Dunlop. 'Spread the word.' Colley and his supporters had outmanoeuvred themselves by rushing to election. Had Lynch given as much notice of his intention to step down as Lemass, he might have been able to call on O'Malley to stand, in the same way that Lemass had called on Lynch himself, but now it was too late. There were only hours before the meeting convened to elect the new leader.

The vote turned out to be largely between the government and the backbenches. 'They were voting to save their jobs,' one backbencher noted, 'and we were voting to save our seats.' When the votes were counted Haughey was shown to have won by 44 to 33.

Colley and some of his supporters took the defeat very badly. One Fianna Fáil deputy later told Garret FitzGerald that 'despite the polling-booth arrangement, some deputies had not felt that the privacy of the ballot had been ensured, because the voting papers, when marked at either end of the room, had to be deposited in a box near the centre of the room. Some deputies claimed they had been told that unless, as they walked back to deposit their votes in the box, they showed them to members of the Haughey camp, they would be assumed to have voted for Colley and would subsequently be treated accordingly.'

Colley's supporters controlled the party mechanism at that stage and if they were not able to ensure a proper election, they were even more incompetent and out of touch with the rest of the party than anyone could have imagined. They really outmanoeuvred themselves by rushing the election, but they could not face up to the reality of their own bungling.

They blamed Haughey for ousting Lynch, even though Haughey had little to do with the campaign against the Taoiseach. Those supporting Haughey had their own selfish reasons for organising their campaign. They were disillusioned with Colley and they believed that they had a better chance of both preferment and re-election with Haughey as leader. Moreover, politicians are usually easily convinced that what is good for themselves is good for their party.

'We were never led by Haughey,' McEllistrim later emphasised repeatedly. 'We were never encouraged by Haughey or anything like that.' Of course, he knew what was going on. 'I'd meet

Haughey in the corridor or something like that and we might just talk about what was happening within the party. But I can say definitely that we were never encouraged by Haughey to do what we were doing and to try and change the leadership of Fianna Fáil. We were never encouraged by Haughey – that's definite.'

It could be argued that as a consequence of the backbench campaign, Lynch stepped down early, but it was O'Donoghue and Colley who persuaded him to do this in order to help Colley. Lynch would personally have preferred Des O'Malley to succeed him, but O'Malley was supporting Colley. There was no doubt that there were people trying to push Lynch, but he decided to jump in an attempt to frustrate them. In the last analysis, the real push came from the electorate, in the way people voted in the European elections and especially by the manner in which the people of Cork city rejected the Fianna Fáil candidate in the recent by-election. It seemed that Lynch had lost his electoral touch, which had always been his strongest political asset. It was time for him to go, and he knew it, even though he could undoubtedly have hung on for a few more months.

'Jack Lynch was a tough man,' Michael Hartnett, one of Haughey's campaign people, noted. 'He might allow you to do a lot of things, but once he had the ball, you could not take it from him. If Jack had wanted to cut us off at the knees, he could have done it with great ease!'

'I wasn't forced out,' Lynch told T. P. O'Mahony. 'I could have held on, and nobody could have forced me out if I didn't want to go.'

21

ONE OF OUR OWN

1979–1999

Immediately after Charles Haughey's election as leader of Fianna Fáil, the ballot papers were burned, and the smoke set off the fire alarm in Leinster House. Some saw this as a portent of things to come. George Colley and Martin O'Donoghue had a long discussion with Des O'Malley as to whether they would actually vote for Haughey as Taoiseach. Garret FitzGerald heard that they were so disillusioned that they might even be prepared to bolt the party rather than support Haughey. The Fine Gael leader sought to appeal to disgruntled members of the Colley wing of Fianna Fáil.

'I must speak not only for the Opposition but for many in Fianna Fáil who may not be free to say what they believe or to express their deep fears for the future of this country under the proposed leadership, people who are not free to reveal what they know and what led them to oppose this man with a commitment far beyond the normal,' FitzGerald told the Dáil during the debate on Haughey's nomination for Taoiseach. 'He comes with a flawed pedigree,' the Fine Gael leader continued. 'His motives can be judged ultimately only by God but we cannot ignore the fact that he differs from all his predecessors in that those motives have been and are widely impugned, most notably, but by no means exclusively, by people within his own party, people close to him who have observed his actions for many years and who have made their human, interim judgement on him. They and others, both in and out of public life, have attributed to him an overweening ambition which they do not see as a simple emanation of a desire to serve but rather as a wish to dominate, even to own the state.'

Others joined in the attacks, including John Kelly and Richie Ryan of Fine Gael and the independent TD, Noël Browne, who described Haughey as a dreadful cross between former President Richard Nixon and the late Portuguese dictator, Antonio Salazar. 'He has used his position unscrupulously in order to get where he is as a politician,' Browne said. 'He has done anything to get power; does anybody believe that he will not do anything to keep power?'

Even in 1932, when the political climate was still poisoned by Civil-War bitterness, Éamon de Valera had not been subjected to such abuse. Every seat in the public gallery and press galleries was full, along with the opposition seats. Across the floor, Haughey sat by himself, with the remainder of the government seats completely empty. He confronted his tormentors alone and refused to allow anyone to reply on his behalf. At the end of the debate he was elected Taoiseach by 82 votes to 62.

He went to great lengths to bind up the wounds in Fianna Fáil. He reappointed most of the outgoing Cabinet, even though the overwhelming majority of them had supported Colley. There was no mass purge of those who had voted against him, in contrast with Albert Reynolds's reshuffle a dozen years later, after he ousted Haughey. Reynolds was actually the only backbencher who had campaigned for Haughey to be given a Cabinet post in 1979. Colley was appointed Tánaiste and given a veto over the appointments of the Ministers for Defence and Justice, but Martin O'Donoghue lost out. He was dropped from the Cabinet and his Department of Economic

Planning was scrapped. The civil servants were transferred elsewhere, many of them to the Taoiseach's own department.

Lynch asked Haughey to appoint O'Donoghue as European Commissioner, but the Taoiseach appointed Michael O'Kennedy. This was a reward for O'Kennedy as he had been the sole Cabinet minister to back Haughey's bid for the party leadership.

As soon as the new government had been appointed, however, Colley seemed to be spoiling for a fight. Even though he had been given unprecedented concessions as a failed challenger for the leadership, Colley still began conspiring against the government almost immediately. On 19 December 1979 he telephoned Bruce Arnold of the *Irish Independent* to say that Haughey was 'dangerous, should have been blocked from the leadership, and should be got out as fast as possible.' He even gave Arnold some details of that day's Cabinet meeting. Colley had told the Cabinet that Haughey had misrepresented him when he told a press conference that Colley had pledged loyalty and support to him as Taoiseach. In view of the campaign that Haughey's supporters had waged against Lynch, Colley indicated that he no longer felt bound to give loyalty to the Taoiseach.

'Since Haughey had been campaigning, or supporting campaigns on his own behalf, for the previous five months,' Bruce Arnold argued, 'it was Haughey, not Colley, who had changed the rule about party loyalty within Fianna Fáil.' However, no evidence has ever been produced that Haughey was actively engaged in the campaign against Lynch. Charlie McCreevy, who later became one of Haughey's most outspoken critics, was adamant that Haughey had never been personally involved. On the other hand, Tom McEllistrim Jr said that Haughey had been kept informed about their moves. Maybe he could have stopped the conspirators, but then they might have thrown their support somewhere else.

At worst, Haughey could be accused of canvassing for the leadership of Fianna Fáil among members of the parliamentary party, whereas Colley went outside the party and sought to enlist the help of the press to oust Haughey. He also publicly disavowed any loyalty to him as leader.

'In my speech at the party meeting,' Colley explained, 'I referred to Mr Haughey's ability, capacity and flair, and I wished him well in the enormous tasks he was taking on. I did not, however, use the words "loyalty" or "support" which he attributed to me.' Colley fully understood how, 'in the excitement and euphoria' of victory, Haughey had misunderstood him, but now the Tánaiste was setting the record straight. As far as he was concerned, the traditional loyalty normally given to the leader of the party had been withheld from Lynch, and it was now legitimate to withhold 'loyalty to, and support for, the elected leader'.

Although Colley and others contended that Haughey effectively drove Lynch from office prematurely, the truth was that it had been Colley and O'Donoghue who persuaded Lynch to step down early and call a surprise leadership election with just two days' notice. Nobody objected, but then both sides believed that they were going to win. By rushing the election, however, the Colley faction outmanoeuvred themselves. They blamed Haughey, rather than their own bungling, and some of the media swallowed their sour grapes.

The transition between Lynch and Haughey was particularly difficult because of their different styles of leadership. Lynch was very much the chairman, whereas Haughey was always the boss. 'The transfer from one political modus operandi to the other almost required the characteristics of a schizophrenic,' according to Frank Dunlop, who worked as government press secretary under both men. 'Lynch's style was sufficiently relaxed to allow his ministers and officials to act almost independently, until such time as he thought it was necessary to intervene,' he continued. 'It was very satisfying to serve Lynch in a capacity where he made it known, verbally and by demeanour, that your advice was valued.

'Lynch never once questioned or countermanded any advice I

gave him,' Dunlop explained. 'Charlie wanted to know why particular advice was given, why it was necessary, and the logic behind it. Charlie laid down the template from day one. He was the boss.' Things had to be done his way. This style of leadership suited 'those who unquestioningly treated him as the boss, those who wished to share the limelight with him and did so to their advantage,' according to Dunlop. He was obviously uneasy with Haughey's style from the outset. 'From now on,' he warned the political correspondents, 'you can't take anything I say on trust.'

Lynch withdrew almost completely from politics but retained a high public profile, opening functions of a non-political nature. Tim Pat Coogan approached him on 10 January 1980 about writing his memoirs. 'You would of course be unmoved by the consideration that a certain piece of legislation which an Irish politician, whose name escapes me, was responsible for introducing will ensure that your earnings from the foregoing will of course be tax-free,' Coogan wrote. It was as if Haughey's name should not be mentioned. It was, of course, Haughey – as Minister for Finance – who introduced the tax exemption for writers and artists in Lynch's first government. Lynch did talk about the possibility of writing his memoirs but never actually did so.

Lynch felt that politics had cost him dearly, both in terms of his private life and his earning capacity, as he thought that he would have earned much more money at the bar. Following the conclusion of his time as Taoiseach, he set out to exploit his political experience in the field of business. He accepted a position as a director of Irish Distillers and joined the Irish board of Algemene, a Dutch bank, as well as the boards of the Smurfit Group and Hibernian Insurance. He also became chairman of Galway Crystal. His business activities involved a good deal of foreign travel. In 1980 he visited the People's Republic of China, and returned home to renewed speculation about the arms crisis.

Vincent Browne of *Magill* magazine had obtained the personal papers of the late Peter Berry. Browne had a private meeting with Lynch to discuss the papers on 6 May, which was the tenth anniversary of the sacking of Haughey and Blaney. In his papers, Berry depicted Lynch as turning a blind eye to the gun-running. Berry insisted that he had told the Taoiseach about the Bailieboro meeting back in October 1969. He added that Michael Moran had told him that he had passed on further information to the Taoiseach in the following months. Prior to Browne's investigation, little effort had been made to examine what Lynch knew and when he knew it.

Lynch denied that Berry had told him about the planned gun-running during the hospital meeting in October. Berry could not have told him about Haughey's involvement, because the Special Branch did not learn of it until December, nor could he have given any details about the plans to fly the weapons in from Austria, because those arms had not even been purchased at that stage. Lynch issued a veiled threat to sue for libel if Browne published Berry's material.

'I suggested to him that he was acting on information which he ought to be careful about, that if he published any allegation against me that would in any way reflect on my integrity, then I would have to consider my situation,' Lynch wrote. He was still a member of the Dáil, so he took part in the debate that ensued the following November on the *Magill* articles. 'I want to say categorically again to the Dáil that I was first informed by Mr Peter Berry of the alleged involvement of the minister on Monday 20 April 1970. That was the first I heard from any source.'

Berry had come to his office that morning. He then 'produced some documents and copies of statements taken from members of the staff of Dublin Airport and the Revenue Commissioners which clearly identified two members of the government as being involved.' The two were Blaney and Haughey, and Lynch emphasised that the name of Gibbons did not appear in those documents.

Lynch confirmed that he had met Berry in hospital in October 1969. "To my lay mind, Mr Berry was obviously a sick man and, as was indicated in the *Magill* articles, had a drip tube inserted in his nose. It is true that the medical staff interrupted frequently during the fifteen to twenty minutes or so I was with him,' the former Taoiseach told the Dáil. 'Mr Berry spoke to me about alleged attempts at importation of small quantities of arms from time to time.' But he said that he was taken totally by surprise by a recent report that the gun used to kill Garda Richard Fallon had been imported shortly before through Dublin Airport.

One of the more sensational disclosures from the Berry papers was the revelation of the secret meeting that Des O'Malley, then the Minister for Justice, had with Haughey a fortnight before the arms trial was due to begin. Lynch was obviously taken aback at the discovery of what went on. 'I had no knowledge of the alleged meeting in Leinster House on 9 September 1970,' he said.

Most of the information about Haughey had been in the public domain for the preceding decade, with the result that the *Magill* series really raised more questions about the roles played by Lynch and O'Malley in the whole affair. As Vincent Browne concluded, 'while Mr Haughey certainly behaved improperly, he was and has been innocent of the more colourful charges that have been laid against him concerning the crisis. It can be argued with some force that he was more a victim of the arms crisis than anything else.'

Some months later, in an interview on Cork local radio, Lynch refused to talk about the arms crisis, because he said that the events were already well covered. He added that Vincent Browne 'did as good a job as one individual could do' in documenting the arms crisis, even though he said there were 'some areas that he has speculated upon that aren't strictly accurate'.

Lynch was conferred with the freedom of the city of Cork along with the long-time Bishop of Cork and Ross, Cornelius Lucey, on 19 December 1980. Lynch was coming to the end of his career after more than thirty years in active politics. In May 1981, he announced that he would not be seeking re-election to the Dáil in the general election to be held the following month. Instead he retired from public life and repeatedly stated that there were 'no circumstances' in which he would stand for the presidency.

'I will not be a candidate for the presidency whenever the next vacancy occurs, and even the next vacancy after that, if I live that long,' he emphasised.

Of course, he did not have to worry about this, because Haughey would probably have blocked his nomination. Even though there is no evidence that Lynch engaged in any kind of active politics after announcing that he would not seek re-election, he remained interested in political matters. His former supporters frequently used Lynch's name to further their own ends. For instance, they were critical of Haughey when he lost power in 1981, and especially after he failed to win an overall majority in February 1982 following the fall of Garret FitzGerald's first government over the rejection of its budget. There were calls for a change of leadership in Fianna Fáil, and Des O'Malley was persuaded to challenge Haughey for the leadership after the general election. He announced his intention to run against Haughey for the party's nomination for Taoiseach, but then, under intense pressure, withdrew his name at the party meeting called to select the nominee.

O'Malley was essentially humiliated and Lynch promptly came to his support by issuing a statement. 'Des O'Malley was right to let his name go forward for consideration as the Fianna Fáil nominee for Taoiseach in the light of the numerous requests from members of the Fianna Fáil Party and organisation to do so following the failure of Fianna Fáil to get an overall majority,' Lynch stated. 'I am confident that he will be a future leader of Fianna Fáil and a future Taoiseach.' Pointedly, Lynch never even mentioned Haughey in the whole of his statement.

Bill Loughnane reacted by accusing Lynch of being 'the main instigator of the O'Malley drive.' This prompted the former Taoiseach to tell RTÉ that he had had no involvement in the abortive heave. 'I make no secret of the fact, as is evident from statements published by me in recent years, and in the one I issued after the parliamentary-party meeting on Thursday, I would favour Des O'Malley as party leader and would wish to see him as a future Taoiseach.'

Fianna Fáil was in opposition in 1984 when the GAA celebrated its centenary. Lynch was selected as a member of the hurling team of the century, which was introduced to the crowd at the all-Ireland hurling final. When Lynch was called on to the field, there was a massive roar from the whole crowd. For some of the Cork supporters in the crowd that day, it was a means of atonement for the by-election defeats of 1979.

In early 1985, Lynch publicly expressed regret over Des O'Malley's expulsion from Fianna Fáil, and he spoke out in favour of the Single European Act in 1987, saying reassuringly that it was no threat to Irish neutrality. In 1990, Lynch told an Irish Association seminar that the time had come to consider seriously the amendment of Articles 2 and 3 of the Constitution in relation to Northern Ireland. He was prepared to give interviews, but he generally shied away from commenting on current politics, and he flatly refused to discuss the arms crisis.

In his final years, Lynch was dogged by ill-health. In 1992, when he was in hospital for treatment, Dick Walsh was in a nearby room. One day Máirín came to visit Walsh. It seemed that Jack had suggested she should bring him a bottle of whiskey. After Máirín left the hospital, Lynch visited Walsh. 'I see you have a nice drop there,' Lynch remarked as he poured out a drink for himself. Walsh had been forbidden whiskey on doctor's orders. For the next few days, Lynch called in regularly for some whiskey, so that when Máirín visited Walsh again the bottle was almost empty.

She remarked that he had made good work of the bottle and added that 'poor Jack' was off the drink completely. In November 1993 Lynch had a stroke and was seriously incapacitated. He went almost totally blind.

Lynch was greatly moved in 1997 when Cork Corporation named the new tunnel under the Lee after him: the Jack Lynch Tunnel. On the former Taoiseach's eightieth birthday the following year, the Lord Mayor of Cork, Dave McCarthy, unveiled a plaque at Lynch's birthplace near Shandon Steeple. He was even recorded singing 'The Banks' on his final birthday on 15 August 1999. He died in the Royal Hospital in Donnybrook, Dublin, on 20 October 1999.

His funeral will probably be remembered as the last great Irish political funeral of the twentieth century. In symbolic terms, it differed enormously from the first great political funeral of the century, that of another Corkman, Jeremiah O'Donovan Rossa, on 1 August 1915. That turned into a clarion call to arms when Patrick Pearse delivered the funeral oration. 'The fools, the fools, the fools,' he said, 'they have left us our Fenian dead, and while Ireland holds these graves, Ireland unfree shall never be at peace.' Pearse used the occasion to establish himself as a spokesman for militant Irish nationalism, and he then used that platform to lead the Easter Rising less than a year later.

In Lynch's case, the funeral provided the opportunity to celebrate the man who had prevented another call to arms in 1970. 'Thirty years ago, as a nation, we were confronted with a stark choice,' Des O'Malley declared in his graveside oration. 'We could have caved in to sinister elements and put our country at mortal risk. Confronted with some of the most difficult decisions to face any Taoiseach in the modern era, he took determined and resolute action to defend democracy and uphold the rule of law. Had the country taken the wrong turn thirty years ago, I fear to think what might have befallen us. We didn't, and for that alone Jack Lynch deserves his place in history.'

Lynch's obsequies were really a celebration of his life. The funeral Mass was not a solemn Requiem Mass, in which black vestments are worn, it was the Mass of the Resurrection, in which all of the concelebrants wear white vestments. Liam Cosgrave was correct when he said that Lynch was 'the most popular leader in Ireland since Daniel O'Connell,' John Buckley, the Bishop of Cork and Ross, told the congregation. 'For a man who was so famous and who achieved so much, he never lost the common touch, always remaining one of our own.'

'I valued our social contacts of latter years,' wrote T. K. Whitaker, who had served under Lynch at the Department of Finance and later provided him with astute advice on Northern Ireland. Whitaker was just one of the men who had worked for Lynch and treasured his friendship. The grief of long-time colleagues like Martin O'Donoghue and Séamus Brennan was etched on their faces at the funeral services, a testament to their admiration and love for the man.

'Jack's whole nature induced loyalty and affection,' Whitaker noted. 'Softness of speech and manner, consideration for others, readiness to listen, absence of pomp, a sense of humour were elements of a most attractive personality which combined modesty and unpretentiousness with good judgement and a deep sense of responsibility and firmness of purpose. I never saw him in a rage or heard him say anything disparaging or hurtful about others.'

Even his most devoted follower could not have called him a particularly innovative politician, but none was more loved by the people as a whole – not just in Cork, but throughout the country. After Lynch was elected leader, Fianna Fáil turned a minority government into a majority one within a year by winning four successive by-elections. In the process Lynch became the most popular Irish leader of the twentieth century. He also became the only leader of Fianna Fáil to gain an overall majority in his first general election as leader. Moreover, the party's percentage of the popular vote increased at each of the following two general elections, even though Fianna Fáil lost power in 1973. In 1977 he led Fianna Fáil to its largest electoral majority ever.

Listening to the people in Cork on the day of his funeral, one sensed that Lynch was already on the road to canonisation. Indeed, some facetiously suggested that he performed his first miracle at his funeral Mass when Charlie Haughey and Des O'Malley sat next to each other and shook hands. Outside the cathedral, Haughey attracted more attention than either the Taoiseach, Bertie Ahern, or the President, Mary McAleese, who were both in attendance. Haughey's celebrity status was tarnished by his notoriety, because of the tribunals investigating his behaviour. Some cheered him, while others jeered, but it was neither the time nor the place for such shows of partisan emotion. Most people remained respectfully silent.

Haughey paid his final respects. It was, in a way, reminiscent of that day in December 1979 when he had sat alone on the Fianna Fáil side of the Dáil and listened in silence to the invective of his tormentors. He did not go to the graveside, but one sensed that he still had a pervasive presence in Des O'Malley's oration.

On his final journey, Lynch's body was driven past the prominent resting places of the heroes of other days to an obscure grave near a far corner of St Finbarr's Cemetery. Unlike other Cork heroes – men like Michael Collins, Tomás Mac Curtain and Terence MacSwiney, who were cut down in the prime of life – Jack Lynch lived a full life in which he made an invaluable contribution to Irish politics, especially in the trying period around the time of the arms crisis.

He was at his best when he was needed most. While he was sailing with a friend one day, someone shouted a warning to Lynch that he was heading for some rocks. 'Don't blame me,' he replied. 'I'm just doing what I'm told – as usual.'

The story could be used to epitomise his political career. Lynch was never an especially ground-breaking minister. His early political actions were seldom newsworthy, yet he was easily elected leader of Fianna Fáil in November 1966. It was during his tenure that Fianna Fáil set up its controversial fund-raising arm, *Taca*, which established close ties with businessmen in the building industry. Those contacts gave rise to suspicions of corruption within Fianna Fáil that were not eradicated during Lynch's lifetime.

Lynch essentially allowed others to chart the course as the country sailed into the stormy waters of the arms crisis. He allowed the Cabinet to draft his famous television address in which he said that this country would not 'stand by' as Northern Ireland descended into the abyss in 1969. The speech had a disastrous impact on people in Northern Ireland. The unionists feared a military incursion from the Republic, while the nationalists mistakenly assumed that the Dublin government was prepared to involve itself directly.

'I knew plenty of good, decent people who were saying, "Why don't we do something more positive?"' Lynch later explained. 'But in those days, to have done anything more would have led to annihilation. I don't mind telling you that I had a hard job maintaining the balance at the time.'

Lynch's political strength was his popularity, but it was also his weakness, because at times he was more intent on being popular than right. Time and again he backed down rather than take a stand, such as when he was confronted with industrial unrest in the early 1960s, and he capitulated in the face of Donogh O'Malley's unauthorised announcement of 'free education' in 1966. Lynch did not seek popularity for some kind of egotistical gratification but because he believed that as a leader it was important to be close to the people. 'Good leadership is staying with the people and certainly not getting too far ahead of them,' he explained to T. P. O'Mahony in a taped interview in 1974. 'There is an obligation on a leader to do what he believes and bring people with him.'

In politics, as in sport, he was always a team player who welcomed a good performance by any colleague. As an ordinary minister he backed up his colleagues. Later as Taoiseach he was content to allow all his ministers to have a virtual free hand. He was slow to stamp his authority on his own Cabinet following his election as Taoiseach and retained a figurative bomb within the Cabinet in the form of Charles Haughey, Neil Blaney, Donogh O'Malley and Kevin Boland. They thought that his more relaxed style was indicative of a lack of ambition and commitment, or even laziness. As a result, they despised him and treated him with virtual contempt, which he tolerated.

They were courageous politicians who were not afraid to take the initiative, but in each case they went too far and lost their effectiveness because not enough people followed them. Boland pushed the government into holding the disastrous PR referendum, while Blaney conspired to arm republicans and in the process threatened to involve the country in a war, without authority. Even though the Taoiseach had declared that his government had 'no intention of mounting an armed invasion of the North', he did nothing when Blaney subsequently stated in Letterkenny that force was not being ruled out. Neither Blaney nor even the government as a whole had a right to engage the country in a war. By not ousting Blaney, or not at least compelling him to retract his outrageous comments, Lynch allowed for dangerous confusion on a fundamental constitutional point, that only the Oireachtas has the right to declare war. He later agreed that he probably 'had not been tough enough' in dealing with the issue; this was really a gross understatement.

The ship of state was probably nearer the proverbial rocks during the arms crisis than it had been at any time since the Civil War. Lynch said that he had no warning of what was going on behind the scenes, but three different people – Peter Berry, the Secretary of the Department of Justice; Jim Gibbons, the Minister for Defence; and Michael Moran, the Minister for Justice – all claimed that they had informed him about what was going on.

Martin O'Donoghue, who became an adviser to the Taoiseach during the crisis, stated in a profile in RTÉ's *Na Taoisigh* series in 2001 that Lynch heard rumours of the planned gun-running, but that he could not act on mere rumours. He could at least have asked those concerned if the rumours were true, but he apparently chose to do nothing, which prompted Peter Berry to conclude that he was turning a blind eye to the whole thing. Berry tried to force the Taoiseach's hand by involving President de Valera in the matter. Lynch initially indicated that he was content with a promise from Haughey and Blaney that they would not engage in any further gun-running attempts. It was not until the following week, when the story was about to break, that he insisted on the resignations of Haughey and Blaney. It was strictly a political decision, not a momentous event of moral significance, as some of Lynch's supporters contended. But from that point on, his handling of the crisis was masterful, as was his role in leading Ireland into what would become the European Union.

When the notion of European unity was being mooted, de Valera warned the Council of Europe that Irish people would be cynical about the idea of the various European countries, with their diverse traditions, uniting in a single entity. 'It is from no desire to interfere with or delay them that some of us here have spoken against the attempt at immediate federation,' he explained in August 1949. 'It is simply that we know the task that would confront us in persuading our people to proceed by that road.'

It was a further ten years before the government of Seán Lemass began planning for membership of what was then called the Common Market. The main task of preparing the Irish people for membership was assigned to Jack Lynch, whose patient dedication and skilful handling of the task must rank as one of the finest pieces of political leadership witnessed since independence.

Less than a quarter of a century after de Valera had warned of the cynical attitude of the Irish people, an overwhelming majority of the electorate – 83 per cent – voted in favour of joining the EEC in the referendum of May 1972. It was a decisive result that killed any further debate on the membership question.

Following his return to power in 1977, Lynch again allowed himself to be manipulated, this time by agreeable elements, in the form of George Colley, Des O'Malley and Martin O'Donoghue. Under their direction, he began steering the country towards economic problems. The economy was already in trouble by the time he stepped down in December 1979. Haughey recognised this, and warned that the country was living beyond its means, but he only exacerbated the state's profligate policies, and Garret FitzGerald's government made things even worse in the mid-1980s. Lynch's last government set a dangerous economic trend, but his successors must bear much of the blame for what happened in the 1980s. Yet it is doubtful that Lynch would have had the will to tackle the problem had he remained in office.

Lynch explained to T. P. O'Mahony that he had objected within the Fianna Fáil parliamentary party to the harsh budget introduced in 1952. 'Why not do a little less than you propose to do, even though you know that the little less isn't honest, as to doing the job properly,' he argued. 'Inevitably it will be very hard to get the necessity of this argument across to the public, and they are going to react.'

'They did react in 1954, and they put Fianna Fáil out of office,' Lynch recalled, 'and I think one of the reasons was that they were too harsh in their budget of 1952, even though it was economically, fiscally and absolutely justifiable; and perhaps absolutely necessary at the time.'

Just as he was slow to confront Neil Blaney over the Letterkenny speech, Lynch failed to confront Síle de Valera over her Fermoy oration, but he was ultimately undermined by his supposed supporters. Jim Gibbons turned the concept of collective Cabinet responsibility on its head by openly refusing to support the contraception bill, but Lynch did nothing.

Lynch was seriously weakened by the results of the European elections in 1979, but the unkindest cut of all was the subsequent loss of the Cork City by-election. With his resolve weakened by the devastating electoral setbacks, he allowed himself to be pushed into early retirement, not by the grubby clique of disgruntled self-seekers who were trying to oust him, but by his own supporters, Martin O'Donoghue and George Colley.

Lynch was not as successful in relation to the Northern Ireland crisis as he had been with regard to Europe, but then at times more than half his team was pulling against him. Should he – could he – have dumped them and still retained the popularity needed to govern? In his modesty he probably underestimated his own popularity, with the result that he was likely to have been in a stronger position than he realised, but there was little that he could do about his misfortune in having to deal at a crucial period with the Conservative government of Ted Heath, whose initial ignorance of Irish affairs was highlighted by his disastrous defence of the prejudiced and biased way in which people were not only arrested and interned without trial but also subjected to 'inhuman and degrading treatment', in the opinion of the European Court of Human Rights. That situation was made even worse by the savage behaviour of British troops on Bloody Sunday. Yet through patience and perseverance Lynch did eventually win Heath over to a more rational policy. Indeed Lynch could claim credit for playing a major role in the process that eventually led to the Sunningdale agreement of 1973, which was a precursor to the Good Friday agreement of a quarter of a century later.

While some of his party colleagues wrapped themselves in the flag and pursued their own notions of greatness, which were sometimes as foreign as they were false, Lynch made a valuable contribution to public life by demonstrating that it was unnecessary to assume airs and graces or surround himself with the trappings of success in order to function as Taoiseach.

He has frequently been described as the first of the new breed of politician, because he was too young to have taken part in the troubles of the 1920s, but in reality he probably belonged with the last of the old breed. He did remember some shooting during the Civil War, and he was the last Taoiseach to have served in government with Éamon de Valera. He was also an old-style gentleman who eschewed personal ambition at a time when people tended to look with suspicion on ambitious politicians. He won the trust of the Irish people. His phenomenal electoral feats were a testament to his popularity, which was the public expression of approval of his serene leadership in keeping the country out of civil war and leading it into Europe. Yet he never lost the common touch. His drink remained a Paddy, or a pint. Power never changed him. He remained a nice fellow, one of our own.

BIBLIOGRAPHY

ARCHIVE SOURCES

Frank Aiken papers, UCD Archives, Dublin; Todd Andrews papers, UCD Archives, Dublin; Department of Education records; Department of Finance records; Department of Industry and Commerce records; Department of the Taoiseach records; John M. Lynch papers, National Archives, Dublin; Seán McEntee papers, UCD Archives, Dublin; James Ryan papers, UCD Archives, Dublin; T. K. Whitaker papers, UCD Archives, Dublin.

NEWSPAPERS AND PERIODICALS

The *Cork Examiner; The Crane Bag; The Economist;* the *Evening Herald;* the *Evening Mail;* the *Evening Press; Hibernia; Hot Press; In Dublin;* the *Irish Independent;* the *Irish Press; The Irish Times; Magill; The (Manchester) Guardian; The New York Times;* the *Sunday Independent;* the *Sunday Press;* the *Sunday Tribune; This Week;* the *Toronto Globe and Mail*

BOOKS

Akenson, Donald Harman. *Conor: A Biography of Conor Cruise O'Brien.* 2 vols. Montreal: McGill University Press, 1994.

Arnold, Bruce. *Haughey: His Life and Unlucky Deeds.* London: Harper Collins, 1993.

_____. *What Kind of Country: Modern Irish Politics, 1968–1983.* London: Jonathan Cape, 1984.

Bell, J. Bowyer. *The Secret Army: A History of the IRA.* London: Anthony Blond Ltd, 1970.

Bew, Paul, Ellen Hazelkorn and Henry Patterson. *The Dynamics of Irish Politics.* London: Lawrence and Wishart, 1989.

Bloch, Jonathan and Patrick Fitzgerald. *British Intelligence and Covert Action: Africa, the Middle East and Europe Since 1945.* Dingle: Brandon Books, 1983.

Boland, Kevin. *The Rise and Decline of Fianna Fáil.* Cork: Mercier Press, 1982.

_____. *Up Dev!* Dublin: privately printed, 1977.

_____. *'We Won't Stand (Idly) By.'* Dublin: privately printed, 1974.

Bowman, John. *De Valera and the Ulster Question, 1917–1973*. Oxford: Clarendon Press, 1982.

Brady, Seamus. *Arms and the Men: Ireland in Turmoil*. Dublin: privately printed, 1971.

Byrne, Gay with Deirdre Purcell. *The Time of My Life: An Autobiography*. Dublin: Gill & Macmillan, 1989.

Callaghan, James. *A House Divided: The Dilemma of Northern Ireland*. London: William Collins, 1973.

Carter, Jimmy. *Keeping Faith: Memoirs of a President*. London: Collins, 1982.

Collins, Stephen. *The Cosgrave Legacy*. Dublin: Blackwater Press, 1996.

_____. *The Haughey File: The Unprecedented Career and Last Years of The Boss*. Dublin: The O'Brien Press, 1992.

_____. *The Power Game: Fianna Fáil Since Lemass*. Dublin: The O'Brien Press, 2000.

_____. *Spring and the Labour Story*. Dublin: The O'Brien Press, 1993.

Coogan, Tim Pat. *De Valera: Long Fellow, Long Shadow*. London: Hutchinson, 1993.

Coombes, David, ed. *Ireland and the European Communities: Ten Years of Membership*. Dublin: Gill & Macmillan, 1983.

Cronin, Seán. *Irish Nationalism: A History of Its Roots and Ideology*. Dublin: The Academy Press, 1980.

_____. *Washington's Irish Policy, 1916–1918*. Dublin: Anvil Books, 1987.

Cruise O'Brien, Conor. *States of Ireland*. London: Hutchinson & Co., 1972.

_____. *Memoirs: My Life and Themes*. Dublin: Poolbeg, 1998.

Curtis, Lis. *Nothing But the Same Old Story: The Roots of Anti-Irish Racism*. London: privately printed, no date.

Dáil Éireann, Dáil Debates, volumes cxii–cccxxviii (1948–1981).

Desmond, Barry. *Finally and In Conclusion*. Dublin: New Island Books, 2000.

Doherty, Paddy. *Paddy Bogside*. Cork: Mercier Press, 2001.

Downey, James. *Lenihan: His Life and Loyalties*. Dublin: New Island Books, 1998.

_____. *Them & Us: Britain, Ireland and the Northern Question, 1969–82*. Dublin: Ward River Press, 1983.

Drower, George. *John Hume: Man of Peace*. London: Vista, 1995.

Dwyer, T. Ryle. *De Valera: The Man and the Myths*. Dublin: Poolbeg, 1990.

_____. *Short Fellow: A Biography of Charles J. Haughey*. Dublin: Marino Books, 1999.

Edmonds, Seán. *The Gun, the Law and the Irish People: From 1912 to the Aftermath of the Arms Trial 1970*. Tralee: Anvil Books, 1971.

Fallon, Ivan. *The Player*. London: Hodder & Stoughton, 1994.

Faulkner, Brian, and John Houston, ed. *Memoirs of a Statesman*. London: Weidenfeld and Nicolson, 1978.

Feehan, John M. *The Statesman: A Study of the Role of Charles J. Haughey in the Ireland of the Future.* Cork: Mercier Press, 1985.

Haines, Joe. *The Politics of Power.* London: Hodder and Stoughton, 1977.

Haldeman, H. R. *The Haldeman Diaries: Inside the Nixon White House.* New York: G. P. Putnam & Sons, 1994.

Hannon, Philip and Jackie Gallagher, eds. *Taking the Long Five: Seventy Years of Fianna Fáil.* Dublin: Blackwater Press, 1996.

Haughey, Charles J., and Martin Mansergh, ed. *Spirit of the Nation: The Speeches of Charles J. Haughey.* Cork: Mercier Press, 1986.

Heath, Edward. *The Course of My Life: My Autobiography.* London: Hodder & Stoughton, 1998.

Horgan, John. *Labour: The Price of Power.* Dublin: Gill & Macmillan, 1986.

_____. *Seán Lemass: The Enigmatic Patriot.* Dublin: Gill & Macmillan, 1997.

_____. *Irish Media: A Critical History Since 1922.* London: Routledge, 2001.

Joannon, Pierre, ed. *De Gaulle and Ireland.* Dublin: Institute of Public Administration, 1991.

Kelly, James. *Orders for the Captain?* Dublin: privately printed, 1971.

_____. *The Thimble Riggers: The Dublin Arms Trials of 1970.* Dublin: privately printed, 1999.

Kennedy, Kieran A. and Brendan R. Dowling. *Economic Growth in Ireland: The Experience Since 1947.* Dublin: Gill and Macmillan, 1975.

MacIntyre, Tom. *Through the Bridewell Gate: A Diary of the Dublin Arms Trial.* London: Faber & Faber, 1971.

Lacouture, Jean. *De Gaulle: The Ruler, 1945–1970.* London: Harvill, 1991.

Lenihan, Brian. *For the Record.* Dublin: Blackwater Press, 1991.

Maher, D. J. *The Tortuous Path: The Course of Ireland's Entry into the EEC, 1948–73.* Dublin: Institute of Public Administration, 1986.

Maloney, Ed and Andy Pollak. *Paisley.* Dublin: Poolbeg Press, 1986.

Manning, Maurice. *James Dillon: A Biography.* Dublin: Wolfhound Press, 1999.

Murray, Raymond. *The SAS in Ireland.* Cork: Mercier Press, 1990.

O'Brien, Justin. *The Arms Trial.* Dublin: Gill & Macmillan, 2000.

O'Byrnes, Stephen. *Hiding Behind a Face: Fine Gael under FitzGerald.* Dublin: Gill & Macmillan, 1986.

O'Connell, Dr John. *Crusading Doctor and Politician.* Dublin: Poolbeg, 1989.

O'Connor, Kevin. *Sweetie.* Dublin: privately printed, 1999.

O'Connor, Ulick. *The Ulick O'Connor Diaries, 1970–1981: A Cavalier Irishman.* London: John Murray, 2001.

Ó Glaisne, Risteárd. *Cearbhall Ó Dálaigh.* Dingle: An Sagart, 2001.

O'Hehir, Michael. *Michael O'Hehir: My Life and Times.* Dublin: Blackwater Press/RTÉ, 1996.

O'Higgins, Thomas F. *A Double Life*. Dublin: Town House, 1996.

O'Malley, Pádraig. *Uncivil Wars: Ireland Today*. Belfast: Blackstaff Press, 1983.

O'Sullivan, Michael. *Seán Lemass: A Biography*. Dublin: Blackwater Press, 1994.

Prior, Jim. *Balance of Power*. London: Hamish Hamilton, 1986.

Rafter, Kevin. *Neil Blaney: A Soldier of Destiny*. Dublin: Blackwater Press, 1993.

Ryan, Tim. *Albert Reynolds: The Longford Leader*. Dublin: Blackwater Press, 1994.

Savage, Robert. *Seán Lemass.* Dublin: Historical Association of Ireland, 1999.

Smith, Raymond. *Charles J. Haughey: The Survivor*. Dublin: Aherlow Publishers, 1983.

_____. *Garret: The Enigma Dr Garret FitzGerald*. Dublin: Aherlow Publishers, 1985.

_____. *Haughey and O'Malley: The Quest for Power*. Dublin: Aherlow Publishers, 1986.

Smyth, Clifford. *Ian Paisley: Voice of Protestant Ulster*. Edinburgh: Scottish Academic Press, 1987.

Sunday Times Insight Team, The. *Ulster*. Harmondsworth: Penguin Books, 1972.

Thatcher, Margaret. *The Downing Street Years*. London: HarperCollins, 1993.

Tobin, Fergal. *The Best of Decades: Ireland in the 1960s*. Dublin: Gill & Macmillan, 1984.

Walsh, C. H. *Oh Really O'Reilly: A Biography of Dr A. J. F. O'Reilly*. Dublin: Bentos Ltd, 1992.

Walsh, Dick. *Des O'Malley: A Political Profile*. Dingle: Brandon Books, 1986.

_____. *The Party: Inside Fianna Fáil*. Dublin: Gill & Macmillan, 1986.

Watts, David. *The Constitution of Northern Ireland: Prospects and Problems*. London: Heinemann, 1981.

Whelan, Ken and Eugene Masterson. *Bertie Ahern: Taoiseach and Peacemaker*. Dublin: Blackwater Press, 1998.

White, Barry. *John Hume: Statesman of the Troubles*. Belfast: Blackstaff Press, 1984.

Whyte, J. H. *Church and State in Modern Ireland, 1923–1979*. Dublin: Gill & Macmillan, 1980.

Young, John N. *Erskine Childers: President of Ireland*. Gerrards Cross: Colin Smythe, 1985.

INDEX

413

414